Reading *Dubliners* Again

Richard Fallis, *Series Editor*

Reading
Dubliners
Again

A Lacanian Perspective

Garry M. Leonard

Syracuse University Press

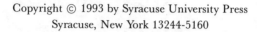

First Edition 1993
93 94 95 96 97 98 99   6 5 4 3 2 1

The paper used in this publication meets the minimum requirements of American National Standard for Information Sciences — Permanence of Paper for Printed Library Materials, ANSI Z39.48-1984. ∞™

Library of Congress Cataloging-in-Publication Data

Leonard, Garry Martin, 1956–
    Reading Dubliners again : a Lacanian perspective / Garry M.
Leonard.
        p.   cm. — (Irish studies)
    Includes bibliographical references and index.
    ISBN 0-8156-2574-X — ISBN 0-8156-2600-2 (pbk.)
    1. Joyce, James, 1882–1941. Dubliners.   2. Lacan, Jacques, 1901–
 — Contributions in criticism.   3. Masculinity (Psychology) in
literature.   4. Dublin (Ireland) in literature.   5. Psychoanalysis
and literature.   I. Title.   II. Series: Irish studies (Syracuse,
N.Y.)
PR6019.09D876   1993
823′.912 — dc20   92-33860

Manufactured in the United States of America

For Kathy, Raymond, and Marshall

GARRY M. LEONARD is assistant professor of English, University of Toronto, Scarborough Campus. His many articles have appeared in the *James Joyce Quarterly, Modern Fiction Studies, Edith Wharton Review, Nineteenth Century Studies, Novel,* and *College Literature.*

Contents

Preface

To be fair, I transcribe here the dream I had while writing this book—the one dream in which James Joyce appeared personally. If Lacan is right, the dream exposes subjectivity as the affect of the gaze of the Other; thus, I have no reliable point of view on the dream I relate and cannot be expected to explain it. I am sitting in the living room of the house where I grew up. It is the formal living room, not the family room, and I wonder why I sit there alone because this is the room used only by my parents for their periodic and arcane ritual of the cocktail party.

But I am not alone. Joyce sits on the couch normally covered with plastic during the long periods when the room was not used. I am thrilled at this chance to interview him, to get the truth. But he looks unspeakably tired. How can I expect him to respond to my questions, questions that cannot fail to be tiresome to him? He looks at me. He is waiting but only because he has nowhere to go. I am about to begin, but I see that the coffee table, which never has anything on it, now has something tossed carelessly on top of it. It looks like lingerie. I cannot believe my bad luck. If I call attention to the article, it will lead away from the interview I envision. If I ignore it, he will know I have done so and respond to my questions with a mocking smile. I gesture toward the coffee table. "That's bizarre," I say. "No," he responds, in what is to be his only comment before my alarm goes off, "that's a brassiere."

I begin—somewhat less enigmatically, perhaps—by relating a story told about P. T. Barnum (a somewhat unacknowledged translator of the language of the unconscious into the language of the marketplace).

It seems he was disturbed because all the people who had paid admission to see the various exhibits in his New York Museum retraced their steps again and again once inside the hall instead of continuing on out the building. They were aware that they had paid money to be inside, and, thus, they experienced a vague and tenuous sense of satisfaction by milling about as long as possible to make the price of admission seem more like a bargain. To admit disenchantment with the exhibits would be to open the question of just what it was they expected to see, and this they preferred not to do. As a result, customers were still outside who had not yet paid to enter. Whenever such an overcrowded situation occurred, Barnum's solution was to display, with much fanfare, an elaborate poster that read: "This way to the Egress." Customers in search of still another spectacle that might yet prove to be whatever it is they required pushed forward eagerly and, of course, found themselves back out on the street in the real world.

In a sense, I am posting a similar sign in the crowded hall of Joyce scholarship. Some readers who follow along will feel tricked; others may be startled into realizing that they have been looking at the same exhibits for too long. Barnum's fakery merely redirected people toward reality, the always already world of brave new words. Likewise, new directions in Joyce criticism are often initially greeted with cries of "fraud!" Yet some of these same approaches will one day be the much stared upon central exhibit in the museum of the classroom. All should be grateful for any moment when, glancing up, one sees a banner never noticed before that reads This Way to the Egress!

Scarborough, Ontario   GARRY M. LEONARD
November 1992

Acknowledgments

One of the most essential resources to me in the writing of this book was the encouragement I received from scholars whose work I respect and admire. I issued the first "publication" of the ideas presented here in the form of fragmentary comments delivered at various conferences. At these conferences, generous comments made by such scholars as Suzette Henke and Ellie Ragland-Sullivan pushed me from the confortably anonymous margin of "just putting forth a few ideas" into the more frightening arena of 'writing a book."

At the Philadelphia Joyce conference in 1988, Sheldon Brivic invited me to participate in a Joyce/Lacan panel, and he has proved to be a steady source of supportive criticism and praise since then. On that same panel, I met Kimberley Devlin, and she has supported my scholarly endeavors both by offering comments on my various manuscripts and by soliciting my opinion of her own work. I also thank Ellen Carol Jones and Robert Spoo who, both as fellow Joyce scholars and as editors (*Modern Fiction Studies* and the *James Joyce Quarterly,* respectively) made me feel that this often difficult project was worth finishing. After submitting the manuscript to Syracuse University Press, I also received very welcome encouragement from Cynthia Maude-Gembler and Richard Fallis. In addition, Bonnie Scott read this manuscript in its entirety and her comments, particularly those relating to the introduction and conclusion, were very helpful. A more general expression of gratitude is due Brandy Kershner, someone who has known me an inconveniently long time — through various scholarly incarnations — yet has always maintained that I could write a good book about Joyce.

Going back quite a bit further, thanks are due my parents who started me on this lifelong obsession with books; indeed, my mother's ingenious response to my insatiable reading habit was to visit various thrift stores and return home with grocery bags full of books. To my three year old, Raymond, I owe, I suppose, an apology: All of your impromptu insertions into the manuscript, unstintingly supplied by you whenever you wandered unnoticed into my office, have been edited out. Perhaps it will be some comfort to you to know that your margi-nalia—although consistently incomprehensible—often appeared to me to have interstellar significance; I cannot shake the feeling that the book has been reduced in scope as a result of my deleting them. Finally, my gratitude and love to KM, who steadfastly supported my efforts to write this book because she could see how much it mattered to me.

Permissions

Permission of W. W. Norton and Company, Inc., to quote from the works of Jacques Lacan is gratefully acknowledged:

Feminine Sexuality (with the école freudienne), edited by Juliet Mitchell and Jacqueline Rose, translated by Jacqueline Rose. English translation copyright © 1982 by Jacqueline Rose. Selection, editorial matter, and introductions copyright © 1982 by Juliet Mitchell and Jacqueline Rose.

The Four Fundamental Concepts of Psycho-Analysis, edited by Jacques-Alain Miller, translated from the French by Alan Sheridan. Transla-tion copyright © 1977 by Alan Sheridan.

The Seminar of Jacques Lacan, Book I, *Freud's Papers on Technique 1953–1954,* edited by Jacques-Alain Miller, translated with notes by John Forrester. English translation copyright © 1988 by Cambridge University Press.

The Seminar of Jacques Lacan, Book II, *The Ego in Freud's Theory and in the Technique of Psychoanalysis 1954–1955,* edited by Jacques-Alain Miller, translated by Sylvana Tomaselli, with notes by John Forrester. English translation copyright © 1988 by Cambridge University Press.

Reading *Dubliners* Again

1

Spilling Whiskey on the Corpus
Jacques Lacan and *Dubliners*

> Why all this fuss and bother about the mystery of the
> unconscious? . . . What about the mystery of the con-
> scious? What do they know about that? (Joyce 1966,
> 3:261)

> The ego is structured exactly like a symptom. At the
> heart of the subject it is only a privileged symptom,
> the human symptom *par excellence,* the mental illness
> of man. (Lacan 1988a, 16)

For several reasons a Lacanian approach to Joyce's fiction constitutes a particularly rewarding interplay of theory and fiction. First,
and most generally, Joyce is, as the above quotation suggests, fascinated
with "the mystery of the conscious." Joyce begins with *Dubliners* to
make the phenomenon of consciousness uncomfortably problematical for his readers. One does not need the insights of contemporary
criticism to see this; it was remarked upon by an anonymous reviewer
of *Dubliners* in 1914: "At least three [stories] would have been better
buried in oblivion. Life has so much that is beautiful, interesting, edu-
cative, amusing, that we do not readily pardon those who insist upon
its more sordid and baser aspects" (Deming 1970, 61). This reviewer
does not object to the stories because they falsify reality but because
they fail to do so!

Joyce's early publishers, who claimed they would be vulnerable to lawsuits if they published the collection because the stories cited the names of actual streets and taverns, betray this same uneasiness that Joyce's fiction is somehow too real. Joyce's prose presents the commonplace as mysterious and in doing so exposes "the mysterious" as a sort of organized ignorance erected to wall out unconscious knowledge *(savoir)*. [1] The initial unease expressed by Joyce's early readers often returned them to the idea that reality was insufficiently fictionalized in the stories.

This anxiety was tempered considerably when the theory of the epiphany became a critical commonplace. Various perceptive and influential critics, most notably Tyndall and Chayes, were then able to impose a metanarrative on the stories that explained how the stories revealed a truth to the reader that was most typically lost on the characters. The implication of their approach was that the stories illustrated a higher truth, and this truth, although certainly beyond the purview of the characters, was, nonetheless, perfectly apparent to a careful and informed reader. Writing in 1946, Chayes explains that patient readers of *Dubliners* will eventually determine the outline of some familiar shape if they allow the meaning of each story to accrue: "In *Dubliners,* claritas is achieved . . . through an apparently trivial incident, action, or single detail which differs from the others making up the story only in that it illuminates them, integrates them, and gives them meaning. It is like the final piece which is added to the child's pile of lettered blocks and completes the spelling of a word or gives form to the 'house' or 'tower' he is building" (361). In essence, she advises readers that 'meaning' will eventually reassert itself as long as they do not panic.

Writing nearly forty years later, Morris Beja succinctly points out why the apparently final note provided by the epiphany never quite stops reverberating: "Constantly in *Dubliners* we see characters come to feel that their past understanding has been limited, or distorted, or downright wrong—so why should we doubt that they may eventually come to see their new sudden spiritual manifestations as false or even perverse?" (1983, 9). Lacan was fascinated by Joyce precisely because in his fiction the letter so revealingly collapses into litter and leaves the subject (the reader) with the uncertain sense that to be conscious is to be a signifier in relation to other signifiers, ad infinitum, with no genuine signifieds that are not self-generated myths. More specifically, Lacan was intrigued by the way Joyce presented his characters as inhabited by a symptom which answers to an absent Other.[2] Indeed, I would push even further than this and suggest that the famous Joycean epiphany achieves claritas only by highlighting the fictional construction of the past and, thus, reveals at the same time a disconcerting glimpse of the as yet unconstructed mythology of the future.[3]

One of the points I argue in this book is that the readers of *Dubliners* are encouraged by Joyce to enjoy transcending the limited perspective of the fictional selves (characters) in the stories but only at the price of becoming uneasily aware that the stories of their own lives also operate as texts that maintain their unity and coherence by forgetting, excluding, or marginalizing whatever contradicts the myth of the self. The dream state organizes what the subject's conscious narration of gender/identity myths elides, and, thus, the language of the unconscious speaks in the gaps of conscious discourse: "The dream classifies and collects the residues of the day's experiences and places them within a well-established organization. This organization is the personal myth of each individual detailing the times in his history when experience was not faced and when trauma ruled. Events which the ego refused to acknowledge, events for which words were forgotten or never known or never recognized, these are represented in the dream and in neurosis" (Schneiderman 1971, 31). For Lacan, the subject is an endlessly pliable version of reality carefully narrated to hold at bay all knowledge of the irreparable fragmentation and disharmony at the base of consciousness that is incontrovertibly Real.[4]

Critics also account for the unease Joyce's stories generate by interpreting the absence of reliable significance in the fiction as a problem only for Joyce's poor, paralyzed *Dubliners*. Thus Brewster Ghiselin characterizes the stories as "one essential history, that of the soul of a people which has confused and weakened its relation to *the source of spiritual life* and cannot restore it" (1956, 41). According to Ghiselin, Joyce does not question "the source of spiritual life," instead he reaffirms its importance by presenting characters who have, for reasons peculiar to them, become estranged from it. At another point he states, "in *Dubliners* from first to last the substitutes are prominent, the true objects are unavailable" (1956, 83). In assuming the existence of "true objects," Ghiselin misses what Lacan promotes as a central tenet of his theory of the subject: objects of desire, as well as linguistic objects (words) are always substitutes for the primordial loss the subject suffers in the mirror stage.[5] Nearly twenty years later, Brown makes essentially the same point as does Ghiselin when he accuses the characters in *Dubliners* of being "unable wholly to give themselves to the world of the here and now" (1972, 47). Brown's insight is valid; his mistake lies in chastising the characters for inabilities that all human subjects demonstrate.

In the first extensive psychoanalytical approach to *Dubliners*, Edward Brandabur voices his discontent with the ready belief in "the Joycean self": "What was the Joycean self? It does not seem enough to define this self as the one who juggled all the masques" (1971, 16). I agree, and at the core of my argument is an antiessentialism, influenced by Lacanian theory, that sees reality, gender, personality, and so on, as the reality effects of a subject seeking to deny a lack-in-being that exists alongside of and, thus, undermines the mythic ideology of unified consciousness.[6] From the first story in *Dubliners*, Joyce's prose attacks this ideology of the "self," thus undermining at the same time the commonplace assumption that consciousness equals "truth." He transforms this overly optimistic equation into a more mysterious one: consciousness equals a fictional construct that performs a masquerade of truth because, to use Lacanian terms, it is attached to signifiers that reside beyond the subject in the Other (and in the unrepresentable sphere of the Real). The writings of both Lacan and Joyce suggest that one makes "a lot of fuss and bother" about the mystery of the unconscious because one does not wish to see consciousness as equally mysterious and a good deal less coherent. One can only misread *Dubliners* as an affirmation of the essential Truth about subjectivity if one imposes a metanarrative on the stories that fills in the unsettling gaps and voids in the body of the text. My approach to the stories, far from filling in gaps, will actually focus upon them and even privilege them as glimpses of the *points de capitons* by which subjects attach their formless beings to the preexisting symbolic order of language, gender, and socially constructed "truth."[7] As Ragland-Sullivan notes, "One sees that a Lacanian reading of Joyce's texts will pay heed not only to jokes, puns, slips of the tongue, and so on, but also to the appearance of the gaze, the voice, or to any equivocation which points to the issue of identifying signifiers" (1990, 75). No organized "self" is serenely present behind the masque of meaning and the mask of identity. Instead, one performs masques because the alternative is to have no sense of destiny at all; one wears masks to keep intact the illusion that behind them one has a real face that must be protected.[8]

Not surprisingly, perhaps, as *Dubliners* became increasingly explainable, the assumption grew that it was more realistic than Joyce's later works.[9] This assumption has come under increasing challenge, most recently by Christine van Boheemen: "Reading *Dubliners* with the insights gained from *Finnegans Wake,* we suddenly discover affinities between the two works which reveal a new complexity in the apparent realism of the earliest epiphanies. . . . The practice of reading 'readerly' fiction like *Dubliners* with the 'writerly' outlook demanded by *Finnegans Wake* might teach us to relativize some of the issues which would seem to divide the profession at present" (1988, 35).

Curiously enough, a glance at a review by a French writer in 1926, written shortly after *Dubliners* was translated into French, reveals a wary appreciation of the way the stories emphasize what Joyce described to Power as "the mystery of consciousness": "He [Joyce] treats—and with a hallucinating truth—only secrets: lusts, despairs, secret or even aborted impulses" (Deming 1970, 72). The truth of consciousness *is* a hallucination because the subject must hallucinate (with language as the phantasmagoric hallucinogen) to see cultural institutions such as the church and ideological institutions such as gender as natural facts rather than constructed reality effects.[10]

As Margot Norris has noted in a recent essay on "The Dead," Lacan's antiessentialism involves "a perception that idealization is the product of complex perceptual structures. These structures—displacements, repressions, extrusions, and the like—that produce sexual desire or the concept of beauty, give to love and beauty political mechanisms and political ends" (1987, 489). One sees as natural facts, reality structures that are not facts and not natural. One does so in order not to see the hallucinating truth of the divided subject that is the well-kept secret of the conscious mind. This mystery contained in the mythical unity of consciousness, like the mystery lurking behind the plague in Thebes, is something that, if one returns to the telling observation of the reviewer in 1914, one should not encourage writers (or kings) to inquire into: "At least three [stories] would have been better buried in oblivion." Significantly, this reviewer does not suggest the stories would have been better left unwritten; instead, the reviewer concedes their right to exist but cannot help wishing that they had been kept secret. And yet, what frightens this reviewer actually excites the iconoclastic Ezra Pound, who recognized, also in 1914, that Joyce depicts a hallucinatory society that will not support any sort of utopic vision of the future: "He does not believe 'life' would be all right if we stopped vivisection or if we instituted a new sort of 'economics.' He gives the thing as it is" (Deming 1970, 676). My study of *Dubliners,* in the light of Lacanian theory, attempts to gaze steadily at gender, culture, and subjectivity as the thing as it is not, rather than the thing as it once was or the thing as it might yet be. Rarely in fiction do characters suffer as exquisitely for the benefit of a reader as they do in *Dubliners,* and I propose that readers explore their kinship with the characters' moral paralysis rather than self-righteously suggest various cures for it.[11]

Lacan, for his part, makes consciousness richly problematical by positing the subject as decentered and self-alienated. He sees Freud's ego as consisting of a mirrored reflection of the outside world. The subject is split between a narcissistic, objectlike total being *(moi)* and a speaking subject *(je)* who tries to validate this (fictional) unity of being by seducing the objective world (the Other) into declaring it authentic. Thus the moi is inherently paranoid because its existence is dependent upon, and solicitous of, outside validation. The je is controlled more than it can afford to realize because the moi exerts constant pressure upon the je to complete the moi's story of self-sufficient autonomy. Beyond this split subject is the Real subject of the unconscious that cannot be represented in imagery or signified in language. It is the remainder (as well as the reminder) of the lack-in-being that the moi is intended to paper over with fantasies of autonomy that constitute what it perceives as reality. The subject depends on others in Real situations (situations that continue to exist beyond the various representations that the subject imposes on them) in order to recognize or reflect its (fictional) unity so as to enable the moi (through the linguistic manipulation of the desire of the other conducted by the je) to reconstitute itself as conscious of reality. Consequently, the subject knows an individual myth of reality, but Truth orbits beyond this representation in the Real (invisible, but not ineffectual) and can only be glimpsed in those decentering moments during which the je fails in its task of linguistic seduction and momentarily experiences the terrifying fact that the moi, the subject's truth, which it desires to serve, is fiction.

Significantly, Lacan himself characterizes Joyce as a symptom and contends, as McGee summarizes it, that "Joyce the symptom illustrates the psychoanalysis that Joyce the subject refuses" (McGee 1988, 2).[12] Ragland-Sullivan makes this same connection and complicates it considerably by linking it to Joyce's often acknowledged role as the father of Modernism: "Joyce's art became a supplement that would give birth to Modernism as that which provokes, but does not answer, and thus pushes 'supposed' masters to interpret, according to Slavoj Zizek. The inert energetics of a jouissance, both unsymbolized and empty yet totally dense and full, that Lacan attributes to the Real, constitutes the painful, silent symptom behind Joyce's language" (1990, 73). McGee characterizes Lacan's remark that Joyce is a symptom as "cryptic," but perhaps it would appear less so if one paired it with a remark Lacan made about the structure of the Freudian ego: "The ego is structured exactly like a symptom. At the heart of the subject, it is only a privileged symptom, the human symptom *par excellence,* the mental illness of man" (1988a, 16).[13] Joyce's characters constantly refuse intimations of reality in order to re-fuse their divided subjectivity (to cure themselves). But they only succeed in slightly altering the structure of their particular ego/symptom, leaving them self-reflective in a temporarily more palatable way but actually no wiser than they were before.[14]

Just as Lacanian analysis invites the subject to see the moi as a fictional construct (as a symptom) that need not be believed implicitly if to do so proves destructive, Joyce's fiction also demonstrates that a slavish allegiance to the script of one's life (a script that has been written by others) only produces a barely manageable despair. Yet this is, to cite one example, what James Duffy prefers to fall back on in "A Painful Case" rather than question the fictional unity of his self-serving moi/je rationalizations. Lacan's scorn for "ego-psychologists" (analysts who shore up subjects' belief in the illusory structure of their moi — rather than generating a dialectic that causes the subjects to challenge this very construct) seems to parallel what I take to be one of Joyce's points in *Dubliners:* One is never so happy as when one is the triumphant hero of one's own story, nor so desolate as when one

is the suddenly vanquished hero of the other story that this same triumphant narrative left untold (this dynamic is neatly presented in the
profound mood swings of the narrator of "Araby").[15] Lacan posits that
some degrees of suffering might be alleviated in the human condition, but the ego itself is necessarily incurable because it papers over
a lack-in-being that can be exposed or denied — but never satiated.
Any sort of cure that a character in Joyce's fiction imagines under-
going merely serves as a prelude for the next identity crisis. Every
time Stephen cures himself in *Portrait,* for example (and he does so
routinely at the close of each chapter), the cure serves as the backdrop
for the debilitating crisis that opens the next chapter (even the cure
at the conclusion of *Portrait* operates as the base for Stephen's multiple
crises on June 16, 1904, in *Ulysses*). Joyce refuses psychoanalysis, I suggest, because he has already faced the terrifying and exhilarating fact
that the structure of consciousness *is* "the mental illness of man." He
is intent on exploring this central paradox of the human condition
rather than pretending to absolve it by strengthening the illusions of
the ego.

    My primary interpretive focus is on Joyce's fiction and not on
Lacan's theory. Although I offer my own readings of Lacan's ideas,
in this book I do not explore the frequent contradictions in Lacan's
theory as it evolved over the space of several decades, nor do I place
the biographical figure of Lacan in a historical and cultural context.
Likewise, analyzing Lacan's deliberate word play in the original French
is beyond the framework of this study. My central purpose is to "Re-
Joyce" *Dubliners,* that is, to present this collection of "easy Joyce" as
an exploration of the mystery of consciousness that is both invigorating and unsettling for the reader. To accomplish this objective, I have
elected to give each story a close textual reading such as it has received only rarely. I have adopted as a goal a challenge that Bonnie
Kime Scott recently set forth: "I have attempted to make newer theory
accessible by . . . seeking clarity of terms, and calling for an abundance of textual references . . . demonstrating that the advent of theory need not herald the disappearance of Joyce's writing" (1988, 15).
Using abundant textual references in play with theoretical concepts
seems particularly appropriate for newer theory because, as Derrida
made clear in his address at the Ninth Joyce Symposium, deconstructive theory itself is inconceivable except as a post-Joycean form of

writing (Benstock 1988b). I work very closely with the text of *Dub-liners* because, in claiming a complex presentation of subjectivity in these stories that bears comparison with later difficult works like *Finne-gans Wake,* I do not want the reader to have to take my word for it.

I will define most Lacanian terms at those points where I am spe-cifically analyzing Joyce's text, but I find it necessary to introduce some of Lacan's central concepts to give the reader a preview of how I will be viewing the cultural and ideological constructs of gender, religion, family, sexual desire, and politics in *Dubliners.* Lacan defines "the Phallus" as a (nonexistent) transcendent signifier that is presumed to bestow monadic self-sufficiency and mastery of the Symbolic Or-der on the masculine subject. The "masculine" subject misrecognizes himself as the unified self he beholds in his mirror image, and he guarantees this fiction that he is "all" by designating the "feminine" subject as "not all." The fact that a man has a penis and a woman does not is a natural enough fact, but the idea that a man possesses "the Phallus" whereas a woman does not is an ideological construct. Indeed, a man must imagine a woman as having been deprived of the Phallus in order to imagine that he has it. The paradox here, for a woman, is that she must pose as not having the phallus precisely because it does not exist. A man, on the other hand, must pose as having what a woman's pose, in fact, designates as an illusion. This *phallocentric* dimension of Lacan's theory has come under attack for appearing to support, as the status quo, the superiority of the mascu-line subject. But Lacan goes on to say that if woman is designated as "not all" in phallocentric discourse, she nevertheless retains a "sup-plementary *jouissance"* that ex-ists beyond a masculine subject's truth and, thus, functions as the ultimate limit upon phallocentric dis-course.[16] For Lacan, the sexual relation consists of two interrelated gender myths: the myth of psychic unity and coherence that is the masculine subject and the corresponding myth of the feminine sub-ject as the site of the otherness and absence that guarantees the supposedly self-evident unity of a man. The irony of this is that by believing in the Phallus, and in the law and order that it represents, a man is symbolically castrated because his penis is, subsequently, just an uneasy rem(a)inder of his insatiable desire that must, henceforth, be completed and authenticated by something outside of himself.[17]

The relevance of this aspect of Lacanian theory to Joyce's fiction has recently been noted by Margot Norris: "The consequences of this perilous construction of sexual identity is that even in adult relations, men and women find the pursuit of desire, the pursuit of the significance and recognition that is a stake in the sexual relationship, elusive except by a series of complex symbolic maneuvers" (1989, 489). The woman, then, becomes crucial to the myth of masculinity because her enigmatic incarnation as "not all" (as lack) serves as a veil in front of the Phallus protecting the masculine subject from the knowledge that the signifier that signifies him does not exist (and, thus, can only perform its function when veiled). "For whoever is encumbered with a phallus what is the woman? A woman is a symptom" (Lacan 1982b, 168). As a symptom, she serves a function similar to that of the ego, or moi; she validates the truthfulness of the fictional construct of masculinity by acting out the fiction of femininity, which is nothing more or less than what is not masculine. She poses as being the phallus so that he, in desiring to have it, will desire her. But in desiring her, because she appears to be it, he is confronted—in the very act of having the phallus—with the fact that he lacks it, too. This paradox is visually represented in the physical act of sex between a man and a woman where a man must lose sight of his penis in order to prove the lack-in-being supposedly made real by a woman's anatomy. The result of this comedy of desire is a strange dance of misrecognition wherein the woman pretends to lack what the man can only pretend he possesses. When the feminine subject fails to perform her part of the masquerade (as do Lily, Molly Ivors, and Gretta in different ways and to varying degrees) the result can be a crisis of gender identity in the masculine subject, a terrifying glimpse into the incertitude of the void upon which gender myths are constructed in the first place: "His [Gabriel's] own identity was fading out into a grey impalpable world" (*D* 223).

In *Dubliners,* I suggest, the masculine subject is shown to be in constant danger of dissolution because of his absolute belief in the fraudulent authority of the phallic signifier and his corresponding abject dependence on the role of the feminine subject as a symptom that provides the veil necessary for the Phallus to perform its (symbolic) function. Women are encouraged by cultural paradigms of femininity to go to greater and greater lengths to guarantee the authenticity of the phallus, but then the resulting insignificance that this imposes on them has the paradoxical effect of rendering their judgment suspect (as in the case of Maria in "Clay" or the slavey in "Two Gallants"). "The males of Dublin," Suzette Henke has observed, "struggle to defend the laws and the word, though reason and logic founder in sentimental drunkenness" (1983, 11). Indeed, the collection is replete with representations of patriarchal authority teetering on the edge of the void: dying, dead, and long-absent priests ("The Sisters," "Araby," "Eveline"), obtuse or drunken uncles who seem to have replaced absent fathers, or older men with perverse desires, or abusive fathers ("Eveline," "Counterparts"), or fathers who feel out of place in their own homes ("A Little Cloud"), or a favorite nephew who unifies a Christmas party in classic patriarchal fashion by giving a speech that is as sentimental as it is insincere, only to collapse in self-doubt when finally left all alone. In the story "Grace," one sees that however disgraceful and abject the fall from patriarchal certitude, there is an enormous effort to res-erect the masculine subject again after his fall from the grace of the masculine gender myth. In this context, it is worth noting that the rehabilitation of Mr. Kernan is exactly paralleled by the rehabilitation of his slightly threadbare silk hat (which, he says, all men must wear if they expect to "pass muster").

In outlining this pattern—a dissolution of the masculine subject that is followed by a strenuous res-erection—I find I have made a claim for *Dubliners* that is similar to a claim Jean-Michel Rabate has made for *Ulysses* and *Finnegans Wake.* I quote it here to reinforce the point made by Van Boheemen (1988) that the reading of *Dubliners* will be radicalized as readers bring to it what they have been taught (somewhat forcibly) by the later works: "The father is constantly denied, dethroned, negated, but also reestablished for a new cycle, to prepare a new fall. He is absent in such a way that he generates the falls, flights, and flourishes of fiction. The legal fiction has really become the law of fiction, linking the performative power of language to the serial signatures of collapsible fathers" (Rabate 1983, 83).

In addition, Ragland-Sullivan outlines some of Lacan's views on *Finnegans Wake* that I argue have relevance for my reading of *Dubliners:* "Lacan says Joyce in *Finnegans Wake* gave up his belief in a substitute or pseudo-father and took the third-person position of one listening to oneself write, rather than the usual second-person position of writer to text. The voice become palpable, if not visible, as a libidinal object that carries signifiers along" (1990, 81). This insight is central to my discussion of Mr. Duffy in "A Painful Case" and Little Chandler in "A Little Cloud." In both cases Joyce shows men who shore up their illusions of "self" by referring to themselves, "from time to time," in the third person. Duffy invents sentences, and Little Chandler "hears" a voice reviewing poems he has not yet written. The anatomical Real of the penis—and the way it visibly manifests incompleteness and infinite desire—actually subverts the symbolic construct of the Phallus that was intended to place the masculine subject at the center of all discourse. To deny the fact that the phallic symbol is constructed in such a way that it is always in danger of subverting itself, this treacherous duality must be seen as coming from outside. Consequently, the masculine subject must be worshipped or denigrated according to whether she confirms or denies the truth of the Phallus (that is, whether she performs the masquerade of femininity that veils its nonexistence and, thus, allows it to perform its function).[18]

Feminine subjects suffer in *Dubliners* because they are expected to repress the question of their own desire in order to guarantee the (fictional) unity of the masculine subject. In this light, I suggest that Mangan's sister is aware of the narrator's attention and helplessly conscious that the boy co-opts the question of her sexuality (in effect, denying it to her). After all, to summarize my argument in a phrase, she is the one who wants to go to Araby! In another example, I argue that Maria's abject helplessness actually makes her a frightening and disconcerting apparition (a witch) because she represents the gaze of the (m)Other—that gaze which first permits the subject's fantasy of phallic autonomy relative to a unified mirror image. Joe, who calls her "my proper mother," labors to get her to authenticate his masculine subjectivity, but in vain. In the end, he still had to be told "where the corkscrew was" (*D* 106). The primary role of confirmation played by the (m)Other is later repressed in the subject's mental economy because he or she must see identity as self-originating in order to preserve the illusion that he or she controls (rather than is controlled by) this Other. "The original moment of consciousness, civilization, and language," Van Boheemen suggests, "may well be the more archaic one of differentiation from the (m)Other—which is covered up, because the text already adopts a strictly patriarchal perspective" (Van Boheemen 1987, 81). The men of "Ivy Day in the Committee Room" gather in a sodden clump and discuss, among other things, the way mothers ruin their children by "cocking them up." They also discuss the execrable way Queen Victoria has prevented her son from ascending the throne, and, finally, (in Hynes's poem) the way "Erin" has taken her poor son Parnell to her breast and will somehow nurture him back to health as a transcendent phallic signifier. No women are present in "Ivy Day," but the alternately frightening and inviting concept of a (m)Other's gaze as the original authenticator of patriarchal order haunts the margins of this story at least as much as the ghost of the dead father (Parnell).

I devote a good deal of my discussion to exposing gender as a social construct, detailing the self-subverting dimension of the Phallic Order, and showing the need for patriarchal order to repress the (m)Other's gaze in order to protect the myth of the self-generation of authority by patriarchal law (what Lacan calls the "Name-of-the-Father"). Because of this emphasis, I think I can fairly claim that my work qualifies as a feminist approach to Joyce. As recently as 1988, Scott cites the need for a study of the construct of gender in Joyce from a feminist perspective: "Feminist versions of Lacan hypothesize a divided subject shaped by the socio-sexual experience of others. Gender marks the parents . . . the mother first supplying semiotic flow, the father later imposing the authority and law of logos. Thus, semiotic, imaginary prelanguage and symbolic, spoken, written logos are gender inflected. The sexual politics of these paradigms in Joyce needs concerted study, certainly in *Finnegans Wake* but also in supposedly realistic tests as early as *Dubliners"* (1984, 161). More generally, in her book *James Joyce,* Scott presents a few charcteristics of a feminist approach to literature that my work aims to fulfill: "Feminists challenge cultural hegemony (established practices, acquiesced to by the masses), attending to various questions and definitions of gender difference . . . exposing the limitations of various behaviors and descourses expected in patriarchal society" (1987, 2). Yet to do this requires, equally, an examination of the masculine gender because one cannot fully understand the desperate origin of the coercive patriarchal forces that insist women must masquerade as worshippers of the Phallic symbol (i.e., masquerade as feminine), unless one understands the integral fraudulence of this symbol of self-sufficient authority that requires something Other (the symptom of "The Woman") to permit the masculine subject to believe in it.

Let me offer an admittedly oversimplified scenario of how the structure of the masculine subject generates the symptom of femininity: In the *Wizard of Oz,* when Dorothy finally reaches the inner sanctum of the Emerald City (after many good and bad witches test the innateness of her femininity) she sees Toto pull back a curtain (the fact that her dog inadvertently performs this action, in her place, preserves her hyperpristine femininity) to expose the wizened wizard (the needy penis as opposed to Oz, the engorged phallic signifier). He is exposed as intently manipulating the tremendously hyperbolic machinery of the Phallic Order. "Pay no attention to the man behind the curtain" cries the little man. This is the pathetic credo of the masculine subject who finds himself at the center of a machine that castrates him to preserve the prior fantasy of his unified existence. This example of the self-denial of a masculine subject (the actual man denies his existence in favor of the existence of the wizard machinery that controls him) highlights the paradox about the Phallic Order and the Name-of-the-Father, which, I think, Lacan outlines and Joyce demonstrates: men victimize others (exert power) precisely because their identity places them in an impossible gender construct in which they can never feel powerful enough. The more a masculine subject subscribes to Phallic Order in an attempt to deny castration anxiety (fear of dissolution), the more he is vulnerable to this precise affect. The more furiously the man operates the machinery of language in a posture of control, the more dependent he is upon the curtain that veils his illusory autonomy.

Correspondingly, women come to grief in their own gender paradox because if they slavishly support the validity of the Phallic Order, they will eventually be spurned and pushed aside; after all, of what use to the masculine subject is the confirmation and admiration of a slave? If they perform the masquerade of femininity poorly, they will not be perceived as women at all. The inability of the Phallic Order to see women who are unfeminine is demonstrated in the story "Clay" where a woman who has never had sex (Maria) is put in a home with other women who made their living out of performing it. The failure to be sufficiently feminine also characterizes, perhaps, the downward spiral of Eveline's relationship with her father (in Joyce's story, "Eveline"); he has denigrated her spirit as much as he can (while continuing to ignore his own problems and his responsibility for them) and will soon move on to beating her physically as well. Alternatively, the women in *Dubliners* who insist on reserving some energy for themselves and refuse to sacrifice it in the service of maintaining a masculine illusion risk varying degrees of social ostracism (Mrs. Mooney, Mrs. Kearney, Molly Ivors).

The final violence of Mr. Farrington in "Counterparts," to cite another example, can be seen as a direct result of Farrington having wrested the admiring gaze of Miss Delacourt from his boss Mr. Alleyne. This generates an enormous lift in his self-esteem that is later dashed when he is snubbed by an anonymous female artiste in a Dublin pub. It is this failure to maintain the authenticating gaze of the (m)Other, coupled with his defeat in arm wrestling, that compels Farrington to search for someone he can *force* to acknowledge the power of the Phallic Order to which he desperately clings. The beating of his son, while an exercise of power, only succeeds in highlighting how helpless he is. Karen Lawrence, in an essay on *Ulysses,* makes an observation that is relative to my approach to *Dubliners:* "Joyce presents the incertitude of paternity even as he demonstrates its power. . . . The maternal silently undermines patriarchal power and the cultural and linguistic structures it underwrites. . . . Maternity . . . is a different kind of 'fiction' than paternity, a fiction of a source before law and identity" (1987, 240).

The corollary of this masculine fall from grace for the feminine subject can be seen in Eveline's depression over her eroding relationship to the "power" of the Phallic Order: her brothers rarely come home any more, and her father's increasingly desperate need to bully is slowly building to the point where he will begin beating her. Her obsession with her mother's request that she keep the family together makes it clear that she sees the crumbling of the Phallic Order as somehow her own fault because she is not feminine enough. As with Farrington, Mr. Hill's inexorable drift toward physical abuse can be analyzed, in the light of Lacanian theory, as an indication of how violence is a frequent response of the masculine subject when the veil put before the phallic signifier (which permits the illusion of patriarchal authority) becomes transparent (through such debilitating circumstances as alcoholism, poverty, unemployment, and failed love affairs).

For several reasons I have focused my study solely on *Dubliners.* First, *Dubliners* has not yet been thoroughly discussed in the light of post-Freudian psychoanalytic theory. Yet, as Fritz Senn noted nearly twenty-five years ago, even in his earliest work Joyce "seemed incapable of using words in one single bare sense only" (1965, 66). Because the later works appear so much more complex than *Dubliners,* critics enter the woods of *Ulysses* and *Finnegans Wake* sprinkling insights about *Dubliners* behind them like so many breadcrumbs that will aid them later when they seek their way back out of the forest. In 1978, Marilyn French used another metaphor gleaned from fairy tales to describe the relative treatment of *Dubliners* by critics: "*Dubliners* remains one of the stepchildren in Joyce studies, receiving less attention than its important siblings, and a fragmented attention more often than not" (443). I suggest that *Dubliners* is a stepchild because it is most often *a stepladder* to the later works. Actually, I see nothing wrong in using *Dubliners* as a gloss on the later works; my only point is that to do so is not the same thing as conducting a painstaking analysis devoted exclusively to this collection.

Although I frequently mention other stories when discussing a particular story, I have chosen to give each story a clearly demarcated section of its own. First, I have tried to preserve the complexity of Lacanian theory to make its interplay with Joyce's fictions as rich as possible, and I have found that hopping from story to story to illustrate an aspect of Lacanian theory makes the collection a stepchild again—this time to post-Freudian theory. Second, although I acknowledge the tremendous importance of those critics who examine how the stories interrelate, an over emphasis on this interrelation can become just another way to domesticate the subversive quality of the text by maintaining that what is inexplicable in one story can be explained by reference to another. By highlighting different aspects of Lacanian theory as I look at each story, I am better able to meet a goal that van Boheemen set forth in her talk on "Deconstruction after Joyce" at the Ninth Joyce Symposium: "We must shed the desire to articulate 'the meaning' of the text—any single meaning will prove to rest upon the reader's strategy of exclusion. Perhaps all that the critic can articulate without falsifying the complexity of the fiction is not *what* the text means, but *how* it means" (1988, 35).

In my discussion of "The Sisters," for example, I detail my understanding of the three Lacanian orders: the Symbolic, the Imaginary and the Real to suggest how the text negotiates the realm between the unconscious and the structure of consciousness, between the inaccessible truth of the real and the fiction of reality. These concepts continue to inform later discussions, but in my analysis of "Eveline," in order to highlight a different dimension of Lacanian theory, I pay particular attention to Lacan's idea that a woman has access to a "supplementary *jouissance*" that places the self-enclosed Phallic Order in question. The text of "Eveline," for example, by presenting Eveline through the gaze of her departing lover, tries to eliminate the threat of supplementarity she represents by perceiving her as beyond the human dimension—as an animal.

Third, I flatter myself that this study might be of particular use in the classroom where these stories are very often taught. A book like *Ulysses* does not lend itself easily to an undergraduate syllabus, so a student's first encounter with Joyce is typically a story from *Dubliners* (or perhaps the collection as a whole). But all the recent exciting discussions of *Ulysses*, conducted in the strobe light of contemporary theory, cannot be easily imported into the classroom using a story from *Dubliners* as the only vehicle. Mindful of this, I have tried to give readings to these stories that are open-ended and provocative. Attridge and Ferrer have written: "One would have thought that the need to make Joyce readable and reputable had long since passed, and that the time had come to take the full measure of his literary revolution" (1984, 7).

Yet *Dubliners* has not benefited much from this literary revolution that may have begun to liberate the later works.[19] Lacan's seminars were famous not because they were alternately brilliant and obscure but because their brilliance necessitated their obscurity. The audience's sense of having discovered something hitherto unknown is a direct result of Lacan subverting what they thought they already knew. The unknown Real beyond the supposedly known reality can only be perceived in teasing glimpses. What one learns, if it is to be of value, must be at the expense of what one thinks one knew; it is when readers feel that they "have learned their lesson" that genuine education ceases. Speaking of Joyce's fiction in general, Sheldon Brivic states: "As the text grows aware that the objects it frames are products of convention, it moves toward finding reality in the structure of its own process" (1990, 183). It is the process of failing to understand that constitutes learning, it is the experience of incomprehension that is the lesson of *Dubliners*. In "The Sisters" it is what the boy cannot see that opens his eyes. In "An Encounter" it is the texts the teacher banishes from the classroom that instruct the boy as to the incertitude of his existence. In "Araby" the narrator sets off for a place he is not sure he can find, for reasons known only by someone else, to bring back something he cannot name; the journey is one he cannot forget because, like the most profound lessons people experience, he can recite it again and again without ever learning it. Perhaps more than anything else, my study of *Dubliners* involves a re-Joycing of the texts that highlights Joyce's extraordinary ability to teach readers what they do not want to know by appearing to offer the sort of comfortingly useless knowledge they consciously crave.

The individual stories from *Dubliners* frequently show up in various anthologies with a brief introduction designed to make them "user friendly" and ready for unambiguous deployment in the classroom. I hope my work, in contrast to this, lives up to Attridge and Ferrer's call for scholars "to produce Joyce's texts in ways designed to challenge rather than comfort, to antagonize instead of assimilate" (1984, 7). My primary thesis about *Dubliners,* then, is that Joyce wanted to present lived experience (consciousness) as an oscillation of bewilderment and conviction that stems from the uncertain social structures that govern individual certitude: identity, gender, and subjectivity. Joyce seemed aware of a force that one might call the unconscious, but, like Lacan, he saw this force as exhibiting itself everywhere through the gaps of a subject's spurious continuity of consciousness.[20] The characters in *Dubliners* struggle to maintain their individual barriers against the steady current of the unrepresented, unsymbolized Real that threatens, in moments of crisis, to sweep them away from all the identity landmarks contained in language and culture. Recently, Morris Beja made the general comment that "critics are beginning to follow Joyce's lead in questioning the traditional gender distinctions . . . and in questioning, indeed, the value of absolute of 'spiritual' distinctions between maternity and paternity in the first place" (Benstock 1988b, 218). I think it is crucial to underline here that Joyce questioned these distinctions — he did not answer them — for to do that would be to erase existing distinctions in order to inscribe new ones.

How does Joyce remove these distinctions while denying himself and the reader the comfort of imposing new ones? He does so by allowing concepts such as authority, paternity, maternity, femininity, and masculinity to plead their cases as long as they want. The very defense that these distinctions are innate always reveals the gaps, ellipses, and misrecognitions that show these natural forces and categories to be elaborate cultural constructs that are designed to protect the subject from the spurious nature of his or her "self." Indeed, innateness is the crucial myth of subjectivity because it precludes the necessity to explain or understand something that "just is." As Vicki Mahaffey has noted, "The source of authoritarian power — whether that of the author, the priest or the reader — is its mystery, its gaps, its selectivity" (1988, 30). In fact, the totalizing drive toward building explanatory paradigms arises from the subject's structural lack-in-being (something very like what Joyce called "the incertitude of the void"). The moi's insistence on verifiability and fixity is meant to obscure the fact that the subject's presumed autonomy depends upon the gaze and desire of what Lacan calls the other (the authenticator of one's unified, presocial self that one first misrecognized during the mirror stage and has designated as true despite all evidence to the contrary).[21] People try to interrogate and impress the Other in their relationships with others and, thus, celebrate the countable unity of the "self" that they see reflected in the other's recognition of them.

Indeed, Joyce's stories operate uncannily like the ideal Lacanian psychoanalyst in that they repeatedly interrupt the readers' self-referential reveries by subverting the continuity of the plot at the very point where they were most inclined to let its mythic unity stand in for their being. All of the stories end with the tantalizing abruptness of the Lacanian "short session" in which the analyst purposely aborts the analysand's discourse by leaving before the end of the session. For Lacan, the purpose of the short session is to terminate the subject's story before he or she "knew." Like Lacan's perfect analyst, Joyce not only interrupts the reader's expectations, he interrupts his own as well. When searching for "what Joyce meant" one must consider the possibility that every time he discerns a thematic pattern in his fiction he interrupts it and, then, dwells on the resulting rip in reality through which the Real momentarily shows through.

I can still remember the sensation of impending certitude I felt as I neared the end of my first reading of "The Sisters." I knew that merely by turning the next page I would discover, along with my surrogate being (the narrator), what, if I had to name it, I would have called "the real secret of Father Flynn." The shock of reading, instead,

Eliza's pseudosummary as it dwindled feebly into an ellipsis, and staring in disbelief at the unknowable blankness of the paper beneath the last line of text, is something from which I have never fully recovered! In that moment, I was thrown back into what Lacan calls "the lumberroom of the mind"—that cluttered room with restricted access, just behind the place where one stages one's existence: the room of scrap parts out of which one first constructed the myth of oneself. James Snead makes this connection between Joyce's creatures of contingency (I suggest this phrase in place of "characters") and Lacan's theory of the fading subject:

> At the mention of "fading" within a larger semantic organization of desire and response, we have almost attained Joyce's mature presentation of characters. Lacan sees character in dialectical fashion. The subject is the interaction of many subjects using a medium, language, based upon absences that repression struggles to hide. Lacan's position presents an advance over the earlier idea that one could understand character by deciphering textual "symptoms"— an idea that really is another version of the "writer's chart" approach. Instead, linguistic figuration creates reality in order to cover up its own lacks. (1988, 144)

Instead of "character," Joyce gives us a subject's moi repetitions, which intertwine with rhetorical strategies of the je to weave a "self" that protects the subject from the primordial disunity and fractured communications that blow steadily from the region of the Other. This leads me to address a question posed by Rabate: "If, finally, *Dubliners* rules out any final recourse to a metalanguage, what are the consequences for the ethics and the politics of reading?" (1982, 46). My preliminary response, which I will elaborate upon in this work, is that the reader, as well as Joyce, reveals through the interplay of consciousness and text that the ego one holds so dear is a symptom, and the text cannot cure this symptom (fortunately!), but it can isolate some of the various threads that form the knot of the "self" and show their inextricable relationship with the Real that informs the texture of reality.[22]

Lacan's theory suggests that all who read or analyze fiction do so to deny the fact of their own castration. People do this whether they are masculine or feminine subjects because both of these gender constructs are attempts to avoid knowledge of the symbolic castration.

Jean Guy Godin contends that Joyce knew this well before Lacan: "In fact, Joyce knows by himself what Lacan teaches. Before this text, before any text, the psychoanalyst's role is not to analyze the author but to let the text teach the psychoanalyst. The way the text functions should be the only criterion" (1988, 211).

For Lacan, castration refers to the fact that people are permanently incomplete and however much they try to complete themselves with language and other signifiers in the Symbolic Order, they are only dealing with substitute objects of desire that merely stand in for the unity they imagined in the mirror phase. The fear, in other words, is not of organ loss but of loss of the (fictional) unity of the "self." In deciphering the meaning of a story and in discovering the motivation of a character, they feel they are confirming the validity of the gender and identity myths that deny the Real of symbolic castration. Instead of seeing the "self" as a fictional construct, dependent upon language, signifying chains in the Symbolic Order, and the gaze and Desire of the Other, they see themselves as autonomous beings in control of the reality that confronts them.

The fear of castration can be understood as fear of falling out of the world of words into the void of the Real. In analyzing a story, readers impose their own discourse on the text and, in effect, occupy the place of the Real relative to what they see as the author's sadly constrained fictional creations. This position allows them to deny their own castration, which is to deny their own construction as fictional beings. But as Helene Cixous makes clear, Joyce's writing is aggressively subversive of the reading subject because it manipulates or frustrates any impulse on the part of the reader to strengthen the illusion of mastery by discerning the meaning of the story.

> This writing which is prodigal and therefore disconcerting because of its economy, which refuses to regulate itself, to give itself laws . . . to impose a rigid grid on the reader, to produce an effect of mastery. . . . It is an extraordinarily free game, which should shatter any habits of reading, which should be continually shaking the reader up, and thus committing this reader to a double apprenticeship: the necessary one which is reading-writing a text whose plurality explodes the painstakingly polished surface: and the one which is, in the very practice of reading, not condemned to linearity, an incessant questioning of the codes which appear to function normally

but which are sometimes suddenly rendered invalid, and then the
next moment are revalidated. (1984, 19)

Joyce is not radical in the typical sense of the word as one who
undermines existing institutions. He is much more frightening than
this because of his tripartite alternation of validation, invalidation, and
revalidation. The revalidated truth must, henceforth, be regarded by
the subject from a perspective of permanent unease because its very
structure as revalidation announces the inevitability of a future invalidation. From a Lacanian perspective, Joyce's prose in *Dubliners* exposes the apparent fact of any sort of institution or ideology as just
another meaning system designed to deny castration and compensate
for a structural lack-in-being. At the same time, the struggling narrators and characters blame themselves for this state of affairs and invite
the reader to do likewise. In essence, Joyce subverts the comforting
idea of characterization by making the boundary of the "self" endlessly permeable. Instead of a self-contained character, he presents the
matrix of contingencies that underlie the mystery of an individual's
consciousness. When one attempts to defuse the text of *Dubliners* by
analyzing the morals and motivations of Joyce's characters, one ignores the fact that neither their morals nor their motivations are their
own. Instead, they are an internalization of what they imagine the
morals and motivations of other people to be — in other words, what
they imagine the Other desires.

Joyce's creatures of contingency in *Dubliners* search for substitute
objects in their world that will complete them and return them once
again to the Edenic mirror stage where they first imagined their unity.
But these substitutions turn out to be empty (Father Flynn's chalice),
or hollow (the empty and dark hall in "Araby"), or false (Gabriel's
elaborate mental scenario in which he imagines Gretta will recognize
his desire for her just by the way he calls her name). The realization
that the object of desire is once again a substitute often seems to serve
as the epiphany of the story. But the epiphany, I will argue, is also
the desperate establishment of a painfully altered "self" before the terrifying facelessness of the implacable and irreducible Real. Although
the text often appears to validate this suddenly altered "self" (e.g., the
crestfallen boy at the close of "Araby"), I hope to demonstrate that
it is precisely this sort of overhasty discovery of truth that allows the

text to expose reality as a fictional construct that permits the split subject to misrecognize the actual indifferent and subversive power of the unrepresentable Real as the imagined benevolent gaze of the Other (i.e., to deny symbolic castration). To merely point out the mistakes of the characters in *Dubliners* or to regard them, from a comfortable distance, as unique victims of the ineffable disease of moral paralysis, is to fantasize one's unity as a literary critic. To feel sorry for them is to avoid feeling sorry for ourselves.

2

The Free Man's Journal
The Making of His[S]tory in "The Sisters"

Just as what is rejected from the symbolic register reappears in the real, in the same way the hole in the real that results from loss, sets the signifier in motion. This hole provides the place for the projection of the missing signifier, which is essential to the structure of the Other. (Lacan 1982a, 38)

Every night as I gazed up at the window I said softly to myself the word paralysis. . . . It sounded to me like the name of some maleficent and sinful being. It filled me with fear, and yet I longed to be nearer to it and to look upon its deadly work. (*D* 9)

Over the last thirty years, "The Sisters" has been persistently analyzed, both as a self-contained story and as an early example of Joyce's complex preoccupations in *Portrait, Ulysses,* and *Finnegans Wake.* The need to explicate the story thoroughly has never had to be defended; after all, it is the first published piece of fiction by one of the most important prose writers of our century.[1] By using some of the insights of Lacanian theory, I show that the boy is thrilled with an increasing command of language that allows him to narrate silently his own story (his[s]tory) in deliberate contrast to the narration of the various adults who frequently surround him — but only rarely include him. Yet he must be careful because, as he parenthetically informs the reader: "It was vacation time" — a time when structured outward demands are suddenly lifted, leaving him to face, perhaps for the first time, the very idea of "this time" (*D* 9). His status as a free man, in turn, generates, also for the first time, the need for him to tell his story in opposition to the role others have assigned him to play in their stories. He is frightened, however, that in gaining the use of the word he may have lost touch with the world (it is clear to him that the adults have).

His defense against the possibility that his reality might be fiction consists of his eschewing all speculative narration in favor of a sequence of literal descriptions that are nearly psychotic in their careful word selection and obsessive concern for fully describing every detail of what he sees. Curiously, a good deal of the boy's vacation time is spent exercising private rituals that fascinate him primarily because the adults who scrutinize him know nothing about them. If he is to discover who he is apart from them, he must have activities that they do not suspect. Father Flynn presided over some of these rituals, which rendered them authoritative, but now he's dead and the boy is suddenly aware of the central dilemma of a human subject: How does one authenticate one's "self"? He has only recently realized that the sisters, his uncle, and Old Cotter are no help in this regard because they only seem to know what they want him to be for them. With no one trustworthy to oversee his rituals during the unstructured time of vacation (nothing given him by another to memorize, nothing to recite to another for possible correction), the boy is wary about making a mistake in his use of language that might cause him to misrepresent the precious facts that the adults around him seem determined to keep to themselves.

He prizes accuracy above all else, and his strategy for concerning himself strictly with reality is to deliberately interrupt his own flights of fancy (which include his recollections of a dream from the night before) and force himself, without a moment's notice, to describe dispassionately some actual item in his immediate environment: the card announcing Flynn's death in one instance, the flowers at the wake in another, Nannie's boot heels, and Father Flynn's nostrils. The curiously paranoid tenor of the boy's narrative results from the undertow of fancy that keeps threatening to erode the outlines of reality. Put another way, the concrete details that the boy strings together are not at all arbitrary.

Increasingly, he is aware of some lack at the center of his own being that he would like to fill with the truth about himself. As a result of this impulse (which can be viewed as Desire in Lacan's sense of the term), he is drawn to those objects whose presence is undercut by an absence (the geometric figure of the gnomon is the primary example). What strikes him first about the flowers is their scent. Immediately, he is alarmed at this disembodied scent, and hastens to name its cause: "There was a heavy odour in the room — the flowers" (*D* 14). The sentence begins ominously and then ends with a reassuring bump — the signifier, after all, has a signified. The narrator's implicit question for objects he sees before him is "Where has it come from?"and his reaction to objects he remembers seeing is "Where has it gone?" He is fascinated by the card announcing Father Flynn's death because this sign has replaced a sign that used to be there, a sign that read "Umbrellas Re-covered." Who removed the sign? Where is it now? In this case, the absence of a sign and its replacement by a new sign does not cause the first sign to disappear; instead, a residue is left in the narrator's mind that he cannot dislodge. A similar dynamic motivates his reluctant fascination with Nannie's boot heel. He is drawn to describing it because something that is missing from it is announced by what remains. What wore down her boot heel? Something so vast as to be unrepresentable. Where has the worn part gone? Somewhere where it can neither be retrieved nor completely forgotten.

Therese Fischer was one of the first critics to feature the enigmatic quality of the story as the point of the story. Fischer eschews explication in favor of excavation — examining what is there rather than bringing something new to the site. After discovering the shortcomings of the narrator, Fischer says, "The reader is prepared for the 'blank spots,' which he will be able to fill, only after having transcended the character's limited, though not altogether unreliable view" (1971, 88–89). But when discussing at what point the narrator is unreliable and why this should be so, Fischer's rhetoric becomes as enigmatic and paradoxical as the text she is discussing: "He is reliable insofar as he does not tell lies purposely" (1971, 89). Can one tell a lie without intending to? How can readers accuse the narrator of misleading them — either on purpose or by accident — when his constant lament is that he does not know what is going on? The only time the narrator adopts an authoritative tone is when he recites matters of public record: "I knew that two candles must be set at the head of a corpse." Or when he tells readers what they already know: "I knew that the old priest was lying still in his coffin as we had seen him" (*D* 18). Concerning the little bit he knows, the narrator is completely reliable; in fact, he takes pains to avoid even the appearance of prevarication by relating the most obvious facts in a tone of daring assertiveness that strikes the ear as odd because what he insists upon is never anything one would think to question: he and the priest were friends; the priest has died; he has seen the dead priest. All three of these facts are verified at least once by other characters in the story.

The persistently odd tone of the narration — where the boy earnestly tries to persuade readers of what they cannot reasonably doubt — creates a feeling of unreliability *in the reader*. The boy is so careful to draw readers' attention to the obvious that after awhile they feel they can take nothing for granted. "There was a heavy odour in the room." Oh really, they collectively think, leaning forward in anticipation of a revelation; "the flowers" the narrator solemnly reassures them. It is as if the boy were playing detective in an environment so safe that ordinary objects must be deliberately misunderstood even to appear dangerous; he insists on turning the apparently pleasant into the possibly vicious. Matters that should be reassuringly clear — that the dead priest is still in his coffin, for instance — are made mysterious because the narrator takes such pains to reassure readers about the truth of what they would never think to verify. After all, who goes to a wake to see if the person is really dead? The situation of the readers, where the obvious is made uncertain, should sound familiar because the narrator is only doing to them what Father Flynn did to him: "His questions showed me how complex and mysterious were certain institutions of the Church which I had always regarded as the simplest acts" (*D* 13). The boy's narrative style, to make my point more directly, is too scrupulous always.

Objects such as the boot heel and the sign announcing the priest's death are reality for the boy, but the absent force that wore down the heel or covered over the sign that was normally visible — a force maleficent, unnamed, and paralyzing — is akin to what Lacan calls the real: something beyond representation that influences all the fictive structures by which one inserts one's 'self' into the narrative of reality. For the readers, the curious effect of the boy's obsessive accuracy is that they begin to view apparent reality as irrelevant and long to uncover what is really going on. Thus, readers lose their transcendent subjectivity in relation to the text and are slowly forced to participate in the boy's fear that words, however scrupulously applied and accounted for, may hide something; as symbols for something that is absent, they are a presence that, however concretely presented, implies a residue of unnameable absence beyond what can be consciously known. The subject constructs meaning by attaching him or herself to a signifier, but this very attachment becomes the mark of a henceforth impossible desire.

Objects such as the priest's window, the candles at the head of the corpse, the flowers, and the chalice, all *pose* as objects of the boy's desire, but these simple objects inevitably become ominous when they are later revealed as yet another substitutive satisfaction for an insatiable desire that always returns. Lacan's description of the function of desire in the structure of subjectivity is particularly relevant to the narrator's repetitive insistence on elevating commonplace objects to a point where they, in their indomitable otherness, become more real than he feels: "The very structure at the basis of desire always lends a note of impossibility to the object of human desire. What characterizes the obsessional neurotic in particular is that he emphasizes the confrontation with this impossibility. In other words, he sets everything up so that the object of his desire becomes the signifier of this impossibility" (Lacan 1982a, 36). Most of the objects described in Joyce's story are incomplete; thus, they stand for and emphasize the impossible structure of his "self" even as they permit him to assert its (fictional) unity.

Certainly, one of Joyce's first editors was unsettled by the narrative tone of "The Sisters," and he was certain that what was unsettling about the story must be something just beyond the grasp of his intellect: "He asked me very narrowly," Joyce wrote his brother Stanislaus, "was there sodomy also in 'The Sisters' and what was 'simony' and if the priest was suspended only for the breaking of the chalice. He asked me also was there more in 'The Dead' than appeared" (Joyce 1966, 2:305–6).

Joyce critics have questioned "narrowly" ever since, but the story consistently reproduces in readers the confusion of the boy who, when introduced by the priest to "books as thick as the *Post Office Directory* and as closely printed as the law notices in the newspaper elucidating . . . intricate questions," accepts that nothing is as it seems, which reduces him to making "no answer or only a very foolish and halting one" (*D* 13). Readers cannot help suspecting that behind the boy's reality is a different reality, located, perhaps, in the blank spots that Fischer says they will be able to fill in if they transcend the boy's narration. Essentially, the challenge of the boy's narration is that if readers cannot complete his story, they cannot be sure of the coherency of their own reality. Filling in the blank spots, after all, does not transcend the boy's narration; it merely replaces it with their own. The story, as told by him, remains hauntingly absent on the margins of analysis, like the absent *"Umbrellas Re-covered"* sign, silently influencing how one creatively misrecognizes the incomplete signifiers of the story.

As critics, readers have become as fascinated with various objects in the story as the narrator (the crackers and wine are a prominent example) and they interrogate each object hoping it will provide them with a glimpse of truth by revealing itself as a signifier with a verifiable signified. But, as Lacan makes clear, an object can only function as an object of desire *because* it embodies within itself the incompleteness readers seek to deny about themselves.

> Through his relationship to the signifier, the subject is deprived of something of himself, of his very life, which has assumed the value of that which binds him to the signifier. The phallus is our term for the signifier of his alienation in signification. When the subject is deprived of this signifier, a particular object becomes for him an object of desire.
>
> The object of desire is essentially different from the object of any need. Something becomes an object in desire when it takes the place of what by its very nature remains concealed from the subject: that self-sacrifice, that pound of flesh which is mortgaged in his relationship to the signifier. (1982a, 28)

A commonplace criticism about this story, for example, is that the boy's refusal to eat the crackers offered to him is a refusal of Holy Communion. Following this interpretation, the boy can be seen by the critic as refusing something that is beyond him (Communion) but which is also, presumably, still available to readers (or to others, or to the boy himself at some later date). By highlighting the boy's fear and confusion as a refusal of a preexisting sacrament (Communion), readers reserve for themselves the possibility of re-fusing their own lives. In other words, they reserve for themselves the privileges of transcendent subjectivity. However, the Real effect of the boy's narration is to highlight the way that objects of desire signify the impossibility of Communion. Every object of desire attracts people by the way it appears to fill a gap in their being (by posing as the Phallus, the signifier that guarantees the existence of a signified) even as it represents the very division in "selves" that makes subjectivity and the structure of the ego (Lacan's moi) a necessary fiction. One sees the boy as refusing Communion rather than seeing the refusal of the signifier to supply communion to the subject's sense of inalterable otherness that inaugurated insatiable desire in the first place.

The narrator does not invent blank spots in the text by inadvertently or deliberately lying. He invents them for just the opposite reason; he proves unable, despite being scrupulously honest, convincingly to cover the blank spots that are contained in the objects around him and in the fiction of his "self" (what Lacan calls a lack-in-being) that corresponds to those objects. Lacan states: "Is the place that I occupy as the subject of a signifier [utterance] concentric or eccentric in relation to the place I occupy as subject of the signified? [statement] — that is the question. It is not a question of knowing whether I speak of myself in a way that conforms to what I am, but rather of knowing whether I am the same as that of which I speak" (1977, 165).

The eccentric relationship, between what the boy says and who he imagines himself to be, makes the reader vaguely aware of the lack-in-being that haunts any human subject. Thus, understanding the story actually becomes, for the reader, an attempt to counteract its paralytic effect by superimposing a meaning on the text that makes the reader coherent and the narrator unreliable. The simplest way to understand the story (and this is the strategy that Joyce's earliest editors and publishers employed) is to assume that something traumatic has happened to the boy that has not happened to the reader (i.e., the narrator has been sodomized by a priest he took to be his friend and is, thus, understandably confused). In this way, the reader blocks the text from confusing his or her understanding of him or herself. But Joyce is extremely careful to have the text offer no real authority for taking this way out. What is often described as the boy's failure to achieve closure or Communion is really his ruthlessly accurate depiction of the impossibility of doing so, which reminds readers of their own impossible structure as speaking beings. So they experience the effect of this text as something maleficent, something signifying their own impossibility; yet, for decades now, they have longed "to be nearer to it and to look upon its deadly work" (*D* 9).

But where do the holes in the subject's story of himself come from? Lacan posits something beyond representation that he calls the Real. It is different from reality because it is the residue of everything unexplainable that threatens to subvert what one takes to be truth; it exists because there is no innate relationship between signifier and signified and no possibility of permanent satisfaction in the relationship between what people lack and what this lack persuades people that they want. Florence Walzl says of the boy's dream, "This dream projects, not the reality of events, but the more gripping reality of doubt and fear" (1973, 413).

Are there two kinds of reality? Or does the "reality of events," which is not all that is real, cover the more gripping reality of doubt and fear that Lacan has designated as the Real—a place beyond representation that silently dictates the manner in which people represent themselves? "Symmetrically," Lacan states, "the hole, the gap of being as such is hollowed out in the real. The notion of being, as soon as we try to grasp it, proves itself to be as ungraspable as that of speech. Because being, the very verb itself, only exists in the register of speech. Speech introduces the hollow of being into the texture of the real, the one and the other holding on to and balancing each other, exactly correlative" (1988b, 229). The narrator wants to understand, to commune with, an object such as Eliza's boot heel, but what makes him feel alive, that is, what makes him talk about it, is that the part of it that is irretrievably missing, the gnomonic quality of the boot heel, is "exactly correlative" to the lack-in-being that lies at the heart of his own subjectivity.

Something Other than the boot heel defines what he sees, and it is not represented in his careful description; something Other than his consciousness defines who he imagines himself to be and is, thus, capable of either authenticating this construct or exposing it as fiction. In his dream, the boy recedes from the world of incomplete objects and encounters instead a "pleasant and vicious region" where the covered umbrella sign and the absent part of a boot heel still reside: the Real.

"Just as what is rejected from the symbolic register reappears in the real, in the same way the hole in the real that results from loss, sets the signifier in motion" (Lacan 1982a, 38). Rejected from the symbolic register is that which people find impossible to express fully in speech: nothing less than the unity of their own being. What cannot be expressed does not disappear, however, but becomes something like the maleficent being that the boy imagines might be lurking behind words—an Other that is watching him when he is not aware of being watched and directing him when he is not aware of being directed. "The real," Lacan says, "is that which always lies behind the automaton" (1981a, 54). It sets the signifier in motion, which inaugurates desire. The subject longs to be nearer to the object of desire—and at the same time fears its deadly work—because the gap he seeks to fill in with the object of desire is also the lack that sets the signifier in motion and that generates his reality as a speaking being. This object can only be a substitute for what he desires because the signifier always crosses through (renders incomplete) the thing that is signified.

Truth is elsewhere in the narration of "The Sisters," but truth is always elsewhere when people use language. This elsewhere is not contained somewhere beyond the margins of Joyce's text or in the mind of what was once Joyce or in the transcendent subjectivity of the scholar or in some as yet undiscovered fact about the composition of the story. Joyce's genius, if I had to express it in a sentence, is that he depicts the absence of verifiable truth in his fiction in a manner that exposes the truth of the reader as fiction. The geometrical figure of a gnomon means something because it lacks something; fill in this lack, however, and one does not explain the gnomon; rather the gnomon recedes in a manner that is not at all the same as disappearing, leaving behind in its place a parallelogram—a figure that it would be easy to designate as true if one could forget that one once saw a gnomon, and that, come to think of it, this reassuring word *parallelogram,* which would appear to be the completed background of a gnomon, this wholesome word *parallelogram,* if one were young and impressionable, might sound a lot like *paralysis.* The line between unity and division in the subject can blur as quickly as the phonetics of *parallelogram* and *paralysis* because the subject depends on objects and on others to experience his own being as something that has been authenticated by the gaze of the Other: "The subject is only ever supposed. It is its condition to be only supposable. If it knows anything, it is only by being itself a subject caused by an object—which is not what it knows, that is, what it imagines it knows. The object which causes it is not the other of knowledge. The object crosses this other through. The other is, thus, the Other, which I write with a capital O" (Lacan 1982b, 164). The impossible structure of Desire renders a human subject an incomplete object of otherness, a gnomon. Sexual identity (gender), and moi repetitions recognized by others as real, help the subject knit a "self" that is capable of translating fragmented messages from the other into a (fictional) unity of being. The narrator of "The Sisters" carefully tells readers what he knows, but he senses, alarmed as he is by the elliptical adult conversation around him, that what one knows is never the whole story. Conscious knowledge is already prestructured in reality and is something to which the subject attaches him or herself to keep unconscious truth in the Real at bay. Knowing, for example, that two candles are set at the head of a corpse allows the narrator to understand death without recognizing its Real influence on how he experiences life.

The seamless clichés of the sisters make clear to him that reality is only the part of the story that denies any lack-in-being in the subject by repressing all awareness of the Real beyond representation. Any Real revelation of truth would have to expose the fictional structure of the subject's sense of self and reveal the dynamic by which it depends on meaning and the recognition of others to suppose its own existence as a unified and coherent "self" that is authenticated by the Other. The boy's dream will provide this glimpse when he sees that the feeble smile of the priest is a reflection of what has become his own expression: "I felt that I too was smiling feebly" (*D* 11). In the course of the story, however, the narrator moves away from this unconscious truth back to his dogged pursual of conscious truth: "I knew that the old priest was lying still in his coffin" (*D* 18). The speaking being, which, for Lacan corresponds to what Freud called the *ego*, is the conscious part of the subject that mistakes a story with holes as the whole story: "Human knowledge, and by the same token the sphere of relations of consciousness, consists in a certain relation to this structure that we call the *ego*, around which the imaginary relation is centered. The latter has taught us that the *ego* is never just the subject, that it is essentially a relation to the other, that it finds its point of departure and its fulcrum in the other" (1988b, 177). The boy's overemphasis of the obvious betrays his unease that his subjectivity is structured so that it is both open to authentification and vulnerable to subversion by forces beyond the reality of his "self" experiences.

So far, the primary intent of my reading follows the advice of Attridge and Ferrer, which "is not to produce an indefinite accumulation of . . . meanings . . . but to look at the mechanisms of its infinite productivity" (1984, 10). What Lacan argues is that the subject's conscious knowledge is ignorant of the knowledge that the unconscious speaks through the subject. As such, conscious discourse with another is to some extent scripted by the unconscious (which operates like a language). In this regard, Lacan spoke of the interrelation of the moi and the je in the formation of the conscious subject.

The moi, which is Lacan's elaboration of what Freud called the ego, is a structure that needs to be verified by others because its unity is fictional. Its origin as fiction, however, is irretrievable in conscious life, which means that it functions like a symptom: "The ego is structured exactly like a symptom. At the heart of the subject, it is only a privileged symptom, the human symptom par excellence, the mental illness of man" (1988a, 16). Lacan subverts the idea that the ego has a synthesizing function, calling it instead "that set of defences, of denials . . . of dams, of inhibitions, of fundamental fantasies which orient and direct the subject" (1988a, 17). The repetitive way in which the subject seeks to confirm the unity of the ego betrays the fact that this unity covers up a basic and permanent lack. The moi, therefore, is the subject of identifications, and the je is the subject of speech. The moi presumes to have already answered the question "Who am I?" but can only do so because the je — as speaking subject — seduces others (or tries to) into supplying the answer to the more Real question of *"Who am I in the gaze of the Other?"*

What one might call the Real subject is unconscious and beyond moi constructions and je dialogues. The moi is the basis of reality perception, but this perception, to confirm the myth of selfhood, can only be the reconstruction of that reality which the je supplies in the form of recognition from others. This recognition, of course, is entirely linguistic or semiotic, that is, of the symbolic Order, and the subject relies on the moi to misrecognize this discourse from the outside as a discourse confirming the innate unity of subjectivity. "What do we call a subject?" Lacan asks. "Quite precisely, what . . . is outside of the object? . . . In the human subject there is something which speaks, which speaks in the full sense of the word, that is to say something which knowingly lies, and without the contribution of consciousness. That restores . . . the dimension of the subject" (1988a, 194). Through the je the moi implicitly seeks recognition and confirmation for what it can only imagine itself to be. To put it another way, when people speak, they seek to seduce others into authenticating their personas or roles (which is how the moi manifests itself) in order to experience the (apparent) certitude of consciousness. In this construct, however, consciousness is only the reality effect produced when one sees one's "self" being seen.

Spoken language, however simply stated, always means more than it says, even as it signifies less than the authentification of consciousness that the subject believes it to mean: "The discovery of the unconscious . . . is that the full significance of meaning far surpasses the signs manipulated by the individual. Man is always cultivating a great many more signs than he thinks. . . . That's what man after Freud is" (1988b, 122). For Lacan, the true subject is the subject of the unconscious—not the ego—and so the conscious subject is irredeemably decentered, or as Lacan phrased it, "ex-centric" in relation to itself. When people speak, they do not think who they are, and when they think who they are, (i.e., imagine their unity) they are speechless. The subject is split between a subject of identifications (moi) and a subject of speech (je). These two unbridgeable forces interrelate with one another even as they remain ignorant of their own insatiable existence (except inasmuch as they experience Desire). As Sheldon Brivic put it in his recent Lacanian approach to *Ulysses*, "When we try to look at the subject, it is gone, but we can see where it used to be by looking at otherness, what is unknown to us and unexpected" (1987, 197). In fact, this sounds intriguingly like the situation of the narrator who sees where the *"Umbrellas Re-covered"* sign used to be because of the unexpected sign announcing Father Flynn's death. The unconscious subverts the conscious subject, despite its presumed status as absence, by insisting that its meaning be conveyed in the gap that exists between the moi and je: "The real is that which always comes back to the same place — to the place where the subject insofar as he thinks . . . does not meet it" (Lacan 1981a, 49). The Real functions as "the encounter insofar as it may be missed, insofar as it is essentially the missed encounter" (Lacan 1981a, 55). Very little happens in "The Sisters" because the boy is fascinated by missed encounters: the sign that is unexpectedly gone (a new one, also unexpected, in its place); the news of the priest's death unexpectedly delivered to him (despite his vigilant attempt to learn of it himself); the murmuring words of the priest in his dream (which he cannot quite hear); and, of course, the ubiquitous unfinished sentences that surround him in his waking hours. What makes the boy uneasy is his vague certainty that all these absences are continuing to affect him although they are very nearly behind his conscious awareness. Or, to put it another way, who is he now (as speaking being, or je) relative to who he presumes himself to be (as spoken being, or moi).

This is why the narrator seeks to persuade the readers of what they cannot reasonably doubt. He is in doubt about himself because he is aware of various missed encounters (which signifies, in Lacanian theory, the pressure of the Real on the structure of the ego). He tells everything he knows, but he does so not to inform us — but to form himself — by trying to seduce something other into authorizing his story: "He [Old Cotter] used to be rather interesting, talking of faints and worms; but I soon grew tired of him and his endless stories about the distillery" (*D* 10). He cares nothing about Old Cotter's unfinished stories, except that they remind him of the necessity to finish his own. What truly alarms and angers him is that, in a sense, he *is* Old Cotter's unfinished sentences because he has relied on him (in the past) to confirm for him his role (moi formation) as a perceptive boy worthy to be initiated into sacred mysteries. One knows that Old Cotter is angry at having been replaced in the boy's interest by Father Flynn: "Old Cotter looked at me for a while. I felt that his little beady black eyes were examining me but I would not satisfy him by looking up from my plate" (*D* 10). No doubt for the same length of time that the boy was interested in him, Old Cotter felt interesting to himself. But the tiresome old man who tells endless stories is replaced by the tired old man who tells the story of his end. "He had often said to me: *I am not long for this world*" (*D* 9).

Put simply, Old Cotter is glad his rival for the boy's attention is dead. (Was he only passing by the priest's house? or Did he have his own interest in the event?) If Lacan is correct in saying that subjects reconstitute themselves for each other, then the estrangement of the boy and Old Cotter is not casual. Moi formations guard against fragmentation by seeking contexts that seem to support the fiction that they operate as the unified basis for perceiving and understanding reality. Thus, the moi is inherently paranoid because the specular logic that dictates its formation leaves it dependent upon, and vulnerable to, the gaze of others, which it has to attract in order to experience itself as an autonomous being authenticated by the gaze of the Other. Significantly, the boy now experiences Old Cotter's gaze, which he at one time apparently courted, as an attack: "I felt that his little beady black eyes were examining me" (*D* 10). Although the boy refuses to look up from his plate, he still is able to describe the old man's eyes in scornful detail, and this bespeaks an earlier time when this gaze was not so unwelcome. Obviously, Old Cotter has disappointed the boy by employing fascinating words only to tell repetitive and boring stories, but, conversely, Old Cotter's elliptical warnings suggest that the boy has also disturbed him with his overly mystical interest in the connotations of words like *faints* and *worms*. Father Flynn is not the only one Old Cotter sees as a "peculiar case." I suspect Old Cotter's endless stories about the distillery represent Cotter's attempt to block the boy from unmooring his words—words like *faints* and *worms*—and, thus, set him afloat as well. Indeed, the boy obviously has a reputation for being dreamy and withdrawn, and this trait has been disturbing enough to the family for the uncle to recite a well-known joke about it. "I'm always saying to that Rosicrucian there: take exercise" (*D* 10–11).

Given this reputation and the family's need to distance themselves from it with humor, I suggest that Old Cotter is as suspicious of the boy as he is of Father Flynn. His view of how children should behave, although generally labeled by him as a theory, is really a specific (although incomplete) indictment against the boy. This would explain why the narrator's hostility is more extreme than one might expect toward someone who is merely boring: "Tiresome old fool! . . . Tiresome old red-nosed imbecile!" (*D* 9–10). These statements, which bracket Old Cotter's elliptical lecture, appear to be inexplicable overstatements unless one sees that the narrator is excruciatingly aware that *he* is the decentered point in the ellipses of Old Cotter's unfinished sentences. In fact, one of Old Cotter's unfinished sentences implies that it is the boy who has been suspiciously aggressive in courting the attention of Father Flynn: "Let a young lad run about and play with young lads of his own age and not be. . . ." (*D* 10, Joyce's ellipses). "Of his own age" is an elaborate qualification for someone as inarticulate as Old Cotter, but I would suggest this phrase is balanced against the incomplete phrase "and not be. . . ." The phrase "of his own age" states obliquely what has been left out: "and not be . . . [seducing old men like me and Father Flynn into playing his perverse, mystical games]." The narrator is the missing (silent) piece that perverts the carefully balanced family mythology—the parallelogram—into a gnomon. He is not talking to them, nor are they to him, and so the boy's je has no chance to translate the Real into some shape in the Symbolic that will support his reality (i.e., his version, filtered through his language and the language of others, of who he is relative to the Real). His cunning silence (exile will have to wait until he is able to live on his own) insists that they do not know who he is, but the priest's death has left the boy vulnerable once more to the "normalizing" gaze of his family.

The gaze by which people formulate the belief in the mythical unity of their moi is designated by Lacan as the Other. It is, essentially, the place of the unconscious, but one imagines it as coming from others. This gaze, although it allows one to reconstruct oneself in reality, also permanently decenters one relative to the Real and makes the "self" a construct dependent upon others for confirmation: "In the scopic relation, the object on which depends the phantasy from which the subject is suspended in an essential vacillation is the gaze" (Lacan 1981a, 83). Because one is a subject relative to the 'other,' the system of belief one calls identity subjects one's ego to the recognition of others: "The system of the ego isn't even conceivable without the system, if one can put it this way, of the other. . . . The level on which the other is experienced locates exactly the level on which, quite literally, the ego exists for the subject" (Lacan 1988a, 50).

The narrator of "The Sisters," to paraphrase Matthew Arnold, is between two fictions (two worlds, each given reality by another): one dead (the persona of "that Rosicrucian" activated first—however inadvertently—by Old Cotter, then by Father Flynn) and the other powerless to be born (himself as a free man independent of the boring Old Cotter and the dead Father Flynn). The boy, therefore, is in an identity crisis because with the death of the priest he has no one to talk to, no one to validate his understanding of himself as a unique boy who is worthy of being shown the secret heart of life. He is surrounded by people who insist, in a style that is mysterious and incomplete, that everything about life is self-evident and self-sufficient. Of course, they present this comforting view entirely in half-finished clichés (which supports Lacan's contention that the more one insists upon speaking one's fate, the more one reveals oneself as having already been spoken). Once the boy's dilemma is clear, the reader sees that the meaning of the cryptic kitchen conversation is not elsewhere. The adults do not decline to finish their sentences; they are unable to because the listening boy's silent presence dictates what they are unable to say.

The appearance that Old Cotter is holding something back is a sure indication that he is revealing all he knows (which is not all he knows, but all that he thinks he knows). As the boy falls asleep, he thinks about Old Cotter's unfinished sentences, but his interest is in extracting meaning from what has been said, not in guessing at what Old Cotter declined to mention: "I puzzled my head to extract meaning from his unfinished sentences" (*D* 11). What Old Cotter does not wish to mean can be extracted from what he wishes he meant (his never verbalized theory). The meaning extracted from his sentences is that he wishes to invalidate Father Flynn's view of the boy—his great wish—as having any basis in reality. The boy successfully extracts this meaning, but only in his dream where Father Flynn's authority to validate him is dissolved by the way the boy and the priest swap the "weak smile" (signifier of a crumbling Phallic Order) back and forth. The smile is what the priest used to display to authenticate and authorize the boy's automatic mass responses. But in the dream, instead of sanctifying a relationship in which the father passes on the authority of the Phallus to the son, the same smile is shown to be a disembodied signifier that marks any masculine signified as a castrated subject. The ability of others to confirm identity recedes in the dream while the phenomenon of experiencing the 'self' only in relation to the gaze of the Other (the talking head of the priest) is highlighted. One glimpses the origin of one's supposed conscious autonomy in dreams, and it is always someone or something that one is watching as it looks back. By imagining what it is that this gaze sees, one conceptualizes oneself."

In a fashion similar to that of Old Cotter, Eliza details the failures and shortcomings of Father Flynn. Her delivery of this information is also elliptical—and even more cautiously presented—but the performance of her narrative in front of the boy masks the same intention: undermine Father Flynn's authority and make the boy dependent, once again, on the message of the family: "You are what we see you as." The hemorrhage in the family has been staunched by the death of Father Flynn, and it now remains for the sisters to apply the tourniquet to the narrator's dangerously extrafamilial sense of self. The accepted story of the boy's family and of the sisters is that the narrator merely brings Father Flynn a gift of snuff from his aunt. But the boy makes it clear he often visits the priest without this pretext: "*Perhaps* my aunt would have given me a packet of High Toast for him" (*D* 12, emphasis added). He visits whether he has snuff or not, and he goes directly to where the priest is, alerting the sisters as little as possible: "Had he not been dead I would have gone into the little dark room behind the shop to find him sitting in his arm-chair" (*D* 12). Clearly, something is a little clandestine about these visits; he comes into the room when he chooses, unannounced by anyone, whether or not the priest is expecting visitors, whether or not he is even awake! The family found the boy's compulsive and repetitive visits to Father Flynn disturbing, perhaps more disturbing than the peculiar behavior of Father Flynn. Significantly, Eliza omits the role of the boy entirely when she declares, "I won't be bringing him in his cup of beef-tea any more, nor you, ma'am, sending him his snuff" (*D* 16). Eliza presents these two things as if they were parallel, but bringing and sending are two quite different actions; for her statement to be truly parallel, she would have to say "I won't be bringing him in his cup of beef-tea and the boy won't be bringing him his snuff [which you are always sending through him]." The Rosicrucian is cut out of the loop by silent consent in this supposedly parallel construction that, in fact, is missing something: the narrator. The boy must narrate his[s]tory— in opposition to their story—because, with Father Flynn gone, Old Cotter hostile, his uncle deliberately obtuse, his aunt strategically pious, and Eliza selectively amnesic, the narrator is in danger of disappearing unless he speaks who he imagines himself to be.

The *je* seeks to translate into language the identity requirements of the *moi* so that the individual's reality appears to correspond to the Real. As Lacan put it: "Reality is only the fantasy on which a thought is sustained, 'reality' doubtlessly, but to be understood as a grimace of the Real" (Ragland-Sullivan 1988, 188). The reader learns from the uncle that the priest's support of the boy's persona was so immense as to be nearly unqualified: "The youngster and he were great friends. The old chap taught him a great deal, mind you; and they say he had a great wish for him" (*D* 10). In the context of the family, however, when the boy seeks confirmation of his persona as an initiate into sacred mysteries, he instantly becomes "that Rosicrucian there"—a comical mystic—and he is urged to take on athleticism and cold baths as his new reality. The sisters make it quite clear that they are capable of containing even madness within the family myth: "We wouldn't see him want for anything while he was in it," Eliza says (*D* 16). If the boy is the subject of the ellipses in this story, then the final unfinished sentence by Eliza must come to him as a warning of how—if he persists in his anticommunal stance toward them—he, too, will be confined within the family until he, too, is discovered "wide-awake and laughing-like to himself" (*D* 18).

In all the conversations in the story something that remains unrepresented haunts the margins of the discourse; from there it struggles to take form in the gaps of the sentences and in the slippage of word choice. Lacan describes two kinds of speech: "Empty speech" *(parole)*, which is controlled by the *moi* and is addressed to someone other than the speaker for the purposes of *moi* recognition (verification of identity), and "full speech" *(langue)*, which is addressed to the Other. Full speech "realizes the truth of the subject," whereas in empty speech "the subject loses himself in the machinations of the system of language, in the labyrinth of referential systems made available to him by the state of cultural affairs to which he is a more or less interested party" (Lacan 1988a, 50). This full speech is implied in slips of the tongue, jokes, and ellipses, but it remains unrepresented by the empty speech, which takes its orders from the *moi*. The job of the analyst, according to Lacan, is not to be seduced by the empty speech of the analysand (his or her conscious presentation of knowledge and intention) but to listen instead for the full speech that is present, although obliquely represented, in the gaps of the analysand's discourse.

When Eliza describes the helpful Father O'Rourke, she presents him as a practical man who performs his duties without complaint or vacillation, "Only for Father O'Rourke I don't know what we'd have done at all" (*D* 16). The implicit comparison to the incompetent Father Flynn is made more overt when she mentions, after the conversation has taken several turns, that "the duties of the priesthood was too much for him" (*D* 17). She intends to put forward "duties" as the subject of the sentence — the reason for Father Flynn's unhappy life — but her choice of verb tense suddenly makes "the priesthood" the subject of her sentence. The slip in verb tense reveals her unconscious knowledge that "the priesthood was too much for him." Duties, the intended subject of her sentence, is revealed as the sort of subject she felt Father Flynn should be — dutiful like Father O'Rourke. This repressed complaint that Father Flynn was insufficiently dutiful returns to her conversation when the only reason she offers for the discovery of Father Flynn's madness is his failure to answer a call (i.e., to perform his duty).

To approach her speech in a different way, her sentence exhibits subject-verb agreement only insofar as it represents unconscious knowledge about what proved too much for Father Flynn. At the same time, the failure of subject-verb agreement, inasmuch as it represents empty speech *(parole),* conveys the conscious knowledge that it was the responsibilities of being a priest — and nothing about the nature of the priesthood itself — that unraveled Father Flynn's sense of himself. Eliza's conscious view of herself, which she seeks to confirm in her remarks, is that she is a woman who has adequately supported the awesome power and authority represented by the priesthood. It is important to her that Father Flynn be thought secondary to the priesthood because she experiences her self-worth strictly in terms of serving this force (and, incidentally, her brother), a force that is now represented by Father O'Rourke. And yet, the full speech, which subverts her grammar, contains a realization that the priesthood itself, and not its duties, operated against her brother as a malevolent force. Eliza details the favors Father O'Rourke has bestowed upon her until she elicits from the boy's aunt a remark concerning Father O'Rourke that approximates what she needs to hear: "Wasn't that good of him?" the aunt says. Eliza's reaction is like that of someone swallowing a potent medicine: "Eliza closed her eyes and shook her head slowly" (*D* 16). Her next statement, when examined closely, is decidedly odd in tone, "Ah, there's no friends like the old friends . . . when all is said and done, no friends that a body can trust" (*D* 16). The cliché in which this statement is couched mitigates its unmistakably bitter tone. The subject of betrayal and trust was certainly not raised by the aunt's benign comment; yet Eliza reacts to her merely polite rejoinder as though it were an invitation to recount the origin of some deep-seated disillusionment. Eliza's disillusionment comes about because of that "disappointed man"—her brother, Father Flynn—whose failure to sustain his faith in the power of the priesthood nearly undermined her own relationship to this symbolic force. Now that she is assured of some attention from the more worthy Father O'Rourke, she seems prepared to state that she is a disappointed woman.

Certainly, the aunt must perceive the subtle turn in Eliza's discourse, and her next remark, "I'm sure now that he's gone to his eternal reward he won't forget you and all your kindness," serves as a reminder to Eliza that the priest is still alive in the sense that he is still watching her (in the gaze of the Other, which is typically how dead people haunt the living in Joyce's fiction). "In our relationship to things," Lacan says, "as constituted by the path of vision and ordered in the figures of representation, something glides, passes, transmits itself from stage to stage, in order always to be in some degree eluded there—It is that which is called the *regard* [gaze]" (Ragland-Sullivan 1988, 44).

To the extent that subjectivity depends on the imagined gaze of the Other, the subject must negotiate his or her relationship with the dead as well as with the living; in the conclusion of "The Dead," for example, Gabriel imagines the inhabitants of an entire graveyard staring through the hotel window at him. The aunt's cautionary remark about the dead man serves its purpose and activates another dimension of Eliza's persona (moi), not the wronged and bitter sister thwarted by a weak-willed brother but the devoted sister who will not even entertain the idea that she deserves compensation. "Ah, poor James! . . . He was no great trouble to us" (*D* 16). In a more general sense, the truth that Eliza's empty speech seeks to block is that her fictional unity—her faith in herself—has been constituted in relation to the Other. Any shift in this relationship (as the narrator finds out in his dream) will be experienced as a fragmentation — a receding to the pleasant and vicious realm (premirror jouissance in the Lacanian schema) before language introduces a mastery of the wor(l)d — a mastery that can be had only at the price of the symbolic castration of the subject (thus inaugurating the binary relationship of self-alienation in relationship to the [imagined] Desire of the Other).

Perhaps because of the aunt's warning about the still-watching Father Flynn, Eliza abandons all implications that Father Flynn's decline was a long, disappointing process and opts instead to narrate the more generally acceptable story that he was a fine priest who suddenly became "queer" because of a single incident (the dropped chalice). The life of a man who "was so nervous" is reduced to a single incident of fumbling that might happen to anyone. Significantly, chronology is completely absent in Eliza's account. How long ago did he drop the chalice? How long was it after that incident before he was discovered in the confessional? Finally, what was the interval between that discovery and his death (and at what point in all this was the boy forbidden to visit any longer)? The story of Father Flynn has been subsumed into Eliza's story, and her bitterness about the duration and cost to herself of her brother's feebleness causes her to omit any reference that might help readers chart the length and degree of the priest's decline. The boy's aunt, for her part, shows a suspicious lack of curiosity about Eliza's sketchy story (probably because she well knows the details) and blandly acts as if this pseudoexplanation were exhaustive: "And was that it? . . . I heard something" (*D* 17).

I turn now to Eliza's famous verbal slips (*"Freeman's general"* for *Freeman's Journal* and "rheumatic wheels" for pneumatic wheels), which may be seen as further examples of full speech subverting empty speech. In essence, the boy's silent and listening presence makes him operate as a symptom that disrupts the intended flow of Eliza's discourse, thus revealing her dependence on the gaze of the Other. Lacan states: "[The symptom] speaks in the Other . . . designating by this Other the very place called upon by a recourse to speech in any relation where it [the symptom] intervenes. If it speaks in the Other, whether or not the subject hears it with his own ears, it is because it is there that the subject, according to a logic prior to any awakening of the signified, finds his signifying place" (1982b, 79).

It is scarcely an exaggeration, then, to suggest that the boy speaks through the gaps in Eliza's discourse. A journal, in the context of *Freeman's Journal,* is a daily account of events that features accuracy, coherency, and factuality as among the highest priorities. To understand the journal/general slip, one must take account of the word that precedes it: *Freeman,* or free man. The boy, who says nothing while Eliza prattles on, remains inscrutable to her. Unlike the aunt, he is not making rejoinders that Eliza can then incorporate into her discourse. Although she can avoid addressing him directly or even referring to him implicitly, she cannot ignore him. In this sense, he is a free man — unpredictably responsive to her discourse and, therefore, potentially destructive to its coherency and truth. Eliza is endangered by a free man's journal — that of the young boy. Eliza's conscious discourse pronounces the name of a newspaper, but the phrase "free man" connects to a chain of signifiers that goes beyond the signified of the particular newspaper. Because the moi depends on the regard of others to recognize its own existence, it is extremely vulnerable, full of conflict, and even, as characterized by Lacan, "paranoid." Certainly, the presence of a potentially hostile other would increase this tension to the point of creating a desire — strong enough to subvert conscious discourse — that the threatening free agent might be ordered to reflect the identification requirements of her moi. She wishes to be the free man's *general* — that is, give him orders he cannot disobey. This would preserve and protect the government of her moi formation from the subversive text of his journal.

My analysis of *rheumatic* for *pneumatic* begins with my assumption that Eliza was not anxious to revisit Irishtown, which Gifford describes as, in 1900, "a poor, working-class slum" (1982, 30). Indeed, the fact that the two sisters and their brother began life in Irishtown gives further proof that Father Flynn was the author of Eliza's great disillusionment, which she can scarcely repress now. Her brother, almost certainly the son of a dock laborer, escaped from the slums, saving Nannie and her in process, and later attended the Irish college in Rome. Gifford tells us: "The fact that Father Flynn was educated at the Irish College implies that he was regarded as an outstanding candidate for the priesthood, the more remarkable since he was born in the lower-class neighborhood of Irishtown."[2] And late in his life, having failed to fulfill the potential that helped him out of the slums, he wants, of all things, to return to Irishtown! One could scarcely expect Eliza to endorse this final and extremely public step downward. The major obstacle in the journey would appear to be renting "one of them new-fangled carriages that makes no noise that Father O'Rourke told him about" (*D* 17). But why is this an obstacle? Father O'Rourke has already been established as the picture of competence. If he told Father Flynn about the carriages, he certainly could have arranged the rental of one for the day. And, anyway, why not use an ordinary carriage? The new-fangled carriage is better, according to Eliza, because it makes no noise. Presumably, the carriage provides a smoother ride as well. Flynn's elaborate fantasy of revisiting Irishtown does not involve only himself but, apparently, must include his sisters: "the three of us together of a Sunday evening," Eliza says. Her deliberate echoing of her brother's actual phrase contains a hint of irony at what a spectacle they would be for the neighbors. Returning to one's origins is quite a validation of one's identity if, like Gallaher, one has "got on," but Father Flynn is a failure, and for him to revisit Irishtown would make him pathetic in the eyes of all who witnessed the procession.

What is being elided here is that the sisters do not wish to go — both for fear of exciting further gossip and for fear of looking upon the place from which their brother took them (and now, with his increasingly peculiar ways, seems determined to return them). The most diplomatic rejection of the plan, rather than defying his wish outright, would be to plead concern for his comfort and their own. Besides, a new-fangled carriage would further support his delusion that he is returning to his origins in splendor. A regular carriage would be too noisy, too bumpy; they are too old for that sort of ride. After all, the narrator has described Nannie as "toil[ing] up the narrow staircase" (*D* 14), and Eliza, when one searches the story for a description of her mobility, is never described as moving at all. The narrator first sees her after he has come back downstairs from paying his respects "seated in his [Father Flynn's] arm-chair in state." Although she is emphatic on two occasions that she always brings "poor James" his soup, the reader sees Nannie doing everything — from ushering guests upstairs to see the corpse, to pouring the sherry "at her sister's bidding," to falling asleep exhausted in her chair — and might well wonder if Eliza performs any chores in the house. Something designed to ease bumps (pneumatic) is required to offset the discomfort of moving about (rheumatic).

It is not surprising that Eliza would have difficulty with a word like *pneumatic;* what *is* surprising is that, instead of stumbling over the word or omitting it, she accurately supplies an equally difficult word, *rheumatic.* The pneumatic wheels would make the ride less bumpy for someone who complains of rheumatic joints. Eliza's verbal slip suddenly supplies the carriage with "rheumatic wheels," and, thus, presents, through the unexpected displacement of words, the reason that it never took them to Irishtown. And when one wonders why Father O'Rourke failed to procure the carriage, one must recall Eliza's oddly vehement tribute to him: "Ah, there's no friends like the old friends . . . no friends that a body can trust" (*D* 16). Father O'Rourke, who knew how and where to rent the carriage, never used his competence to actually procure one for Father Flynn. Eliza's empty speech presents the failure to visit Irishtown as one more unfortunate disappointment in the life of a disappointed man. But once again something is insisting from beyond her discourse. Her full speech, the slip of her tongue, betrays something else: a determined woman who frustrates a dying man's wish in her bitter attempt to hold together the appearance of normalcy and propriety he has so incomprehensibly compromised. Eliza's moi is both stable and adrift at the same time (as is anyone's). Something remains floating in the Real that her conscious discourse seeks to elide. Eliza's identity question is posed to the Other via the other (the aunt), and for this reason the aunt's responses can never be entirely adequate: Eliza still waits for a return message from the dead—represented by Father Flynn. She desires to know *(journal; pneumatic)* and to escape knowing *(general; rheumatic)* who she is for the Other: "She stopped suddenly as if to listen. I too listened; but there was no sound in the house" (*D* 18).

At first, for the narrator of "The Sisters," words merely "sounded strangely," but with the creation of a permanent sense of otherness, words "now . . . sounded to me like the name of some maleficent and sinful being" (*D* 9). In essence, the boy has exchanged fusion with the mother for selfhood, or otherness, represented by the Name-of-the-Father. The narrator visits Father Flynn, again and again, because the visits further his flight from nature to culture: "Sometimes he had amused himself by putting difficult questions to me. . . . His questions showed me how complex and mysterious were certain institutions of the Church which I had always regarded as the simplest acts"

(*D* 13). this flight into culture generates a feeling of alienation in the boy that renders him inarticulate and yet increasingly dependent on the endless substitutive strategies of the law that forms reality by resisting and negating all that it can of the Real: "He told me that the fathers of the Church had written books as thick as the *Post Office Directory* and as closely printed as the law notices in the newspaper, elucidating all these intricate questions. Often when I thought of this I could make no answer or only a very foolish and halting one" (*D* 13). "All questions" may be elucidated in this text "as thick as the *Post Office Directory*," but it is equally true that this huge text is only comforting inasmuch as it remains unread. Curiously, the boy's narration does not recount a single fact from the hours spent reciting law for Father Flynn. What he recalls instead is the unnameable complexity of the law, which seems to name him.

The narrator shows an increasing awareness in the course of the story that knowledge is not a question of facts; it is a process of narration. He does not struggle to correct the history presented by Eliza; he seeks to protect the right to tell his own story. Controlling the right to narrate one's own story is more important than being correct, or maintaining the authority to speak is the same thing as being correct. What the boy is vying for in the story is the right to convincingly misrepresent his "self" in a text that will persuade other people to confirm what he imagines he knows. Surrounded by history, he struggles to preserve the boundaries of his story. He recognizes that who he is told to be by the family can only be counteracted by getting others to recognize him as being something else. In essence, he writes his life at the same time that he reluctantly lives within a script that has already been written. Put another way, he narrates the myth of himself as he vacillates between the illusory unity of the Imaginary Order and the self-confirming alienation of the Symbolic Order. To describe this dynamic in terms of the image of the geometrical figure that haunts him, I suggest that once he felt that he was a parallelogram (unified), then the law and the Name-of-the-Father reduced him to a stammering gnomon (no man), and now he must — using conscious knowledge — construct a myth of himself over the void of his own incertitude (a know man).

But a gnomon is a figure in its own right and not merely an incomplete parallelogram. To assume it is incomplete is to support the

Imaginary Order fantasy that the gnomon can be completed if only the missing piece can be found. The gnomon is a feminine shape in the sense that what is missing is only imagined as lost (castrated) so that a masculine parallelogram may pose as complete (as having the Phallus). Neither the gnomon nor the parallelogram can be defined without reference to the other; the fact that there is a gnomon means there is no such thing as a parallelogram—and vice versa.

As Joyce's obscure title for this story suggests, the narrator is very much in the company of women, and he is excited by this unlawful, gnomonic atmosphere, but he also has heard his uncle's warning to "box his corner," to become a man. The figure of the gnomon and the parallelogram can also be viewed as representing the intertwined dynamic of the speaking subject. When the subject sees himself as unified, he is other than he is, and the fragments of knowledge that challenge this unity fade into the unconscious; he is a parallelogram fearing the lack represented by a gnomon. When a subject sees himself by inserting the recognition of another person into the place of his lack, the moi disappears, and the subject experiences himself as a gnomon dreaming about becoming a parallelogram. Language is the centerpiece of this paradox because, as Lacan insists, the word is a presence made of absence that allows absence to be named. Rabate, while discussing *Ulysses,* characterizes a dynamic in Joyce's fiction that is relevant to my analysis of "The Sisters": "Through language, a play of absence, difference, and incertitude are brought to bear upon one's own kinship. . . . as soon as the subject attempts to define himself, he needs the symbolic order of language as conditioned by the absent father, so that he may wander through meaning in quest of a father" (1983, 83). Thrust from the no-man's land of the symbiotic mirror identification into the know-man's land of the Name-of-the-Father, the narrator assumes an identity by inserting himself into a chain of signifiers (his three precious words operate like an incantation in the opening of the story) that produces in him the affect of subjectivity.

The subject's truth becomes his lack of being, and what he has left out of the chain in order to be included in it recedes to the Other, where it regards him steadily and either confirms or subverts the seamless fabric of his narrative. When Real events cannot be entirely subsumed into the boy's reality (the death of the priest), this gaze of the

Other rips through the weave of the boy's story, thus revealing that all the loose threads (chains of signifiers) that present the fabric of his identity are no more than a metaphor for presence that allows absence to be named and, thus, elided.[3] Reality is fiction—and vice versa—and beyond them both is the unrepresented truth of the Real that the subject never experiences as anything but the silence that makes his discourse audible. The conscious subject blends moi formations with je expressions so that an-other becomes an ideal reflection of who the subject believes he appears to be in the gaze of the Other; it reveals that the privileged Cartesian subject who thinks himself into being is in fact a composite. Dreams appear fragmented, but that is an inversion of the fictional unity of the subject who tries to recall them. The boy's dream shows (from a backstage perspective that is never seen by the other) the various bits of lumber and cloth that produce the backdrop of subjectivity before which his conscious thoughts and experiences are played out. Lacan states that "in the so-called waking state, there is an elision of the gaze, and an elision of the fact that not only does it look, it also shows. In the field of the dream . . . what characterizes the images is that it shows. . . . Our position in the dream is profoundly that of someone who does not see" (1981a, 75). The centerpiece of the boy's dream is the priest's smiling face, which follows him even though the blanket is over his head and his eyes are shut; by the conclusion of the dream, the narrator is still looking at nothing, but he is doing so with an imprint of the priest's expression on *his* face. The sin that remains inexpressible in the dream despite all the murmuring and all the desire for penance is that the boy and the priest, all through their friendship, were permanently alienated from one another. This alienation was the inevitable result of their mutual desire to seduce the other into acting as a benevolent representative of the (imagined) Desire of the Other.

In conscious life, the moi is regarded as indivisible. The gaze of the Other is experienced as a natural part of one's own being that is comforting and validating (although in moments of incertitude, like the one Gabriel Conroy has after talking to Lily, it may also be experienced as judgmental and censorious).[4] In his dream, the narrator's "self" reveals itself as something that must be seen in order to imagine itself as seeing: "In the dark of my room I imagined that I saw again the heavy grey face of the paralytic" (*D* 11). Initially, this would appear to be an act of observation, but when the boy covers his head with the blanket, what he "sees" is that he is being seen: "I drew the blankets over my head and tried to think of Christmas. But the grey face still followed me" (*D* 11). By "thinking of Christmas," the boy strives to erect numerous chains of conscious signifiers between himself and the gaze of the priest in order to protect the myth that he is the indivisible author of his own meaning. But, instead, the words *paralysis* and *simony,* which earlier he consciously juxtaposed as signifying *him,* suddenly appear as signifiers of Father Flynn: "the heavy grey face of the paralytic"; "I too was smiling feebly as if to absolve the simoniac of his sin" (*D* 11). What comes into play in the dream is the semantic instability overlooked by the ego (which constitutes the conscious inertia we experience as piece/peace of mind). The reflection of one's own image in relations with others is masked in conscious interactions and this lends credence to what one takes to be reality.

"The reflection of the subject, its mirror image, is always found somewhere in every perceptual picture, and that is what gives it a quality, a special inertia. . . . But in the dream because of an alleviation of the imaginary relations [the friendship of the boy and the priest], it [the masked image of ourselves in the other] is easily revealed at every moment, all the more so to the extent that the point of anxiety where the subject encounters the experience of his being torn apart, of his isolation in relation to the world, has been attained" (Lacan 1988b, 167). Because the dream signifies the boy's relation to the world as torn apart, his identity recedes to a curious limbo where it can be neither vanquished nor confirmed: "I felt my soul receding into some pleasant and vicious region" (*D* 11). The priest, equally stripped of identity (and now referred to as "it"), is waiting there for the boy. In essence, the dream details and summarizes all the times — outside the mythic history of the subject and, therefore, unrealized — when the ego, by aggressively putting forth what it knows, refuses to acknowledge that residue of interpretation in the Real that is generated by understanding the experience of reality. What the individual knows is always a translation of the Real into whatever the subject can afford to understand; knowledge operates as a sort of organized ignorance, and the primary effect on the subject is a feeling of stability and indivisibility. Any dream, then, does not reveal Lacan's real, but it does demonstrate the influence of the real on the signifying structure of the subject whose reality is delimited by his or her dependence on the gaze of the Other: "A dream is conscious. This imaginary iridescence, these moving images, this is something which belongs entirely to the same order as that illusory aspect of the image on which we insist in relation to the formation of the ego. The dream is very much akin to reading in the mirror" (1988b, 57). Dreams and conscious discourse are inversely related; the non-sense so prevalent in dreams is the residue from the sense of the speaking subject. Language, which the boy tries to employ in this story with a conspicuous truthfulness, functions as a defense against unconscious truth.

In a dream, there is no way to pose successfully as someone signified (as someone having an autonomous identity) because the gaze of the Other is no longer obscured as some sort of ego ideal (other person) who confirms the autonomy of the "self." In fact, Father Flynn becomes "it"—the maleficent being the boy imagines as lurking behind the language of his conscious discourse. What operates as substitutive displacements in the boy's conscious life appear in the dream as the reference points of the boy's unitary impossibility. Whereas the narrator tells his story to send a message to the Other to be verified, in the dream he *becomes* a message *from* the Other: "I understood that it desired to confess something. I felt my soul receding into some pleasant and vicious region" (*D* 11). The meaning of the dream, therefore, "is taken as a network, and is represented, not at all term by term, but through a set of interlacings" (1988a, 266). The unconscious knowledge about being a message is represented the next morning by the boy's strong urge to walk "slowly along the sunny side of the street, reading all the theatrical advertisements in the shop-windows as I went" (*D* 12). The boy's reading is not at all selective or casual; he reads all. This is the option he turns to now that his habit of visiting the priest has been foreclosed.

No one advertisement is more appealing than any other; he is not interested in their messages but in the fact that they are messages. He is drawn to their pure signifying power. In a sense, while he is doing this, he is still dreaming (one might say reading his subjectivity in the mirror) because, as Lacan goes on to say: "Each signifying element of the dream, each image, includes a reference to a whole set of things to be signified, and inversely, each thing to be signified is represented in several signifiers" (1988a, 266). In reading the messages in the shop windows, the narrator feels he is controlling them, but he is in fact inserting himself—as just another message—among them. As in the opening paragraph of the story, he surrounds himself with words so that he can imagine himself as their organizing force. The very activity of doing this, however, betrays his need to be constantly spoken. To put it most simply, he becomes a link in the chain through which signifiers pass, and this generates within him that illusion of linguistic mastery that enables him to function as a speaking (because already spoken) subject.

A Lacanian interpretation of this dream suggests that the dream reveals itself as a repository of all the subject's actualities that the ego refuses to sanction even as possibilities. The "pleasant and vicious region" is where the narrator ex-ists without benefit of the supposedly existent "self" (ego)—that symptomatic structure that allows the subject to believe in closure and origin. The dream can be seen as a message from the Other to the moi, which conscious thought denies. One knows from the dream, for example, that the boy is uneasy about smiling the priest's smile because if the priest's smile is transferrable (that is to day, without origin), then the law of the Name-of-the-Father is free floating and not attached to the phallic signifier in the Other? At the wake therefore, he consciously fancies that the dead priest will be continually smiling (as he would prefer to have it in the dream) so that the coherency of his own thoughts will appear secure: "I pretended to pray but I could not gather my thoughts because the old woman's mutterings distracted me. . . . The fancy came to me that the old priest was smiling as he lay there in his coffin" (*D* 14). In this sequence of events, the old woman's muttering reminds him of his earlier patter of the Mass responses. As he is consciously hearing Nannie's mutterings, he is returned to the position of his dream where he listened to the dead priest's murmuring voice and saw that his subjectivity depended on his being seen. And what is this voice in the dream murmuring as the narrator smiles feebly and listens? Nothing more or less than his own earlier conscious je ramblings that he pattered while Father Flynn smiled. The je discourse, although apparently dominant and original in conscious life, comes from the Other in dream thoughts and, thus, is revealed as not being original utterance at all but empty speech that functions solely as a defense against unconscious truth.

In taking on the smile in the dream, the boy, like the mad Father Flynn, hears his own confession.

Juxtaposing the boy's dream with his conscious moi and je formations suggests that the normal subject who sees does so because language has stablized perception by providing a way to translate the Real into reality (which allows the subject to elide the prior Real represented by the Gaze). The dream, to borrow the phrasing of horror show titles, is "The Return of the Real." The boy's use of the Symbolic Order of language in the opening paragraph of the story hollows out a place for him in the Real, but the dream reveals this reality as always already constructed by the Other whose gaze authenticates him. Lacan asks: "Is not the dream essentially . . . an act of homage to the missed reality—the reality that can no longer produce itself except by repeating itself endlessly, in some never attained awakening?" (1981a, 58). One can see that misrecognition in conscious life is the purpose of the moi, which can only perform this function if it does not know the truth that the dream threatens to reveal—that it, the moi, does not exist, but rather ex-ists in the sense that it functions as an unrepresentable symptom that allows the subject to believe in the myth of him or herself.

Walking down the sunny side of the street, the boy remembers another detail of the dream involving long velvet curtains. Here one sees him balanced delicately between the meaning of his dream and the papered-over void of his moi constructions because *curtains* is a displaced term for the sister's house where he first met Father Flynn; a house, the reader is told, that is "registered under the vague name of *Drapery*" (*D* 11). On the door of the same house, there is usually a notice saying "Umbrellas Re-covered," but this has been covered over by closed shutters, and now the only visible sign is the one announcing Father Flynn's death. Curiously, the boy remembers this sign that has been covered over ("Umbrellas Re-Covered") as he begins reading theatrical advertisements. By becoming a message immersed in other messages, he is able to re-cover the umbrella of conscious "self" that screens out the distorted messages from the Real, which threaten to subvert his reality when he is dreaming.

The narrator's interpretation of the death of Father Flynn in the opening of the story is only partly translated from the Real by his three conscious words. The rest of this interpretation surfaces in his dream in which it is the death of his own moi that he mourns. In the "never attained awakening" of conscious life, he feels absolved of the burden of his own unnatural existence because of the death of the father, and he experiences the imaginary unity that constitutes the moi as being freed by something. Thus, one sees the origins of conscious knowledge as having arisen out of the need to misrecognize the residue of interpretation that, repressed from conscious life, returns in the dream. This misrecognition is a reinterpretation of the Real as a reality that can never fail to be a distortion of what is beyond representation in the Real. One knows that the narrator, despite his elaborate and painstaking pose as a creature of certainty, is, in fact, a creature of contingency: at the very moment he experiences "a sense of freedom as if [he] had been freed from something by [Father Flynn's] death," he is compulsively reading theater advertisements in an attempt to recover the rips in the fabric of his story that the dream made real (although not Real) by leaking through them the night before.[5] The smile that he allowed to be his umbrella turns out to have been the free-floating smile of the imagined Other. This Real smile survives in his dreams even as the unsmiling and dead Father Flynn is lying still in his coffin.

3

The Detective and the Cowboy
Desire, Gender, and Perversion
in "An Encounter"

> The pervert is he who, in short circuit, more directly
> than any other, succeeds in his aim, by integrating
> in the most profound way his function as subject with
> his existence as desire (Lacan 1981a, 206)

> He gave me the impression that he was repeating
> something which he had learned by heart or that,
> magnetised by some words of his own speech, his
> mind was slowly circling round and round in the same
> orbit. (*D* 26)

By the end of his conversation with the old man, the narrator of
"An Encounter" is obviously very frightened: "I went up the slope
calmly but my heart was beating quickly with fear that he would seize
me by the ankles" (*D* 28). But Joyce's subtle presentation of the complex relationship between gender and desire is destroyed if one accepts fear and repulsion as the only emotions that the boy experiences
and then reproduces those feelings in one's own analysis. Senn noted
quite a few years ago that there is "something generally human" in
the old man "in whom we may recognize ourselves" (1969, 32).[1] If fear
were the single and overriding impulse of the narrator, then why his
carefully feigned appearance of calm ("I went up the slope calmly")?
I suggest that the boy is aware that he has sailed into a sexual adven-

ture of Odyssean proportions. Because he has had an adventure such as heroes might endure, how he exits this scene is as important as how he conducts himself during it. His favorite adventure stories, significantly, are not the Westerns, so popular among his peers, stories where men murder any other men who challenge their phallic supremacy. Instead, he favors "American detective stories" in which a world-weary man struggles to maintain his sexual equilibrium despite being constantly exposed to glimpses of the lawlessness just beneath the surface of compulsive gender complementarity: "I liked better some American detective stories which were traversed from time to time by unkempt fierce and beautiful girls" (*D* 20). In this world, the detective survives the chronicle of disorder in which he is inadvertently enmeshed, yet he knows his survival is no more than a temporary restoration of reality carved out of the inscrutable Real (the Circean damsel in distress may return in yet another treacherous form).[2] The attitude of even a successful detective is often wary; the Real world may approach him again in the future — once more in apparent innocence — and once again undermine his sense of masculine subjectivity.

The heroes of western adventures, on the other hand, confront a catastrophic Phallic disorder that is eventually reconstructed into a complete restoration of the phallic economy. This economy, it is usually implied, will now reign permanently having once been tested and found true. To present my point simply, when the Lone Ranger finally decides it is time for him to ride away from the anonymous little town where he has restored order — and someone inquires in hushed tones, "Who was that masked man?"— the clear implication is that he has restored the people's faith in the mighty signifier that authenticates their worth as signifieds and that the legend that he (who?) once visited them will, henceforth, obfuscate the fact that he has no identity and his authority is a self-generated myth. The detective drama often makes the point that order has been restored and that the Circean wiles of unkempt and fierce women have once again been withstood, but the orderly conclusion is often ominously undercut when the detective admits that, human desire being the inexplicable thing that it is, terrifying crises of gender and identity are bound to occur again in the future. The priceless Maltese Falcon, for example, is rendered harmless as an object of desire. But at the same time, Bogart concedes that other, as yet unspecified, objects of desire will cause similar crises in the future.

To present the distinction between the hero of the detective story and the hero of the cowboy story within the schema of Joyce's story, the narrator is the detective who enters the distorted world of the old man in an attempt to solve the mystery behind it. Mahony, on the other hand, is the cowboy who doesn't really notice the old man except to remark offhandedly that he is a "queer old josser." Mahony only views as threatening those things that physically encroach on whatever he determines is his territory. From his point of view, the old man is too physically pathetic even to bother running him out of town. Only open combat with a clearly defined opponent can be considered manly. In fact, while the narrator finds himself being drawn deeper and deeper into the metaphorical obscurity of the old man's narrative, the bored Mahony spots a stray cat and instantly designates this intruder as a far more worthy and legitimate test of his manhood than "the queer old josser."

Leo Dillon and his brother Joe also prefer Western adventures. The narrator accepts this preference (none of the children seem to ever want to play at being detectives) and hides as best as he can his status as a "reluctant Indian." I interpret this reluctance as indicating a sense on the narrator's part that the world of the Western is too cut and dried in terms of gender and desire to account for his own disturbing and confusing impulses. The Western is a world where men are men and women keep the homefires burning (or patch up the bloodied but unbowed men so they can continue their fight to prove the existence and indomitability of phallic power). The narrator feels that his sexual nature defies and exceeds these boundaries and that is why his encounter with the polymorphously perverse old man fascinates him initially. Eventually, the old man's entirely permeable sexual discourse proves too alarming for the narrator and causes him to suddenly appreciate the much more straightforward cowboy morals of Mahony: "[Mahony] ran as if to bring me aid. And I was penitent; for in my heart I had always despised him a little" (*D* 28). Western adventures "bring aid" to young boys because they present an extremely clear picture of what is masculine and what is feminine to a group of individuals who are still busily trying to learn these vital distinctions (which, of course, must be learned because there is nothing innate about them). It is just speculation on my part, but my sense is that the narrator, having been terrified by the old man, will be reading Westerns for a while.

Those who subscribe to the world of the Western learn that one must either be the Phallus (the assertive masculine role) or desire to serve it (the supportive feminine role). But some confusion about this priniciple is introduced by the opening paragraph of the story in which the reader learns that Joe Dillon, the craziest Indian of them all, eventually decided to become a priest. I take this glimpse into the future on the part of the narrator as a warning that "wild" Indians who profess complete faith in their masculinity are actually more subject to the ideological controls of their culture than "reluctant" Indians. Everyone is incredulous at the news that Joe Dillon could be so thoroughly domesticated from his wild Indian days, but the narrator makes it clear that Joe Dillon's world, unlike that of the harried and doubtful American detective, has rarely been traversed by unkempt, fierce, and beautiful girls: "His parents went to eight-o'clock mass every morning in Gardiner Street and the peaceful odour of Mrs. Dillon was prevalent in the hall of the house" (*D* 19).

One can surmise from this, in part, that Joe Dillon is fierce ("he played too fiercely for us who were younger and more timid") because his mother is not ("the peaceful odour of Mrs. Dillon"). Joe, it would seem, is quite certain he is what he has been taught a man should be, and this confidence gives him the ability to always conclude everything with the sort of ecstatic climax that any hero of a Western would admire: "However well we fought, we never won siege or battle and all our bouts ended with Joe Dillon's war dance of victory" (*D* 19). Joe Dillon's younger brother, Leo, also shows an apparent fierceness that is likewise easily controlled. When he is discovered with a copy of *The Apache Chief,* the public rebuke Father Butler administers has a far-reaching effect. When the narrator plans "a day's miching" just before the summer holidays, Leo seems to go along with it. His concern, however, that they should not go to the Pigeon House because they "might meet Father Butler" demonstrates his fear that the law-affirming Father might appear anywhere, at any time, to punish his transgressions.

The curious paradox of becoming masculine is that the intervention of the Father's law, far from strengthening the child, cuts him off from the (m)Other's gaze, thus permanently banishing him from the jouissance of the mirror stage (where the subject first misrecognizes his unified mirror image as the equivalent of a coherent subjectivity). This symbolic castration creates a permanent lack-in-being in the boy that can only be appeased by a rigid adherence to the gender myth of masculinity. The subsequent fear for the masculine subject is not fear of organ loss (physical castration) but fear that the mythical construct of gender itself will prove false, thus bringing on an unbearable dissolution of being (symbolic castration). In the aftermath of this transformation, the masculine subject fears the condemnation of patriarchal institutions because he has granted them the power and authority to "cut him off" from his identity as a man should he prove inadequate in any way that this system deems other (feminine). Lacan stresses that the loss of symbiosis with one's mirror image—which is actually the loss of jouissance sanctified by the authenticating gaze of the (m)Other—is repressed and displaced by the subject but symbolically felt as a lack-in-being that inaugurates an insatiable search for the object of Desire that could fill this void. The structure of Desire in the human subject is proof of a Real castration, and gender myths of masculinity and femininity seek to compensate for the experience of symbolic castration and, thus, deny its paralyzing effects.

The absurdity of Leo's fear that Father Butler is somehow everywhere shows how extremely dependent masculine cowboys like Joe and Leo Dillon are to the edicts of patriarchal authority. They pay excessive homage to any institution that demonstrates phallic authority (that is, to all institutions whose original authority is posited as having come from the "Name-of-the Father") not because they have a penis—but because they do not have the Phallus—that fetishized representation of the penis that only ex-ists as the fantasy upon which the myth of masculinity is based. Not surprisingly, even though Leo pooled his allowance for the adventure, he does not show up at the allotted time. The narrator, in direct contrast to the Western certitude about gender, consistently demonstrates a lack of faith in the truth of the masculine gender myth. He admits, for example, that he keeps his own counsel about this incertitude, especially in the midst of his more exuberant peers. The best characterization he can offer of himself along these lines is that he is "a reluctant Indian." Accordingly, Father Butler's reproach in "the daylight hours" awakens only one of the boy's consciences — the one that through superficial conformity to the myth of masculinity tries to avoid undue scrutiny from Phallic-thought police like Father Butler (Leo and Joe Dillon only have one conscience and it is thoroughly cowed by patriarchal authority figures like Father Butler). In this regard, Father Butler is a new incarnation of the scrutinizing Old Cotter in "The Sisters," just as the old man that the boy encounters is a new incarnation of the enigmatic Father Flynn.

The narrator of "An Encounter," much like the narrator of "The Sisters," is repelled by paradigms of rigid masculinity and powerfully drawn to characters who seem unable to subscribe to this myth. The penalty for failing to subscribe adequately is horrendous, as both narrators realize, and includes such dangers as social ostracism and even the loss of one's sanity. Consequently, the narrator of "An Encounter" is thrilled to meet a man whose objects of desire are as variable and unstructured as his own. There is no clear evidence that the old man is what one would now characterize as a pedophile or a homosexual. Critics who have characterized him as one or both of these have had to assume that his first monologue about the allure of girls is a deliberate and crafty falsification (to lure the boy into his confidence) and that his second monologue reveals the true structure of his desire (as a homosexual and a pedophile). But the narrator is struck by the fact that the old man gets mesmerized by his own rhetoric *in both cases.* The old man is perverse in the sense that he is polymorphously perverse — he demonstrates the directionless sexual instinct of a child. Only reference to the thoughtless and naive onanism of a young child could supply a precedent for the old man's absurdly spontaneous act of masturbation. As Colin MacCabe points out, "The pervert is articulated around the lack that the neurotic refuses to acknowledge" (1979, 123).

Rather than denying his lack-in-being, the old man appears to celebrate it by endlessly taking note of it: "His mind was slowly circling round and round in the same orbit" (*D* 26). Lacking any sense of himself as masculine, the structure of the old man's Desire is not goal oriented in the least. To put it another way, there is no privileged object of desire in his discourse and, thus, he has no ability to arrest the process of desire by subscribing to the acceptable goals of the gender myth of masculinity. In his second monologue (about whipping boys who desire girls) the narrator tells us, "His mind . . . seemed to circle slowly round and round its new centre" (*D* 27). The old man's polymorphous perversity (desire endlessly circulating around continually varied objects and, therefore, not indicative of any gender whatsoever) can be clearly seen once one appreciates that both monologues excite the old man.

What is so disorienting about the old man's discourse is that his twin monologues expose the fictional construct of all sexual preferences, including heterosexuality. He is capable of exciting himself, in the second monologue, by imagining that he is punishing the very perspective that excited him in the first monologue! In other words, the old man of the first monologue, in order to fetishize the female form as an object of desire, presents a view of little girls that the subject of the second monologue would have to regard as perverse. In the same way, the old man of the second monologue excites himself about the male body by fantasizing a need to punish and correct the perverse structure of Desire that he depicted as being normal only minutes earlier ("Every boy . . . has a sweetheart"). By speaking authoritatively for two radically different structures of Desire, the old man demonstrates to the terrified and fascinated boy the illusion of phallic authority. The two contradictory lessons the old man gives to the boy parody and deconstruct the earlier lesson of Father Butler.[3]

Indeed, the rhetorical structure of Father Butler's public denouncement of *The Apache Chief* is worth examining in more detail. He begins by declaring the book outside the bounds of worthwhile reading material: "What is this rubbish? . . . Is this what you read instead of studying your Roman History? Let me not find any more of this wretched stuff in this college" (*D* 20). Next he speculates that the author of such rubbish is likewise outside the bounds of decency: "The man who wrote it, I suppose, was some wretched scribbler that writes these things for a drink" (*D* 20). His final categorical judgment — and his most ominous one — is that while they enjoy all the comforts and privileges accorded to those students residing within the acceptable bounds of the law, if something in their natures should prove to be unexpectedly perverse, then they will be cast out and made wretched as well: "I'm surprised at boys like you, educated, reading such stuff. I could understand it if you were . . . National School boys" (*D* 20). Readers learn later, when the old man speaks of whipping, that, for the narrator, this allusion to "National School boys" comes to represent that area beyond the boundaries of correctly structured Desire where Phallic authority ceases to cajole students into assuming the role of masculinity and, instead, forces conformity through corporal punishment: "We were not National School boys to be *whipped,* as he called it" (*D* 27). In essence, Father Butler's rebuke insists, much like the old man, that there are correct goals toward which their energies should be directed, and any other impulses they indulge might expose them to severe punishment. Father Butler presents a monolithic and seamless narrative of normal masculinity. But the old man, whose contradictory manner highlights the void at the center of any structure of Desire, inadvertently reveals that Father Butler's totalizing drive toward building a meaning system denies the structural lack-in-being (the symbolic castration) that it is based upon. In short, the old man subverts something the narrator already doubts — the ability of the masculine gender myth to deny symbolic castration.[4]

One who ignores the content of the old man's two speeches for a moment might notice that their rhetorical structure, much like the rebuke of Father Butler, alternates between describing acceptable goals for one's [sexual] energy and unacceptable ones and, therefore, punishable. The narrator's encounter with the old man confirms (all too vividly) something he already suspects: patriarchal figures are directing him toward appropriate objects of desire that will satisfy his lack-in-being, but these objects are arbitrary and substitutive, and the guarantee of fulfillment is a myth. The Phallic Order designates some objects as satisfactory and others as perverse in order to deny that all objects of Desire are substitutes that promise to reunify the subject. Curiously, the narrator treats the old man with the same exaggerated respect we would expect him to show Father Butler: He does not interrupt him, he does not contradict him, he betrays no misgivings about what he has been told. Indeed, because it does not even occur to him that he might refuse to give his name if asked, he takes the precaution of making up an alias beforehand. He extends his courtesy so far as to avoid breaking away from the old man while he is still talking: "I waited till his monologue paused again. Then I stood up abruptly. Lest I should betray my agitation I delayed a few moments pretending to fix my shoe properly and then, saying that I was obliged to go, I bade him good-day" (*D* 27–28). Joyce's selection of detail is very rich here as he shows us the boy preparing to return to the myth of normalcy and masculinity via an act of overly solicitous correction (tying his shoe). All of these strategies, in addition to showing respect, mimic the typical interview strategy of the hero of a detective story who pretends to know everything that is told to him in an effort to plunge as deeply as possible into the depths of forbidden knowledge: "I pretended that I had read every book he mentioned" (*D* 25). But also, like a detective hero, he learns more than he can afford to know in the course of his investigation. The knowledge he gains only forces him to confront the terrifying amount he does not know. Consequently, the boy retreats from the pleasant and vicious realm of the unrepresented Real back to the comforting illusions of the Symbolic Order. In effecting this transition, he grows ashamed of his investigative stratagems and becomes enamored of Mahony's cowboy persona — a persona that accepts the correctness of the Phallic Order without question: "He ran as if to bring me aid. And I was penitent; for in my heart I had always despised him a little" (*D* 28).

As I pointed out earlier, readers of this story have settled on the idea that the old man is a pedophile, but his perversity is much more polymorphous than this. After all, he begins his monologue with a fetishistic appreciation of the hands and hair of young girls. His description is too detailed to be merely a trap for the narrator, and it is actually his speech on the beauty of girls that causes him to go off and masturbate. Lacan maintains it is not the object of the sexual drive that matters but the process of that drive. Culturally defined gender myths such as masculinity and femininity seek to obscure this fact by insisting that the opposite sexes complement one another perfectly. The pervert, on the other hand, simply has no belief in the phallic signifier and, therefore, no respect for culturally constructed sexual differences: "In adults, we are aware of the palpable richness of perversion. Perversion, in sum, is the privileged exploration of an existential possibility of human nature — its internal tearing apart, its gap, through which the supra-natural world of the symbolic was able to make its entry" (Lacan 1988a, 218). Because the "self" is based on external, inconstant sources, the human sexual drive always searches for more than it can possibly find. Gender myths presume that the presence of Desire in a subject implies the possibility of self-induced satisfaction, but the opposite is true. Subjectivity, gender, and identity are all reality effects generated by a structure of Desire that must designate certain objects of desire as correct because it is a structure based on a lack-in-being that may be temporarily eased by substitution but never permanently satisfied.

Because the old man keeps arbitrarily substituting different objects as the object of his desire (a girl's hair, a girl's hands, a bad boy, the act of whipping, the narrator's attention), what the boy witnesses, in a completely exposed format, is the process of the drive rather than the attainment of its objects. Culture imposes various ideologies on the subject (what Father Butler would term education) to make the case that the object of the drive is naturally designated, and that only proper objects are capable of correctly channeling the process of the drive. The pervert does not believe in the existence of the Phallus, which is to say there are no objects the pervert is willing to imbue with transcendent symbolic significance, including, and especially, the penis. Instead, as in the case of the old man in "An Encounter," the pervert becomes mesmerized by the process of the drive, repeating phrases in a circular manner that has no end point, and always being careful to "come" just short of privileging a particular object. Because it is obsessively circular, the pattern of his speech is also rigorously meaningless and does not masquerade as something obsessively linear that will eventually achieve closure (as do all of Father Butler's pronouncements).

As a result, the old man short-circuits desire because he refuses to let the sexual drive be properly channelled through the culturally certified appliance of masculinity. Gender, like a complex stereo system, elaborately controls and directs sexual electricity, but, as everyone knows, electricity can also operate a toaster or a hairdryer or even directly shock the subject when no objectives are interposed as effective resistance: "In the profound relation of the drive, what is essential is that the movement by which the arrow that sets out towards the target fulfills its function only by really re-emerging from it, and returning on to the subject. In this sense, the pervert is he who, in short circuit, more directly than any other, succeeds in his aim, by integrating in the most profound way his function as subject with his existence as desire (Lacan 1981a, 206). The old man does not masquerade as a gendered subject who desires this or that object. Instead of functioning as a subject, he repetitively demonstrates the precise dysfunction of Desire (its insatiable dimension) that the gendered subject denies. His discourse, suspended over the incertitude of the void, is devoid of the sense of purpose and aura of usefulness that permeates Father Butler's speech. The old man does not believe in the monadic authority of the phallic signifier, so he has no need to connect himself to preexisting gender myths that typically help the masculine subject deny symbolic castration. Because the artificial constructs of culture, conscience, and education are nowhere honored in his monologues, his manner of speaking implies that all locution is a circumlocution that surrounds the subject's ex-istence with meaning. "The phantasy is the support of desire;" Lacan writes, "it is not the object that is the support of desire" (1981a, 185). The structure of perversion, therefore, "is an inverted effect of the phantasy. It is the subject who determines himself as object, in his encounter with the division of subjectivity" (1981a, 185).

In essence, Father Butler urges the students to sublimate their sexual drive into the approved channels dictated by the Phallic Order and thereby discover the legitimate objects that will appear to support their desire. This approach to reality requires that one perfect a subjectivity that recognizes the landmarks of gender, identity, class, culture, and education. The subject becomes split because unconscious, unrepresented elements of the drive constitute the Real, which, in turn, constantly undermines and occasionally subverts the reality the subject perceives. These uncataloged impulses (which the narrator generically designates as "a spirit of unruliness") send cryptic messages to the conscious subject in dream fragments that are never made whole by any given object of desire. Father Butler warns the students that they must effectively sublimate the sexual drive if they hope to participate in the (spurious) phenomenon of transcendent subjectivity that their identity, class privilege, and gender bestow upon them. His promise to them is that appropriate object(s) of desire will support the fantasy of themselves. But their continued fervid fantasy play outside the sober hours of school, as well as its spillover into the communal and secretive reading of *The Halfpenny Marvel* during school, makes it clear that their perfunctory acceptance of Father Butler's summary of reality is also what gives rise to their unruly spirit. This spirit seems to be constituted by everything that is not accounted for, recognized, or represented by the Phallocentric structure of Desire. It is unruly in that it subverts the rules of reality, thus exposing, however briefly, the mysterious and insatiable pull of the unrepresentable Real. The old man is the incarnation of everything that is unruly, and it is his polymorphous perversity, completely uncharted by the usual signposts of the Symbolic Order (such as gender) that sends the frightened narrator in the direction of that unconquered cowboy, Mahony.

For Lacan, the subject who is engaged in satisfying the drive through sublimation is also engaged in the act of satisfying the sexual drive, whether or not he is engaged in any sort of physical act. The physical act is not the support of desire—the fantasy is the support of desire—and one can indulge the fantasy without resorting to the act. Any given fantasy of satisfaction is equivalent to any given physical act because the physical act only satisfies to the extent that it is supported by a given fantasy. Indeed, the old man's verbal ejaculations seem to satisfy him more profoundly than his physical one. The climax of his speech has a physical counterpart in his masturbation, but clearly the act of masturbation is a mere side effect to the much more potent linguistic masturbation where his words surround his existence and designate his "self" as an object of desire. In this light, Father Butler's rigid fascination with sublimation can be seen as revealing his interest in arousing the desire of the boys in front of him ("Now, Dillon, up!"). He is, in fact, every bit as intent on satisfying the sexual drive as his perverted counterpart. Lacan interprets Freud as having deliberately erased the distinction between the symbolic search for satisfaction (sublimation) and the physical one (orgasm).

> Freud tells us repeatedly that sublimation is also satisfaction of the drive, whereas it is *zielgehemmt*, inhibited as to its aim—it does not attain it. Sublimation is nonetheless satisfaction of the drive, without repression.
>
> In other words—for the moment, I am not fucking, I am talking to you. Well! I can have exactly the same satisfaction as if I were fucking. That's what it means. Indeed, it raises the question of whether in fact I am not fucking at this moment. Between these two terms—drive and satisfaction—there is set up an extreme antinomy that reminds us that the use of the function of the drive has for me no other purpose than to put in question what is meant by satisfaction. (1981a, 165–66)

Whereas the goal of the normal subject's drive is "to realise itself in the field of the Other and to find in that field the object which is eternally lacking," the drive of the pervert constantly leaves open the question of satisfaction of the drive by refusing to seek out an object in the field of the Other that bestows satisfaction by representing Truth. Both Father Dillon and the old man, one as masculine and the other as perverse, are fucking as they speak.[5]

Rather then generating substitute objects to fill the gap of human desire, the pervert hovers over the void of his own incertitude ("his mind was circling round and round in the same orbit"), and this attitude makes a mockery of absolute and complementary divisions such as masculinity and femininity. Lacan states, "To disguise this gap by relying on the virtue of the 'genital' to resolve it through the maturation of tenderness (that is by a recourse to the Other solely as reality), however piously intended, is none the less a fraud" (1982b, 81). Father Butler's no-nonsense lecture during the sober hours is intended to cause the difficulty of gender, sexuality, and identity to be properly channeled and, thus, to disappear. Significantly, the narrative Father Butler tells Leo Dillon to study more diligently—Caesar's *Commentaries on the Gallic Wars*—is a text that describes many battles by beginning with the somewhat clichéd preface "hardly had the day dawned." What is important to note is that *The Apache Chief* describes much the same thing (i.e., a series of battles fought with courage and conviction) except that Indians attack the accepted text of Western settlements (civilization)! These colonizers assumed, as did the British colonizers of Ireland, that they had a prior right to exist anywhere on the globe, regardless of what sort of unrepresentable savages had settled there before them.[6] Caesar, unlike the Apache chief, is a warrior whose goals have been cataloged and approved by historians of Western culture. It is not, therefore, civilized war that Father Butler denigrates but the adventures of reluctant Indians who haunt the margins of Western culture like an unruly spirit that might call its fictional unity into doubt at any time. Similarly, the fictional text of masculinity is both sustained and threatened by the marginalized and unruly spirit of femininity: "I liked better some American detective stories which were traversed from time to time by unkempt fierce and beautiful girls" (*D* 20). Clearly, the old man traverses (acts in opposition to) Father Butler's patriarchal scoldings; he is the Apache chief, and the narrator reluctantly becomes his Indian.

Even though Caesar is quite similar to the Apache chief (he spends a good deal of his time on the warpath), Father Butler confidently presents this warrior to his students as the original example of what can be accomplished when a masculine subject channels his sexual drive in a civilized (sublimated) and goal-oriented manner. The narrative of the Gallic Wars presents the warrior Caesar as one who participated in the teleological march toward God that Mr. Deasy so approves of in the "Nestor" chapter of *Ulysses*. The Apache chief, on the other hand, is a perverse warrior who threatens to undermine the truth of Caesar's monological and monocausal account of the world. The monocausal theory of history, which the *Commentaries on the Gallic Wars* subscribes to, is being undermined by the presence in the classroom of another text that presents a different myth; Indian warriors were famous for precipitous raids (glimpses of the Real) as opposed to self-righteous campaigns (paranoid moi formations). The deconstructive dynamic of having both these texts in the same classroom is reproduced in the story by the later self-destructive structure of the old man's dualistic/duellistic two-part monologue. The difference, of course, is that in the first instance the structure of the class is shown to be split (between an unruly spirit and the sober hours of school). In the second instance, the prior cause of this division is exposed: the split in the subject himself between the Real (unruly spirit) and reality (sober hours).

Just as the old man draws attention to the artificial structure of Desire by presenting a normal and perverse account of it, the dual presence of *Commentaries on the Gallic Wars* and *The Apache Chief* exposes narratives of history as a social construct that, like patriarchal authority and gender, recounts experience with a coherency that is entirely mythical. During the sober hours of school, the students recite approved history word by word. Outside of the class, however, their unruly spirit recites the perverse text as something that is beyond language: "[Joe Dillon] looked like some kind of an Indian when he capered round the garden, an old tea-cosy on his head, beating a tin with his fist and yelling:—Ya! yaka, yake, yaka!" (*D* 19). Here, Joe Dillon's yell corresponds with Stephen's idea of history and God as a very unteleological "shout in the street." If one accepts Lacan's theory that the object of the drives is incidental to the fantasy that Desire is based upon and that it is the process—whether sublimated or not—that yields all the satisfaction it is possible for the subject to obtain, one can then conclude that both Caesar and the Apache chief, while fighting, "experience exactly the same satisfaction as if [they] were fucking." Father Butler's preference, in other words, is strictly based on the fact that Caesar was a normal masculine subject and the Apache chief (not to mention the wretched alcoholic who created him) was a pervert. Or, to make the same distinction by contrasting the style of these two warriors' own narratives, Father Butler privileges Caesar's measured prose—with all its implications of a monocausal truth in the Other about to be unfolded—and denigrates the Apache chief's circular and supplementary (rather than complementary) shout of jouissance that undermines the notion of Truth and foregrounds instead the unfathomable, absolute, and infinite gap at the base of human desire (which is the Real truth).

Father Butler and the narrative of Caesar, the narrator tells us, awakened one of his consciences. This conscience is the part of the split subject that seeks to correlate itself completely with reality by pursuing an acceptable object of desire in the field of the Other, thus affirming the possibility of Truth by insisting upon the impossibility of any other conscience (i.e., on any other structure of desire). But the narrator, by referring to this as only one of his consciences, makes it clear that he has by no means banished the spirit of unruliness that is embedded in narratives such as those in American detective stories and Westerns. What he wants are "real adventures" such as the sort that cannot happen "to people who remain at home" (*D* 21). The old man, then, as the Apache chief, appeals to the second conscience—that repressed part of the split subject that corresponds, inscrutably, with the unrepresentable Real (through dreams and slips of the tongue, etc.). In setting out to find adventure, the narrator seeks more knowledge about the perverse texts that Father Butler banished from the classroom. This banishment does not awaken his conscience but, as he puts it, *one* of his consciences, which means that it awakened, at the same time, a sense that this conscience—only one structure among other possible structures—is a construction. Where boundaries exist around a unified construction, there must also be an ex-istence of excluded and marginalized experience that forms what Lacan calls the Real. The awakening of one conscience simultaneously prompts the realization in the narrator that some residue of meaning ex-ists (in an unrepresented form) beyond the false closure of the signifier/signified that go together—like cowboy and his horse—in the social construction of masculinity.

The cowboy persona of Leo Dillon, one must presume, regards Father Butler's reprimand as a pronouncement of truth that awakens the only conscience it is possible to have — the unified conscience of a masculine subject. What the narrator hopes to acquire in the land abroad where real adventures take place is the sort of knowledge Father Butler seems to have forbidden him to know. His initial pose is to act as one who knows everything in the hopes of proving himself worthy to be initiated into further mysteries. But what he encounters in his brief intersubjective involvement with the old man is not an increase in his knowledge about reality but a brief glimpse of the Real which, far from filling in the gaps in his knowledge, instead highlights them as indicative of the insatiable lack-in-being that is the basis of social constructions such as reality, identity, and Truth. He finally leaves home and has a Real adventure where knowledge itself is revealed as one more stopgap measure to paper over the insatiable lack-of-being that is the basis for the impossible structure of desire in the split subject. During this story, then, the narrator encounters two father figures who represent the two sides of the split upon which his own subjectivity is based; one believes in the Phallus, the other does not. One believes Truth can be discovered by desiring to become whatever the Other desires one to be, the other sees the field of the Other as illusion and monotonously celebrates the incertitude of the void; it is teleology (Father Butler) versus tedium (the old man).

In the end, the narrator seeks out the company of Mahony with a fervor he has never felt before. Mahony's lack of knowledge, previously the source of the narrator's scorn for his friend, now seems an odd source of strength. Mahony, after all, has completely confounded the old man's attempt to fascinate him by declaring he has no less than three "totties" (objects of desire) and then asking him, point-blank, how many he has (the old man's evasive response is that he had lots of sweethearts — when he was their age).

"Neurosis is dream rather than perversion," Lacan has stated. "Neurotics have none of the characteristics of the pervert. They simply dream that they have, which is natural, since how else could they reach their partner?" (1982b, 157). In the conclusion of Joyce's story, the narrator calls for Mahony as if he (the narrator) were drowning and Mahony were standing safely on land with a rope: "How my heart beat as he came running across the field to me! He ran as if to bring me aid. And I was penitent; for in my heart I had always despised him a little"

(*D* 28). The narrator retreats to Fort Masculinity to save himself from further random attacks by the Apache chief. The intense relief on the part of the narrator, now that he has extricated himself from the debasing effect of the old man's endlessly circular desire, is described in a manner that calls to mind the relief experienced by anyone who has awoken from an encounter that had appeared terrifying Real — the chronicles of disorder — only to discover (gratefully!) a more familiar reality that relegates this previous encounter to the ambiguous status of having been "only a dream."

4

The Question and the Quest
The Story of Mangan's Sister

The displacement of the signifier determines the subjects in their acts, in their destiny, in their refusals,
in their blindness, in their end and in their fate.
(Lacan 1988c, 43–44)

Gazing up into the darkness I saw myself as a creature
driven and derided by vanity; and my eyes burned
with anguish and anger. (*D* 35)

I had read "Araby" several times before I noticed and became curious about the fact that the Araby Bazaar is really the place
where Mangan's sister wishes to go. The surprise and confusion of
the boy's aunt when he asks if he may go makes it clear that he has
not mentioned the event until after his conversation with Mangan's
sister. She is the one who introduces "the magical name" that is also
the title of the story, but what is her story? If she is not the protagonist of the story, can she be seen as the contagonist whose powerful
absence makes the boy's presence in his own narrative possible?

Blanche Gelfant, in her introduction to a panel entitled "A Frame
of Her Own: Joyce's Women in *Dubliners* Reviewed" at the Ninth Joyce
Symposium, cites the boy's fantasy relationship to Mangan's sister
as typical of what male critics have done with the women they have
come upon in Joyce's fiction: "The reader can see Mangan's sister
only as she has been appropriated by a male viewer—indeed, three

male viewers: the deluded boy, the retrospective narrator, and the author. A fourth must be added, the male critic, whose objectivity as observer of Joyce's women has until recently gone unchallenged" (1988, 263). One has only to look over some of the male commentaries on "Araby" from the sixties and seventies to see that Gelfant's indictment of the male critic is justifiable.[1]

But is Joyce really the third male appropriator standing between the reader and Mangan's sister? I do not think so, and Marilyn French, in the panel that Gelfant introduces, also suggests otherwise: "Joyce's women are not mere mythic figures, types, such as appear in the work of so many other male authors. They have a reality of their own which is palpable even though the men who occupy the foreground of the stories largely ignore it" (1988, 267). Male critics have often appropriated the women in Joyce's fiction with at least as much ingenuity as any of the male characters in *Dubliners*. Mangan's sister, for example, has been featured as a virgin, a whore, Ireland, simony, and so on, in various essays. Like the boy of the story, male essayists have too often discovered that Mangan's sister represents the very thing they fear is lacking in their own arguments. And yet it is her frustrated desire that calls the boy into being. I suggest that her unspoken story speaks who the narrator becomes in the course of what he presents as his story.[2]

The narrator says, "I kept her brown figure always in my eye." Once readers refuse to take his word for it, they see that this is not so. What he always keeps, as the symmetry of this phrase suggests, is his *I*, which is constructed in relation to the representation of Mangan's sister that he has appropriated by his "eye." It is this that allows him to believe in the fictional unity of his masculine identity, which in turn grants him the illusion of bearing his chalice (his presumed subjectivity) safely through a throng of foes (what Lacan terms the Real).[3] I go even further and suggest that the subject of "Araby" is the desire of Mangan's sister in the sense that her function in the boy's narration as absence and lack is what permits his subjective presence. He represses awareness of the question of her desire by incorporating it into what he presents as his quest. As a result, what he takes to be his identity has been constructed relative to another (Mangan's sister) and is destined to be taken apart in relation to someone else (the shop girl at the bazaar). The appropriating gaze he directs to Mangan's sister is reflected back to him — in an inverted and disorienting form — by the indifferent gaze of the shop girl who asks if he wants to buy something. As the delirious subjectivity when setting out on his quest founders, the question of woman returns, and the boy becomes the object of another's gaze: "Once or twice the young lady glanced at me over her shoulder. I lingered before her stall, though I knew my stay was useless, to make my interest in her wares seem the more real" (*D* 35). The masculine quester becomes the feminine question — masquerading to appear "more real."

By moving from the subject controlling the gaze to the object controlled by it, the narrator moves from the exhilaration of having the Phallus to the more debilitating posture of consciously pretending to be the Phallus for the benefit of an-other's desire ("I lingered . . . to make my interest in her wares seem the more real"). More real for whom? Certainly not the narrator; although he now knows he is pretending, earlier he knew he was the real thing, both of these moments equally represent reality inasmuch as both misrepresent the Real. The illusion of having the phallus (based on the lack of Mangan's sister — her inability to satisfy her desire to go to the Araby Bazaar) allows the boy to emerge as the only one worthy to go in search of the one, true (nonexistent) object of desire (the Holy Grail). He is a selected signifier destined to bring back the elected signified. Certainly the narrator feels found out by the end of this story (which was never his story), but his final epiphany is a new pose. Like so many of Joyce's characters, he is learning that in the masque of subjectivity — in disguising the face of the slave — sincerity is crucial; once you can fake that you have it made.

The boy sees Mangan's sister as a representation of what Lacan calls the woman; he imagines who he has become by positing his completeness on her lack.[4] He lives in a world of words, rather than the world itself — what Lacan calls the Real — which is whatever has not been represented, distorted, interpreted, or reconstructed in the Symbolic Order of language. In this kingdom of words he is able to imagine himself as king, and this allows him to believe in himself as a subject. But in the world of words, the subject is a signifier with no signified. The subject takes its place in a signifying chain and is, henceforth, forced to model its very being on the moment of the signifying chain that traverses consciousness. A woman who appears to the masculine subject as feminine — as the Woman — appears as the locus of the question about the masculine subject's identity. She seems to represent the response given by the subject to the question of knowing what he is for the 'other.' Essentially, the Other is a concept designating the reference point from which one establishes identity — between consciousness and unconsciousness, between others and language, somewhere between one's sense of what is inside and outside. If the masculine subject could only possess the *original* signifier — which does not exist and which Lacan calls the Phallus — then he would no longer be merely a signifier that acts as a signifier for another signifier in a chain that goes on forever. But this can never be because there is nothing certain in the Symbolic Order — nothing that directly corresponds to the Real — that is capable of stopping the chain reaction.

For the narrator, Mangan's sister is a representation of femininity — the opposite of masculinity — which is to say she does not exist for him except as the representation of lack that confirms the fullness and authenticity of his masculine subjectivity. The Woman represents to the masculine subject the Other, which is the locus from which the subject's question of his existence is presented to him. This question can bathe and support the subject, but it can also invade him and tear him apart. When a woman is taken to be the Woman by a masculine subject, she is perceived as enigmatic and powerful because she appears to have the power to nurture or destroy — to confirm the authenticity of his identity or to undermine it. In fact, she has the power to do neither; the enigma of femininity merely reflects back to the masculine subject a division that already exists within him.

But does Mangan's sister exist outside the boy's "I/eye" — outside his representation of her as the Woman? Joyce shows us she does by allowing the possibility that, although the boy's narrative seeks to repress it, *she has noticed him looking and is looking back at him.* A commonplace criticism about this story is that the girl does not notice the narrator — perhaps because he is too young or, perhaps, because he has kept his confused adoration a secret. But I argue for the opposite assumption: she has seen him looking at her and that is why she begins their conversation (a fact as curiously easy to skip over as the fact that she brings up the subject of the Araby Bazaar). To begin with, he must have distinguished himself from her brother in her eyes because he consistently refuses to take part in his attitude of playful disobedience toward her: "Her brother always teased her before he obeyed and I stood by the railings looking at her" (*D* 30). Certainly, the narrator wishes to worship her in private, but he really has two impulses, and the second one has been insufficiently noted: one impulse is to remain unseen while seeing her (he pulls the window blind to within an inch of the sash), and the other is to have her see him while he appears to be looking elsewhere (every morning he contrives to cross her path as though by chance).

What can it mean, then, when he says *"at last* she spoke to me" (emphasis added) except that she has noticed him noticing her and has finally decided to act? And, when she does speak, her remarks (and the narrator heralds these remarks as "the first words," making it clear that he has been expecting something to begin), although narrated indirectly by the boy and, thus, apparently haphazard and indifferent are, in fact, rather cleverly designed to test the extent and nature of his attraction to her without risking embarrassment or rejection on her part. She is a girl curious about her recently discovered ability to attract the male gaze (a discovery selected by Molly Bloom as an extremely important one in a girl's life). The fact that the narrator is young and naïve is precisely the point; she would scarcely experiment with this new dimension of her being with someone like Blazes Boylan, because he would certainly lack the subtlety to interpret it in a manner flattering to herself. That her words to the boy come "at last" suggest that she has been fascinated by the game and even prolonged it. Finally, her choice of remark, asking him if he is going to an event that she cannot possibly attend, by rule of her parents, is not at all arbitrary but a clever way of drawing out his attention while at the same time protecting herself from it; she is still a little frightened of what his gaze might mean, but she longs to be nearer to it.

In an important essay, Devlin points out that a major component of Leopold Bloom's enjoyment of Gertie McDowell (his consumption of her image) depends on his belief that she is only stimulated by being looked at, not by looking at him: "Oddly enough, Bloom does not think of women being stimulated visually, through provocative sights, in an elision of the possibility of female scopophilia. . . . He fails to think of her as a voyeur or recognize the full extent of her own visual pleasure, refusing to see her as the pruriently viewing subject, himself as the exhibitionistic object. But after all, since when is a fairly overt masturbation not an exhibitionistic act?" (1988, 140).[5] They boy also exhibits himself to the girl morning after morning (although certainly less overtly than Bloom). My point is that the excitement of both Bloom and the narrator of "Araby" is contingent on the dynamic of their upholding their *I* by keeping the figure of a woman in their *eye*. But how is it possible to maintain this illusion about the unity of their subjectivity if the women they have appropriated for the purposes of stimulation have also or, in the case of Mangan's sister, have already appropriated their image in order to stimulate themselves?

Mangan's sister speaks to him first, and as she does so she turns a silver bracelet "round and round her wrist." Is this self-consciously sexual, a subtle variation of Gerty leaning farther back? Not necessarily, but I insist this shows that she is concentrating on what she is doing and saying and experimenting with her ability to direct the boy's gaze. The point is made that the narrator's two friends are fighting one another for each other's caps, and yet he is standing quietly before her staring at her hand and the movement of her bracelet. She would have to be conscious of his quiescent attitude against a backdrop of puerile high jinks. She could not possibly confuse his attitude of reverence with their attitude of juvenile disregard. While she turns the bracelet, the narrator describes her as "bowing her head towards me" (*D* 32). This gesture is not the same thing, I would like to point out, as bowing her head down (as looking at the ground and away from him). I argue she is looking at him, even moving her face closer to him, and the proof is the curious absence in the narrator's extremely detailed description of any mention of her face or her eyes. Instead, he details the light of the lamp, her hand on the railing, the curve of her neck, and the border of her petticoat. Taken all in all, this is the observational standpoint of someone who is avoiding the gaze of the person he is looking at. She is watching him watch her and he, not wishing to understand this, looks elsewhere.[6]

After he is alone, the narrator gives the reader the impression that he has created an image of Mangan's sister in precise detail: "I may have stood there for an hour, seeing nothing but the brown-clad figure cast by my imagination, touched discreetly by the lamplight at the curved neck, at the hand upon the railings and at the border below the dress" (*D* 33). But this projection of her image is not a duplication at all; it has been edited significantly. There is no re-creation, for example, of her hand turning her bracelet, nor is there any recollection of her head bowing toward him. That the narrator forgets these two movements is evidence that he has already repressed the question of her desire, which these gestures betray, in order to appropriate her image as the negative of his own. After dressing her in this image he needs to see, the boy strips her of language; although she brought up the subject of Araby, she is silent in his image of her while he burns with impatient desire to go to this same bazaar. Thus, the mediated image of Mangan's sister that Gelfant complains of is, in fact, the girl in the boy's imagination, but Mangan's sister exists alongside the boy's narration and can be glimpsed through those gaps in the text where the boy's story falters. Her desire is the subject of the story because it is the subject of the boy's unconscious where it directs — right alongside but outside of his awareness — his conscious intentions that he misrecognizes as a call to destiny.

Having taken the unusual tack of discussing this story as though it were the story of Mangan's sister, I need to explain why she is absent from the narrator's story (although not from Joyce's). Pearce describes a narrative paradox that forces the reader, in the interest of wholeness, to present a narrative with holes. He gives several explanations for this, but one is most pertinent: "Some holes result from the failure to recognize or the need to suppress stories that are not valued or might be threatening; that is, the stories of woman." (1988, 79).

The boy in "Araby" must suppress the story of Mangan's sister (specifically of the awakening of her own confused desire) in order to tell his story — in order to have a story — so that he can believe in the myth of himself and, thus, bear his chalice safely through a throng of foes. This strategy will work until he comes upon another woman at the bazaar who is also enjoying and resisting the pleasure of looking and being looked at by two men. In essence, what was repressed returns because he has been displaced to a new position where he observes what he would not see when he was in the same position as the two men. He sees that the shop girl is looking back, that she is informing the structure of the conversation while appearing to be indifferent to it. In essence, he sees that she is looking, and in the only signifiers that are available to him (and too often to male critics) this makes her lewd, and himself as well, because it forces his earlier voyeurism into a strictly physical register unmitigated by the ennobling features of chivalry or courtly love. The shop girl's candid flirtation does not offend him — it indicts him. What the narrator retreats from in the closing moments of the story is the vague dread that something exists beyond the representations available to him — what Lacan calls the Real — that calls his being, (represented by his quest) into (quest)ion. The boy's concluding observation about himself is a reinterpretation of the Real and, thus, is no more true than his earlier perception of Mangan's sister, but it does restore reality to him because instead of the intolerable scenario of seeing himself being seen by Mangan's sister, and by the annoyed and distracted shop girl, he now reports *I saw myself* as a creature" (*D* 35). It is better to be his own creature than to be feminized by the objectifying gaze of a woman.

To reiterate, a woman is perceived by the masculine subject as what Lacan calls the Woman. A man comes upon this image and takes it to be the Other who has knowledge of the impossible signifier that gives meaning to the endless play of signifiers. For the masculine subject, the relief of discovering the Woman is something like the relief of a traveler, lost and bewildered in a snow storm that seems to represent first one thing and then another to him, who suddenly trips on something and, crouching down to examine it more closely, takes it to be his own doorstep. Marching resolutely through the storm of words that speak who he is, a man seeks the meaning of his own past in the future that the enigma of femininity seems to promise. The feminine mystery seems to contain for him something previous to, and outside of, the murderous signification of the Symbolic Order that, as Lacan puts it, speaks through him and directs him: "We make our destiny, because we talk. We believe that we say what we want, but it is what others wanted, most particularly our family, which speaks us. . . . We are spoken, and because of that, we make of the accidents that push us, something 'plotted'" (Ragland-Sullivan 1988, 118).

Lacan designates this "something beyond" in the Woman as *jouissance*. This complex term refers to a sense of fusion and naturalness — before cultural myths, before speech — that is comparable to the infant's pleasure in the object constancy provided by his own mirror reflection. By making Mangan's sister fictional, the boy is able to plot the fact of his own destiny, which seems to harmonize his body in a manner outside the linguistic manipulations of the Symbolic Order: "My

body was like a harp and her words and gestures were like fingers running upon the wires" (*D* 31). Here, words and gestures — precisely what
was elided from his fantasy image of her — return as confirmation of
his identity rather than a challenge to it. A suggestion of a mirror
response is in this description (every movement of the girl generates
a reflective movement in the boy) except that he, not Mangan's sister,
has become the mirror image constructed relative to another. Under
the guise of worshipping her image, he is worshipping his image — the
imaginary stage mirror reflection of fusion and wholeness outside and
previous to the Symbolic Order (the mythical fusion, certainty and
oneness of what Lacan calls the Imaginary Order). Significantly, he
cannot account for her importance to him in language: "Her name
sprang to my lips at moments in strange prayers and praises which
I myself did not understand. My eyes were often full of tears (I could
not tell why)" (*D* 31). We see from this passage that he knows her name,
yet he withholds it from the story, for to name her would be to make
her equivalent to a word, and this would once more close himself off
from the prespeech fusion and sense of oneness that lies beyond representation. Gabriel Conroy's early love letters exhibit this same fear
that using a woman's name will murder what is beyond the sign that
seems to unify him: "Why is it that words like these seem to me so
dull and cold? Is it because there is no word tender enough to be your
name?" (*D* 214).

The overheard conversation of the shop girl — her display of desire beyond his representation of what the feminine is — subverts his
fiction of Mangan's sister and would subvert his subjectivity as well
if he did not reinterpret the real under the guise of self-enlightenment.
At the conclusion of the story, he sees himself in order not to see that
he is being seen and that his "self" is nothing but what he imagines
the Other sees: "In the scopic field, everything is articulated between
two terms that act in an antinomic way — on the side of things, there
is the gaze that is to say, things look at me, and yet I see them. This
is how one should understand those words, so strongly stressed, in
the Gospel, *They have eyes that they might not see.* That they might not
see what? Precisely, that things are looking at them" (Lacan 1981a,
109). For the boy to know that the shop girl has glanced at him once
or twice, he must be, at least as far as he is aware, staring at her steadily.
But this time the girl's sporadic glance overmasters his steady gaze

because he knows that she knows that he is looking at her. "This is the phantasy to be found in the Platonic perspective of an absolute being to whom is transferred the quality of being all-seeing. At the very level of the phenomenal experience of contemplation this all-seeing aspect is to be found in the satisfaction of a woman who knows that she is being looked at, on condition that one does not show her that one knows that she knows" (Lacan 1981a, 75). Mangan's sister presents a more teasing and exciting image to the boy because it does not occur to him that she knows he is looking at her, yet, as I have already argued, every shift of posture is, on her part, a conscious reaction to the effect of being gazed upon. Likewise, in an antinomic way, there is nothing erotic, nothing supportive of the myth of the "self" in the exchange of looks because she sees that he knows that she knows that he is looking at her. Neither can pose as an object of desire for the other because it is the structure of desire that is based on a lack in being, not the illusion of an object that will satisfy and complete them, that has been made visible by their exchange of looks. "If I go I will bring you something" the narrator says to Mangan's sister (*D* 32), and it is the fact that the object is unnameable that gives it an alluring status as the thing that will complete him. Once he is standing before items for sale at the bazaar, however, he is faced with a simple and tawdry commercial transaction; it is not only the shop girl's dutiful surveillance that unnerves him but also her sudden demand that he say what he wants: "She asked me did I wish to buy anything" (*D* 35). Her realistic question, impossible to appropriate as a reflection of his own desire (he does not know what he wants), derails his Real, and illusory, quest.

The advantage for the masculine subject of converting an individual woman into what Lacan calls the Woman—an image of femininity that does not exist—is that this image then operates (to extend the boy's analogy) as a chalice wherein the bread and wine of fragmented experience is converted into the body and blood of unified subjectivity. Accompanied by the sacred image of the Woman, the narrator is able to move through any scene, however variegated and threatening, without fear of dissolution. For the masculine subject, a woman becomes a symptom that helps ward off any discovery of how tenuous his subjectivity really is. Mangan's sister—somewhere beyond representation—plays the harp that is his body. If he did not imagine her, he could not believe in his masculine subjectivity as an instrument of certitude capable of endless harmony. The world is lost for the sake of the word. What is needed is possession of an object that will authenticate all other objects. The boy's quest for the Holy Grail is a search for what Lacan designates as the Phallus. It is not an anatomical object for several reasons — the primary one being that it does not exist. So rather than despair of finding it, the masculine subject embarks on a lifelong campaign of mistaking different objects for this primary signifier.

Indeed, when the subject looks for the Phallus, the search must result not in finding it or failing to find it (both alternatives lead toward psychosis) but in repeating the act of losing it. This repetition keeps alive the illusion that the Phallus exists and may yet be found again, and this illusion, in turn, creates a crucial effect on the masculine subject that is nothing less than the experience of consciousness. The mythical unity of this consciousness is always on the verge of being subverted by the unconscious, which exists not before it or underneath it but in tandem with it. Thus, the boy's spurious certitude is presented by Joyce as precariously balanced over an abyss of oblivion: "All my senses seemed to desire to veil themselves and, feeling that I was about to slip from them, I pressed the palms of my hands together until they trembled, murmuring: *O love! O love!* many times" (*D* 31). The word love, repeated like a chant, wards off the danger that the other for whom the boy has constructed himself (Mangan's sister, who authenticates him) may be alien and dangerous. Because she confirms his unity, she is also uniquely capable of reminding him that he is permanently alienated into the otherness that exists in the gap between the word and the world. This impossible state of things that makes things possible is what Lacan calls desire.

Lacanian Desire, therefore, is essential and insatiable because it is the result of a fundamental lack-of-being that the subject consciously denies. The impossibility of satisfying desire actually permits the effect of subjectivity because it allows the subject to continue past each new object of desire as it inevitably proves fraudulent. The object of desire appears to frustrate the subject when, in fact, it contains within its structure the unbridgeable division that is always already present in the subject; the enigma of femininity, for example, merely reflects to the masculine subject the division that already exists within him. In patriarchial culture, an ideological world helps hide this fact and defines the feminine solely as that which is not masculine, as that negativity that authenticates masculine identity by embodying enigmatic anonymity. This same ideology relegates the female to an identity limbo where she is taught to mask her lack of identity to guarantee the spurious certitude of the masculine subject. The cultural praise she accrues for successfully doing this helps to mitigate the vertiginous effects of denying the problematics of her own sexual identity.

For Lacan, the Woman is a mythical species that, like Tinkerbell, does not exist beyond a masculine subject's belief in her. This imaginary being that confirms their fictional unity is then perceived by the masculine subject as either enchanting (Mangan's sister) or treacherous (the shop girl). Mangan's sister is enchanting in that she seems to promise wholeness only to the narrator, and the shop girl is treacherous in that she seems to offer wholeness to everyone but the narrator. From his displaced position as alienated observer at the Araby Bazaar, he witnesses the masquerade of femininity and sees how the masculine subjects participate in its construction (thus unconsciously directing the construction of themselves). He then loses faith in the Woman, which simultaneously deconstructs the myth of himself and forces him to begin telling his story anew, this time as a blinded and humbled Samson rather than Sir Lancelot. Femininity is absence, or lack, for the narrator—a placeholder like zero in the numerical system of the boy's narrative—it can neither betray nor bestow anything. But a masculine subject is compelled to view it as always doing one thing or the other in order to continue believing in the fictional unity of his subjective consciousness. In other words, it is the subject that is fraudulent not the object of desire. Put in the context of "Araby," it is the narrator who is fictional, not Mangan's sister. Both Mangan's sister and the shop girl exist in his narrative and beyond it by remaining nameless, yet some part of them (jouissance) subverts the narrator's representation of them; it is their unrepresented story that writes his story.

In Lacan's analogy about how the subject constructs himself, he describes the subject as attaching himself at various points to the existing Symbolic Order the way upholstery is anchored to the existing wooden frame of a chair. This gives shape to an otherwise shapeless chair, just as attaching one's self to the existing Symbolic Order gives identity to an otherwise fragmented subject. The buttons that secure the upholstery to the frame (Lacan calls these buttons *points de capitons*) are key signifiers that anchor the subject to the existing linguistic code. The subject does not know what the key signifiers mean; he only knows they imbue him with a sense of meaning. And it is this buttoning down of the self to the linguistic code that generates a sense of being. The linguistic code to which the subject buttons himself, such as the representation of the Woman, takes on the role of the Other. It presents the question to which the subject imagines himself to be the answer. But if it imbues him with certitude, it can just as easily invade him with incertitude. It can hold him together or tear him apart. Neither state is based in the Real, although each may be said to represent the two poles of the subject's reality. What is real is that the strategies and avenues of fulfillment that are available to a given subject are given by this code and in many ways predetermine what the subject is often fond of calling his destiny.

The narrator tells Mangan's sister that if he goes to Araby he will bring back something for her. She has not asked him to go, and she does not tell him what she wants. He wants to get her what she does not even know to ask for, hoping that she will then give him what she does not possess; this is the powerful masquerade around a non-relation that Lacan calls love. Mangan's sister, as an object of desire, causes the narrator to desire, but she has no signified for him. Whatever he might bring her from the fair, it will not be what she wants, but only what he imagines she wants. The image of Mangan's sister as the Woman, in its metaphorical function as a symptom, has linked the narrator's conscious and unconscious desires in such a way that unconscious fantasy is able to force its way into the signifying chain in a fervent quest to obtain something he cannot name for someone who has not asked for it.

The result is a complete shift in the boy's interests, away from everything that has been of interest in the past toward a quest for what the Other knows about who he is. But there is no Other of the Other (even though the Woman would be this Other of the Other if she existed). Once a woman is transformed into the representation of the Woman, the search for the knowledge in the Other that verifies the masculine subject's existence is made possible. But, on the other hand, this same transformation, although it authorizes the quest, also makes absolute the impossibility of the subject ever completing it. So those moments where the narrator murmurs incoherent prayers to the image of Mangan's sister allow him to "bear his chalice safely through a throng of foes" because his belief in her, although she does not exist, is sufficient to cover the reality that he does not exist either (that the presumed unity of his masculine subjectivity is a fiction). By linking the narrator's conscious and unconscious desire, the image of the Woman connects subject and system as a point de capiton, and this determines both the necessity of his quest and the certainty of its failure. One does not find, or fail to find, the Phallus; one repeats the act of failing to have it, which is then understood as having lost it. Only through narration can the boy misrecognize this scenario of repetition as his destiny.

Unable to acknowledge the impossibility of satisfaction that the structure of desire has forced upon him, the narrator quickly introduces an obstacle to his goal by saying he will bring her something. In this way, the obstacle between him and what he takes to be the object of his desire will seem real and, therefore, surmountable rather than Real and, therefore, impossible to represent or overcome. He is caught in a structure in which the object of his desire becomes the signifier of his own impossibility. Every knight-in-armor, rather than face the debilitating nonrelation of the sexes, chooses to embark on a difficult and dangerous journey with an image of the Woman burning in his breast. The quest is a necessary obstacle, not an unfortunate one, on the interminable path to true love although it will be perceived as difficult and burdensome by the amorous knight. The male subject *must* go on a quest so that the inevitable failure to complete himself—to find the phallus—will seem to be the failure of the quest and not of the quest(ion) of his own subjectivity. In this way, the nonrelation of the sexes between the knight and his lady will be obscured by the erection of an impossible object (the Phallus). Put another way, by seeing femininity as an enigma, by seeing the desire of the Woman as inscrutably elsewhere, the knight is able to imagine a bridge over the unbridgeable division upon which he has founded the supposed unity of his subjective consciousness; the bridge will appear real as long as the Woman appears mythical. In short, the narrator of "Araby" has employed for himself the convention of courtly love that Lacan charaterizes as "an altogether refined way of making up for the absence of sexual relation by pretending that it is we who put an obstacle to it. . . . For the man, whose lady was entirely, in the most servile sense of the term, his female subject, courtly love is the only way of coming off elegantly from the absence of sexual relation" (1982b, 141).

Femininity is not an essence; it is a representation. As such, it is a constructed identity—constructed by the male subject—and the representation does not contain or account for female desire. He desires it—the representation—rather than her because the masquerade of femininity appears to him as a lack-in-being that he gratefully defines as not masculine. The Woman masquerades as feminine—as the Phallus—to reassure a man that she does not have it, but at the same time her masquerade proves that it must—somewhere—exist or how could she know to imitate it? Of course, she has learned to perform what he needs to see, not anything that actually is, and so the masculine and the feminine waltz around the nonrelation of the sexes with a two-step of mutual misrecognition. Lacan says, "It is in order to be the phallus, that is to say, the signifier of the desire of the Other, that the woman will reject an essential part of her femininity, notably all its attributes through masquerade. It is for what she is not that she expects to be desired as well as loved. But she finds the signifier of her own desire in the body of the one to whom she addresses her demand for love" (1982, 84). A woman thus desires the Phallus, and so a man struggles to appear as if he has it. She desires the ability to bestow on him the gift he demands of her so that he can feel that he has had it all along. The Phallus can only play its role when it is veiled because there is nothing behind the veil. The erection of meaning that it enjoins on the masculine subject involves the subject in constant slippage because what is meaningful always contains its own vanishing point. In short, meaning does not reflect the sexual order; it compensates for a supposed unity that is fictional. Courtly love—the boy's quest on behalf of Mangan's sister—elevates her to a place where her inaccessibility disguises his lack. Thus, she becomes a symptom for him that wards off his unconscious and ensures the consistency of his relation to the phallic term.[7]

The Woman shows in her masquerade of femininity what she does not have by pretending that she has it and, thus, becomes what he desires but at the price of having no way to pronounce the quest(ion) of her own desire. She serves for the narrator as a metaphor for the phallus and, thus, becomes for him a symptom that disguises his lack. As a symptom standing in the place of the Other, Mangan's sister represents for him the initial signifier upon which his divided subjectivity is based. She appears to answer the question of who he is and this allows his self-ordained quest to subsume all previous concerns: "I could not call my wandering thoughts together. I had hardly any patience with the serious work of life which, now that it stood between me and my desire, seemed to me child's play, ugly monotonous child's play" (*D* 32). He has reinterpreted the Real to form a new reality, and the self-deprecating tone in this sentence will surface again at the close of the story when he does the same thing. The representation of femininity that the narrator worships is the only signifier that cannot signify anything. Because the image of Mangan's sister has been constructed to signify nothing, it can signify him.

In traveling to the Araby Bazaar, the boy boards a special train. People press against the doors in an attempt to enter, but they are pushed back and told that it is "a special train for the bazaar" (*D* 34). For the entire trip past "ruinous houses," the boy remains "alone in the bare carriage." At the end of the ride, the uniqueness of his journey persists as he steps out of the train on to "an improvised wooden platform" just recently constructed. Standing alone on the deserted platform, he sees in front of him "a large building which displayed the magical name." All these details suggest that the boy sees his journey as traveling to someplace other than Dublin. It is different from anywhere; it is magical. The boy's fantastic hope for the place gives it a fairy tale quality. The tawdry building seems enchanted to him only because of an enormous act of faith on his part. Its status as magical is as tenuous as the fantastic unity of his subjective consciousness. The magical power of symbolization begins when a child realizes something is missing. The power of language to evoke what is not present depends on the feeling that something is lacking. His later realization that the bazaar is a commercial sham, perpetrated on the naïve for profit, will destroy the place as symbol but will have no effect on the powerful dynamic of symbolization. The narrator experiences his sexual awakening as the advent of unity, whereas Joyce's story of the presence of Mangan's sister outside the confines of the boy's narrative gives an opposite account of sexuality based solely on its divisions (division of the subject, division between subjects). It is her representation in the boy's narrative as the Woman and her absence from it as *a* woman that makes his story of himself possible. "Araby" is not about the loss or gain of this or that object, it is about the impossible structure of desire for both the masculine and feminine subjects.

The boy on the improvised platform sees displayed before him what is described as "the magical name" rather than the word "Araby." Like Mangan's sister, the bazaar implies something beyond what can be named or represented. What the narrator hopes he will see is the world before it has been crossed through by the word. The actual bazaar is irrelevant; in his own mind, he has traveled beyond time and space to the land of the Other, authorized to do so by a woman who, as The Woman, represents this land. This magical name does not exist anymore than she does. He hopes to discover the lost object that would end the primacy of the signifier over his subjectivity. He presumes she must desire this most precious of all signifiers because it was her appearance to him as lack — as feminine — that convinced him of the existence of a Holy Grail that could authenticate who he is. The magical bazaar could return him to the imaginary pristine duality of the mirror stage before he seized the false scepter of language and began to rule a world within the world where words are always ruling him (the boy, like Martha Clifford in *Ulysses,* does not like "that other world").

The Araby Bazaar is magical for the boy because he believes it will be a place beyond mere representation where the lost object he needs to complete himself will be found. This object is not hidden in a geometrical or an anatomical space; if that were so, he would have found it long ago. It is not hidden at all; it is always elsewhere "in" a symbolic structure that can only be perceived in its effect. In taking upon himself her pilgrimage, he is inevitably drawn into becoming the object of her desire, even as he tries to make her subject to his desire. Like the minister in Poe's story "The Purloined Letter," which Lacan analyzed, the narrator of "Araby" appears to be in control while he observes Mangan's sister; he understands everything she does relative to himself. But when he is displaced to her position at the close of the story, suddenly he demonstrates the traits of femininity (passivity and self-effacement) that he had previously attributed to her (likewise, after the minister steals the letter from the queen, he assumes her position, passively waiting for someone to steal it from him). The structural shift at the close of "Araby" makes the point that femininity and masculinity are effects of one's position in the Symbolic Order rather than inherently biological. Only the presence or absence of the phallus marks the distinction between the two positions. Whoever pretends to possess the Phallus is placed under the banner "feminine" and whoever struggles to represent it lines up under the banner "masculine" (which is why Lacan defines a man as someone who finds himself male without knowing what to do about it).

In front of the booth displaying the vases, the narrator witnesses another woman masquerading with two men as feminine in the sexual waltz of nonrelation; she has said something that the men want to possess. Curiously, they do not repeat what she has said (do not put it into words) but only insist that she has expressed it, each man calling on the other one to verify this, which, as one can see by now, is no verification at all. The boy is suddenly observing people who believe themselves to be unseen. In this new shift of position, he witnesses a scene of flirtation from which he is absent. In seeing the anonymous shop girl flirting with the two men — in seeing her looking at them — he is, in effect, seeing the earlier version of himself being watched when he had believed himself to be unseen. As Lacan makes clear, the Symbolic Order constitutes the subject, and if the subject's position within this order shifts, then the orientation of his subjectivity, which the subject receives from the itinerary of a signifier, will shift as well (1988c, 29). By watching and overhearing the girl and the two men, he views the earlier construct of his subjectivity, now revealed as imaginary, which, at the moment the quest began, he took to be himself. The look of Mangan's sister, repressed at that time for the sake of a seamless narrative, returns. The Real, which is the endless return of the moment of the subject's own impossibility, threatens to break through and show the fabric of his story to be no more complete than a complex weave that is made up of as many unconscious gaps as it is of conscious threads.

But this gap in subjectivity — what Lacan calls aphanisis — is equally present in his earlier conversation with Mangan's sister. When she asks him if he is going to the bazaar, he hears her saying, "Will you go and bring something back," thus transforming her question into his quest. Were he to tell her she has said this, she would have to respond, like the shop girl, "I never said such a thing!" What follows her question is, to my reading, the most significant sentence in the story: "I forget whether I answered yes or no." What a strange ellipsis in the narration of his story. He is not in doubt about anything else he has narrated up to this point. He forgets *what* he answers because he wishes to pose *as* the answer. At the moment the quest is inaugurated, the boy as subject (as question) disappears. He loses his authority at the precise moment she authorizes his quest. Later in his narration, as the meaningful dimension of the quest starts to fade, the boy's sense of his own subjectivity once more restricts him to the self-conscious and the trivial rather than the unified and heroical: "Remembering with difficulty why I had come I went over to one of the stalls and examined porcelain vases and flower tea-sets. . . . I lingered before her stall, though I knew my stay was useless, to make my interest in her wares seem the more real" (*D* 35).

The narrator's consciousness flickers back and forth between these two moments of forgetfulness that mark the beginning and end of his quest. The two moments are threaded together by various acts of interpretation that are motivated by desire (indeed, Lacan says interpretation operates in the same manner as desire) and controlled by language. The quest, which he had hoped would untie the knot of the Symbolic Order, only succeeds in repeating the act of tying it. The boy's quest, which outlines the structure of desire, is impossible. He sets out to find the phallus/chalice because the desire of Mangan's sister, which he has appropriated as his desire, convinces him that it must exist and that it is the thing he requires to complete himself. What sets the quest in motion is the discovery that she lacks something. But in order for her to verify that he is something (masculine), she must be seen as nothing, (feminine). Put most simply, the divided structure that constitutes the narrator's subjectivity is inevitably reproduced in what becomes the unattainable object of his desire.

The conversation of the woman and the two men revolves around the issue of whether or not she has *said* something. "O, I never said such a thing!" the woman begins. "O, but you did!" one man counters. "O, but I didn't," she responds in perfect counterpoint. "Didn't she say that?" one man says to the other. "Yes. I heard her," he replies. "O, there's a . . . fib!" says the woman. Once more, one sees that it is the woman's desire that is unspoken. What has she said? The men keep her in a posture of negativity that allows them to affirm one another. ("Didn't she say that?" "Yes. I heard her.") There is another significant ellipsis when she says: "O, there's a . . . fib!" (*D* 35). What word does she veer away from? We cannot know, but certainly the word *lie* is a strong possibility. A fib is a lie, but it is a lie about something that is trivial in substance or significance. What has been made trivial (and she participates in this as part of the masquerade of femininity) is the substance of her desire. She is locked into a continual masquerade of absence that confirms their presence. In this conversation she is, in her essence, not all. The men repress the fact of her desire — her jouissance — by representing it themselves. Once more the unspeakable dictates what gets spoken in a Maypole dance around the nonexistent Phallus. "On the one hand," Lacan says, "the woman becomes, or is produced, precisely as what he is not . . . and on the other, as what he has to renounce, that is, *jouissance*" (1982b, 49). The men reserve for themselves the right to interpret, the woman supports that right by posing as enigmatic. The content of her statement — what she actually said — is not relevant, and this allows their narrative to become so.[8]

What the narrator wishes to find at the Araby Bazaar is something that will not set him forth on another repetition or shift him into a new register of signification that requires a fresh act of faith about his subjectivity. What he yearns for is an ending — the discovery of certitude beyond the forever shifting signifiers of language. Were he to find the Holy Grail/Phallus, his subjectivity would seem like a chalice that could neither be spilled nor declared empty. In beginning his search for what Mangan's sister lacks, for what she means, he has begun a search for what *he* means. But interpretation does not lead to knowledge (the two men are not interested in what the shop girl has actually said), it leads to the point where knowledge stumbles over the Woman. Her jouissance is an area of excess that is supplementary to male desire, not complementary to it, and knowledge, as it comes to the male subject, is merely the organized renunciation of jouissance. Most commentators on "Araby" agree that, by the end of the story, the narrator has learned something about himself. Yes, but this knowledge will become the new obstacle he will place between himself and the objects of his desire. It is not frustration of a particular desire of the narrator that occurs in this story—after all, he is never able to say what he wants—rather it is to use Lacan's phrase, "frustration by an object in which his desire is alienated and which the more it is elaborated, the more profound the alienation from its *jouissance* becomes for the subject" (1981b, 11).

Significantly, the boy's famous closing insight about himself is not presented in terms of looking inward but in terms of seeing himself: "Gazing up into the darkness I saw myself as a creature driven and derided by vanity; and my eyes burned with anguish and anger" (*D* 35). Far from putting an end to the myth of himself, he inaugurates a new fiction of what he imagines the gaze of the Other sees, which he has now learned must be who he is *really*. He reinterprets the Real, denigrates his earlier interpretation, and presents his new interpretation as the reality that was behind the appearances all along. But insight is just another guess at what it is the Other sees. The subject responds anew to the itinerary of the signifier in a manner that incorporates its directives while still preserving the subject's illusion of an autonomous identity and a satiable desire. "Epiphanic light," Ragland-Sullivan has stated in a recent overview of Joyce and Lacan, "is the return of the void into the Real of phallic meaning, where the void shows the place of division and the 'truth' of loss around which humans elaborate lives" (1988, 122). Elaborating on this, I would say the Joycean epiphany is the imaginary light that staves off Real darkness. The subject imagines himself to make the world real. In his new identity, the narrator is "derided by vanity." To be derided is to be laughed at contemptuously, to be subjected to ridicule. But how much better it is to be subjected to ridicule than not to be a subject at all. Who would not consent to wear a mask if the alternative was to have no face at all? Driven by vanity? The narrator will continue to be so driven. A vanity is a piece of furniture where a woman puts on her makeup, when she becomes a representation of femininity, when she is encouraged by the mirror to abandon the question of who she is and imagine herself instead as something that initiates a man's quest. At her vanity, a woman becomes the Woman; she masquerades as lack so the man can masquerade as completeness. Her vanity protects him from knowledge of his emptiness, that is, of *his* vanity. The two types of vanity are the two sides of the division over which he builds a bridge from one moment of forgetfulness to the next.

The necessity of the boy's humiliation, which he presents to himself as "knowledge," is certainly a painful realization, but it is one that protects him from realizing the greater pain of psychic and symbolic castration. Not perceiving his own castration, he feels free to act again, to set another scene where he will imagine himself as seeing a woman while remaining unseen. He does not hear the the signifier that Lacan gives voice to as follows: "'You think you act when I stir you at the mercy of the bonds through which I knot your desires. Thus do they grow in force and multiply in objects, bringing you back to the fragmentation of your shattered childhood'" (Lacan 1988c, 52). In his final observation of himself, the boy's discovery of himself is, in fact, yet another discovery of who he is not. In telling readers who he is now, he is not lying, only telling a fib.

5

Wondering Where All the Dust Comes From

Jouissance in "Eveline"

The woman only becomes the support of this relation [the masculine subject's relation to the 'Other']
in a second stage and at that level of fiction which
is commonly labelled sexual commerce. In this the
woman will play her part, but it is of course elsewhere
that she upholds the question of her own *jouissance.*
(Lacan 1982b, 121)

But in her own home, in a distant unknown country,
it would not be like that. Then she would be married
—she, Eveline. People would treat her with respect
then. (*D* 37)

Because she is a housekeeper who performs her cleaning tasks regularly, Eveline has often wondered how it is that dust silently accumulates on all the surfaces of the room: "Home! She looked round the room, reviewing all its familiar objects which she had dusted once a week for so many years, wondering where on earth all the dust came from" (*D* 37). Dust may appear insignificant, but it is also impossible, without extraordinary effort, to stop it entirely or control it completely. Curiously, one becomes aware of it in those quiet intervals in which neither a string of words nor a train of thought distracts one.

95

> She sat at the window watching the evening invade the avenue.
> Her head was leaned against the window curtains and in her nostrils
> was the odour of dusty cretonne. (*D* 36)

> Her time was running out but she continued to sit by the win-
> dow, leaning her head against the window curtain, inhaling the odour
> of dusty cretonne. (*D* 39)

"Eveline" is the most sparingly written story in *Dubliners,* yet Joyce twice
takes the time, in deliberately similar sentence structures, to highlight the pervasive and invasive presence of dust. That this odour is
"in her nostrils" and that in between her complex reveries she "inhales"
it, suggests that she takes a somber comfort from this action: she
breathes it to calm herself. Dust, after all, is typically beneath notice;
it is not important. It is Eveline's weekly job to make sure none of
the men in the household have any cause to notice it. But however
much they ignore it, the dust silently accumulates on everything in
their known world—even more unobtrusively, yet more insistently,
than the snow in "The Dead." The difference between Eveline and
her father is nowhere more starkly contrasted than in the fact that
he knows nothing about it while she is so familiar with it as to wonder about its origin.

The only other person who knows something about the curious
fact of dust—Eveline's mother—*is* dust, and it is her relationship with
her mother that Eveline is trying to resurrect and strengthen during
this frightening lull in her life, a lull that almost certainly precedes
the occasion of being beaten for the first time by her father. Although
it is not clear what is specifically involved in the promise Eveline made
to her mother to "keep the home together as long as she could," certainly dusting routinely would be one of the "commonplace sacrifices"
she would be expected to make. A sacrifice involves surrendering or
destroying something for the sake of something else. What is Eveline
sacrificing and for whom?

At first glance, she would appear to be sacrificing her personal
freedom for the sake of the home. If one recasts this into a Lacanian
mold, however, one can see that she is expected to sacrifice the question of her sexual desire in order to help veil the illusion of patriarchial power. As Van Boheemen points out, the "plot" of patriarchy

"is the exclusion of the presence of the 'other'" (1988, 30). This exclusion becomes "the supportive scaffold for meaning and identity" and must, henceforth, be represented as that which cannot be represented (as the masquerade of femininity). Woman's place is ecstasy—in the Latin sense of *ex-stasis* —to put out of place. As such, the figuration of a woman becomes an aspect of the male condition that the male cannot face—symbolic castration. His not entirely convincing denial of not being whole is projected on to her hole (her lack of an organ, which is misrecognized by the man as her lack of phallic power).

Mykyta points out, "It is by seeing the woman as an object that does not speak or look that the man can believe he is approaching her when what he approaches is only the cause of his desire (for her)" (1983, 54). In short, the masquerade of femininity hides the fact that masculine sexuality is a myth. But what does it feel like to be designated as "an object that does not speak or look" when one remains, in spite of this patriarchal construction, a subject who cannot stop desiring to do both of these things? Eveline's mother, acting on behalf of patriarchy's need to pose as a monolithic authority with no beginning and no end, has her daughter promise to sacrifice her quest to be whole in order to pose as the question of a veiled hole.[1] Henceforth, Eveline's ex-istence — her absent sexuality that inaugurates a persistent presence beyond patriarchal reality—places her in her mother's former role as a secret supplement and a necessary veil before the myth of coherence and completion that the father sporadically enjoys. Eveline's submission, however, is the repressed origin of her father's increasingly tenuous autonomy; as his illusion of a complete "self" wears thin, his hatred of her apparent helplessness can only deepen. What are the voices and visions of the silenced and blinded object (the feminine) that yet has eyes to see and a mouth with which to speak? The residue of such a being's self-censored (unrepresented) sexuality settles down, invisible and indivisible, on to every surface of the patriarchal world—like dust.

Lacan maintains that woman is defined within patriarchal culture as "not all." Yet it is precisely this masculine projection of lack upon her that causes her to have a supplementary jouissance beyond the phallus (beyond man's Truth) that is, according to Lacan, what one has always called God. The woman's silence (her representation as the veiled hole—what cannot be represented) is also the ultimate limit to any discourse articulated by man. Likewise, a woman's "absent" gaze represents the impossible Real that both guarantees the illusion and nullifies the fact of the phallic autonomy of the Name-of-the-Father. She is man's symptom because she comes away from her encounter with the law of the father castrated of her own sexuality. So does a man, for that matter, but a man assumes he has lost the phallus and that he might yet regain it. The difference between a man and a woman in this (symbolic) regard is that she learns consciously to play the role he can only perform unconsciously; that of the subject castrated from his or her sexuality by the substitutive structure of Desire within the Symbolic Order.

Although much of Eveline's anxiety appears to come from whether or not she will feel right about leaving her father, the more primary question is whether or not she can break her promise to her mother. Can she leave the secret world of dust that connects her to her dead mother? Actually, the final request made by her mother (asking her to promise to keep the home together) is not what Eveline recalls most vividly. She recalls, with much more drama and persistence, her mother's final incoherence (her words from beyond the limits of representation): "She trembled as she heard again her mother's voice saying constantly with foolish insistence: — *Derevaun Seraun! Derevaun Seraun!*" (*D* 40). Eveline cannot know what these words mean, but her mind and body instinctively interpret the tone of her mother's last pronouncement as conveying a clear (even if nonsemantic) warning to her to leave while she still can: "She stood up in a sudden impulse of terror. Escape! She must escape!" (*D* 40). The dilemma Eveline is faced with is whether she should honor her mother's "commonplace" request, which eventually will lead to a nervous breakdown of her own, or to heed the uninhibited tone of her mother's "final craziness," which urges her to flee from the house at her first opportunity.[2]

In her early musings, Eveline hesitantly catalogs her father's failings: his alcoholism, his increasingly violent attitude toward her, and his consistent and truculent disparagement of her attempt to keep the home together. She tries to offset her growing awareness of his worsening condition by recalling a couple of vague memories: Her father reading her a ghost story and making her toast when she was ill and a picnic years ago where he wore her mother's bonnet to amuse the children. And yet this attempt to offset the bad qualities with the good reveals itself as rather desperate because she is attempting to excuse her father's routine and systematic abuse by citing two isolated incidents of behavior that she naïvely interprets as indicating a latent tenderness in him. Once could much more easily argue that these brief displays are casual performances of minimal commitment craftily designed to sate Eveline's (and the family's) necessarily modest demands for his affection. In addition, Eveline's attempt to, as she thinks of it, "weigh each side of the question," ignores the fact that her father's conduct is growing steadily more violent. While she may exclude this fact from her discourse, her body elicits the early signs of the nervous breakdown that clouded her mother's sanity: "She knew it was that [her father's potential violence] that had given her the palpitations" (*D* 38). There is something pathetic and telling about the fact that she uses a cliché of patriarchal justice (weighing each side of the question) to gloss over her place in this equation as something that has no weight at all.

Because of her father's deteriorating view of his masculinity, one can presume that even the images that feature him in various attitudes of affection in Eveline's slender mental scrapbook will soon be overlaid with more immediate ones of intimidation and violence. The real balance in question is a matter of gender; her father's worsening alcoholic condition and his corresponding slide toward poverty have made the illusion of being a self-generated patriarch nearly impossible to maintain. His response to this impending dissolution is to try and increase still further his control over the feminine counterpart (Eveline) whose masquerade is supposed to guarantee his authenticity. He gets away with it, in part, because Eveline has been well instructed by her mother on the importance of actively participating in her own oppression. She has accepted the equation that because it is within her power to shore up her father's crumbling self-image (it is most certainly *not* within her power), any punishment he visits upon her is merely the unfortunate result of her own feminine inadequacy. Indeed, Eveline's inability to judge accurately her father's increasingly brutal behavior is the corollary of her belief that he grows more violent only in direct correspondence with her increasing failure to be sufficiently feminine. She cannot condemn him without first condemning herself.

The question, therefore, of whether or not Eveline will leave Dublin cannot be phrased solely in terms of whether or not she will be able to leave her father (in weighing the question there is no question that the balance tips toward the necessity to escape). The question is whether or not she will disobey her mother's comprehensible request to heed her incomprehensible warning. Certainly the mother's initial request is clear enough: engage in all the commonplace sacrifices necessary to keep the home together. But what of the second, and final, utterance which, by its desperate tone and repetitious quality, seems to be the more vital pronouncement? Because Mrs. Hill formed her self-identity (what Lacan terms the moi) strictly in accordance with what her husband desired to have her complement in him, is it not inevitable that when expressing something motivated by her own desire she would express it in a mode that is incomprehensible?[3] Whatever Mrs. Hill means to convey with this phrase that she repeats with "foolish insistence," it is not complementary to the desire of her husband, but supplementary to it. And, naturally, it is Eveline's recollection of this phrase that initiates her timid (nearly unconscious) exploration of what about her sexuality exists independently of her father, her brothers, and her lover, Frank. She turns away, in other words, from masquerading as the question and inaugurates her own quest (which is represented by the vague name Buenos Ayres just as Mangan's sister wanted to journey to a bazaar with the magical name "Araby").

In Lacanian terms, her struggle is to discover who or what she is beyond being an object of symbolic exchange within the phallic function.[4] Eveline's visceral recollection of her mother's final crazy chant functions as a sort of mental umbilical cord that brings her unexpected and unsettling nourishment from the unseen and barely suspected world beyond the normal masquerade of femininity. The feeling this recollection gives her — that there is something unrepresented beyond what is visible and comprehensible — is akin to her more commonplace musing while performing household chores, when she wonders "where on earth all the dust came from" (*D* 37). This parallel I am drawing between the settling of dust and the unsettling of paternity is a practical reading of a phenomenon that Lawrence sees in all of Joyce's work: "Joyce presents the incertitude of paternity even as he demonstrates its power. . . . The maternal silently undermines patriarchal power and the cultural and linguistic structures it under-

writes. . . . Maternity . . . is a different kind of 'fiction' than paternity, a fiction of a source before law and identity, the 'alphabed' of
Anna Livia—paternal signature and maternal stain; the ink itself comes
before the signature" (1987, 240). The Woman is expected to uphold
the wholeness of the phallic order by virtue of her holeness—her lack
of the male organ (upon which identity is symbolically based). "The
woman only becomes the support of this relation [the male subject's
relation to the Other] in a second stage, and at that level of fiction
which is commonly labelled sexual commerce. In this the woman will
play her part, but it is of course elsewhere that she upholds the question of her own *jouissance*" (1982, 120–21). In essence, Mrs. Hill has requested that her daughter should play her part as long as she can, but
her final craziness, which gives rise to her incomprehensible litany,
"Derevaun Seraun," has also given Eveline a glimpse of this elsewhere
where she upholds (unconsciously) the question of her own jouissance.[5]
As a unit of exchange in a sexual commerce, Eveline is the daughter
of her father and the sweetheart of Frank, but her life as the daughter
of her mother is an ex-istence that is as worthless as dust.

On the face of it, of course, Eveline's decision to run off with
Frank is still very much a part of the feminine masquerade whereby
she hopes Frank will prove to be a "nice" father: "Frank would save
her. . . . Frank would take her in his arms, fold her in his arms. He
would save her" (*D* 40). The hope that Frank will be an uncondition-
ally loving father is the result of a feminine fantasy on her part about
belonging to a benevolent phallic economy that would regard her as
a particularly valuable object of exchange. The fictional quality of this
desire (which is not her desire, but rather an approximation of what
she imagines her desire should be) is revealed when she expects Frank
to manifest himself as a Saviour. Instead, he actually disappears from
her view (even though her gaze is directed solely at him): "Her eyes
gave him no sign of love or farewell or recognition" (*D* 41). What draws
Eveline to Frank, I suggest, is not who he is, but rather where he has
been. Like Desdemona, Eveline is fascinated with all the "elsewheres"
that Frank describes to her: "He had tales of distant countries. . . .
He told her the names of the ships he had been on and the names
of the different services. He had sailed through the Straits of Magellan
and he told her stories of the terrible Patagonians" (*D* 39). Added to
this, is the fact that he has promised to take her to "Buenos Ayres."

Previous to this, elsewhere, for Eveline, was nothing more than the place from where dust mysteriously materialized. Now it is a land where she can play her part in the phallic function *and,* somehow, be herself, as opposed to an image of the phallus that sustains male desires (her father's "self"). In this fantasyland, she is able to fulfill both promises to her mother: "to keep the home together" *and* to 'Escape!': "But in her new home, in a distant unknown country, it would not be like that. Then she would be married — she, Eveline. People would treat her with respect then. She would not be treated as her mother had been" (*D* 37). In this chain of thoughts, the only hope Eveline has for escaping her mother's fate is to discover, and travel to, "a distant unknown country" (elsewhere) where "she" is *equivalent* to "Eveline." Only elsewhere can she represent her 'self' from a perspective other than a patriarchal point of view. When she states, "she would not be treated as her mother had been," she cannot possibly be referring to the idea of being married (this is precisely what caused the mother to be treated as she was). Instead, she must be thinking of something else. This something else is represented by its absence from her fantasy. In other words, this "Eveline" she refers to, the one who escapes her mother's fate, can only be represented as something that is unrepresentable — even in the midst of her own fantasy of what life would be like for her "elsewhere." The impossibility of representing female desire within the Symbolic Order is presented with admirable economy by Van Boheemen: "Representation is itself a patriarchal undertaking and must necessarily issue from the patriarchal point of view, but in order to inscribe itself, patriarchy needs the figure and idea of woman as the 'other' that confirms its self-presence" (1987, 38–39). One can see this dynamic in action in the closing seconds of the story when Eveline's gaze becomes, from Frank's perspective, no more comprehensible than an animal's. The trance she is in, as I will point out in detail, has no meaning from the patriarchal point of view, yet it is this very manifestation of her "ex-istence" that gives Frank's patriarchal point of view its meaning.

Another reason Eveline is forced to pose questions of self-reliance that hint at an elsewhere beyond the phallic function is that all her previously secure attachments to various men have been severed. Ernest, the older brother who "had been her favourite" is dead; Harry, who "she liked . . . too," works as a church decorator and is "nearly always down somewhere in the country" (*D* 38). Her father, whom she has tried to associate with security (by obsessively recalling his making her toast when she was ill) has increasingly revealed himself as her chief attacker. All of her expectations of male security now focus upon Frank. But, as I have already suggested, she is only able to fantasize him as a more generous and loving version of her father. She is excluded, in other words, from the most elementary benefit of playing her part within the phallic function: the protection that is normally afforded a valuable object of exchange. In the end (in fact, all along), her unlikely and unexpected protectorate is her dead mother: "latterly he [her father] had begun to threaten her and say what he would do to her only for her dead mother's sake" (*D* 38). How is it that her mother, who was a victim unable to defend herself while alive, becomes the only force protecting Eveline from paternal violence now that she is dead? Apparently, her father benefits a great deal from abusing a particular woman, but the idea of Woman is something that he dares not desecrate. The same woman who was controlled and denigrated to prevent her from becoming a subject (while she is alive) is paradoxically worshipped once she is irretrievably an object (once she is dead).

As object, the Woman guarantees the steadily benevolent gaze of the Other that the masculine subject requires in order to believe in the illusion of oneness and autonomy that the Phallus represents. The female object must be made to sustain male desire, and any indication that this object has its own point of view — a different structure of desire — must be repressed systematically. Put another way, she must not be allowed to develop any sense of "self" unless the experience of this "self" (or "identity") appears to be a reward for the effectiveness and persuasiveness of her "feminine" masquerade. In performing this masquerade persuasively, as judged by the male gaze, Eveline upholds the mythically monolithic structure of the phallic economy. Within this economy, she is always an object of exchange whose value is determined by how well she acts as a veil before the phallus. Because the phallus does not exist, it can only perform its function as guarantor of masculine autonomy when it is veiled.[6] Therefore, the less feminine Eveline is from a masculine perspective, the less "valuable she is as an object of exchange. In the phallic economy, only a man (masculine subject) can bestow "value," yet Eveline's poignant attempt to decipher her mother's final message suggests how desperately she would like to see herself as something other than an object of exchange among men.

Not surprisingly, as an object of exchange in the phallic economy, Eveline is forced to turn over the value of her labor to her father. The part she plays in the phallic economy must be a role of increasingly humiliating self-effacement to keep pace with her father's deteriorating self-esteem (increasingly eroded by old age, well-earned loneliness, and alcoholism): "She always gave her entire wages — seven shillings — and Harry always sent up what he could but the trouble was to get any money from her father. He said she used to squander the money, that she had no head, that he wasn't going to give her his hard-earned money to throw about the streets. . . . In the end he would give her the money and ask her had she any intention of buying Sunday's dinner" (*D* 38). Clearly, he is the one who "squanders" the money (primarily on drink, one suspects); at least some portion of his "hard-earned money" (the majority, one suspects) is actually *her* hard-earned money, which she has previously turned over to him. She is so unconsciously trapped within the phallic economy that she characterizes the problem by lamenting that "the trouble was to get any money *from* her father" (*D* 38). The trouble, actually, is how to get *her* money back from him. First, he takes it; then he informs her "she has no head" (because she no longer possesses her money), and, finally, he returns it to her in a manner that transforms her into the undeserving recipient of his largesse. Eveline's two brothers occasionally contribute money, and Mr. Hill may have resources of his own. Eveline's wages, then, are a supplement to male earnings and, as such, they must be strictly accounted for and rigidly controlled. In the framework of the family, her ability to generate money is a fact that is repressed the better to preserve the crumbling patriarchal structure of the household economy; likewise, her (supplementary) sexuality is repressed to benefit the phallic economy. Here, one might recall that the orgasm of a Victorian gentleman was characterized as "spending," and Mr. Hill is careful to make sure that Eveline always spends for him, even when she has generated the money herself.[7]

In a sense, her paycheck is laundered by the phallic economy in a process that severs the connection between the fact that Eveline is spending money and the fact that it is her money that she is spending.

Her father's calculated delay in handing over money for food guarantees that her experience in the marketplace will be that of a servant who is tardy in performing the will of her master rather than a consumer indulging her own desire: "She had to rush out as quickly as she could and do her marketing, holding her black leather purse tightly in her hand as she elbowed her way through the crowds and returning home late under her load of provisions" (D 38). Small wonder that in this weekly interaction with her father her position as someone capable of earning money is converted into proof that she "has no head" (that is to say, no subjectivity, no point of view), and that she "squanders" those riches that she is "given" (as though she were unworthy to receive them) by the all-powerful generosity of the self-perpetuating phallic economy. Small wonder that this state of affairs, above all others, has "begun to weary her unspeakably"—just as it must have wearied her mother (D 38).

What is the effect on Eveline of spending her own money within a framework that insists she has only been granted permission to spend for someone else? She is excluded from representing the power of choice, a power she is, nonetheless, exercising (as a consumer). She experiences it as a supplementary power—one that can neither be spoken nor represented—a power that disempowers because it is impossible to speak of it: "There is woman only as excluded by the nature of things which is the nature of words. . . . If she is excluded by the nature of things, it is precisely that in being not all, she has, in relation to what the phallic function designates of *jouissance,* a supplementary *jouissance.* Note that I said *supplementary.* Had I said *complementary,* where would we be! We'd fall right back into the all" (Lacan 1982b, 144).

At the same time that this exclusion designates Eveline's status in the phallic economy as "useless" (as an indifferent object of exchange, with a variable market value imposed from without), it also places her outside discourse and renders the question of her desire inscrutable and enigmatic. "There is a *jouissance* proper to her, to this 'her' which does not exist and which signifies nothing" (Lacan 1982b, 145). The irony here is that a woman's place within the phallic economy as "not all" (her nonexistence) is precisely what generates her ex-istence (beyond the Name-of-the-Father) as the ultimate limit to any discourse articulated by patriarchy; her jouissance is a question about value within sexual commerce which, because it is, itself, without value, makes invaluable the masculine quest for meaning.

To put this another way, a woman's place is elsewhere — outside and beyond the symbolic; she can only be apprehended by the male subject as that which it is impossible to represent — as a 'hole' that sustains the male wholeness falsely represented by the truly nonexistent Phallus. As what cannot be fully represented, a woman's place becomes representative of Truth or the Other — something whose limits cannot be overcome because it is beyond what can be represented consciously or dialectically. Female desire, which is unaccounted for in the structure of the Woman (a structure which, after all, constitutes itself as a symptom of masculinity) operates as the absent God ruling the wor(l)d of the Symbolic Order. This paradox of the all-powerful woman who is "not all" corresponds to the paradoxical attitude of Eveline's father who refrains from beating Eveline because of the idea of her dead mother (a woman he was quite able to treat poorly while she was alive). Thus, he demonstrates that a woman may well be especially excluded and denigrated by the male subject even as he, at the same time, worships and fears the incomprehensible *idea* of the Woman — the projected structure that operates as a symptom protecting him from knowledge of his own divided subjectivity.

What is curious about Eveline's experience at the North Wall is that she is led to a moment of decision and realization like the narrators of "an Encounter" and "Araby." But whereas those masculine epiphanies featured a state of hyper self-reflection on the part of the narrator, the effect of such a moment on Eveline becomes the black "hole" that Frank stares into as his ship pulls away from the dock. The stupendous moment shows a terrified woman mumbling incoherent prayers to the Name-of-the-Father as she is drawn into the fascinating and sickening whirlpool of an experience beyond representation — a mystical experience of jouissance that Lacan likened to orgasm.

> Could she still draw back after all he had done for her? Her distress awoke a nausea in her body and she kept moving her lips in silent fervent prayer.
>
> A bell clanged upon her heart. She felt him seize her hand:
> — *Come!*
>
> All the seas of the world tumbled about her heart. He was drawing her into them: he would drown her. She gripped with both hands at the iron railing.

— *Come!*

No! No! No! It was impossible. Her hands clutched the iron in frenzy. Amid the seas she sent a cry of anguish! (*D* 40–41, my emphasis)

How completely nonverbal and, therefore, unreal, the feelings evoked in Eveline are. Frank's urgings (Come! Come!) threaten to push her beyond the barriers of the known world. The familiar world, which excludes her, is overwhelmed by sensations beyond representation: "All the seas of the world tumbled about her heart." As I have already suggested, these exotic seas represent the path to the elsewhere where she might truly *be* Eveline, rather than everyone's idea of Eveline.[8]

But this boundary she is on the verge of crossing also entails a dissolution of the moi identity—the feminine masquerade she has formulated in accordance with the male gaze—which she has labored to perform all her life. Nothing appears pleasurable about this sensation, which might make suspect my characterization of it as jouissance, but Lacan's point is that jouissance "goes beyond" the law of constancy associated with the pleasure principle.[9] The subject's moi clings to the pleasure principle because of its tendency to keep the quantity of excitation constant, thus, apparently freezing the surging incoherencies of conscious sensation into the apparently monolithic unity of moi identity. Jouissance goes beyond pleasure, beyond representation, beyond the phallic function. It is currency that is both valueless and invaluable in its relationship to the phallic economy.

Whereas the narrator of "Araby" rearranges his sense of 'self' under duress, Eveline imagines herself passing beyond the barrier where Frank has gone, thus *becoming* Eveline. The terrifying release of jouissance tips over from pleasure to panic because it involves the death of the subject: "He rushed beyond the barrier and called to her to follow. . . . She set her white face to him, passive, like a helpless animal. Her eyes gave *him* no sign of love or farewell or recognition" (*D* 41, my emphasis). Unlike Eveline, Frank is not crossing a barrier beyond himself because masculine, sexuality (for better and for worse), has been defined within the phallic function. For him, in contradistinction to Eveline, nothing about Buenos Aires represents an "elsewhere" beyond representation. For Eveline, it is a place where her excluded sexuality may have been secretly developing independent of the phallic function that insists on representing it as something un-representable (as a hole). His sexuality is comprehensible to him (at least in terms of clichés and received ideas) because the Symbolic Or-der designates the phallic signifier as the central symbol upon which all other symbols depend. The question of Eveline's sexuality, how-ever has been banished by Eveline herself to permit her to masquer-ade as the lack (castration) that con'firms' the (fictional) reality of the phallic signifier.

As Eveline's moment beyond pleasure climaxes, in the final line of the story, Joyce abruptly shifts from her point of view to that of Frank—a character whose point of view the reader has not shared, even for a moment, elsewhere in the story. To him, she looks like "a helpless animal." How else could a man describe a woman who has moved beyond the barrier of language and the phallic function (a woman who has ceased to appear as the Woman)? "Naturally," she would appear to be a creature without language—an animal. Readers are told what the look she gives him looks like, but the real question—her question—is What does it feel like to look like this? There is no way to say. Were Frank allowed to go on describing what he sees in Eveline's white face he might fall back on the cliché that she appeared to be in another world. Her attitude is one of ecstasy (ex-stasis) such as a saint might display when having a vision—a view of something unrepresentable in reality that exists in the real. When trying to talk about the unapproachable and indomitable otherness of female jouis-sance, Lacan cites a posture and physical expression of Saint Theresa in a statue by Bernini: "As for Saint Theresa—you only have to go and look at Bernini's statue in Rome to understand immediately that she's coming, there is no doubt about it. And what is her *jouissance,* her *coming* from? It is clear that the essential testimony of the mystics is that they are experiencing it but know nothing about it" (1982b, 147). From the point of view of St. Theresa, it is experience without testimony, an unsymbolized text impossible to interpret. Yet, as I will discuss, the fathers of the church imposed exhaustive interpretations on the visions of female saints, interpretations that confirm patriar-chal existence by appropriating female ex-istence (jouissance).

Eveline has been excluded from selfhood throughout this story, but in the concluding line it is we the readers (along with Frank) who are excluded from her jouissance. What startles Frank (and readers of the story) into accepting Eveline's pose as that of a helpless animal is that it is not a pose at all; there is nothing in her expression that supports the phallic function. It is precisely the fact that her pose signifies nothing that makes it so terrible to behold. What is most disturbing about her inscrutable expression is that suddenly a hole is where her face was (like the holy Saint Theresa), and this hole subverts (however fleetingly) the wholeness of the reader's self-evident autonomy.[10] Ironically, as Frank steams toward what Eveline imagined as her "elsewhere," it is her face that Frank is forced to glimpse as the unrepresented and unpromised land that he can never visit.

So Eveline, in her final moment, has glimpsed "a distant unknown country" where "she, Eveline" ex-ists. She is a mystic who experiences this without knowing anything about it. It is a barrier her mother crossed, before turning back to her to shout, in her newly found native tongue *"Derevaun Seraun!"* Significantly, one of the "familiar objects" Eveline regularly dusts is "the coloured print of the promises made to Blessed Margaret Mary Alacoque" (*D* 37). At the time that Joyce wrote this story, Margaret Mary Alacoque had only been beatified (it was later that she was canonized as a saint). As Gifford tells us, Alacoque "experienced a sustained sequence of visions" (1982, 49). How is it that while Eveline's vision of "all the seas of the world tumbl[ing] about her heart" is so frightening that it is described as an expression of inhuman blankness the vision of her counterpart, Margaret Mary Alacoque, inspires a list of household directives (as well as promises of "eternal" reward for following these directives) that is hung on the walls of Dublin's most patriarchal households?

The answer, I suggest, is that Eveline's experience, unknown and unpublicized, is safely left uninterpreted by the phallic order. Alacoque's visions, on the other hand, were exhaustively interpreted by *the Fathers* of the church, and were "found" (surprise!) to contain twelve promises that share a single theme: the necessity for a woman to sacrifice the question of her own desire to masquerade as the lack that sustains the unified desire of the phallic signifier or, in plain language, the necessity for a woman to make "commonplace sacrifices" to "keep the home together as long as she can."

1. I will give them all the graces necessary in their state in life.
2. I will establish peace in their homes.

3. I will comfort them in all their afflictions.
4. I will be their secure refuge during life, and above all in death.
6. Sinners shall find in My Heart the source and the infinite ocean of mercy.

. . . . .

11. Those who promote this devotion shall have their names written in My heart never to be effaced. (Gifford 1982, 49–50)

Because this is something Eveline has dusted every week for years, readers can plausibly see in the sixth promise the source for the metaphorical structure with which, at the close of the story, she frames the experience of her jouissance: "All the seas of the world tumbled about her heart" (*D* 41). What interests me about the way the walls are decorated in Eveline's house is that one wall hanging makes the mysteries of Margaret Alcoque's visions abundantly clear, whereas the picture hanging next to it—a simple photograph of a priest—represents for Eveline a mystery that has never been solved. "During all those years she had never found out the name of the priest whose yellowing photograph hung on the wall above the broken harmonium beside the coloured print of the promises made to Blessed Margaret Mary Alacoque" (*D* 37). There is, indeed, a broken harmony between this female saint whose visions have been beaten into platitudes, and this nameless priest who presides over the enormous feminine sacrifice that St. Alacoque requests from the women of the household. Like Eveline's father, the identity of the priest has not been made any more secure as a result of Eveline's subservience and sacrifice.

"Eveline" is a remarkable story because it presents a woman who, although profoundly powerless in both her household and her culture, nonetheless, glimpses and silently signifies a supplementary world beyond the represented reality that excludes her. The poignancy of Joyce's characterization of her lies in the fact that he forces the reader to appreciate that her inability to represent her desire does not in any way exempt her from experiencing it. As Lacan puts it: "Her being not all in the phallic function does not mean that she is not in it at all. She is in it *not* not at all. She is right in it. But there is something more . . . a *jouissance* of the body which is . . . *beyond the phallus*" (1982b, 145). After all, what Eveline wants most from her escape with Frank is not love but something she persists in calling "life"—a right that she feels has been unfairly denied her: "He would give her life, perhaps love, too. But she wanted to live. Why should she be unhappy? She had a right to happiness. Frank would take her in his arms, fold her in his arms. He would save her" (*D* 40).

If she is to have life, her chain of thought begins, he must give it. Love is worth no more than a parenthetical mention because love between a man and a woman within the phallic economy means she must imagine her existence as something made permanent somewhere else by the commonplace act of her sacrificing it in the here and now. Or, as Alacoque promises, "Those who promote this devotion shall have their names written in My heart never to be effaced." If she successfully poses as "not-all," so the logic of this promise runs, then she guarantees just what Margaret Mary Alcoque purportedly promised — that her unrepresentable "self" is written down elsewhere.

But she is not "not in it"; she is still right in it as "not not-all." Why must she depend on his giving what she has a right to? Why is her identity, inasmuch as it exists anywhere, always elsewhere? In her final spasm at the iron rail, her ecstasy is appalling to witness because in this unearthly moment she demonstrates — although she knows nothing about this — that it is neither Ireland nor her father nor Frank from which she comes! She thinks vaguely that Frank will save her, but what she confronts in her equation of love and life is the paradox that, as a feminine subject, "she finds the signifier of her own desire in the body of the one to whom she addresses her demand for love" (Lacan 1982b, 84). Because the man insists on posing as the phallus (and the phallic economy insists that the woman should make this imposture seem real), his presumption that her desire is complementary to his own is the very thing she is asked to accept as the satisfaction of feminine desire. But no matter how much the phallic order tries to recuperate female desire as perfectly complementary to masculine needs (in the case of Margaret Mary Alacoque by translating it into twelve promises that demand the systematic repression of the question of female desire), her jouissance still remains supplementary to the phallic economy. So the unassimilated jouissance of Eveline, unlike that of her domesticated counterpart, St. Margaret Mary Alacoque, freezes her face into a supposedly blank expression, an unveiled hole that Frank can only gaze into as through a glass darkly — that face beyond language, which is God's. Yet, although female jouissance can only present itself to the masculine gaze as a terrifying rip in the fabric of reality, a fabric that normally veils the nonexistent phallic signifier, the male orgasm is revered, rather defensively, as such a monumental event that a good deal of Christian myth revolves around the question of how much longer it will be before God comes again![11]

6

Living for the Other in "After the Race"

The unconscious is that part of the concrete discourse
in so far as it is trans-individual, which is not at the
disposition of the subject to re-establish the continuity
of his conscious discourse. (Lacan 1981b, 20)

Jimmy had to strain forward to catch the quick phrase.
This was not altogether pleasant for him, as he had
nearly always to make a deft guess at the meaning
and shout back a suitable answer in the teeth of a
high wind. (D 44)

Certainly the young Jimmy Doyle gets around a good deal more
than Eveline and at a rate of speed that leaves him breathless.
Life itself seems to be a vehicle that hurries Jimmy from one point
to another, never letting him quite catch his breath. Nothing is supplementary about Doyle's desire and, therefore, nothing is threatening or unsettling about it for others. He is neither more nor less than
what the recognition of others appears to make him. It is because he
is so obligingly functional as a mirror for other people that he is such
a highly tolerated companion for people who would otherwise have
no use for him. He is performing the role of cavalier youthfulness
for the sake of his father, who amassed his fortune by never acting
cavalier or youthful. Thus, the son is actually living the fantasy that
actually kept the older man going. Of course, living someone else's
nostalgic fantasy is bound to leave one always a little out of breath
and rather unpleasantly excited. For Jimmy Doyle, the recognition of

others feeds his ideal image as a dashing and contemporary man about town (the very image that his father, with good-natured grumbling, is anxious to purchase for him). Doyle's difficulty is that this recognition can never feel real except when he is talking about it with others.[1] As Lacan states: "The ego is constituted in relation to the other. It is correlative. The level on which the other is experienced locates exactly the level on which, quite literally, the ego exists for the subject" (1988a, 50). The irony of Jimmy Doyle's evening with his friends is that he is always guessing at what it is his listener wants to hear, and in doing so, he is trying to "hear himself."

As the story opens, Doyle is in an expensive racing machine with a group of high-spirited men. The two Frenchmen are happy because their financial future appears secure, and the third companion, Villona, is content because he knows where his next meal is coming from. Only Doyle is described as being "too excited to be genuinely happy" (*D* 43). Doyle's state of excitement, which is not entirely pleasant, is both supported and threatened by the "cargo of hilarious youth" in which he finds himself. Indeed, all his heightened senses are devoted to discerning how best to conduct himself in a manner that will most closely approximate what he imagines the others expect him to be: "The Frenchmen flung their laughter and light words over their shoulders and often Jimmy had to strain forward to catch the quick phrase. This was not altogether pleasant for him, as he had nearly always to make a deft guess at the meaning and shout back a suitable answer in the teeth of a high wind" (*D* 44). His anxiety is not, for instance, about whether his response could be judged as intelligent or witty. He is more concerned that his words appear suitable. He feels, in other words, that his response should complement and, thereby, compliment what the others have said. But, in a situation similar to what Lacan describes as the relation of the subject to the 'other,' Jimmy Doyle can never be sure he has correctly heard what it is the others are saying or that what he says in return represents what it is the 'other' desires.

When he is not striving to construct a correct response to what he cannot quite hear, Jimmy Doyle contents himself with seeing himself as he would like to be seen. "He had been seen by many of his friends that day in the company of these Continentals" (*D* 44). The final pillar upholding Doyle's ideal image of himself is that Segouin, the driver of the car, has recognized him to the extent that he has introduced him to a fellow driver: "Segouin had presented him to one of the French competitors and, in answer to his confused murmur of compliment, the swarthy face of the driver had disclosed a line of shining white teeth. It was pleasant after that honour to return to the profane world of spectators amid nudges and significant looks" (*D* 44). Joyce's description makes it clear that all the French driver has recognized is someone whose otherness can be consumed to further nurture his own sense of "self." Doyle's murmured compliment, too abject and confused to be even coherent, fails to elicit any words at all from the driver — only "a line of shining white teeth" are "disclosed." This charade underlines the general dynamic of Doyle's friendships with all the Continentals where he masquerades as the object of their desire so that their attention will seem to authenticate the fiction of himself. This, in turn, allows him to move through the "profane world of spectators" with a self-aggrandizing impunity that guarantees his ideal image.

Throughout this story, people seem aware of what Jimmy represents, but very few pay any attention to anything he actually says. This position is imposed on readers, as well because they are told several times that Jimmy has spoken, but they never actually hear anything that he says. Jimmy Doyle's literal discourse is uniformly meaningless because it is completely unconscious (it is dictated by the structure of the 'Other,' within which he desires to embed himself). Lacan states: "The unconscious is that part of the concrete discourse insofar as it is trans-individual, which is not at the disposition of the subject to re-establish the continuity of his conscious discourse. . . . The unconscious participates in the functions of ideation, and even of thought" (1981b, 20). The reader learns, during the story, that Doyle has invested a good deal of his father's money in Segouin's new motor establishment. This obvious explanation for Segouin's casual indulgence of him is rigorously avoided by Doyle — so much so that he gratefully interprets, as another sign of recognition, Segouin's dismissive comment (probably not even true) that he is only being allowed to invest "the mite of Irish money" because of "a favour of friendship" (*D* 45). Doyle's need to preserve the myth of Segouin's friendship contributes to his later misinterpretation of what is done to him during the game of cards. Indeed, his companions fleece him of money he does not even possess because they urge his drunken participation in a game where the implications of the symbolic structure entirely escape him: "Jimmy did not know exactly who was winning but he knew that he was losing. But it was his own fault for he frequently mistook his cards and the other men had to calculate his I.O.U.'s for him. They were devils of fellows but he wished they would stop" (*D* 48). Doyle is so excited to be part of the whirl of what his father once imagined was "the life" that he feels it would be quibbling to admit that the sensation it provides is almost wholly unpleasant (like the sensation of being carried forth at a terrifying rate of speed by a vehicle you are not driving).

If one views "After the Race" as a presentation of Jimmy Doyle's slavish dependence on the Other to authenticate the myth of himself, one can draw a connection between Jimmy Doyle's behavior of leaning forward to hear the comments of his friends and his later folly of betting wildly on cards he cannot quite read. In both cases, he is striving to hear what it is the Other wants from him so that he can conduct himself according to its desire. To offer another example of the same dynamic, when he does speak at the party aboard Farley's yacht, he has no idea what he has said but judges that it must have been a good speech because Villona shouts "Hear! Hear!" as he speaks, and Farley claps him on the back when he is finished. Thus, he is gratified by behavior on their part that demonstrates their sense of amusement at his powerless posturing as an Irishman under the influence of alcohol. He is playing the hero of his father's unlived story, even as he plays the fool for the French musketeers who need him to provide a foil for their own dubious sophistication.[2]

There is an excruciating ratchetlike dynamic in this story whereby Jimmy Doyle is driven to greater and greater folly by his pursuit of an ideal image that he imagines is reflected in the gaze and recognition of others. Joyce's design for this story shows that the exhilaration generated by recognition from the Other also leads to a desperate sense of alienation that requires a constant reprisal of this recognition in the verbal and symbolic register. This alienation (or lack-in-being), makes subjects somnambulists who walk through reality with obstinate conviction while ignorantly bruising themselves on the ineluctable Real that consistently undermines the conscious fictions by which they live.

Although Jimmy Doyle's lack-of-being is profound indeed, in a significant moment at the height of the chaotic party a sensation of absurdity gets through to him. It is not a moment of particular clarity, and it is quickly drowned out by the noise of "living," but for a split second Doyle realizes his relationship to his supposed friends: "Cards! Cards! The table was cleared. Villona returned quietly to his piano and played voluntaries for them. The other men played game after game, flinging themselves boldly into the adventure. They drank the health of the Queen of Hearts and the Queen of Diamonds. Jimmy felt obscurely the lack of an audience" (*D* 48). It is in this obscure moment that Jimmy feels no one is watching him, that the eyes of the 'other,' which appear to be turned always in his direction, in fact only stare vacantly at him with a gaze that is blind. But to see this is no longer to be able to imagine himself, and a desperate sense of excitement quickly returns: "What excitement! Jimmy was excited too; he would lose, of course" (*D* 48).

7

Men in Love

The Woman as Object of Exchange in "Two Gallants"

Each time the subject apprehends himself as form and as ego . . . his desire is projected outside. From whence arises the impossibility of all human coexistence. (Lacan 1988a, 171)

—You're what I call a gay Lothario, said Lenehan. And the proper kind of a Lothario, too!

A shade of mockery relieved the servility of his manner. To save himself he had the habit of leaving his flattery open to the interpretation of raillery. But Corley had not a subtle mind. (*D* 52)

Early in "Two Gallants" one sees Corley swaggering down the hill of Rutland Square. He is at the height of his self-induced glory because Lenehan is keeping pace with him and obligingly skipping off the path and into the road whenever Corley's hyperbolic narrative causes him to take over the entire pathway they are presumably sharing. Initially, Joyce presents the relationship of the two men merely by describing how they walk together. Initially, he does not even refer to them by name but describes them vaguely (and inaccurately) as "two young men." Their anonymity relative to their surroundings is established in the opening paragraph of the story where the city of Dublin is described from an aerial point of view, and they are not mentioned at all: "The grey warm evening of August has descended upon the city and a mild warm air, a memory of summer, circulated in the streets. The streets, shuttered for the repose of Sunday, swarmed with a gaily coloured crowd. Like illumined pearls the lamps shone from the summits of their tall poles upon the living texture below which, changing shape and hue unceasingly, sent up into the warm grey evening air an unchanging unceasing murmur" (*D* 49).

The best indentification one can make is that they must be somewhere in the "gaily coloured crowd." This opening makes the point that, despite the vigorous way Corley and Lenehan put forth their importance, they are merely two threads in the "living texture" of a crowd. Their conversation, which will shortly be presented in complete detail, is also characterized as one tiny contribution to "an unchanging unceasing murmur." The appearance of the crowd changes unceasingly, while its murmur is unchanging. The manifestation of people asserting their individuality presents a kaleidoscopic spectacle, but the manner in which they do so—talking—is "unchanging and unceasing."

Indeed, the narrative tone continues to undermine the swaggering incertitude of these "two gallants" for the rest of the story. At several critical points, when either the conversation or the plotting of Corley and Lenehan is at an impasse, the two men—privately and not for the benefit of the other—gaze at the moon. We learn, for example, that while Corley samples the passing girls with his smile, "Lenehan's gaze was fixed on the large faint moon. . . . He watched earnestly the passing of the grey web of twilight across its face" (*D* 52). Later, after Corley recalls one girl in his past who was "a bit of all right," silence overtakes him: "He too gazed at the pale disc of the moon, now nearly veiled, and seemed to meditate" (*D* 53). Silence descends on them both after passing the harpist playing *O Moyle,* and only crossing the road and blending in again with "the gaily coloured crowd" restores them to conversation: "The two young men walked up the street without speaking, the mournful music following them. When they reached Stephen's Green they crossed the road. Here the noise of trams, the lights and the crowd released them from their silence" (*D* 54). In other words, a force beyond their dialogue makes their conversation possible and also bestows upon it a diminutive quality because it reveals the two gallants as just the smallest bit of patchwork in "the gaily coloured crowd."

Corley and Lenehan each qualify as what Lacan calls "the man of today" who "entertains a certain conception of himself" that he takes to be "the result of a natural inclination, whereas in fact, in the present state of civilization, it comes to him from all sides" (1988a, 4). Corley, for example, conducts himself throughout the story with a confidence rendered absurd by the fact that his belligerent certitude is only made possible by the fact that he is dauntingly obtuse. Lenehan is a good deal more subtle, but the only advantage he appears to gain by this is that his self-deception is that much more refined. Both of the gallants move through the crowd with a studied nonchalance that is intended to mask the fact that they are creatures of a grim necessity and not at all in command of their surroundings, their attitude toward one another, or even the nature of their conversation. Corley is particularly an invention of the city of Dublin because he is currently "about town," that is, living directly off the energy generated by the city by ferrying to the police any information he considers sellable: "He was often to be seen walking with policemen in plain clothes, talking earnestly. He knew the inner side of all affairs" (*D* 51). If Corley specializes in knowing the inner side of all affairs, Lenehan specializes in living off the empty rhetoric that surrounds and obscures everything unsavory in the nature of these affairs. People have a vague distrust of him as "a leech," yet he profits from the begrudging acceptance accorded to him by people who benefit from his skill at getting them to extemporize at length about the unacknowledged "fact" of their own importance. Corley sells information about other people's lives, whereas Lenehan's service to his fellow Dubliners is to make a living off their need to talk in order to live with themselves.

Because a free bout of all-night drinking depends upon it, Lenehan is particularly anxious about whether or not he has made himself sufficiently important to Corley. In essence, he subtly divines the structure of Corley's ego to make himself absolutely necessary to the continuance of this inherently insupportable structure. In a sense, Lenehan is eager to serve as an ego psychologist for the crudely constructed Corley—promising to confirm the coherency of his contradictory moi in exchange for a consideration. In fact, the nature of his work is startlingly like the sort of psychoanalyst Lacan railed against because, in effect, he glorifies the false structure of Corley's ego to strengthen its illusory properties and, thus, ensure that the analysis will prove interminable (and, for him, profitable). Superficially, Lenehan acts the simpleminded role of an inferior friend who is transported out of himself by the fine qualities of his companion (he is a cynical Jimmy Doyle): "The narrative to which he listened made constant waves of expression break forth over his face. . . . Little jets of wheezing laughter followed one another out of his convulsed body" (*D* 49). But all this athletic and false merriment is a cover for Lenehan's constant monitoring of how Corley is reacting to his own insincere encouragement that he go on talking: "[Lenehan's] eyes, twinkling with cunning enjoyment, glanced at every moment towards his companion's face" (*D* 49-50). Corley, of course, does not realize that Lenehan has to observe him closely to determine how best to punctuate, with artificial laughter, Corley's tedious monologue.

Lacan describes "empty speech" as that which the subject addresses to the other in an attempt to get this other to confirm the subject's imaginary concept of himself as a being who is unified in a particular way. "Full speech," on the other hand, is addressed to the Other — that point beyond language and the ego to which the subject constantly (and unconsciously) directs the question, "Who am I for you?" "Full speech" emanates from the unconscious and speaks the subject (in dreams, jokes, slips) in a way that the ego stubbornly misrecognizes as the conscious production of an anonymous "self." Lenehan's service for Corley is to make empty speech feel like full speech by posing as the Other and, thus, accurately reflecting back to Corley the image of himself his empty speech is anxious to confirm. In this dialectic, Corley experiences the repetition of his meager repertoire of rhetorical tricks, performed in conjunction with Lenehan's urgings, as evidence of his "personality." In fact, his absurd posturing for the completely cynical audience of Lenehan indicates the absence of such a structure. "Well!" Lenehan says at the completion of each rhetorical turn, as if rewarding a dog for a well-executed trick, "That takes the biscuit!" (*D* 50). Indeed, the physical effect produced on Corley by Lenehan's highest praise ("that emphatically takes the biscuit") is not unlike what can be achieved by praising a dog: "Corley's stride acknowledged the compliment" (*D* 51).

The gist of all Corley's narratives circles around what he presents as his indomitable masculinity. According to him, women yield to his charms as readily as men yield to his opinions. People are so anxious to have contact with him (women especially) that they regard the opportunity of being exploited by him as a pleasant surprise. The truth is he sells information about anyone to whomever will pay for it, and he sells the illusion of himself as a possible husband to women who will be trapped in permanent employment as slaveys or prostitutes if they fail to marry. The force of his personality, in other words, is an illusion based on the systematic manipulation of needy people. Nothing recommends Corley to Lenehan except that his ethical vacuity and dim-witted greed often produces the price of a drink. Certainly, Lenehan would shove off with little or no excuse if he did not like Corley's prospects of buying a few rounds later in the evening (Lenehan does not just pick the odds on horses).

Preserving some semblance of his own ideal image is an even trickier business for the superficially subservient Lenehan. He depends on Corley's complete indifference to him to permit him to make snide remarks that support his sense of himself as a superior person: "To save himself he [Lenehan] had the habit of leaving his flattery open to the interpretation of raillery. But Corley had not a subtle mind" (*D* 52). The subtle mind of Lenehan and the obtuse egotism of Corley permit, as Lacan would see it, a sort of see saw relationship that is uneasy and only temporarily stabilizing because it is inherently aggressive.

> The relation of the subject to his . . . *Idealich* [ideal image], through which he enters into the imaginary function and learns to recognise himself as a form can always see-saw. Each time the subject apprehends himself as form and as ego, each time that he constitutes himself in his status, in his stature, in his static, his desire is projected outside. From whence arises the impossibility of all human coexistence.
>
> But, thank God, the subject inhabits the world of the symbol, that is to say a world of others who speak. That is why his desire is susceptible to the mediation of recognition. Without which every human function would simply exhaust itself in the unspecified wish for the destruction of the other as such. (1988a, 17)

How is it that Lenehan and Corley do not come to blows when they clearly despise their unacknowledged dependence upon one another? They avoid acting upon the implicitly violent imaginary

relation by recognizing one another on the symbolic plane and mutually designating a woman as "other" who becomes the object of value
within their mutually affirming phallic economy: "And where did you
pick her up, Corley?" Lenehan asks. Corley informs him that "one
night" he "spotted a fine tart" (*D* 50). This anonymous woman, picked
by Corley with the same sort of discerning eye any shopper might
employ in selecting pastry in a bakery, becomes an object of exchange
that validates their (spurious) phallic economy.

Her exchange value, determined by the two men with no reference to anything inherent in her (or in any woman), will cause her
to represent the abstract value that permits their unholy communion
as mutual wholeness. Irigaray's interpretation of Lacan on this point
is particularly illuminating: "A commodity—a woman—is divided into
two irreconcilable 'bodies': her 'natural' body and her socially valued,
exchangeable body, which is a particularly mimetic expression of masculine values. . . . At the most, the commodities—or rather the relationships among them—are the material alibi for the desire for relations
among men. To this end, the commodity is disinvested of its body
and reclothed in a form that makes it suitable for exchange among
men" (1985, 179–80). As the reader will see, her activity of procuring
for them the gold coin from the master's house hollows out a space
for these two gallants within the indifferent Real of the city. The joke
played on the reader in this story is that the men seem to be convers-
ing about whether or not Corley will have sex with this woman when,
in fact, the question is whether or not he will be able to persuade her
to steal for him.

The "use value" of her body is made subordinate to her exchange
value. She is, to use Irigaray's phrase, "reclothed in a form that makes
it suitable for exchange among men." The coin stands outside the imaginary relation of the two gallants and authenticates, for each of them,
the mirror image of themselves that they have forced each other to
represent. Indeed, on the level of the symbolic order, it is Corley and
Lenehan who "make love" by converting the use value of this woman
(Corley's acts of intercourse with her) into an exchange value (her
willingness to steal). Lenehan's paranoia that Corley may "give him
the slip" after he gets money from the girl can be read as similar to
that of a deflowered maiden's fear that now that her lover has taken
from her what he wants (Corley has "had his way" with Lenehan in the

sense that he absorbed all of his praise and offered nothing in return), he will never return to offer any recompense for her sacrifice. Certainly, the way Corley presents the gold coin to Lenehan mimics the actions of a man who feigns indifference to his lover to increase her delight when she sees the evidence that he has not forgotten her: "Corley halted at the first lamp and stared grimly before him. Then with a grave gesture he extended a hand towards the light and, smiling, opened it slowly to the gaze of his disciple. A small gold coin shone in the palm" (*D* 60). Although the woman in question does her best to present herself as a valuable commodity ("She had her Sunday finery on"), she only serves the men as the third term that validates the self-enclosed phallic economy of Corley and Lenehan. Again, Irigaray's comments on this phenomenon seem particularly apt.

> Putting men in touch with each other, in relations among themselves, women only fulfill this role by relinquishing their right to speech and even to animality. (1985, 189–190)
>
> . .   .   .   .
>
> Woman exists only as an occasion for mediation, transaction, transition, transference, between man and his fellow man, indeed between man and himself. (1985, 196)[1]

Despite their complete alienation from and hatred of each other, Corley and Lenehan are able to act as authenticating subjects for one another because the "fine tart" (significantly nameless and silent) acts as an object of exchange for both of them.

Corley's account, narrated at Lenehan's request, of how the relationship with this woman has progressed to date tells us nothing about the woman and explains instead how Corley has managed to engage her interest while withholding every detail of his identity. His narration organizes itself along two separate histories: how his physical intimacy with her developed and how the intimacy was converted, at every stage, from a natural use value to an exchange value: "I put my arm round her and squeezed her a bit that night. Then next Sunday, man, I met her by appointment. We went out to Donnybrook and I brought her into a field there. She told me she used to go with a dairyman. . . . It was fine, man. Cigarettes every night she'd bring me and paying the tram out and back. And one night she brought me two bloody fine cigars—O the real cheese, you know, that the old fellow used to smoke" (*D* 50–51, Joyce's ellipses). What Corley thinks "fine" is not their physical relationship but the relentless way he has converted the act of sex into a transaction of goods that he can proudly boast of to another man.

Corley, through Lenchan's skillful framing of his rambling monologue, is able to perceive himself as "a gay Lothario" who "takes the solitary, unique, and, if I may so call it, *recherche* biscuit!" In fact, the true nature of Corley's profession is ironically contained in how he pronounces his own name. Gifford points out that in aspirating "the first letter of his name after the manner of Florentines," Corley would pronounce his name "Whorley" (1982, 57). But that is not what Lenehan names him: "You're what I call a gay Lothario . . . And the proper kind of a Lothario, too!" (*D* 52). So Corley becomes, in terms of his ideal "self," a seducer, one who bends others to his will from a position of power, rather than a whore, one who debases his own being in the absence of anything else to sell. As long as a woman remains an object, without her own source of desire and, thus, without a point of view, then her gaze has been effaced and she can be reconstructed—completely independent of anything she might be—as an image of the phallus sustaining the male fantasy of the 'self.'

The relationship of Corley and Lenehan can be interpreted in the light of Lacan's observation that "the woman only becomes the support of [the subject's relation to the Other] in a second stage, and at that level of fiction which is commonly labelled sexual commerce" (1982b, 121). This, in turn, allows us to see Lenehan as left in the feminized position of a woman waiting for her hitherto faithful lover to meet her once again. In fact, Lenehan takes up the position of waiting the woman held earlier while Corley deliberately prolongs his monologue. His terror is that Corley will "give him the slip" and go "spend" with another man (!) whatever money he manages to procure: "All at once the idea struck him that perhaps Corley had seen her home by another way and given him the slip. . . . Would Corley do a thing like that?" (*D* 59). This is the jittery lament of an insecure lover. Corley, for his part, enjoys Lenehan's dependence upon him. During the story, Corley moves from being Lenehan's puppet to becoming his messiah. The earlier ironic distance, which Lenehan had provided for himself with his mock servility, collapses as the two men gaze together at a symbol that has materialized from the dark continent of a woman's desire. Although the men feel they have captured her through the teamwork of producing this coin, it is only the cause of their own desire at which they stare.

Desire, as Lacan insists, is not a question of the satisfaction gained from a symbolic exchange but of the successful intervention of speech that permits an exchange of recognition: "What is overlooked in analysis is quite obviously speech as a function of recognition. Speech is that dimension through which the desire of the subject is authentically integrated onto the symbolic plane. It is only once it is formulated, named in the presence of the other, that desire, whatever it is, is recognized in the full sense of the term. It is not a question of the satisfaction of desire . . . but, quite precisely of the recognition of desire" (1982b, 183). The relation to the Other is fraught with peril for Corley and Lenehan because their impression of themselves is so at odds with the Real.

Their relationship to this coin, however, which functions as a token of recognition from the 'other,' is ecstatically straightforward. On the symbolic plane, Corley and Lenehan achieve a simultaneous jouissance — a sort of mutual orgasm — when they stare together at the coin. The story, significantly, does not end with Lenehan gazing at the coin but with them basking in the glow of the coin which is "gazing" at them: "A small gold coin shone in the palm" (*D* 60). The mystery of the woman's body (represented by the closed fist) is now forced open by Corley to reveal a phallic signifier that confirms who they are relative to each other. In light of this, one can now view the earlier conversation of Corley and Lenehan as elaborate linguistic foreplay designed to heighten this carefully staged moment of surrender when Corley relaxes his fist and lets Lenehan gaze unimpeded at the secret gaze of the Other shining just for them in the palm of his hand. The subjectivity this bestows upon them is authenticated on the symbolic plane. For each of them, the fiction of their ideal image is made true in the same way that a symptom is believable — as reality that seems to represent, and be equivalent to, all there is in the Real. This triumph of reconstructed subjectivity on the part of Corley and Lenehan, however, remains undercut by Joyce's presentation of the opening sentence of the story in which the indifferent city silently presides over the two anonymous men lost in the "changing shape" of the crowd.

In the Dublin economy, the gold coin merely represents a gratifyingly large number of pints. What makes the coin far more special than this is the way it functions in the economy of masculine desire. The subject's desire, put most simply, desires the desire of the other to determine who it "is" in relation to the Other. Corley's desire is a good deal more complex than an urge for physical satisfaction; he has already had this, and he dismisses it as a means to an end. All desire is really a desire to be valued — to be recognized — to be the cause of another's desire: "She's all right, said Corley. I know the way to get around her, man. She's a bit gone on me" (*D* 52). One demands recognition from others by seeking to posit our selves as the cause of their desire, but this recognition never seems particular enough to permanently authenticate what one calls *I* or *me*. One's desire, therefore, never finds a permanently satisfying object of desire and, accordingly, moves from object to object (neutralized subjects, really) setting up elaborate scenes of symbolic authentification. Corley delights in making his date wait, for example, because he can assume that while she is waiting she is thinking of him. This situation lends to him a dimension of reality that Lenehan is there to recognize (although readers already know how cynical Lenehan's recognition of Corley really is). What he ignores, of course, is that while he delays their rendezvous, he is also thinking of what she represents to him. His sense of his own identity is still on that imaginary plane where he presumes that someone else is thinking of him, and, therefore, what she is thinking verifies who he is; but he can only imagine what she is thinking (he can only imagine himself). When describing the nature of desire between two subjects, Lacan writes: "Now learn to distinguish love as an imaginary passion from the active gift which it constitutes on the symbolic plane. Love, the love of the person who desires to be loved, is essentially an attempt to capture the other in oneself, in oneself as object" (1988a, 276). Naturally, then, the gift one expects from another is not anything that they could possibly give because it is something one only imagines one lacks.

One learns, for example, through Corley's oblique narration, that he once treated women with the expectation that they might bestow this gift upon him if they should so choose. "I used to spend money on them right enough," he tells Lenehan, "in a convincing tone, as if he were conscious of being disbelieved" (*D* 52). Later he reversed this approach because, as he puts it, "damn the thing I ever got out of it. . . . Only off of one of them" (*D* 52, Joyce's ellipses). What did he get "off of her," and what went wrong? Not surprisingly, his answer to these questions is a silence bracketed by words: "She was . . . a bit of all right, he said regretfully" (*D* 53, Joyce's ellipsis). After another silence, he adds "she's on the turf now." Here we see the problem: he took her to be his lost complement, but if she is able to serve this function for others, how could it be *his* lost complement? One can even guess at how the relationship began to unravel when Corley insists: "There were others at her before me. . . . Didn't she tell me herself?" (*D* 53). What apparently happened is that he interrogated this love object that had given him an "active gift" on the symbolic plane only to discover that she had given it to others before him. He moves from accepting her love for him as a unique gift confirming his particularity to seeing her as no more discerning than a bitch in heat ("there were others *at her* before me," my emphasis). A woman who successfully operates as an object of exchange for one man simultaneously betrays the fact that, like any other sort of commodity, she is only temporarily suspended from a marketplace where she is capable of functioning as an object of exchange for any man. The danger of a man viewing a woman as that symptom which makes the myth of masculinity believable (the danger of viewing a woman as the Woman) is that all women become a sort of mythical species that make all men possible. The interchangeablility of the Woman as symptom, then, threatens to call attention to the mental illness of the masculine ego.

The solution is to regard the basic human nature of women as animalistic and, therefore, treacherous (the last resort of Frank in "Eveline"). In this way, their failure to operate effectively as a symbol becomes an inherent flaw in the feminine rather than an unbridgeable gap in masculinity. Indeed, Corley seeks to domesticate women by regarding them as obliging animals (as livestock). Of his "fine tart" he says, "We went out to Donnybrook and I brought her into a field there. She told me she used to go with a dairyman" (*D* 50–51). His recollection of this bit of information and the significant pause that follows it suggest that one see a connection between his "bringing her into a field" (such as cows inhabit) and his remembering her former boyfriend was a dairyman. Corley insists that the women he uses have all had former partners because this strengthens his resolve to abuse them. Paradoxically, the anonymous woman who steals a coin at his bidding bolsters his identity even though he has withheld from her his name and lied about where he works. "I told her I was in Pim's," he tells Lenehan. As Gifford points out, the received idea about Pim's, for Dubliners, was that the proprieters were Quakers, and all who worked there were "models of sober commercial reliability" (1982, 57). Corley is able to present this fantasy to her because Lenehan knows the truth about who he really is. In the end, it is Lenehan he is seducing because it is Lenehan who must confirm for him (recognize) that he has become the cause of "the Woman's" desire; as a representation that confirms his subjectivity (rather than an actual subject) she has no ability to do this in a manner that can be trusted. Corley and Lenehan each assume the other is confirming what they, in fact, each see as the fiction of the other's being. The woman serves as a place holder in this drama of misrecognition — "a hole" — a representative of the Other who can deliver to them the precious message of who they are in the gaze outside themselves that they must presume sees them whole.

They authenticate each other by converting a woman to an object of exchange (the Woman) so that their desire is, to use Lacan's phrase, "susceptible to the mediation of recognition." It is this recognition (a misrecognition, really) that permits an uneasy communion ("takes the biscuit") and diverts their hostility toward one another. Lacan describes this hostility as "the unspecified wish for the destruction of the other as such." Significantly, the manner in which the narrator describes what the woman is wearing makes it clear that she imagined what a male gaze would see while she was dressing herself: "The ends of her tulle collarette had been carefully disordered" (*D* 55). The deliberate disorder she carefully superimposes on her collarette (such a detail is, apparently, in fashion) is intended to correspond to what she imagines a man will recognize as the incarnation of his symptom — the Woman. Like Gerty MacDowell in "Nausicaa," she recognizes, on a subliminal level, a woman must dress in fashion to compete with other women who are also striving to approximate the current constellation of signs that signify the Woman to a man.

'Femininity' is a role, an image, a value, imposed upon women by male systems of representation. . . . This masquerade of feminin-

ity . . . requires an effort on her part for which she is not compen-
sated. Unless her pleasure comes simply from being chosen as an
object of consumption or of desire by a masculine 'subject.' And,
moreover, how can she do otherwise without being 'out of circulation'?

In our social order, women are 'products' used and exchanged
by men. Their status is that of merchandise, 'commodities.' How
can such objects of use and transaction claim the right to speak and
to participate in exchange in general? (Irigaray 1985, 84)[2]

Yet although Joyce's depiction of the slavey as merely an object
of exchange is severe and uncompromising, there is still the tiniest
suggestion that a real woman ex-ists behind the masquerade: "A big
bunch of red flowers was pinned in her bosom, stems upwards" (*D*
55). The woman betrays her subjectivity because of a disorder in her
masquerade that is *not* deliberate. But who notices this slip? Certainly
not the woman, who would correct it if she did; certainly not Lenehan
who, readers are told, "noted approvingly her stout short muscular
body" (back to livestock imagery). No, it is the narrator who notes
this mistake, and, in doing so, the suggestion is made that if the masquerade of femininity is the only language a woman is allowed to speak,
than it is the breaks, elisions, and omissions in that language, as in
any language, that is most revealing—a Freudian *slip*, indeed![3] In this
significant way, the narrator breaks faith with the reader, who has been
encouraged up to this point to see the woman in the same light by
which Corley and Lenehan see her. As with "Araby," Joyce's narration
leaves the reader with the uncomfortable feeling that the composition
of Corley and Lenehan's story has only been made possible by the
decomposition of a woman's story (and her subsequent recomposition
as the Woman).

What one can see in the formation of Corley and Lenehan's desire
in this story is that the subject's fantasy about an object of desire supports the signifying structure through which one "captures" the desire of the other: "The phantasy is the support of desire; it is not the
object that is the support of desire. The subject sustains himself as
desiring in relation to an ever more complex signifying ensemble"
(Lacan 1981a, 185). In "Two Gallants," Joyce seems to be at pains to
show that one's primary desire is to know who one is, *but only as long
as this knowledge collaborates what one already imagines oneself to be.* Likewise,

Lacan insists that we have no conscious desires other than those that manifest themselves when one strives to become the cause of desire in another. In short, one experiences one's subjectivity only by becoming an object for someone else: "The subject cannot desire without itself dissolving, and without seeing, because of this very fact, the object escaping it, in a series of infinite displacements. . . . And the tension between the subject—which cannot desire without being fundamentally separated from the object—and the *ego,* where the gaze towards the object starts, is the starting point for the dialectic of consciousness" (1988b, 177). Both Corley and Lenehan, in order not to "dissolve," define themselves in relation to the alienating gaze of the 'other'—even though this dependence introduces a permanent division in their subjectivity that can only be bridged by controlling, exchanging, worshiping, or despising the Woman who exists (in the form of a symptom) as the third term representing the authenticating gaze of the Other. Their exploitation of the female slavey allows them to misrecognize their fragmented and anonymous love for one another as proof of their healthy masculine status as "two gallants."[4]

8

Ejaculations and Silence
Sex and the Symbolic Order in "The Boarding House"

It is the man — by which I mean he who finds himself
male without knowing what to do about it, for all that
he is a speaking being — who takes on the woman, or
who can believe he takes her on. . . . Except that what
he takes on is the cause of his desire, the cause I have
designated as the *objet a.* (Lacan 1982b, 143)

Polly Mooney, the Madam's daughter, would also
sing. She sang:

> *I'm a . . . naughty girl.*
> *You needn't sham:*
> *You know I am.* (*D* 62)

O ne could make a case that "The Boarding House" is a story where
the lives of three people — Mrs. Mooney, Polly Mooney, and
Bob Doran — are demonstrably altered as a result of several crucial
interviews among them. It is worth noting, then, that the text of the
story nowhere records direct dialogue except in the closing lines when
Polly answers her mother's call to come downstairs, "Mr. Doran wants
to speak to you" (*D* 69). Yet, even after this announcement of someone about to speak, one never hears what Mr. Doran has to say. This
is such an abrupt inversion of the situation in "Two Gallants" in which

Corley and Lenehan talk at length and the slavey is not heard from at all, that one might justifiably regard it as deliberate.

In "The Boarding House," readers are made to understand that the position from which characters speak is far more important than any particular things they might say. Mrs. Mooney realizes that Bob Doran is the sort of man who will say what he does not mean to preserve what he thinks is true. Thus, she makes a clear distinction between him and a man like Bantam Lyons who has long since ceased to preserve any illusions about love or truth or desire. Mrs. Mooney, correctly enough, views power as operating at the base of everything perceivable. The reader is repelled by her because she abdicates her feminine role, which is to support the importance of the phallic order (and, thus, authenticate its moral imperative as justice). Joyce's wonderful irony, of course, is that her cynical manipulation of socially upheld morality helps her to achieve all her goals by forcing Bob and Polly to "do the right thing." How can we call Mrs. Mooney immoral when she orchestrates the exceedingly moral symphony of voices featuring Mr. Doran's priest, his employer, and Bob Doran's conscience, thus instilling within him the conviction that "reparation must be made in such cases"? Mrs. Mooney well understands Polly's value as an object of exchange in her house full of men. Even before Bob Doran arrived on the scene, she appreciated the abstract value to her business of Polly walking about. Perhaps the most infuriating and indomitable trait of Mrs. Mooney is that she scrupulously plays by the rules and never lets herself be played by them. She understands that love and sex are a game—a game with winners and losers. In knowing this, she is no more cynical than Corley and Lenehan, just a good deal wiser and more efficient about the use she makes of this knowledge in her long-term planning.

The primary price Mrs. Mooney has had to pay for her formidable ability to manipulate social convention for her own ends is that she has never imagined herself to be in love. Like Mrs. Kearney, she has never accepted a man's adulation as proof of her femininity. She married the boss's son not so much for his money (Mrs. Mooney is not afraid to work hard) but because he, as a son, was in a position where he would inherit something, and, quite simply, she was not. Not surprisingly perhaps, her husband quickly turns to alcohol to support those illusions about himself for which she cares nothing. His eventual attack with a cleaver upon the author of all his pain is so expected that she smoothly converts this attempted murder into the excuse she needs to enlist the aid of a priest in getting him out of the house. Again, I do not think she would have necessarily insisted on this particular denouement of her marriage; her sole principle with regard to men is that she has no interest in helping them out with their problem of being masculine. Something seems to be unspeakably horrid in her dismissive attitude toward her husband. The extent of her crime, however, is that she at first pretended interest in him, and then, a little bit later, she stopped pretending. My guess is that he never did very much for her either, but the difference in their two positions is that she never expected that he would. I find it difficult to dislike Mrs. Mooney because I believe her clear-sighted attitude about the fragile structure of the Phallic Order, and her recognition of its compulsion to victimize when possible, allows her to protect Polly from the grim life being led by the slavey in "Two Gallants" (and other women who are "on the turf").

Her crime, in short, is that she understands men, and, despite understanding them, she still does not pity them. The reader is encouraged by the narrator to see Polly as treacherous and conniving (especially with that famous description of her as "a little perverse madonna," which I will discuss shortly). But looked at from a different perspective — one that is outside the phallic economy that says a woman must pose as "not all" if she is to be of value — Polly can be seen as a high-spirited girl, gleefully aware of the effect on men of her flirting, dancing, and singing.[1] She does not yet have any clear idea of what she wants men to do for her or of how her ability to mesmerize them might benefit her (in this last quality, she seems very like Mangan's sister). In addition, she has a theatrical flair that manifests itself in three modes: her public performance as a naughty girl; her more private performance as a virgin on her bath night; and her final star turn as a seduced, possibly suicidal maiden. But what is so sinister in all this? She seems treacherous solely because one can sense, even before one reads of Bob Doran again in *Ulysses,* that her masquerade, even should she continue it, will not be enough to save him. One wants to condemn her performance as feminine because it is so flawlessly executed one cannot fail to see it as performance rather than natural female behavior. It is solely Polly's observable performance with Bob

Doran that causes Mrs. Mooney to notice "something [is] going on between Polly and one of the young men" (*D* 63). She does not know, for instance, anything they have said to one another, yet she is sufficiently impressed with the manner in which they conduct their conversations to abort her plan to send Polly back to the corn-factor's office (where she thought she might be more likely to meet a young man who "meant business").

Throughout this story, it is the context in which a conversation is conducted that is presented to the reader, not the actual words that are exchanged. Other interviews that are presented by Joyce as a sort of psychological dumb show include the one in which Mrs. Mooney confronts her daughter, the one in which she confronts Bob Doran, and the one in which Bob Doran proposes to Polly (having barely survived an interview with his priest the night before, which also is not recounted to readers). One can add to this all the several possible interviews that Bob Doran imagines he now will have to endure because "something has gone on" between Polly and him. There is, first of all, Mr. Leonard, his boss at the great Catholic wine merchant's office where he has worked for thirteen years: "He felt his heart leap warmly in his throat as he heard in his excited imagination old Mr. Leonard calling out in his rasping voice: *Send Mr Doran here, please*" (*D* 66). Here, finally, is a bit of direct dialogue, but it is from an interview that has not yet occurred! Another bit of direct dialogue plays in Doran's mind as he "hears" the talk of his friends: "He could imagine his friends talking of the affair and laughing" (*D* 66). Doran "hears" this direct dialogue through the perspective of his laughing friends, and then he "hears" Polly speaking in the manner that will provoke such talk: "She *was* a little vulgar, sometimes she said *I seen* and *If I had've known*" (*D* 66). Even the phrase that periodically distinguishes itself in his mind from the competing noise of all the other phrases is not original to him: "He echoed her phrase, applying it to himself: *What am I to do?*" (*D* 67). One final piece of dialogue—Jack's vow that "if any fellow tried that sort of a game on with *his* sister he'd bloody well put his teeth down his throat, so he would" (*D* 68)—filters through Doran's mind. Joyce's use of italics makes it clear that Doran's consciousness exists against a background of static, with an occasional phrase tuning in to give the effect of subjectivity; as soon as Mrs. Mooney figures out the various wavelengths he operates within, it is a simple matter for her to push his buttons. Looking over this list, it seems fair to say that Doran's "self" consists of conversations he has had, conversations he has overheard, and conversations he hopes to avoid. He seems a particularly apt example of Lacan's point that consciousness is a constellation of remembered speech that is undermined by speech that has been forgotten. In short, Doran's subjectivity is presented by Joyce as a cacophony of shouting and accusing voices, none of them his, yet all of them intermingling to form the broadcast of himself.[2]

By the time Doran puts on his coat and waist coat to go to his interview with Mrs. Mooney ("more helpless than ever"), he has the motion of a reluctant robot powered by the dynamic of all the voices in his head: "A force pushed him downstairs step by step. The implacable faces of his employer and of the Madam stared upon his discomfiture" (*D* 68). The fragmented discourse going through his head suggests that what he takes to be his personality is actually what he imagines other people see when they speak of him or to him. Of Jack Mooney's vow to protect his sister's virtue, he simply assumes he is the implied audience. Mrs. Mooney and Mr. Leonard represent all the people who Bob Doran has imagined confirming who he takes himself to be. That is, they occupy the space of the Other through which Bob Doran constitutes the structure of his subjectivity. For Lacan, the subject is one who must interview someone else, an other, to center his identity in a reality generated by language. Language constitutes people as a subject, and, thus, the difference between "self" and society is only an imaginary distinction that protects people from the realization that they are not distinct entities, but signifiers who act as signifiers of other signifiers (other subjects).

Lacan states: "Through the work—already a presence made of absence—absence gives itself a name. . . . There is born the world of meaning of a particular language in which the world of things will come to be arranged" (1977, 65). One needs to hear voices to avoid being driven mad by unremitting static and undecipherable echoes. Mrs. Mooney's boarding house can be seen as a universe of representation within the Symbolic Order—a universe as necessary as it is distorted. The wider Dublin world of music halls, drunken former husbands, horse racing and churchgoers is "the world of things" that "come to be arranged" within the carefully constructed reality of the boarding house. On a more specific and personal level, the boarding house is the signifying structure within which Bob Doran takes what he imagines is "his place" (but is, instead, just the place of one more signifier in an endless chain of signifiers).

The random and inexplicable world beyond the boarding house is made meaningful (although not at all true) within the walls of the house. For example, Jack's penchant for violence is explained as that of an older brother protecting his sister; Polly's accurate imitation of a music hall vamp is publicly explained as asexual innocence (the madonna) and privately consumed as titillating evidence of her boundless carnality (the *perverse* madonna): "On Sunday nights there would often be a reunion in Mrs. Mooney's front drawing-room. The music-hall artistes would oblige; and Sheridan played waltzes and polkas and vamped accompaniments. Polly Mooney, the Madam's daughter, would also sing. She sang: *I'm a . . . naughty girl. / You needn't sham: / You know I am"* (D 62). What are Polly's mannerisms during the tantalizing ellipses in the first line of her song? The break in speech strongly suggests the foregrounding of a gesture and look. How a female artiste sang a song was often far more provocative than the superficially naughty lyrics. My guess is that Polly takes this moment to do what she typically does, at some point, when speaking to anyone: "Her eyes . . . had a habit of glancing upwards when she spoke with anyone, which made her look like a little perverse madonna" (D 62). The narrator does not say *she* glanced up, but that her eyes did, which means that this habit is being interpreted strictly from the point of view of an observer who meets her gaze. Bob Doran, of course, is my nomination for who this observer would be. I envision him watching the Sunday night festivities from the outskirts of the room and recording the details of Polly's upward glance with the same reverential attitude he will later devote to his recollection of everything that transpired when she visited his room on her bath night. On that occasion, the obsessively detailed recollection of Polly is accounted for as a product of "the curious patient memory of the celibate" (D 67).

Within the representational universe of the boarding house, Polly pretends to be the naughty girl so popular on the music hall stage; like any good little perverse madonna, she performs the erotic masquerade on Sunday. And yet the lyrics of the song tell the male listener that he need not pretend to think her innocent because she knows she is not. The lyrics of her song insist that her performance as a temptress is real, and it is a man's denial of this reality that would be a sham. And yet her surroundings—Sunday night in her mother's house with her mother watching—insist that she is too innocent to understand her song. To put this paradox another way, in the drawing room Polly pretends to know something about masculine desire, yet in Bob Doran's bedroom she pretends to know nothing about it at all. This contradictory symbolic ordering presents Polly to Bob Doran as an erotic madonna: a woman who recognizes and encourages his desire and then forgives him after he has expressed it. Polly becomes the female object of desire who does not look, but whose look is co-opted as the recognition that bridges the gap at the base of male desire. Doran thinks to himself later: "He could not make up his mind whether to like her or despise her for what she had done. Of course he had done it too" (*D* 66). The two-part structure of Doran's thought makes it clear that they have each done something; what the duality of his thought implies is that they have not each done the same thing.

Bob Doran is drawn irresistibly to Polly because her body—her look, her voice, her gestures, in both public and private modes—has been adequately coded to represent the contradictory structure of his own desires. This is the intersubjective hall of mirrors between the masculine and feminine subject (optimistically known to most people as "the sexual relation") that Lacan characterizes as fantastic: "In the case of the speaking being the relation between the sexes does not take place, since it is only on this basis that what makes up for that relation can be stated" (1982b, 138). The body and being of Polly, encoded as it has been into the Symbolic Order as both madonna and whore, allows Bob Doran to believe in the possibility of loving himself. But because this "self" is illusory, he experiences her effect on him as "delirium." As madonna she becomes the maternal gaze that confirms the authenticity of his unified being; as whore she becomes the object of desire that appears to satisfy his lack-in-being, a lack that is caused, in the first place, by his subjectivity depending upon the regard of a reflection (the gaze of the mother, or madonna). In essence, Bob desires Polly in order to recognize his desire so that her recognition (or masquerade as feminine) will obscure the lack that his desire is based on in the first place.

In Lacanian terms, he sees Polly as the phallic signifier (as *being* the phallus) that would make of him a signified (*having* the phallus).

He is in love with her "sham," which permits him to say, "I am" (his sham). Joyce makes it clear that although the sexual drive plays a central role in the establishment of their relationship, it is the symbolic structure surrounding them in the boarding house that interprets this event and generates what Doran comes to believe in (rather feebly) as fate. This fate, which presents itself to him as inexorable and unavoidable, actually is more of a linguistic construct than a destiny. As Lacan notes, "Symbols in fact envelop the life of man in a network so total that they join together, before he comes in the world, those who are going to engender him 'by flesh and blood'; so total that they bring to his birth, along with the gifts of the stars, if not with the gifts of the fairies, the shape of his destiny" (1977, 63).[3] Bob Doran's reality is the subject's distortion of the Real into the representable universe of the Symbolic Order; the secret of Mrs. Mooney's extraordinary power over him is that she has discerned the constellation of voices, morals — and just plain words — that dictate how he must act to remain true to himself. To put this another way, she can predict with confidence how he will speak to her because she understands — much better than he does — the manner in which he has been spoken.

Polly, by masquerading as feminine, persuades Doran, at least briefly, that he is everything (that he possesses the phallus). Mrs. Mooney intervenes in his love affair (a love affair with his ideal mirror image) by imposing the course of action he must follow if he is to preserve the illusion of himself that Polly represents. Of course, Bob Doran is already a little unsure why his affair with Polly, which began on such a surge of feeling, now seems to entail complex social obligations he wishes to avoid. As he so succinctly puts it, "delirium passes." There can be no question of permanent satisfaction in his desire for Polly because his attraction to her is both symbolic and physical. In seeing Polly as "not all," Bob Doran assumes her essence will confirm his essence — that her desire is merely to recognize his desire. But she can support this assumption only by masquerading as what he needs to see. Rather than giving him something, she is simply allowing him to reimagine the mirror-stage jouissance where he first misrecognized his integrated reflection as the visual equivalent of the narrative myth of the 'self.' Lacan states: "If it is the case that the man manages to satisfy his demand for love in his relationship to the woman to the extent that the signifier of the phallus constitutes her precisely as giving in love what she does not have — conversely, his own desire for the phallus will throw up its signifier in the form of a persistent divergence towards 'another woman' who can signify this phallus under various guises, whether as a virgin or a prostitute" (1982b, 84). Inevitably, then, according to Lacan, a woman will come to be seen by the masculine subject as yet another fraudulent object of desire — a tease pretending to be the phallus. Her masquerade will be denounced as treacherous or deceiving when it is no more and no less than an acting out of the division that lies at the base of his own insatiable masculine desire.[4]

Polly's affect on Bob Doran (what he characterizes as delirium) stems from the fact that she is both 'a woman' and 'another woman' — both virgin and whore. She is a woman who, in a room full of men, unabashedly declares she is a naughty girl; later, in a private performance, she is the virginal girl with the white instep and furry slippers who "one night as he was undressing for bed . . . had tapped at his door, timidly" (*D* 67).[5] In *Ulysses* one learns that Mrs. Bob Doran has effortlessly achieved a third incarnation as a proper matron; yet one also learns, from the ever-observant Bloom, that Doran frequently can be seen "sloping into the Empire [theatre]" — surreptitiously reliving in the music halls the delirium first experienced in the drawing room of Mrs. Mooney's boarding house. On that earlier stage, Polly vamped by glancing up "like a little perverse madonna" while singing her naughty girl song. The image of Polly as a naughty girl is a signifying construct that Bob Doran revisits in the dark hall of the Empire whenever he can. The fact that there is no literal connection between who he married and what he sees on stage only reinforces the point that he was made delirious not so much by Polly (whoever she is) as by what she represented for him:[6] "It is the man — by which I mean he who finds himself male without knowing what to do about it, for all that he is a speaking being — who takes on the woman, or who can believe he takes her on. . . . Except that what he takes on is the cause of his desire, the cause I have designated as the *objet a*. That is the act of love. . . . The act of love is the polymorphous perversion of the male, in the case of the speaking being" (Lacan 1982b, 143). For Lacan, the *objet a* is any object people invest with their desire and presume to be the lost object they need to complete themselves. But it provides no satisfaction because it is just another signifier that means something only in relation to other signifiers, which is to say it is a substitute for the lost object the subject once imagined was Real.

Doran has been enthralled by an image and symbol of femininity. This is all the man can ever see of a woman because, according to Lacan, "images and symbols *for* the woman cannot be isolated from images and symbols *of* the woman. It is representation . . . the representation of feminine sexuality, whether repressed or not, which conditions how it comes into play, and it is the displaced offshoots of this representation . . . which decide the outcome of its tendencies, however naturally roughed out one may take such tendencies to be" (1982b, 90). The look of the "little perverse madonna" (not Polly) from which Bob Doran suspends himself is a look that has been invented and perfected by music hall vamps in accordance with the greater or lesser enthusiasm shown by the men in the audience. In the Empire, this look, which is always a masquerade, actually is featured as a theatrical production. For her part, Polly sees Bob Doran as someone who believes in her performance, and his credulity lends substance to her fantasy that the various roles she plays as the Woman may be somehow real after all. His devout belief in her as feminine means that, despite her acting like the wronged heroine of a creaky melodrama ("she would put an end to herself, she said"), he sees her performance as so genuine that he has no choice but to cast himself in a role as either her seducer or her comforter, and he chooses the latter: "He comforted her feebly, telling her not to cry, that it would be all right, never fear" (*D* 66). In front of an audience, this scenario would seem painfully contrived, but before the specific audience of Bob Doran, Polly is able to feel completely genuine and honestly suicidal because this "self" that she pitifully offers to "do away with" has been constructed and authorized by his desire, a desire she has authenticated and reflected back to him as accurately as any masquerade can. If Polly were to "do away" with the role of the Woman in the midst of performing it for both of them, it would affect them both like an act of suicide.

Significantly though, after he leaves, she "does away with herself" very nicely by moving unconsciously from the role of the imperiled maiden to that of the offstage actress preparing herself for a new role in front of the masculine gaze of her mirror: "She looked at herself in profile and readjusted a hairpin above her ear" (*D* 68). A bobby pin set awry is a convincing detail for a girl contemplating suicide but not for one contemplating an offer of marriage. Yet I stress that there is nothing cynically hypocritical in the gesture. What one sees when one watches Polly after Bob Doran has left the room is the unconscious existence of an actress between scenes. She is not, for a brief period, masquerading as feminine for any man, and, because her sense of self is normally generated through this function, she occupies her time reviewing her most effective performances: "She regarded the pillows for a long time and the sight of them awakened in her mind secret amiable memories. . . . There was no longer any perturbation visible on her face. . . . She waited on patiently, almost cheerfully, without alarm, her memories gradually giving place to hopes and visions of the future. Her hopes and visions were so intricate that she no longer saw the white pillows on which her gaze was fixed or remembered that she was waiting for anything" (*D* 69). The men for whom she has performed are as anonymous to her as masculine members of the audience are to the female music hall artistes. Her next role, now that this show is closing, will be as a matron—a respectably married woman. From now on, Bob Doran will have to "slope into the Empire" to see a revival of "perverse madonna" construct that first persuaded him he could yet regain the imaginary unity he once experienced as delirium (jouissance) in the mirror stage.

In essence, Polly is vaguely aware she has marketed her femininity successfully and that her mother, acting as a sort of broker, will now be able to fetch a fair price for her in the marketplace. (As readers will see, Mrs. Mooney prepares for her performance with equal dexterity.) Still, their silent partnership is far from sexual entrapment; Polly is an unmarried girl, not a siren; her mother is a businesswoman, not a panderer. Polly's success in posing as the phallus for Bob Doran requires that she ignore the question of her own sexual identity to answer the question of his. This leads, as Polly's unconscious adjustment of her bobby pin suggests, to "a quasi-total extinction of sexual life, except possibly in the domain of verbal parade. An extinction which the women in question are not even aware of, but which strikes them as quite normal, that is, as belonging in the order of things. In short, they do not see it as having the value of a symptom but rather as adding to their 'value'" (1982b, 128).[7] Polly's song comes under the heading of verbal parade, as does her offer (as heartfelt as it is theatrical) to "do away with herself."

To increase her value, and to have him authenticate that increased value, the question of her sexuality is left out of the exchange all together. Within the Symbolic Order, women are persuaded that by corresponding as closely as possible to the phallus a man lacks (something that requires them to locate the question of their own jouissance elsewhere) they will be able to establish their value in the world of sexual commerce. It is not a woman's unmediated experience of sexuality that is in play but various representations of that sexuality. Desire is insatiable for the subject, despite his or her finding and focusing upon an *objet a* because the *objet a* is only what causes a subject to desire without being able to satisfy it. Because the substitute object has no signified, the subject will inevitably slide from one *objet a* to another in a perpetually hopeful (yet completely hopeless) search for satisfaction and wholeness; this is how the representation of a woman as the Woman operates as a symptom for the masculine subject.[8]

Because the subject is a signifier for which there is not a signified, "it only ever relates as a partner to the *objet a* inscribed on the other side of the bar. It can never reach its sexual partner, which is the Other, except by way of mediation as the cause of its desire" (Lacan 1982b, 151). Polly and Bob Doran do not so much have a sexual affair as they call one another's soul into existence for each other; each guarantees, as genuine, the performance of the other. Polly answers for Bob Doran the question of who he is for the Other, and Bob Doran designates Polly's value within the Symbolic Order. Polly's soul, therefore, is completely actualized by her market value. To appear to Bob Doran as a supposedly infatuated version of the 'other' (thus causing his delirium), Polly must accept this delirium as the answer to the question of who she is. Lacan states: "The soul's existence can . . . be placed in question — cause being the appropriate term with which to ask if the soul be not love's effect. In effect, as long as soul souls for soul . . . there is no sex in the affair. Sex does not count. The soul is conjured out of what is *homosexual,* as is perfectly legible from history" (1982b, 1955).

Yet, the sexual act — whether it took place or not, whether it is a sin, what sort of reparation is called for — is what all the people in the boarding house focus upon, and they focus upon it by not talking about it openly. All the people, that is, except Polly; she is merely pleased at having successfully accomplished something (her mother's studied silence is correctly read as approval), even if she does not seem consciously involved with any of the practical measures she took to accomplish it. Her "secret amiable memories," whatever they may be, do not appear to include Bob Doran because, if they did, she could not have forgotten what she was waiting for. What she is waiting for, of course, is really only what she is supposed to be waiting for according to the conventions of courtship (the subject is only ever supposable). Once Doran is out of the room, she effortlessly slips out of one character and into another. What she forgets, therefore, is the role of the seduced virgin. There is nothing deliberate or especially manipulative about her behavior because the masquerade of femininity (like a man's imitation of phallic autonomy) is a contextual performance that, while a person is performing it, feels like consciousness (real life).

Lacan insists it is not an actual partner or a literal act that shapes the other as an internal image for the subject but fantasies of who the person is and what the act means. Lacan says of the *objet a,* "nothing . . . is thinkable — except that everything which is thought of as a subject, the being one imagines as being, is determined by it" (1982b, 165). An exchange of caresses is meaningful only in the wider field of the exchange of symbols; femininity and masculinity cannot be understood outside the symbolic process through which each is constituted. "The human being only sees his form materialised, whole, the mirage of himself, outside of himself. . . . It is through the exchange of symbols that we locate our different selves in relation to one another" (Lacan 1988a, 140). In short, subjectivity is not an essence but a set of relationships. Language is the preexisting symbolic system that allows the individual to shape — through connecting points, or point de capitons — his or her identity. The primary shock for Bob Doran in this story (as it is for Gabriel in "The Dead") is that he is not who he thought he was. Almost all literal discourse (exchange of symbols through language) is marginalized by Joyce. By focusing on the behavior that the exchange of symbols causes, rather than the exchange itself, he is able to show that conversations involving Bob Doran, as well as those featuring him, intermingle to determine his actions. These discourses — indirect, imagined, remembered or literal — become the force pushing Bob Doran down the stairs and through his final interview with Mrs. Mooney.

Mrs. Mooney operates as the third term that splits the mirrorings of Polly and Bob Doran and assigns the affair its meaning. She deliberately avoids any dialogue with Polly or Bob Doran, even after others in the house have begun to talk of the affair. She is not interested in what others think but in what Polly and Bob Doran think of each other. Likewise, she is less interested in knowing the precise time when they may have had sex and more interested in discerning at what point they feel compelled to make sense of what has happened between them. Thus, her cue to intervene is that "Polly began to grow a little strange in her manner and the young man was evidently perturbed" (*D* 63). She plans, in a brief and highly staged encounter, not to ask Bob Doran what has happened but to tell him, "She dealt with moral problems as a cleaver deals with meat: and in this case she had made up her mind: (*D* 63). Indeed it is seventeen minutes past eleven, and she plans to "have the matter out with him" and still make the short mass at twelve o'clock on Marlborough Street. Mrs. Mooney must play by the rules to avoid being played by them. Outside her window, "worshippers, singly or in groups, traversed the little circus before the church, revealing their purpose by their self-contained demeanour no less than by the little volumes in their gloved hands" (*D* 63). If these worshippers are self-contained, to whom are they revealing their purpose? They, too, are performers — complete with deliberately selected and artfully arranged props and costumes ("the little volumes in their gloved hands"). This is a public example of the performative as normative as opposed to Mrs. Mooney's more private performance.

Mrs. Mooney looks forward to her conversation with Bob Doran with the keen anticipation of a gambler about to take over everyone else's chips with the symbolically powerful selection of cards she is holding: "She counted all her cards again before sending Mary up to Mr Doran's room to say that she wished to speak with him. She felt sure she would win" (*D* 65). Like a poker player, Mrs. Mooney can predict her success because she has learned that the cards that anyone holds obtain their value only in relation to the cards that everyone holds; reality is an effect of symbolic exchange. What she is so certain of is that Bob Doran requires her interpretation (her blessing as the supposedly self-contained people in front of the church might refer to it) to make sense of what has happened. Bantam Lyons, however, would be all too capable of interpreting a tryst with Polly for himself—counting it a lucky draw of the cards. Polly may have recognized his masculinity, but only Mrs. Mooney can recognize him as a *man* in the social sense of that term.

In counting her cards, Mrs. Mooney first goes over the latent public shame (which she could make manifest) that is inherent in Mr. Doran's private actions. In speaking to Mr. Doran, she fully intends to speak for him; indeed, her remarkable nonchalance about the impending interview with Mr. Doran can be explained by noting she need not threaten, cajole, or even debate with him because it is the essential mirage of his own identity that is at stake should he dare to defy her. The problem that readers witness being worked out in "The Boarding House" is how the act of sex—about which nothing is expressible—will be translated onto the symbolic plane so that Mr. Doran's desire can be signified in language, and his identity made to appear Real, in relation to what he knows he is and believes he is not. There can be no subject except in representation, but no representation can signify the subject's desire completely. "What would grammar matter, Mr. Doran thinks, if he really loved her?" (*D* 66). But grammar is *why* he loves her; love is the signifier that stands in for the intolerable absence generated by the sexual act. Joyce's story presents a half-dozen discourses about love, all of which attempt to "speak" the unspeakable act that produces inarticulate and undecipherable delirium. The word *delirium* is commonly understood as a mental disturbance featuring disordered speech and hallucinations—an apt description of the fragmentation and loss that operates in secret behind the symbolically ordered performance of subjectivity.

Jack speaks of the act of sex in terms of ownership and revenge, Mrs. Mooney in terms of reparation, a priest in terms of penance, a man in terms of public exposure, and a young woman in terms of being naughty, but everyone in the story is really talking about a symbolic relation that defines his or her position as subjects or objects of desire for one another. It only remains for Bob Doran to accept his role for all the other people to be authenticated in their roles. Joyce gives us almost none of Mr. Doran's earlier life, (his background) and this increases the reader's sense that subjectivity surpasses the sum of individual experiences. Years of cautious living avail Mr. Doran nothing as he feels himself being forced down the stairs. The organized system of symbols that constitute a subject can easily override such fond notions as maturity and development. He is aware that his regular life accounts for only nine-tenths of his existence, but the other ten percent is delirium. When descending the stairs, Bob Doran thinks nothing at all except that he is being thought into being by everyone else. He experiences his *I* as the focal point of a constellation of eyes; his subjectivity, the presumed center of his universe, is just another planet circling around the 'other.'

Although Mr. Doran hastily reviews his past before going down the stairs, his previous attempts to be a freethinker offer him no leverage in his present circumstance: "As a young man he had sown his wild oats, of course; he had boasted of his free-thinking and denied the existence of God to his companions in public-houses. But that was all passed and done with . . . nearly" (*D* 66). The ellipsis signifies the ten percent of Mr. Doran's life that is silence. The closer characters get to discussing the phenomenon of sexuality, or the act of sex, the more they rely on a silence—an absence in their discourse—that is then encoded by the symbolic configurations that frame this silence (configurations that compensate for the permanent lack that it reveals). Mrs. Mooney, for example, speaks of "the news"; the boarders call it "the affair"; Bob Doran says "the sin was there," and otherwise refers to the incident as 'it': "Of course, he had done it too. . . . It was not altogether his fault that it had happened" (*D* 66). Bob Doran's subjectivity, much like the absent topic of sex (and all the absent actual dialogue that Joyce consistently presents solely through its effects), is constituted by what surrounds a center that is absence and lack. Identity is an absence that takes its meaning from the Symbolic Order in which it finds itself situated. Mr. Doran slenderly maintains in his own mind his identity as a free-thinker by his habit of buying "a copy of *Reynold's Newspaper* every week" (*D* 66).[9]

But this action, and what he believes it represents about his reality, has no Real influence on what position he takes up (or, rather, is unable to refuse) in the Symbolic Order. Bob Doran acts like a signified, but he is a signified who is directed in his performance of certitude by the chain of signifiers he perpetually slides under. In this regard especially, he answers very nicely to what Lacan describes as "the man of today": "The man of today entertains a certain conception of himself, which lies half-way between naiveté and sophistication. The belief he holds that he is constituted in this or that way partakes in a certain current of diffuse, culturally accepted notions. He may think that it is the result of a natural inclination, whereas in fact, in the present state of civilization, it comes to him from all sides" (1988b, 4). So Bob Doran may faithfully pick up his copy of *Reynold's Newspaper,* a Sunday newspaper that, according to Gifford, was characterized by a contemporary as "a formidable spokesman for the most irreconcilable portions of the community" (1982, 65). The futility of this habit is highlighted by his other occasional habit (depicted in the "Cyclops" episode of *Ulysses*) of going on a several-day drunk to vent the incoherent ten percent of his life that Polly once helped him to experience as delirium.

9

"Why had he married the eyes in the photograph?"
The Gaze in "A Little Cloud"

> Let us once again take up . . . the relation to the gaze.
> We are at war. I am moving forward over a plain,
> and I assume myself to be under a gaze lying in wait
> for me. . . . What matters the most to me is knowing
> what the other imagines, what the other detects of
> these intentions of mine. (Lacan 1988a, 224)

> The bar seemed to him to be full of people and he
> felt that the people were observing him curiously. He
> glanced quickly to right and left (frowning slightly
> to make his errand appear serious), but when his sight
> cleared a little he saw that nobody had turned to look
> at him. (*D* 74)

Little Chandler is extraordinarily self-conscious about the likelihood that, at any given moment, people might be looking at him. His first line of defense, refined to the point of unconscious habit, is to always be sure that his appearance is neat: "He took the greatest care of his fair silken hair and moustache and used perfume discreetly on his handkerchief. The half-moons of his nails were perfect" (*D* 70). The manner of his personal grooming is rigorously consistent as if seeking to guarantee that, whenever people look at him, they will always see the same thing. Thus, he expects to be looked at, yet he takes

pains to avoid drawing undue attention to himself. His carefully mani-
cured fingernails correspond to his timid personality, which is carefully trimmed of all excesses. When Little Chandler walks the public
streets during the day, readers are told, "It was his habit to walk swiftly."
At night, he does so "apprehensively and excitedly" (*D* 72). He is
terrified that someone will apprehend him, yet he is excited by this
very prospect. In fact, he sometimes deliberately increases this feeling
of delicious terror by choosing the darkest and narrowest streets and
then trembling like a leaf at the thought that he is attracting the gaze
of "wandering silent figures" and that his hurrying form might be the
subject "of low fugitive laughter" (*D* 72).

His later rather fervid and circumspect questioning of Gallaher
on the subject of prostitutes suggests to me that the narrow streets
are those frequented by prostitutes and the low fugitive laughter that
frightens and excites him comes from women anxious to encourage
him to stop awhile and pay them for their services.[1] There seems little
likelihood that Little Chandler will ever respond, but the not entirely
unpleasant thrill he gets by subjecting himself to their siren calls will
help readers understand his odd pose with Gallaher as a strictly moral
man who, nonetheless, insistently inquires about immoralities in other
cities.

When walking these narrow streets, Chandler experiences vague
longings—some pleasant, some alarming—all because he assumes he
is being seen. Similarly, he watches himself entering Corless's bar by
first assuming that everyone is looking at him and then imagining that
he is able to control what they see: "The bar seemed to him to be full
of people and he felt that the people were observing him curiously.
He glanced quickly to right and left (frowning slightly to make his
errand appear serious), but when his sight cleared a little he saw that
nobody had turned to look at him" (*D* 74). In his momentary play-
acting (parenthetically described), Chandler consciously represents
himself as someone other than who he feels he is, as if what others
imagine him to be is more real than who he actually is. He considers
himself to be serious, yet he immediately contradicts this possibility
by pretending to be serious in the hopes that the people watching (no
one is watching) will authenticate what is in fact a deliberate pose.
This is a reenactment of the paradox of the mirror stage in which one
introduces a permanent self-alienation into the structure of subjec-

tivity by embracing a mythical identity that can only be verified by someone other than oneself. What Little Chandler sees as himself is not real unless it corresponds to what he thinks other people see. The real Real is that they see nothing, they are the blind gaze by which he suspends the symptom of his ego. When he perceives "nobody [has] turned to look at him," he drops this overly subtle guise and advances toward his friend Gallaher. For whom did Chandler wish to appear serious? Gallaher is the only person he can expect to know in this bar that he has never entered before. Why must anonymous observers (who are, in fact, not looking) be convinced that he is there on a serious errand? Lacan asserts that one experiences oneself by seducing the other into seeing what one imagines the Other desires one to be. Little Chandler's performance for a gaze that is blind is similar to the dilemma of the subject who performs for the (blind) gaze of the Other. Chandler's assumption in entering the bar and acting serious seems to be that a real person is behind this pose who is choosing to act. But this pose creates the effect of subjectivity for Little Chandler. It is, in fact, his attempt to carve a pocket of reality for himself out of the Real (the same effect he produces when he chooses to be thrilled and chilled by suddenly ducking down a shadowy street).

The subject first forms the moi by misrecognizing its mirror image as proof of its unified identity. The subject knows himself by imagining how the Other views him, and then the speaking subject (je) tries to verify this ideal image by seducing others into seeing it too. This myth of a coherent self, based on the gaze of the Other (manifested in the form of the gaze of an-other) becomes the basis of the phenomenon whereby the subject experiences "self" by imagining the Other, like the original mirror, sees a unified whole when it looks at him or her. Following Chandler's entry into the bar, for example (where the myth of himself precedes him to make Real his own entry), readers see that his demeanor and the tone of his responses quickly incite Gallaher into verbalizing *the very image Chandler mentally projected* when he first entered the bar (that he was on a "serious errand"): "Tommy . . . I see you haven't changed an atom. You're the very same serious person" (*D* 76). The fact that Gallaher would use the same adjective that is so dear to Little Chandler's fantasy of himself can be seen as Joyce's way of insisting that the words people might use to describe themselves are often the same words that they prompt others to use when verbalizing for people who it is they imagine them to be.

According to Lacan, people experience the fiction of identity by first imagining what the 'other' sees and then seducing an other into narrating for them the story of themselves: "The subject exhausts himself in pursuing the desire of the other, which he will never be able to grasp as his own desire, because his own desire is the desire of the other. It is himself whom he pursues. Therein lies the drama of this jealous passion, which is also a form of the imaginary intersubjective relation" (1988a, 221). Chandler desires Gallaher to recognize that he has an exceptional artistic temperament, however latent it might be, and then offer — good friend that he is! — to ply his connections in London to help him get a start. Little Chandler ignores the fact that Gallaher's connections, even if they were used on his behalf, could scarcely help place the "slender volume of poems" that he feels capable of writing. The kind of poetic temperament that Little Chandler timidly believes himself to have would only be a liability in the brash and boisterous world of international journalism that Gallaher inhabits. It scarcely matters, in any event, because Gallaher has no intention of advancing Little Chandler. Chandler, for his own part, is battling the uneasy sense that his success as a journalist has little to do with intrinsic merit and that his cosmopolitan image that plays so well in Dublin may, in fact, cause snickers in more sophisticated cities like Paris. Accordingly, he has sought out Chandler as someone who will envy what he has done and, thus, reinvigorate his admiration for himself.

In both cases, the two subjects are poised to destroy each other to verify themselves. Gallaher must belittle little Chandler (who must *be little* if he is to accommodate him) to exalt himself. Little Chandler has a more difficult task than Gallaher because he has already valorized Gallaher's point of view as representative of the 'other' (which is why he is so reluctant to acknowledge during his conversation with Gallaher, that he is an object of Gallaher's ridicule). Gallaher's double bind, however, is that the more successfully he ridicules Little Chandler, the less value he can attach to the envy of his diminutive "friend." Correspondingly, the less Little Chandler is able to think of Gallaher as someone "unspoiled by . . . success" who "deserved to win" (his initial description of Gallaher in the opening paragraph of the story), the more overwhelmed he will be by the fact that his "friend" is a vulgar, self-centered man who is not regarding him as anything but a mirror that unifies the fictional coherence of his identity. This is the paradox of the subject having to conceptualize his own desire by misrecognizing himself in the desire of the other. The "imaginary intersubjective relation" drives people to destroy the other in their perpetually doomed attempt to bask permanently and securely in the gaze of the Other. Aggression toward the other only leads to subjects discovering, yet again, the vanishing point of their own (fictional) unity. Gallaher, for example, feels compelled to negate Chandler's description of Paris as "beautiful," even though he then immediately reissues the same word Chandler uses as a new word that has been authenticated by him.

> —Have you seen Paris?
> —I should think I have! I've knocked about there a little.
> —And is it really so beautiful as they say? asked Little Chandler. He sipped a little of his drink while Ignatius Gallaher finished his boldly.
> —Beautiful? said Ignatius Gallaher, pausing on the word and on the flavour of his drink. *It's not so beautiful, you know. Of course, it is beautiful. . . .* But it's the life of Paris; that's the thing. Ah, there's no city like Paris for gaiety, movement, excitement. (*D* 76, emphasis added, Joyce's ellipses)

The "Paris" of "gaiety" that Gallaher describes is no more real than the "beautiful Paris" that Little Chandler imagines. *Both* these generalizations are tourist clichés. Little Chandler's description of Paris, as one would expect of him, uses the cliché appropriate for polite company. He speaks of that Paris where he could bring his wife, even as he fantasizes about—as though it were one of his narrow streets—the one he would like to visit alone. Gallaher, unable to contradict this cliché, instead superimposes on it, ironically enough, Little Chandler's fantasy city—gay, exciting Paris, which functions as the magical "Araby" toward which the sexually frustrated male Dubliner yearns to travel.

What is at issue in their conversation is not Paris at all but who is going to verify whom in their battle of life-styles. Little Chandler hopes that a worldly man like Gallaher will ease the constant sense of regret that burns in him by confirming for him the fundamental decency of staying in Dublin and sacrificing the pursuit of personal pleasure in order to support a family. Gallaher, however, intends to warm himself by fanning the smouldering regret that is so obviously the cause of Chandler's carefully controlled melancholy. The fact is, Gallaher's unsolicited boast that he has been to the Moulin Rouge and the Bohemian cafes merely reveals that his sophisticated knowledge of Paris has not taken him beyond visiting all of the more lurid tourist traps that anyone with a weekend to spare might also experience. Indeed, Gallaher inadvertently admits as much when he tells Little Chandler how best to confirm all his (imprecise) stories about London: "You ask Hogan, my boy. I showed him a bit about London when he was over there. He'd open your eye" (*D* 77). Gallaher has tried repeatedly, and with no success, to discover the very Paris he is anxious to have Little Chandler believe in. Little Chandler's mounting envy, however, reproduces in him the feeling of having visited this clichéd Paris he has never actually been able to find.

Gallaher would have all his friends believe that these cities (Paris and London) could supply them with the missing dimension of their lives, which could convert the gnomonic structure of their desire into a perpetually satisfied parallelogram. But, in fact, he has returned to Dublin to reacquaint himself with where he has been by learning where it is Chandler and his other Dublin friends wish they could go. He poses as someone who has achieved what others desire, and he does so to generate the belief, which will be authenticated by their envious gaze, that he has satisfied himself. He is, in fact, pursuing himself by interrogating the desire of the other. Later in their conversation, when the nature of Little Chandler's desire grows uncomfortably inscrutable for Gallaher, and the extent of his envy becomes problematic, then Gallaher's earlier eagerness to patronize Chandler's quaintly provincial desire suddenly reveals itself as having been—all along—a ruthless effort to reduce Little Chandler to nothing but a mirror wherein he could perceive the unified image of himself: "I don't fancy tying myself up to one woman, you know. He imitated with his mouth the act of tasting and made a wry face. —Must get a bit stale, I should think, he said" (*D* 82).

Readers witness in this story of the reunion of Little Chandler and Gallaher a rapid collapse from an occasion of elaborate friendliness to one of unmitigated hostility. This suggests the fragility of the seesaw relationship that always exists between subjects who are constantly reconstituting themselves for each other (by validating each other's moi by exchanging language through the je, or speaking subject). The moi is inherently paranoid because it is a mirage upon which the subject bases the validity of existence, yet it can only be experienced as real in relation to the desire and gaze of others. The speaking subject (je) tries to project an aura of spontaneity and originality in its impromptu conversations, but it is a slave of the paranoid moi, struggling to generate those messages in the other that the moi requires in order to believe in its existence relative to the Other.

Thus, Little Chandler opens the conversation with a cliché that supports his elaborately moral life; "is [Paris] so beautiful as they say?" (*D* 76). Gallaher rhetorically digests this adjective to nurture his own discourse: "It's not so beautiful, you know. Of course, it is beautiful. . . . But it's the life of Paris; that's the thing" (*D* 76). Gallaher is determined to convert Chandler's oblique niceties into a no-holds-barred discussion of what is required "if you want to enjoy yourself properly." In such a discussion, of course, Gallaher will emerge as a sort of hedonistic Hercules and Chandler as a pathetic Sisyphus dutifully pushing the weight of his civic responsibilities up the same obscure hill forever. But Little Chandler is not so easily bested. Although Gallaher has sidestepped his received idea about Paris as "beautiful" by superimposing the received idea that it is a city alive with sexual excitement, Chandler does not challenge this characterization. Instead, he superimposes yet another received idea that such pleasure, furtively enjoyed in the sections of Paris that are not beautiful, must therefore be immoral.

> Little Chandler took four or five sips from his glass.
> —Tell me, he said, is it true that Paris is so . . . immoral as they say?
> Ignatius Gallaher made a catholic gesture with his right arm.
> — Every place is immoral, he said. Of course you do find spicy bits in Paris. Go to one of the students' balls, for instance. That's lively, if you like, when the *cocottes* begin to let themselves loose. You know what they are, I suppose?
> — I've heard of them, said Little Chandler.
> Ignatius Gallaher drank off his whisky and shook his head.
> —Ah, he said, you may say what you like.
> There's no woman like the Parisienne — for style, for go.

> Then it is an immoral city, said Little Chandler with timid insis-
> tence—I mean, compared with London or Dublin?
> —London! said Ignatius Gallaher. It's six of one and half-a-dozen
> of the other. (*D* 77)

Gallaher is forever trying to introduce his light hearted adjectives:
"Ah, there's no city like Paris for gaiety, movement, excitement. . . .
There's no woman like the Parisienne—for style, for go" (*D* 76–77),
whereas Chandler, just as obsessively, insists that whatever is not beautiful must be immoral, according to what "they" say. This introduces
a further irony into their conversation: Gallaher has succeeded, better than he can know, in increasing Chandler's suspicion that some
of what they say is immoral may also be beautiful. Yet Gallaher's dogged
resistance to this suspicion is precisely what aggravates Chandler's
suspicion that all Gallaher's exploits in the seamier districts of con-
tinental Europe amounted to nothing more than being professionally
fleeced by a sexual industry specifically designed to appeal to the over-
developed fantasies of the Irishman.[2] "And mind you," Ignatius Gallaher says—with unconscious irony—"they've a great feeling for the Irish
there. When they heard I was from Ireland they were ready to eat
me, man" (*D* 77). Gallaher and Little Chandler each want the other
to verify (to see) who they imagine themselves to be. Paradoxically,
though, to do this they must invent fictions that communicate the structure of their moi to the other person who is supposed to authenticate
it. In doing so, however, they experience their ideal selves as mirages
that continually recede before them the more they (rhetorically) seek
to approach closer to them.

In trying to actualize and authenticate their (fictional) identity,
they become objects in the very discourse that was intended to call
forth their subjectivity for the eyes of the other. Their unconscious
need to be recognized by the Other speaks through them so completely
that they are present in this conversation in Corless's bar only in the
sense that they are watching the other watch them—trying to manipulate the gaze into "seeing who they are." But the more they are forced
to expose their dependence on the gaze, the more hostile they become
to this other who, to preserve the illusion of its own autonomy, sees
who they are as only who they imagine themselves to be—as just a
pose of who they are not.

Let us once again take up . . . the relation to the gaze.

We are at war. I am moving forward over a plain, and I assume myself to be under a gaze lying in wait for me. If I am assuming that, it is not so much that I am afraid of some sign of my enemy, some attack, because as soon as that happens the situation becomes more relaxed and I know who I am dealing with. What matters the most to me is knowing what the other imagines, what the other detects of these intentions of mine, I who am moving forward, because I must screen my movements from him. It is a matter of ruse.

The dialectic of the gaze is maintained on this plane. What counts is not that the other sees where I am, but that he sees where I am going, that is to say, quite precisely, that he sees where I am not. In every analysis of the intersubjective relation, what is essential is not what is there, what is seen. What structures it is what is not there. (Lacan 1988a, 224)

What is "there" in the conversation is that Little Chandler and Gallaher are the most sincere friends. "I wish you and yours every joy in life," Gallaher says when congratulating Little Chandler on his marriage. The fact that these congratulations are two years late ("I didn't know your address") does not dissuade Gallaher from insisting that this is "the wish of a sincere friend, an old friend. You know that?" (*D* 79). One key to Gallaher's success, of course, is that he has learned how to fake sincerity.

After Gallaher lamely declines to accept Chandler's invitation to visit his home, Chandler sees that what is unseen is structuring what is Real: "He saw behind Gallaher's refusal of his invitation. Gallaher was only patronising him by his friendliness just as he was patronising Ireland by his visit" (*D* 80). But as Lacan suggests, intersubjective dialogue is a matter of ruse, so Little Chandler keeps this valuable new insight to himself to flush Gallaher out from his Real position: "Who knows?" Chandler says, "When you come next year I may have the pleasure of wishing long life and happiness to Mr. and Mrs. Ignatius Gallaher" (*D* 81). Little Chandler's strategy here is very clever. In general, I might add, the quality of his conversational strategy with Gallaher has been underappreciated—perhaps because his later collapse at home is so abject. His deliberate thrust against Gallaher's pose as being a man of the world is couched in the rhetorical framework of a toast to a married couple—the very framework that Gallaher used (in a cynical show of "sincerity") to assure Chandler of his friendship. But now, Little Chandler has ceased to operate for him as a mirror that authenticates the unity of his moi, and Gallaher exposes this earlier cynicism by suddenly characterizing marriage as putting his head in a sack: "I'm going to have my fling first and see a bit of life and the world before I put my head in the sack — if I ever do" (*D* 81). Gallaher contradicts his earlier offer of sincere congratulations regarding his friend's marriage by suddenly implying that this marriage is ample evidence of a failure in life on Little Chandler's part, a failure every bit as satisfying to him as that of the alcoholic O'Hara. He depends, in other words, on the failures of his friends to shore up his own dubious success. Gallaher's reason for avoiding marriage, in order to "have my fling first and see a bit of life," inadvertently reveals something that he has taken pains to hide — that he does not feel he has done so even yet. His response — spoken in haste — to Little Chandler's attack betrays all the latent aggression and unsatisfied desire informing his carefully structured pose as a sincere, well-wishing friend of Chandler's who is so content with his own enviable life that he has nothing but boundless benevolence for the sadly stunted lives of others.

To understand why Little Chandler strains to admire Gallaher against mounting evidence that he is being used by him, readers need to glance back at his attitude toward Gallaher, which he expressed a few hours before their meeting in Corless's: "Gallaher's heart was in the right place and he had deserved to win. It was something to have a friend like that" (*D* 70). The delight that Chandler takes in the unexpected attention of Gallaher is so profound that his walk through public streets — normally an activity fraught with anxiety and contradictory impulses — suddenly becomes an act of absolute certitude: "For the first time in his life he felt himself superior to the people he passed" (*D* 73). This moment, in turn, gives him the courage to reconsider his fantasy about becoming, at some point in the future, a published poet admired by a select group of readers. In essence, his extremely high opinion of Gallaher allows him to elevate his own self-esteem. He suddenly experiences the possible gaze of people on the street as unambivalent support of his inherent merits. For the first time, he is modestly confident that unknown reviewers will look upon him and recognize the full complexity of his hidden and unappreciated nature: "Every step brought him nearer to London, farther from his own sober inartistic life. A light began to tremble on the horizon of his mind. . . . He tried to weigh his soul to see if it was a poet's soul. . . . If he could give expression to it in a book of poems perhaps men would listen. . . . The English critics, perhaps, would recognize him as one of the Celtic school" (*D* 73–74). He interprets Gallaher's invitation as bestowing upon him a gaze that opens up his repressed discourse with the gaze of the Other. It is the enormous importance of this discourse (which is usually operating on him unconsciously) that prevents him from discerning Gallaher's obviously self-serving treatment of him.

Even after he is somewhat disillusioned by something vulgar in his friend, Chandler reassured himself that "the old personal charm was still there under this new gaudy manner. And, after all, Gallaher had lived, he had seen the world. Little Chandler looked at his friend enviously" (*D* 77). What Little Chandler finds painful to acknowledge is that Gallaher's regard for him, imagined earlier as a light trembling "on the horizon of his mind," is now exposed as nothing other than his fictional construction of his "self." "The subjective half of the pre-mirror experience," Lacan says, "is the paralytic who cannot move about by himself except in an uncoordinated and clumsy way. What masters him is the image of the ego, which is blind, and which carries him. . . . And the paralytic, whose perspective this is, can only identify with his unity in a fascinated fashion, in the fundamental immobility whereby he finishes up corresponding to the gaze he is under, the blind gaze" (1988b, 50). The subject's dependence on authenticating his identity by recapturing the supposed unity of the mirror stage forces him to perform in the present for a gaze that at some later point will reveal itself as having been a blind gaze—as having "seen" nothing! In this sense, Little Chandler's "self" is very much like his unwritten collection of poems, which he imagines as being observed and evaluated by some omniscient reviewer (the Other), despite the fact that their only claim to existence is his imagined review of what does not exist.

The ego that "carries" Chandler through the Dublin streets is, in a manner never experienced before by him, sure of itself. Chandler feels unified, superior—even poetic. He walks the streets unaware of the crumbling buildings or the desperately poor children. In imagining himself as valorized by Gallaher's gaze, he loses sight of the fact

that the truth of this moment is purely a matter of structuration that
falsely presents reality as all there is of the Real. He can no longer
fail to realize, however, after Gallaher brutally characterizes his marriage as "putting your head in the sack," that Gallaher's gaze seeks
to cancel him out rather than recognize him: "Ignatius Gallaher turned
his orange tie and slate-blue eyes full upon his friend" (*D* 81).[3] Chandler stands up to this hostile scrutiny, but betrays himself in the process "You'll put your head in the sack, repeated Little Chandler stoutly,
like everyone else if you can find the girl" (*D* 81). He betrays not merely
that he is angry but that he is unhappy. In trying to thrust Gallaher's
destructive metaphor back into his face, he has inadvertently confirmed
what he has taken pains to deny—that he finds the phrase an apt enough
description of his situation, "He had slightly emphasised his tone and
he was aware that he had betrayed himself" (*D* 81). This, after all,
is what Gallaher has been angling to discover since the beginning.
All that remains for Gallaher, to win this dueling discourse, is to reiterate the variety of his options compared to those of a married
Dubliner. This he does, promptly, by insisting that the women in his
future will provide him with an unlimited source of wealth and sensual satisfaction.

In essence, Gallaher defeats Little Chandler because Little Chandler bases the validity of himself on the premise that Gallaher admires
him. The reason he does so is that Gallaher's imagined regard happened to connect to his buried discourse between himself and the
Other that relates to his fantasy of becoming a known writer. Gallaher is in a safer position because the fictional gazes that sustain him—
the eyes of French cocottes and wealthy Jewesses—are "elsewhere."
All Gallaher has to do to win the day is display his scorn for Little
Chandler, and this is scarcely an effort because he has barely been
able to keep it in check since the moment when the conversation began. Significantly, Gallaher's final insult about being "tied up to one
woman" is already present *in latent form* in the word choice he employed
when congratulating Chandler on his marriage.

> —Hogan told me you had . . . *tasted* the joys of connubial bliss"
> (*D* 78).

. . . . .

—But I'm in no hurry. They can wait. I don't fancy tying myself
up to one woman, you know.

He imitated with his mouth the act of tasting and made a wry face.

—Must get a bit stale, I should think, he said. (*D* 82)

The idea of all these wealthy, sensual women anxiously waiting for
Gallaher is, of course, ludicrous. The fact, therefore, that Little
Chandler never takes up sarcasm as a weapon, although Gallaher's
ridiculous posturing invites it, and the fact that he confirms, rather
than challenges, Gallaher's brutal characterization of marriage, even
though it directly contradicts his earlier "sincere" congratulations, all
bespeak the frightening depth of Little Chandler's need to believe in
the Gallaher he has invented.

As Lacan's theory of the gaze suggests, Little Chandler cannot
attack Gallaher without tearing himself apart: "In the scopic relation
the object on which depends the phantasy from which the subject is
suspended in an essential vacillation is the gaze. Its privilege . . . derives from its very structure. . . . From the moment that this gaze
appears, the subject tries to adapt himself to it, he becomes that punctiform object, that point of vanishing being with which the subject
confuses his own failure" (1981a, 83). Little Chandler has privileged
Gallaher's gaze to the point where it represents the gaze of the Other.
Like Lacan's "punctiform object," he fantasizes himself as suspended
from the gaze of "Gallaher" (the Gallaher he has invented), and he
cannot challenge the fantasy of "Gallaher" without snapping the fantastic thread that binds him to the desire of the 'other' (and guarantees
his subjectivity). Any revelation that Gallaher's gaze is "blind" reduces
Chandler to that very vanishing point that his adaptation to the gaze
was intended to forestall. Joyce introduces an ellipsis into the narrative
just after Gallaher's comment that being tied to one woman must "get
a bit stale." Did their conversation end at this point? This seems unlikely to me because I imagine Gallaher would take his leave of Chandler with the same elaborate fraudulence he displayed earlier when
he wished him "joy" as a "sincere friend." The conversation, the fancy
bar, the bewildering whiskey—all vanish with the sort of instantaneous
Poof! that one might associate with the conclusion of a magical spell
in a fairy tale. Joyce's dislocation of the narrative shows that Little

Chandler "disappears" at the same moment that Gallaher's gaze is revealed as "blind." It seems certain to me that various awkward pleasantries were to be exchanged by the men as they hastened to leave each other's presence. Their conversation, however, as Joyce's ellipses indicates, is indeed over.[4]

When readers see Chandler again, he is as dispirited as any Cinderella caught out after midnight: "Little Chandler sat in the room off the hall, holding a child in his arms" (*D* 82). Any solace he might have expected at home has been forfeited because he forgot the simple errand that his wife requested of him (to bring home coffee from Bewley's). Judging from the very little one sees of Annie Chandler, one can surmise that she has been housebound with the child and is disappointed at her husband's lateness but assumes he would not be so completely indifferent to the household as to forget the coffee. But readers know that Chandler thinks as little as possible about his home because it represents a demeaning and humiliating trap to him relative to the "freedom" that Gallaher enjoys. His realization that Gallaher scorns him and feels superior to him has only increased the depth of Chandler's envy. What he sees when he looks at Gallaher (despite his "friend's" formidable vulgarity) is a man who is complete, one who has found a way to satisfy all his desires, whenever he chooses, without any dependence on the opinion (or gaze) of others. Gallaher, of course, promotes this image of self-sufficiency by insisting he rules the Symbolic Order of language and women (the objects of exchange that serve as the basis of patriarchal authority): "I've only to say the word and tomorrow I can have the woman and the cash" (*D* 81). Of course, Gallaher's pronouncement is so obviously the result of fear and incertitude that it contains its own negation. Gallaher needs Little Chandler as much as Little Chandler needs him, but, as Lacan points out, it is the peculiar fate of people who are envious to imagine the subject of their envy as possessing in abundance precisely what they lack.

What appalls the envious subject is that the apparent "completeness" of this other person exacerbates latent feelings of fragmentation: "Everyone knows that envy is usually aroused by the possession of goods which would be of no use to the person who is envious of them, and about the true nature of which he does not have the least idea. Such is true envy—that envy that makes the subject pale before the image of a completeness closed upon itself, before the idea that the *petit a,* the separated *a* from which he is hanging, may be for another the possession that gives satisfaction" (Lacan 1981a, 116). In terms of the dialectical discourse between Chandler and Gallaher, one can see that Chandler initially "hangs" from what he imagines to be Gallaher's benevolent gaze; later, he comes to believe that this gaze is something that Gallaher controls, and that Gallaher's possession of it builds his identity into a daunting and unassailable fortress of permanent satisfaction. Unfortunately this leaves him with the impression that the "all-powerful" Gallaher has *declined* to recognize him, instead of understanding that Gallaher's blind gaze has no relationship to the gaze of the Other that Little Chandler dreams of satisfying.

In fact, after Gallaher has discerned that Chandler is becoming less and less willing to flatter him without reserve, he asserts the indomitable quality of his personality more and more vehemently: "Why, man alive, said Ignatius Gallaher, vehemently, do you know what it is? I've only to say the word and tomorrow I can have the woman and the cash. You don't believe it? Well, I know it. There are hundreds — what am I saying? — thousands of rich Germans and Jews, rotten with money, that'd only be too glad" (*D* 81). Too glad to do what? Marry him, presumably, but Gallaher leaves the sentence hanging because he means more than he can say. These "thousands" of women wait for him to say the word so that they might become whatever he needs them to be. Of course, he has no real idea what that is, so the sentence trails off into silence — his silence.[5] Quoted outside the larger context of Chandlers' "identity" drama, Gallaher's impromptu speech, because of what it is unable to say, sounds like the absurd (even desperate) assertions of a lonely, bitter, and insecure man.

But, astoundingly, Gallaher's privileged position as the objet a from which Chandler is hanging lends, even to hyperbole such as this, an authenticity which convinces Chandler that his friend possesses in abundance the missing object without which he can never be happy. The profound impression Gallaher's clumsy bragging has made upon Chandler is not apparent until readers see him look at a photograph of his wife. He compares, unfavorably, the gaze that looks out at him with the gaze he imagines as always looking steadily at Gallaher.

> He looked coldly into the eyes of the photograph and they answered
> coldly. Certainly they were pretty and the face itself was pretty. But
> he found something mean in it. Why was it so unconscious and lady-
> like? The composure of the eyes irritated him. They repelled him
> and defied him: there was no passion in them, no rapture. He thought
> of what Gallaher had said about rich Jewesses. Those dark Oriental
> eyes, he thought, how full they are of passion, of voluptuous long-
> ing! . . . Why had he married the eyes in the photograph? (*D* 83,
> Joyce's ellipses)[6]

In essence, Chandler replaces the actual look of his wife with a gaze
he can only imagine. "Those Oriental eyes," he says. What "Oriental
eyes" does he mean? He is holding a picture of his wife — where is this
other pair of eyes located? "The gaze I encounter . . . is, not a seen
gaze, but a gaze imagined by me in the field of the Other" (Lacan
1981a, 84). It is significant that Little Chandler's sentence trails off
as he imagines this 'other' displaying desire for him with her gaze,
much the way Gallaher's sentence trailed off earlier. In both sentences,
the ellipses occur at the point where the subjects imagine the gaze
(in the position of the objet a) as desiring them.

This sudden void in both sentences gives evidence that the ego,
or the moi, is merely the residue of the relationship between the other
and the Other, rather than anything inherent in the subject. The unconscious of the subject is that which the ego misrecognizes by resorting to silence when its presence is felt. "The system of the ego,"
Lacan states, "isn't even conceivable without the system, if one can
put it this way, of the other. . . . The level on which the other is experienced locates exactly the level on which, quite literally, the ego
exists for the subject" (1988a, 50). The ego is the position from which
we are able to imagine ourselves as the desire of the 'other'; as such,
the ego can be understood as the point at which the subject knows
himself — but only by seeing himself as being seen. The subject experiences the freedom of the ego only by internalizing a sense of "self"
as the object of someone else's gaze thus forfeiting all autonomy. In
this context, one should recall Chandler's exhilaration during his walk
to meet Gallaher, "For the first time he felt himself superior to the
people he passed." This superiority has been constructed relative to
another's gaze and, thus, will be revealed as a fictional reality that
is fragmented in the real.

    Chandler unquestionably is expecting too much when he despises his wife's photograph simply because of his interpretation of her expression. He wants to find in it a gaze he can only conceptualize by describing how secure and ecstatic it would make him feel — if it existed. But in reviling his wife's expression because he finds it insufficiently supportive of himself, he is simply doing to her what Gallaher has just finished doing to him. The photograph is doubly defiant to him because in it Annie is wearing the summer blouse that he bought for her "one Saturday." What he remembers about this purchase is how embarrassed he felt while buying it. He is imagining the present will bring an expression to his wife's face that will somehow reflect that she desires him. His sense of this happening is so acute that he cannot meet the gaze of the shop girls, and he recalls "striving to hide his blushes as he left the shop by examining the parcel to see if it was securely tied" (*D* 82–83) (much like the little boy in "An Encounter" who pretends to check his shoelaces or Gabriel, who compulsively polishes his already shiny shoes). Like Gabriel in "The Dead," Chandler imagines an important, although necessarily vague, scenario wherein his giving of the present will unleash an expression of "voluptuous longing" in his wife that will designate him as its cause. In Gabriel Conroy's elaborate scenario it is the tone of voice he uses in calling Gretta that he imagines will cause her to look at him with a gaze that recognizes his ideal image. Needless to say, the tired glance she gives Gabriel unmans him as much as Annie's prim look unmans Little Chandler.

    Instead of responding to Little Chandler's interior scenario, Annie inquires after the price of the blouse, pronounces it a swindle, and only gradually comes around to thanking him for it. "She was delighted with it, especially with the make of the sleeves, and kissed him and said he was very good to think of her" (*D* 83). What he had been thinking of, of course, is the way that the present would make *her* think of *him!* Joyce devotes a single paragraph to Chandler's response, and the whole of that paragraph is an inarticulate sound followed by an ellipsis: "Hm! . . ." (*D* 83, Joyce's ellipsis). Rather than being reasonably critical of Gallaher, Little Chandler becomes unreasonably critical of his wife. His repressed feeling that he has been defeated by Gallaher brings to consciousness his overdeveloped sense that he has been betrayed by his wife (or, more precisely, by her "prim, lady-like" gaze).

Chandler's sense of his wife as someone whose gaze should exist solely to authenticate him is so overwhelming that, while staring at the photograph, the question of her independent existence—of her desire— disappears altogether and her eyes become a commodity that has turned out to be a bad bargain (unlike the "rich" eyes of Gallaher's wealthy and sensual Jewesses): "Why had he married *the eyes* in the photograph?" (*D* 83, emphasis added).

The crying of the infant introduces an unformed identity who is even more indifferent to other people's search for satisfaction and completion than either Chandler or Gallaher! Chandler's reaction (rocking the child faster and faster while attempting to read the next verse of Byron's poetry) is an apt exemplar of his conduct throughout the day: intently trying to read his own story aloud in the gaze of others while screening out the wailings of their own unsatisfied desire (desire which, once heard, makes their gaze blind relative to him). "It was useless. He couldn't read. He couldn't do anything. The wailing of the child pierced the drum of his ear. It was useless, useless! He was a prisoner for life. His arms trembled with anger and suddenly bending to the child's face he shouted: —Stop!" (*D* 84). His increasingly desperate repetition of the word *useless,* his sudden leap of logic from the literal observation that he "couldn't read" to the conclusion that "he couldn't do anything," and his summation of complete hopelessness that "he was a prisoner for life," all make it clear that Chandler is shouting "Stop!" not so much at his child, but at the world of uncontrollable desire and ceaseless yearning that the child's crying represents. When Annie returns, the irony of Chandler's construction of "the eyes in the photograph" deepens because her literal eyes, which he denigrated as "unconscious and lady-like," now regard him with an open hostility that exposes the self-serving dimension of his earlier construction: "Little Chandler sustained for one moment the gaze of her eyes and his heart closed together as he met the hatred in them. He began to stammer: "—It's nothing. . . . He . . . he began to cry. . . . I couldn't . . . I didn't do anything. . . . What?" (*D* 85, Joyce's ellipses). It is significant that the passion in her gaze, unexpectedly hostile, completely fractures his power of speech. It may not even be the hostility of the expression that unmans him as much as his realization that her expression is unconscious of what he imagines as himself.

My sense is that Annie is exhausted and exasperated—not full of hatred in any profound or permanent sense — when she glares at her husband. We know, for instance, that there is not much money in the family budget ("to save money they kept no servant"). In addition, she has dealt with the child all day while looking forward to Little Chandler's return with the coffee. He has forgotten it, and when she returns from rushing out before the store closes, the child she has tended all day is now screaming inconsolably. Little Chandler's extreme reaction to the look she gives him is also understandable given that he has been critiquing her gaze in excruciating detail the entire time she has been gone. In addition to citing the absence of "passion" or "voluptuousness" in the eyes he married, he also finds "something mean" in them that seems to have imbued the very furniture in the room with a similar quality of meanness: "He found something mean in the pretty furniture. . . . Annie had chosen it herself and it reminded him of her" (*D* 83). I need scarcely point out that Little Chandler's ungracious and petty attitude toward Annie seems more "mean" than any imagined quality in his wife's gaze.

Annie's efforts to make the home pretty are resented by Chandler because he is anxious to see his surroundings as something that entraps him, rather than as a refuge within which he has chosen to hide himself: "A dull resentment against his wife awoke within him. Could he not escape from his little house? Was it too late for him to try to live bravely like Gallaher? Could he go to London? There was the furniture still to be paid for. If he could only write a book and get it published, that might open the way for him" (*D* 83). His association of the very furniture in the room with his wife's "lady-like gaze reveals much more about his own predicament (a subject dependent on another's gaze and, therefore, forced to experience himself as an object) than it does about his wife's personality. "The gaze is not located just at the level of the eyes," Lacan states. "The eyes may very well not appear, they may be masked. The gaze is not necessarily the face of our fellow being, it could just as easily be the window behind which we assume he is lying in wait for us. It is an *x*, the object when faced with which the subject becomes object" (1988a, 220). Chandler's insistence that, but for the unpaid furniture, he might yet become a published author in London is an attempt to give some sort of concrete form to the *x* whose regard alternately buoys up and sinks his sense of subjectivity.

Indeed, both the "gaze" of the furniture and the "gaze" of Chandler's books from his "bachelor days . . . in the little room off the hall" represent that *x*, which the subject imagines as representing the gaze of the 'other'. "Many an evening," Chandler reflects in the early part of the story, "he had been tempted to take one down from the bookshelf and read out something to his wife. But shyness had always held him back; and so the books had remained on their shelves. At times he repeated lines to himself and this consoled him" (*D* 71). The "gaze" of these books, whose existence he associates with his bachelor days clearly have an enduring, even daily, presence for Chandler. The rest of the house is ruled by the primness of the decorations, the "pretty" quality of the furniture, and the dispassionate gaze emanating from his wife's photograph. Chandler drives himself into a near frenzy by fully indulging his resentment of this atmosphere, but one could also argue that they protect him from the gaze of the past — the gaze that constituted "Little Chandler" as a bachelor. Even if Annie has no appreciation or interest in poetry (she certainly has no leisure time to study it), it is unlikely she would refuse, on every occasion, to listen while he read some aloud. What he assumes would be her disinterest is really his own — he hears nothing in the bit of Byron verse that he reads except "the melancholy of his soul," which he longs to "express . . . in verse." He does not want to write poetry, he wants to be regarded as a poet, which is why he is able to "hear" the wording of a review for poems he has not written. The omnipresence of his wife's dispassionate gaze in the photograph and even in the furniture (a gaze before which he will not even read poetry aloud) protects him from having to discover that he has not "a poet's soul."

Little Chandler's perverse insistence on viewing Gallaher's tiresome bragging (and fibbing) about his vulgar exploits as "living bravely" also suggests that he places a much higher premium on being recognized as a poet than on expressing, through the medium of poetry, his soul. The meeting with Gallaher has clearly upset the balance Chandler struggles to maintain between keeping alive the expectations of his bachelor days, while submitting to a highly structured and mortgaged lifestyle ("the furniture still to be paid for") that allows him to protect those expectations from ever being exposed to the actual scrutiny of others. The reviews in his head are, of course written by a reliably benevolent 'other'. The amount of hostility Chandler feels toward his furniture — and toward his wife — cannot be viewed as permanent (any more than her look of hatred when she snatches the crying child from his arms) because one has seen how earnestly he has invited Gallaher to come to this very house and meet his wife. In fact, one could make a case that he actually has a defensive loyalty about his family because it is the keenness of his disappointment at Gallaher's casual refusal of his dinner invitation that finally activates his distrust of Gallaher's motives for having a drink with him. One needs to appreciate how profoundly Gallaher's conversation both bolsters and buffets the secret discourse of Chandler's soul in order to understand how it is that, on this particular evening, Chandler has no ideal image that he "sees" others gazing at and, therefore, no idea at all why he married "the eyes in the photograph."[7]

10

In No Case Shall the Said Bernard Bernard Bodley Be . . .
Repetition and Being in "Counterparts"

> The object is encountered and is structured along the path of a repetition — to find the object again, to repeat the object. Except, it never is the same object which the subject encounters. (Lacan 1988b, 100)

> As he walked on he preconsidered the terms in which he would narrate the incident to the boys:
> —So, I just looked at him — coolly, you know, and looked at her. Then I looked back at him again — taking my time, you know. *I don't think that's a fair question to put to me, says I.* (D 93)

Farrington's problem, in Mr. Alleyne's eyes, is that he is insufficiently machinelike. Ironically, Farrington's hatred and rage, which he directs at himself as well as others, comes about because all his attempts to break free of mechanical routines end up revealing more cruelly the extent to which he lives his life as though he were an automaton. It is precisely because Farrington feels too much like a machine that he is not able to imitate one to the extent that would satisfy Mr. Alleyne. Little in Farrington's life makes him feel unique, and, as a result, he cannot afford to excel at mechanical tasks (mindless repetitions) that describe all too accurately the way he experiences life. To complicate matters, Mr. Alleyne treats Farrington with a compulsive, systematic scorn because he knows that Farrington knows that there is nothing inherently superior in his (Mr. Alleyne's) character that might justify this sort of treatment. Mr. Alleyne, like Gallaher, needs to belittle other men in order to feel good about himself. Like Gallaher, also, he quickly grows to resent the denigrated other whose very humiliation suddenly stands forth as a silent signifier of his own desperate incertitude.

The inescapable fact is that Mr. Alleyne needs Farrington in order to assert his self-worth, whereas Farrington only needs the paycheck that Mr. Alleyne is in a position to withhold from him (Farrington's self-worth depends on his performance in the pub scene). To put this another way, Farrington knows beforehand the use Mr. Alleyne will make of him and, thus, is able (usually) to suffer it with a sense of detachment. The unpleasant relationship of these two men reveals the inevitable hatred that arises from the fact that one can only see oneself as one thinks others see one. One's ego (Lacan's moi) is inherently paranoid because the successful preservation of its (fictional) identity depends on recognition by others (which precludes others from having a point of view of their own). Alleyne and Farrington are locked in the Hegelian master / slave paradigm—a paradigm Lacan discussed to make the point that one desires, rhetorically, to enslave others in an attempt to make them recognize one as who one imagines oneself to be. Yet the more successfully people force an-other to recognize them (that is, the more they master this 'other'), the more they are forced to doubt its worthiness to reflect back to them the ideal 'selves' they believe themselves to be. In other words, masters may feel powerful while they are forcing slaves to degrade their own identities to better reflect the masters'—but of what real use is it, finally, to have secured the recognition of slaves? It is also clear, although Alleyne chooses not to see this, that it is only in the context of his job that Farrington grants him superior status. Were a stranger in a pub to speak to Farrington in the same way, there is little doubt that Farrington would give him a thrashing.

Alleyne repeatedly demands recognition from Farrington, but the repetitive quality of his conduct further reveals the insatiable need for recognition that this very behavior is intended to satisfy. Alleyne has put himself in a position in which his sense of completeness—his self-confidence—depends upon his being recognized by someone he systematically scorns at every opportunity. When people refuse to recognize one, one either retreats in the face of their indomitable otherness (often envying it as Real, which is what Little Chandler does) or one plots to seduce/coerce it into recognizing us. Defeating otherness with this latter strategy, however, only means one is now being recognized by something that — because one has vanquished its point of view — has proven itself unworthy to represent and authenticate the totalized mirror image of ourselves that guarantees the myth of one's own identity. People want others to operate as mirrors for them, Lacan states, but the peculiar structure of the moi — a structure that uses others to verify its own self-sufficiency — puts the subjects in positions of alternately fearing people who refuse to recognize the subjects' selves or compulsively denigrating those people who do offer it. If one coerces or seduces a person into displaying only those reactions that are a reflection of one's own desires (or, if of the feminine gender, only those desires constructed by a masculine culture), then the degraded status of this individual as a mere reflector makes him or her suspect as representative of that something Other needed to authenticate one's being. To state this paradox most simply, the subject is caught in the Groucho Marx paradox of not wanting to belong to any club that would agree to have him as its member.

Mr. Alleyne abuses Farrington by interrupting his speech, and then repeating back to him his own half-finished phrases (as if Farrington had intended them to be complete sentences):

—But Mr Shelley said, sir—
—*Mr Shelly said, sir. . . . Kindly attend to what I say and not to what Mr. Shelly says, sir.* (*D* 87)

. . . . .

—Eh? Are you going to stand there all day? Upon my word, Farrington, you take things easy!
—I was just waiting to see . . .
—Very good, you needn't wait to see. (*D* 88, Joyce's ellipses)

One effect of this tactic is to promote Mr. Alleyne as the phallic signifier who generates the meaning of language. His repetition of Farrington's partially completed statements bestows a meaning on them *only within the context of his own words.* Another effect of this conversational tactic is that Mr. Alleyne reduces Farrington to the level of a malfunctioning machine that must be adjusted rather than a subject who must be listened to. Mr. Alleyne listens to Farrington only long enough to hear a phrase that he can co-opt into his own discourse and designate as the nonsense that makes his own meaning sensical. In this sense, he understands what Farrington has said, even though Farrington has not finished, and he is able to repeat Farrington's fragment as evidence of a malfunction that needs correction. As a result, Farrington is as inscrutable to him as a broken machine: "I might as well be talking to the wall as talking to you" (*D* 87). Mr. Alleyne does not so much "correct" Farrington as he seeks to reprogram him. A machine "says" what one expects to hear, or it merely repeats the phrase "I am broken."[1]

Ironically, Farrington's defense against being ruthlessly transformed into a machine is to deliberately act like one: "Mr. Alleyne began a tirade of abuse, saying that two letters were missing. The man answered that he knew nothing about them, that he had made a faithful copy" (*D* 91). Farrington hides behind the logic that if his purpose is to perform designated tasks with machinelike precision and accuracy, than all mistakes must be the fault of the mind that has programmed him. Accordingly, he adopts a pose that is as stupid and uncomprehending as possible: "I know nothing about any other two letters, he said stupidly. *— You — know — nothing.* Of course you know nothing, said Mr. Alleyne" (*D* 91). Here Farrington has made a complete statement, and this forces Mr. Alleyne to truncate it to continue reducing Farrington's language use to that which, like a machine, either breaks down or performs an expected function. Mr. Alleyne ridicules Farrington as vehemently as possible, but the hysterical quality of his ridicule emphasizes his helplessness in the face of his own creation. Of course this is no ordinary file that has been left incomplete — it is the Delacour file and Miss Delacour, in person, is the principle audience for Mr. Alleyne's self-conscious tirade. It is not surprising, then, that his attack on the otherness of Farrington is even more direct and preemptive than usual. He knows she is watching, and failure to demonstrate autonomy and phallic power in her eyes would constitute a failure to be recognized by the gaze of the Other which, for him, she represents.[2]

In this particular encounter, Farrington has an unexpected advantage over Mr. Alleyne because he has no particular relationship to Miss Delacour. He can appear utterly blank and anonymous in front of her without having to feel that her gaze verifies this anonymous pose as a Real manifestation of his identity. He has never thought of himself in terms of what he imagines she thinks of him, so the coherency and unity of his ideal image is not directly in question. Mr. Alleyne, however, has everything to lose because he has only himself to gain. That is, he has endowed Miss Delacour's gaze with the power to confirm or deflate him. Farrington will be in an identical fix but not until later when he is in Davy Byrne's pub and decides to try and capture the gaze of the woman wearing the bright yellow gloves. Once he has committed himself to doing this, her casual departure from the pub, without so much as a backward glance, nearly proves intolerable. Mr. Alleyne unwittingly increases the degree of his own vulnerability by asking his "machine" (Farrington) to express an opinion about the nature of his identity. He does so in the belief that Miss Delacour will confirm his ideal image of himself as a supremely unified subject who is impervious to disintegration: "Tell me, he added, glancing first for approval to the lady beside him, do you take me for a fool? Do you think me an utter fool?" (*D* 91). The point Mr. Alleyne wishes to make — a point that must be approved by Miss Delacour — is that his sense of "self" is so fantastically immune to fragmentation that he can deliberately call into question his own credibility as a subject and still force a man (whom he is in the act of humiliating) into confirming its unity — even when this confirmation comes at the expense of his own identity.

Once Alleyne has raised the question of whether or not he is a fool, all Farrington needs to do is leave the question open. "The man glanced from the lady's face to the little egg-shaped head and back again and, almost before he was aware of it, his tongue had found a felicitous moment, "I don't think, sir, he said, that that's a fair question to put to me" (*D* 91). Farrington's response (perhaps, because it is almost unconscious) is quite brilliant in that he unexpectedly asserts the indomitability of *his* moi at Mr. Alleyne's expense. His answer explains — for Miss Delacour's benefit, no less — that he *must refrain* fron answering Mr. Alleyne's tirade of abuse, not because he is a robot who merely performs according to the will of others but because it is Mr. Alleyne who has no more control over himself than a machine, and, therefore, his tantrums have no more validity than a sudden burst of static from a blown speaker. Miss Delacour's expression makes it clear that his point is well-taken: "Miss Delacour, who was a stout amiable person, began to smile broadly" (*D* 91). Previous to this reaction on her part, the deliberate glancing of Farrington and Mr. Alleyne established that final possession of Miss Delcour's approving gaze was the feminine prize for which they were vying.[3]

They are like two jousters from the court of King Arthur — Farrington, the pathetic and unlikely challenger dressed in rags, and Mr. Alleyne, outfitted in his armor of burnished steel and brandishing his unbreakable lance. But it is Mr. Alleyne who is decisively unseated from his rhetorical horse — in plain view of the princess who will now bestow her smile on his vanquisher. Farrington's unseating of Mr. Alleyne is so successful that his tormentor is reduced to the ineffectual and ridiculous repetition of a broken machine: "He shook his fist in the man's face till it seemed to vibrate like the knob of some electric machine: —You impertinent ruffian! You impertinent ruffian!" (*D* 91).[4] Mr. Alleyne's subsequent howling for Farrington's apology only underlines the extent of his defeat. By using threats to extract respect from Farrington, he only verifies Farrington's point that asking him to express himself freely on the question of Mr. Alleyne's intelligence is *not* "a fair question." Farrington's apology to Mr. Alleyne, however abject and slavish, cannot fail to reinforce the point that the master depends upon recognition from the slave.

"Speech is mother to the misrecognised . . . part of the subject" (1988b, 43), Lacan writes. In the exchange between Farrington and Mr. Alleyne, each subject strives to establish that the other is a reflection of his own desire. Mr. Alleyne tries to reduce Farrington to the status of an automaton — a mere object. But it is Farrington who routs Mr. Alleyne with a rejoinder that exposes the little man's bluster and rage as the frightened ravings of a decentered nexus hoping to verify his unilateral fantasy of autonomous being. This does not mean, of course, that Farrington is inherently a subject and Mr. Alleyne inherently an object. It simply means that as a result of this particular exchange, witnessed by Miss Delacour, these are the two positions they occupy in relation to one another at the frantic conclusion of their conversation. A given conversation is a bit like a game of chess: careful strategy on the part of both opponents may lead to a draw, but if one person gains an advantage, the game slowly winds down with this person in control of the entire board and the other person unable to move in any direction without precipitating the annihilation of their own moi: "The human being only sees his form materialised, whole, the mirage of himself, outside of himself. . . . It is through the exchange of symbols that we locate our different selves [mois] in relation to one another. . . . It's the symbolic relation which defines the position of the subject as seeing. It is speech, the symbolic relation, which determines the greater or lesser degree of perfection, of completeness, of approximation of the imaginary" (Lacan 1988a, 140–41). Farrington verifies his (fictional) unity in their exchange (his rise in spirits and confidence when he leaves the office is dramatic), and, inversely, Mr. Alleyne experiences the dissolution of this same unity.

"If the object perceived from without has its own identity," Lacan writes, "the latter places the man who sees it in a state of tension, because he sees himself as desire, and as unsatisfied desire" (1988b, 166). In the case of Farrington, *the object unexpectedly becomes a subject* when he utters his (soon to be) famous retort, "I don't think that that's a fair question to put to me," and with that Mr. Alleyne is electrified into a quivering pose of chaotic and unsatisfied desire: "Mr. Alleyne flushed to the hue of a wild rose and his mouth twitched with a dwarf's passion. He shook his fist in the man's face till it seemed to vibrate like the knob of some electric machine" (*D* 91). Even though Farrington briefly experiences a sense of himself as an autonomous being, the only way for him to retain this feeling is to repeat the experience. Subjectivity is the effect of a symbolic exchange between subjects (each trying to reduce the other to an object); it can neither be manufactured nor preserved unilaterally by the subject. The Symbolic Order of language, by which one imagines how the Other sees one, is how one maintains a sense of "self" when alone (dreams, of course, reveal the fragmentary nature of this "self").

This was Lacan's view of Freud's discovery of the repetition compulsion. Freud first identified this compulsion when he watched a child, whose mother had left the room, first toss an object away while uttering the word *fort* (gone), and then pull the object back toward himself while uttering the word *da* (here): "The activity as a whole symbolizes repetition, but not at all that of some need that might demand the return of the mother, and which would be expressed quite simply in a cry. It is the repetition of the mother's departure as cause of a *Spaltung* in the subject — overcome by the alternating game, *fort-da*, which is a here or there, and whose aim, in its alternation is simply that of being the *fort* of a da, and the *da* of a *fort*. It is aimed at what, essentially, is not there" (Lacan 1981a, 62–63). Lacan insisted that the purpose of the game for the child was not to pretend that the mother was returning, but to set up a tension whereby the subject perceives his "self" as lacking something. This initiates human desire, and the child then experiences his own subjectivity by repeating, again and again, the loss and recovery of this missing object needed to complete the "self."

The identity that language allows the subject to call into being is the result of "a process of pure repetition which revolve[s] around the object as lost" (Mitchell and Rose 1982, 34). There is no original object to be found (even though the phallic signifier poses as this original object) because what the subject is seeking is a jouissance with its original "integrated" mirror image. Nonetheless, the subject, through language, repeats, over and over, the discovery of this original object — even though it always turns out to be a substitute for it. Because identity with the original mirror image cannot be consciously "remembered," the act of losing the object is repeated in behavior as a substitution for this lost original moment of jouissance: "The object is encountered and is structured along the path of a repetition — to find the object again, to repeat the object. Except, it never is the same object which the subject encounters. In other words he never ceases generating substitutive objects. . . . We find then, at a materialist level, of the process of the function of repetition as structuring the world of objects" (Lacan 1988b, 100). Because the found object is always a substitute, finding an object offers only the briefest reprieve, even as it inaugurates a renewal of desire.

Farrington's moment of triumph over Mr. Alleyne is extremely brief and begins to erode immediately as he quickly offers him an apology, begins to fear for his job in the future, and returns almost immediately to his earlier anxiety of how to secure money for an evening of drinking. Farrington will devote the rest of the evening to a continual and strenuous effort to repeat this moment of triumph. His anticipation of being called on to tell the story again and again allows him to pawn his watch, comforted with the single cheerful thought that this will provide him with the money necessary to secure a forum in the pub to tell his story. Upon leaving the pawnshop, he demonstrates a security and sense of certitude that has not been seen in him all day: "The man passed through the crowd, looking on the spectacle generally with proud satisfaction and staring masterfully at the office-girls. . . . His nose already sniffed the curling fumes of punch. As he walked on he preconsidered the terms in which he would narrate the incident to the boys: —So, I just looked at him—coolly, you know, and looked at her. Then I looked back at him again—taking my time, you know. *I don't think that's a fair question to put to me,* says I" (*D* 93). Everything that Mr. Alleyne ranted about following Farrington's remark is edited in this first repetition of the story in order to further isolate, elevate, and prolong his moment of triumph. In this preconsideration of how he will tell the story, Farrington immediately deletes the word *sir,* which was part of his original statement. Equally significant, however, is what he retains: the arbitrating presence of Miss Delacour's gaze. What disappears from Farrington's revised account of the event is any evidence of his humiliation and rage. His retort, which one knows popped out of his mouth to his own surprise, is now presented as a careful and deliberate statement, calmly delivered in a manner calculated to ensure maximum effect.

During this mental recitation, Farrington "stare[s] masterfully at the office-girls" because he feels himself to be validated (still) by Miss Delacour's amused and approving smile. One can see that repetition of the event reaffirms the unity of his moi (he seems immune to the fact, for the moment, that he has given up his watch and that Mr. Alleyne's belittlement of him will be even worse tomorrow). Upon entering Davy Byrne's pub, Farrington gets the ball rolling by telling his version of the event to Nosey Flynn. Ater O'Halloran and Paddy Leonard arrive, "the story was repeated to them" (*D* 93). Just as this second recital is winding down, in comes Higgins who witnessed the event: "Of course he had to join in with the others. The men asked him to give his version of it, and he did so with great vivacity" (*D* 93). Significantly, when imitating Mr. Alleyne, "he showed the way in which Mr. Alleyne shook his fist in Farrington's face" (*D* 93). Then, juxtaposed with this picture of incoherent fury, he presents a portrait of the cool and masterful Farrington: "Then he imitated Farrington, saying, *And here was my nabs, as cool as you please,* while Farrington looked at the company out of his heavy dirty eyes, smiling" (*D* 93–94). Imitation of this sort (as opposed to Alleyne's preemptive mockery) is the sincerest form of flattery because it presents a symbolic proof of the integrity of one's existence. Of course, the calm and masterful "Farrington" that Higgins is imitating *was not present* during the scene with Mr. Alleyne. Farrington is watching, with his "heavy dirty eyes," the ideal mirror image of himself implicit in Higgins's imitation of him. In the same way that one's mirror image appears to be perfectly integrated, the image of Farrington presented by Higgins betrays no hint of all the confusion, humiliation, and anger that had rioted chaotically in Farrington's brain when he was forced to absorb the brunt of Mr. Alleyne's tantrum: "The tirade continued: it was so bitter and violent that the man could hardly restrain his fist from descending upon the head of the manikin before him" (*D* 91).

An individual cannot remember any unconscious truth about his past (all recollections are distorted to observe the spurious unification of the moi), yet this same inscrutable truth — the fact that identity is an imaginary unification of conscious and unconscious fragments of the real that exist beyond language — is being acted out all the time along the path of compulsive repetition. The repetitive action, during the moment it is enacted, bestows the appearance of unified subjectivity on a conscious psyche that is always being undermined by the fragmented truth in the unconscious that this unification represses. As Ragland Sullivan summarizes, "Repetition binds the various fragments of the subject together by constantly reaffirming the *moi* as a principle of unity in Real situations" (1986, 112). When Farrington retells his story of the afternoon, and then watches and listens as others tell it, he feels complete because what he has lost (*fort!*) appears to be returning to him via Higgins's performance (*da!*). But in performing this symbolical trick, Farrington's desire demonstrates itself always to be the desire of an-other: "*fort! da!* It is precisely in his solitude that the desire of the little child has already become the desire of another of an *alter ego* who dominates him and whose object of desire is henceforth his own affliction" (Lacan 1982b, 104). If an-other can provide him with a convincing substitute for the lost object of jouissance, it is still only a matter of time before some other strips him of this same object. For this reason, one can see that the repetition compulsion is not the result of frustrated desire, but the lack of recognition of a desire in the Other. Farrington looks for someone other to acknowledge his desire in order for him to then recognize it as his own. Of course, it is not his own, but this recognition of the other permits him to imagine that it is. Thus, Farrington will be able to stare "masterfully at the office-girls" for as long as he is able to repeat in his head the prize-winning comment that won him Miss Delacour's approving gaze).

This drama where repetition mimics the integrity of identity has also been acted out in the nature of Farrington's work. He is a copyist, which is to say he essentially repeats things for a living. Naturally, he takes no interest in the content of what he is transcribing because his job is to reproduce it, not understand it. But on this particular day he has been unable to complete a phrase because it has come to his notice as a strange procession of words: "He stared intently at the incomplete phrase: *In no case shall the said Bernard Bodley be . . .* and thought how strange it was that the last three words began with the same letter" (*D* 90, Joyce's ellipses). Later, when Farrington tries to continue his copying, the reader never learns what Bernard Bodley will or will not "be." Instead, distracted by an impulse toward violence, which will be precisely repeated when he faces Mr. Alleyne later, Farrington writes again the first name Bernard: "He longed to execrate aloud, to bring his fist down on something violently. He was so enraged that he wrote *Bernard Bernard* instead of *Bernard Bodley* and had to begin again on a clean sheet" (*D* 90). This mistake imposes a mood on Farrington that is in distinct contrast to his later masterful mood as he leaves the pawn shop: "His body ached to do something, to rush out and revel in violence. All the indignities of his life enraged him" (*D* 90). This clerical breakdown nearly results in a nervous breakdown and underlines, in concentrated and stark terms, that in no case shall Farrington be — although the "Fort! Da!" repetition compulsion of Farrington/"Farrington" is a viable construct as long as no one notices the mistake.

In Davy Byrne's pub, it is only a matter of time before Farrington seeks further recognition of himself and is disappointed. When the counterpart of Miss Delacour enters the bar, her exotic and colorful dress attracts Farrington's eye: "Farrington's eyes wandered at every moment in the direction of one of the young women. There was something striking in her appearance" (*D* 95). Not surprisingly, he is even more interested in attracting her gaze.

> [W]hen, after a little time, she answered his gaze he admired still more her large dark brown eyes. The oblique staring expression in them fascinated him. She glanced at him once or twice and, when the party was leaving the room, she brushed against his chair and said O, pardon! in a London accent. *He watched her leave the room in the hope that she would glance back at him, but he was disappointed.* He cursed his want of money and cursed all the rounds he had stood, particularly all the whiskies and Apollinaris which he had stood to Weathers. If there was one thing that he hated it was a sponge. He was so angry that he lost count of the conversation of his friends. (*D* 95, emphasis added)

What is significant in this description is that Farrington does not desire this woman solely in the animal sense of wanting access to her body for his own pleasure. On a more complex level, he demonstrates human desire in that what he longs for is not the body of but the Desire of the other. As I have already suggested, to desire the Desire of another is to demand recognition from that other. Lacan writes, "It is indeed through the mediation of demand that the sexual function enters into the circuit of desire. But the predominance of demand is precisely what characterises the neurotic in his dependency on the demand of the Other, as he flees from the point where his desire places his being in question" (1982b, 121). The evidence suggests that the woman from the Tivoli has indeed noted his interest in her but has not thought much of it. This combination — of her having noticed him, but only with an "oblique staring expression" — puts in doubt the earlier recognition scene with Miss Delacour. Accordingly, Farrington loses himself once more, as he did after inadvertently repeating the name Bernard, in a maelstrom of incoherent rage, unbearable longing, and a sense of fragmentation that is so profound he can no longer comprehend the conversation of his friends in the pub.

Farrington cannot rest assured that his earlier acquisition of the gaze of Miss Delacour will be made permanent because this past event depends upon his maintaining a masterful future: "What did I try to get across with the mirror stage? That whatever in man is loosened up, fragmented, anarchic, establishes its relation to his perceptions on a plane with a completely original tension. The image of his body is the principle of every unity he perceives in objects. Now, he only perceives the unity of this specific image from the outside, and in an anticipated manner. Because of this double relation which he has with himself, all the objects of his world are always structured around the wandering shadow of his own ego" (Lacan 1988b, 166). If Farrington cannot sustain a sense of unity and mastery in the present, then, retroactively, past moments of seeming jouissance are subverted and revealed as self-delusion. Gabriel Conroy has a similar moment of retroactive self-hatred that is actually experienced relative to his mirror image: "He saw himself as a ludicrous figure, acting as a pennyboy for his aunts . . . the pitiable fatuous fellow he had caught a glimpse of in the mirror" (*D* 219–220). Farrington's subsequent loss to the artiste, Weathers (undertaken for the "National honour" of Ireland, no less), in full view of all his drinking buddies, unexpectedly strips Farrington of a recognition he had enjoyed among other men. Once alone and, thus, unobserved by anyone, he tabulates this loss, along with the loss of the approving gaze of Miss Delacour (who is represented, interchangeably, by the woman from the Tivoli): "He had lost his reputation as a strong man, having been defeated twice by a mere boy. His heart swelled with fury and, when he thought of the woman in the big hat who had brushed against him and said *Pardon!* his fury nearly choked him" (*D* 96–97).

This sets the stage for Farrington's final attempt to reincarnate his selfhood. By beating his child for letting the fire go out, Farrington "becomes" Mr. Alleyne. This is the most pathetic defeat of all during his miserable day because slaves who imitate the brutality of their masters have given up the search for their own autonomy. By imitating Mr. Alleyne (in a dark repetition of the way Higgins imitated him earlier in the evening), Farrington submits himself to the all-powerful authentic 'otherness' of the master. Like Mr. Alleyne, Farrington selects for his abuse someone who depends upon him for his livelihood and who, therefore, cannot escape or call attention to the unfairness of the treatment given to him. Paradoxically, in his position astride another human being whom he is beating with a stick, Farrington is a more abject slave than he was at the beginning of the story because he no longer recognizes the dependence of Mr. Alleyne on the gaze of the Other. Instead, similar to what Little Chandler does with

Gallaher, Mr. Alleyne is elevated to the status of the 'other' as that which must be imitated in order to authenticate identity. The boy, however, even in the posture of the completely helpless slave ("seeing no way of escape [the boy] fell on his knees"), intuitively understands the appalling lack in being of the man who is beating him. In his desperation, the boy formulates a remarkably astute strategy; he offers to pray, in a manner honored by Catholic convention, for the return to his father of the lost gaze of "the Woman": "— O, pa! he cried. Don't beat me, pa! And I'll . . . I'll say a *Hail Mary* for you. . . . I'll say a *Hail Mary* for you, pa, if you don't beat me. . . . I'll say a *Hail Mary*" (*D* 98, Joyce's ellipses).[5]

11

Where the Corkscrew Was
The Purpose of Insignificance in Joyce's "Clay"

> For whoever is encumbered with the phallus, what
> is a woman?
>   A woman is a symptom. (Lacan 1982b, 168)

> Maria understood that it was wrong that time and
> so she had to do it over again: and this time she got
> the prayer-book. (*D* 105)

What relief the character of Maria provides for the reader of *Dubliners!* For once, Joyce's hidden meaning is seductively unambiguous, even if it is subtly presented: Maria wishes she were married, but because there is no longer the least likelihood of this, she cannot afford to acknowledge this desire. As a result, her every encounter—from her pathetic courtship with "the colonel-looking" drunkard on the bus to her mistake in repeating the first verse of "I Dreamt that I Dwelt"—has a dual significance. On one level, she insists that everything is "so nice," yet readers are consistently in the masterful position of seeing this is not so. What Maria compulsively labels as "nice," readers see as a near miss on her part with the central repressed truth of her life, which is that her disappointing failure to marry not only dictates all she does but also supports all she fails to do. If read this way, the story has an element of suspense to it: Will Maria be forced to see herself as readers see her? and What will happen if she is directly confronted with the pathos of her own condition?[1] But my question is the inverse of this one: What happens to the reader if Maria's condition is not all that pathetic or, at least, no less pathetic than Joe Donnelly's, for example? What if her helplessness is in part a masquerade that makes her the central component of Joe's sense of himself and, therefore, makes her crucial to him as "his proper mother"?[2] It is her function as what Lacan calls the (m)Other that makes her a crucial player in the Donnelly family romance that is acted out, once again, on All Hallow's Eve. Critics love to quote the unsung second verse about "suitors on bended knee" to explain Maria.[3] My argument is that the narrator lets *the reader* sing this second verse and does not try to show readers their mistake.

In a recent essay, Margot Norris has helped make a reexamination of this story possible by implicating the reader as a cause of Maria's problems: "It is we, as critical and perceptive readers, who create the pressures that necessitate Maria's defensive maneuvers in the way she invents her story" (1987, 214). She goes on to expose the other defensive critical ploy in reading this story, which is to assign Maria grandiose metaphorical status as the Virgin Mary, Ireland, the Whore of Babylon, and so on: "Readers and critics can no more accept the possibility of Maria's insignificance than can Maria herself" (1987, 206).[4] My argument begins by accepting that Maria is insignificant and that the efforts by various critics to assign her significance as a metaphorical figure have obscured Joyce's more central purpose, which is, as Norris notes, to explore "her need, and her strategies, for promoting herself" (1987, 206). Yet Norris's phrase "promoting herself" seems a qualification of her assertion that Maria is insignificant. To be promoted, after all, either by one's own efforts or the effort of others, is to advance in station, to rise, to move up a grade—to become more significant. Maria, however, does not succeed in making herself more significant (although many critics have succeeded for her). I wish to argue that *what Maria promotes is her insignificance!* Her naïve, childlike dependence on people is what makes her indispensable to them.

Lacan makes the point that a woman learns to pose as lack—as something castrated and outside the domain of phallic power—to become something indispensable for the male subject who seeks to reify masculinity. The fact is, neither men nor women possess the phallic signifier that would make them a bastion of certitude or fountain of truth, so women pretend to have lost it so that men can believe they might yet find it again. After all, it is better to believe the signifier of the unified self is temporarily lost rather than discover it is a permanent illusion (and that masculinity is a permanent illusion). Yes, Maria is insignificant — but who is not? Significance is a matter of attitude and position toward the nonexistent phallus. Joyce explores Maria's need for strategies of self-promotion, but in doing so he exposes the readers' strategies as well. I suggest that because significance is a construct and an attitude, insignificance must be as well. I have long been uneasy in teaching this story to undergraduates because as their admiration for my presentation of the story grows, I am forced, not unlike Joe Donnelly, to see that *I need Maria* in order to enjoy my role as a master explicator. In a collection of stories where so many characters are too much like the readers, it is Maria's profound and unambiguous insignificance, relentlessly presented in all the minutiae of her trip across town, that makes her so important to the reader.

Again, I agree with Norris when she explains the dynamic that powers Maria's strategies of self-promotion: "The symptoms the old maid's lacks produce are therefore not solitary brooding and depression but social strategies designed to capture significance by winning the approval of the 'other'" (1987, 207). What I cannot accept is the implication that this dynamic is unique to Maria and, somehow, the sad result of her particular insignificance. To highlight Maria's "paltry stratagems," Norris points out that anyone visiting the laundry where Maria works "finds its status as a laundered whorehouse advertised on its wall. . . . The narrative voice skillfully keeps the true purpose of the laundry a secret" (1987, 209). but what is the "true" purpose of these tracts? Maria, quite legitimately I think, dislikes them because they only tell her what she means to the people who maintain this charity. Her marginal life, as this marginalia makes clear, helps center people. The walls of the laundry are the male gaze passing judgment on errant femininity and defining the negativity of these "lost" women as the sign that makes the positive quality of masculinity visible. This is — as close as one can figure — the "true" purpose of these tracts. Certainly, Joyce was aware of Blake's aphorism from "The Marriage of Heaven and Hell": "Prisons are built with stones of Law, Brothels with bricks of Religion." Certainly the *Dublin by Lamplight Laundry* has been built with the bricks of polite Dublin society who are happy to support this institution because it acts as a foil that allows their own spurious virtue to shine forth. Joyce describes a similar dynamic when explaining to Stanislaus the meaning of "Dublin by Lamplight" in the story: "The phrase *Dublin by Lamplight* means that Dublin by lamplight is a wicked place full of wicked and lost women whom a kindly committee gathers together for the good work of washing my dirty shirts" (Ellmann 1975, 157). Joyce's repetition of "wicked" and his ironic reference to the committee as "kindly" suggest that in his explanation to Stanislaus he is deliberately parodying the tone of the self-aggrandizing tracts that Maria has to look at every day. The committee for the Dublin by Lamplight Laundry presents its concern for these women as charitable; but in fact, it is a place where their dirty laundry is washed both literally and symbolically while they praise their own self-sacrifice and Christian virtue; now *that* is a "paltry stratagem," and Norris is unwittingly aligning herself with it when she scorns Maria's instinctive resistance to it.

Hugh Kenner has termed Joe's wife "another Mrs. Mooney," referring to the redoubtable woman who coerces Bob Doran into proposing to her daughter Polly. Kenner says that Mrs. Donnelly "has eased [Maria] into the laundry and one may suspect will soon ease her into a convent" (1956, 57). Maybe, but wherever she sends Maria, she will never get rid of her because Maria is more important to Joe than she is. Indeed, if one looks past one's need to portray Maria as pathetic, one can see that she dominates the evening at the Donnelly's because Joe spends the entire evening trying to impress her with his job, his wit, and his hosting abilities. Maria's obvious impotence drives him to represent himself as powerful, and his failure to do so convincingly sends him drifting into the past toward some point where he recalls being unified and certain of himself. It is from this dangerous drift that Joe seeks to save himself when he asks his wife to tell him where the corkscrew is.

And readers who gaze at Maria are comfortable with her profound incompetence, not fully aware, perhaps, that their strenuous attempts to delimit the extent of her pathos puts them squarely in the hopeless position of Joe Donnelly. They marvel that she does not seem to be suffering despite her limitations and miss the fact that the story closes, not on Maria but on a description of Joe's reaction to her song: "[Joe] said that there was no time like the long ago and no music for him like poor old Balfe, whatever other people might say; and his eyes

filled up so much with tears that he could not find what he was looking for and in the end he had to ask his wife to tell him where the
corkscrew was" (*D* 106).[5] I suggest that he experiences a dissolution
of personality nearly as dramatic as Gabriel's at the close of "The Dead,"
and he does so not because Maria has failed to move on to the second
verse but because her repetition of the first verse mirrors his own paralytic repetitiveness where he yearns, in an obviously well-established
pattern, for an imagined unity of being in "the long ago."[6] His defen-
siveness about this regressive point of view ("whatever other people
might say") makes it clear that others, from time to time, have tried
to push him into "the second verse" of his life.

The first verse that Maria sings says at least as much about herself
and Joe as the famous forgotten verse. A girl remembers, as if in a
dream, a time when she was wealthy, satisfied, and loved.[7] This time,
part memory and part fantasy, corresponds to what Lacan called the
Imaginary Order, which is a period of time in which individuals mistake their mirror images for themselves, that is, as proof that they
are unified and autonomous beings.[8] The Imaginary, in Lacan's sense
of the term, seeks to subvert the Symbolic Order of rules and substitutions that places the subject in a permanent round of insatiable 'desire' that lacks the jouissance, the effortless fusion, of "the long ago."
Consciousness is, in fact, a fragmented phenomenon, alternately shored
up by ideal ego identifications and torn down by unconscious Desire,
but the subject dimly recalls this prior time of effortless unity and unqualified certitude and tries, in present time, to recapture the certainty
of this earlier misrecognition.

Joe's weepy breakdown at the close of this story suggests that he
has been ambushed by the Imaginary, and the inertia that causes Maria
to repeat the first verse is the same inertia that causes him to sit down
with her by the fire "talking over old times" (*D* 101). Joe's feeble attempt to impress Maria with some smart remark he made at work
only seems to have revealed to him what an awkward construct his
current persona is. When subjects try to confirm the myth of themselves by seducing another into authenticating it for them, they are
in danger of perceiving the fictional dimension that underlies the truth
about themselves. As Lacan puts it, "Does the subject not become
engaged in an evergrowing dispossession of that being of his . . . he
ends up by recognizing that this being has never been anything more

than his construct in the Imaginary and that this construct disappoints all certitudes" (1981b, 11). I suggest this describes the downward trajectory of Joe Donnelly from a braggart to a confused and hesitant man. The "lost" Maria living at the laundry is certainly no more lost than the Joe Donnelly readers witness in the concluding moments of the story.

Maria sings, "I dreamt that I dwelt in marble halls / With vassals and serfs at my side / And of all who assembled within those walls / That I was the hope and the pride." (*D* 106). In this state of mind, the subject's sense of self is assured, and others exist only as confirmation of that "self." But there is a second part of the dream, which the singer identifies as more important than the first: "But I also dreamt, which pleased me most, / That you loved me still the same" (*D* 106). The certitude of the first part of the dream depends upon Maria being the desire of what Lacan designates as the Other. The Other is the fantasized place to which subjects direct the question of their identities. It is the place where the subject presumes that knowledge and certitude reside because this place guarantees the authenticity of the ideal mirror image. One of the earliest representations of the gaze of the Other for a child is the gaze of the Mother (hence, Lacan's collapsing of these two terms into the word *(m)Other*). All night long Joe has been performing for Maria's gaze, but it is, perhaps, while listening to her song that he sees that she is lost in the fantasy of her own mirror stage; she may be his "proper mother / (m)Other," but she is not looking at him, which leaves him nowhere. Instead, she is dreaming of her ideal unity and imagining herself as a subject certified by the Other ("*I* was the hope and the pride. . . . *you* [the ideal image] loved me still the same"). This is a self-confirming dialectic that leaves no place for Joe, and he fades out, just like Gabriel at the conclusion of "The Dead," although readers are not privy to his thoughts. One could make a case that Joe would have been *relieved* to hear the second verse of the song where he could have at least found a place for himself among the many suitors gathered at Maria's knee.

Critics shake their rhetorical heads at the sadly deluded Maria when she looks in the mirror and sees "the diminutive body which she had so often adorned. In spite of its years she found it a nice tidy little body" (*D* 101). After all, so the argument runs, she *must* be wrinkled and ugly, but it is Maria's consciousness that is being described, not her body. The critic who views her appreciation of her body as sadly deluded is betraying the patriarchal illusion that a woman's body can only have the value assigned to it by the gaze of a man. Indeed, one reason Maria frightens and disconcerts people is that she seems capable of valuing herself despite the nearly complete absence of social accolades. Maria's private review of her body is remarkably unmediated by an imagined male gaze (contrast it with Gerty MacDowell and Molly Bloom). What is astonishing about her perception (and this may begin to explain why she is not as miserable as readers think she should be) is that she still sees her image and her consciousness as equally unified. Compare this to Gabriel's perception of his reflection: "As he passed in the way of the cheval-glass he caught sight of himself in full length, his broad, well-filled shirt-front, the face whose expression always puzzled him when he saw it in a mirror and his glimmering gilt-rimmed eyeglasses" (D 218). Gabriel feels his own fragmented consciousness to be at odds with the unified man in a "well-filled shirt-front" that looks out at him. When shame overwhelms him, he compares his state of mind once again to his mirror image: "He saw himself as a ludicrous figure, acting as a penny-boy for his aunts, a nervous well-meaning sentimentalist, orating to vulgarians and idealizing his own clownish lusts, the pitiable fatuous fellow he had caught a glimpse of in the mirror" (D 219–20). The unified mirror image is clearly seen as fraudulent — a facade whose apparent seamlessness covers a wavering consciousness that is constantly at the beck and call of others, in an endless pursuit for recognition.

Yet readers of *Dubliners* insist that it is Maria who is the helpless one. It is true that, from a social and cultural purview (the realm of what Lacan calls the Symbolic Order), she has been excluded, circumvented and ignored, but paradoxically this has made her a powerful childlike figure. Joe and the reader alike are at a loss to explain how it is she could be existing at all. One's collective horror about Maria's plight betrays one's own privileging of the Symbolic Order of language and culture. The paradox of Maria is that because she is outside the privileges of the patriarchial order and deprived of the phallus — because she is an alarming incarnation of otherness — she possesses the powerful gaze of the (m)Other that upholds the Phallic Order of which she is so significantly not a part. So one experiences a feeling of horror, that is really relief, at the appalling helplessness of an elderly woman whose 'self' construct is so transparent. The transparency and self-deception of Maria allow the reader to appropriate her desire and place it at the center point of the reader's own certitude.

Readers are so caught up in shoring up their "selves" at Maria's expense, they fail to see how poorly Joe is doing in his attempt to do the same thing. All night long he has been trying to get her to recognize him and acknowledge him as the object of her desire. In Lacanian terms, Joe is distracted and nearly exhausted from pretending to have the Phallus (which would make him masculine), and Maria is a good deal calmer because her role is to be helpless in order to demonstrate that she does *not* have the Phallus. Because the Phallus does not exist as an imagined signifier for unity and certitude, masquerading as one who possesses the Phallus (masculine) can be as debilitating as posing as one who does not (feminine). Certainly, Maria has been disempowered by a partiarchial culture that cannot see her worth — cannot see her at all — because she is a virgin past childbearing age (that is, neither a whore nor a madonna). From the point of view of the patriarchial order, she is dead, and it is appropriate that her annual visit to the Donnelly's takes place on Halloween, when the dead walk. But ghosts, as Hamlet and Stephen Dedalus well knew, have a far greater capacity to disturb life than do the living. Because Maria is a child, her presence allows Joe's childhood to haunt him; because she nursed him, her function as his (m)Other makes her gaze something that Joe tries to capture as the authentification of his mirror image "long ago" when he once was (so he believes) the unified subject he now must imagine himself to be.

In Lacanian theory, a signifier can only signify something by being opposed to another signifier. This means that there is no signified — only signifiers that pose as signifieds in a given discourse (and, thus, are always subject to shifts in meaning). The subject reacts to the dislocation of losing a sense of primordial unity with the mother (castration) by becoming masculine or feminine. One lines up under one banner or the other in accordance with one's relationship to the phallic signifier that stands for the difference and lack in the linguistic and Symbolic Order that permits substitutive Desire. In this regard, one can say that the phallic signifier guarantees meaning and knowledge by establishing an insatiable wanting. The male, because he has a penis, poses as having the Phallus. But this pose is false because the phallic

signifier represents the fact that language is a system of constant substitutions based on lack, with no signifier ever achieving the status
of an absolute signified. The paradox, as Rose explains, is that "the
phallus can only take up its place by indicating the precariousness
of any identity assumed by the subject on the basis of its token" (Mitchell
and Rose 1982, 40). Anatomical difference means nothing in terms
of inferiority and superiority until it is made to figure gender difference. The penis exists, but its representation as a guarantee of certitude in the figure of the phallus is false.

A woman masquerades as not having the Phallus so as to convince a man that he does have it, and this comedy of nonrelation is
what Lacan calls love. The difficulty for a woman is that all her power
in the Symbolic Order is obtained by her only inasmuch as she is convincingly helpless. The difficulty for a man is that he must appear
as complete and powerful when he is no less helpless than the woman.
As Lacan puts it, "What might be called a man, the male speaking
being, strictly disappears as an effect of discourse, . . . by being inscribed within it solely as castration" (1982b, 44). The phallus, therefore, is something of seeming value that can only perform its function
when its fraudulent dimension is veiled. When one sees Joe preempt
Maria's distress about the missing plum cake by declaring, "It didn't
matter," one learns that what does matter is that she must listen to
his stories about work: "[He] made her sit down by the fire. He was
very nice with her. He told her all that went on in his office, repeating
for her a smart answer which he had made to the manager. Maria
did not understand why Joe laughed so much over the answer he had
made" (*D* 101).[9] Here the absurdity of their intersubjective exchange
is highlighted: Joe tries to get her to verify his superiority to "the
manager" — to acknowledge his possession of the phallus — and she, as
a result of a lifetime of cultivating helplessness and ignorance of "a
man's world" — does not know what he is talking about! Significantly,
readers never hear Joe's "smart answer": Joe, to use Lacan's term,
"strictly disappears" because his fraudulent posture as being the Phallus, presented to someone who would never presume to have it, in-
scribes him into his own discourse as castrated.

Maria does not understand "why Joe laughed so much over the
answer," but it is really the same reason why, when Lizzie Fleming
says she'll get the ring (get married and align herself with phallic power),

"Maria had to laugh and say she didn't want any ring or man either" (*D* 101). Joe is laughing longer than necessary because Maria is not laughing at all, and her inability to shore up his "smart answer" reveals to him that he is only exposing his incertitude with the very story intended to confirm his completeness. Maria's incomprehension cannot fail to leave his own stratagems rather threadbare. Characters in *Dubliners* frequently laugh, not because they are happy, but because no one else is, and, therefore, they must pretend to be. When Farrington makes his "smart answer" to Mr. Alleyne, no one laughs. Because there was a woman present when he made the remark (the very reason he was prompted to make it), Farrington knows he will be further subjected to Alleyne's wrath in the future.

Instead of laughing, Maria tells Joe, "The manager must have been a very overbearing person to deal with." But Joe has switched tactics; if he cannot get Maria to confirm his masculinity, he also cannot endorse her potentially subversive assessment of all displays of masculinity as overbearing: "Joe said he wasn't so bad when you knew how to take him, that he was a decent sort so long as you didn't rub him the wrong way" (*D* 104). The manager, whom Joe pretended to dominate, is now a powerful force around whom he is happy to tiptoe. Following this exchange, readers learn of the first missing item in the story: "Nobody could find the nutcrackers and Joe was nearly getting cross over it and asked how did they expect Maria to crack nuts without a nutcracker" (*D* 104). Readers know the next-door girls have seen to it that the nuts have been "handed round," so Joe's anger that *Maria* has been prevented from cracking the nuts is significant. Whenever Joe fails to demonstrate wholeness and mastery, he looks to the women in the story to help him out. [10] This behavior is repeated at the end of the story when Maria's song reduces him to a state in which "he could not find what he was looking for and in the end he had to ask his wife to tell him where the corkscrew was" (*D* 106). Here I wish to stress that the corkscrew is more than what one routinely calls a phallic symbol. Its function is that of a missing object, which would, if present, grant Joe the ability to open a bottle he is otherwise helpless to open. This presents the corkscrew as a phallic signifier in Lacan's more complex use of that term as a fantasy object intended to complete and authenticate subjectivity.

When Maria says she does not want "any ring or man either," she is not denying the obvious (that she desperately wants a man) but stating the truth of what is apparent to no one but herself: she is too young to think seriously of marriage.[11] Her disclaimers, accompanied by blushing and nervous laughter, are those of a young girl. Just before she views her "nice tidy body in the mirror," she thinks "of how she used to dress for mass on Sunday morning when she was a young girl" (*D* 101). One can gather that every time she prepares herself for Sunday mass she recalls herself as a young girl, and this allows for a constant return of a mental image of youth (which may help shape her perspective of her figure as "a nice tidy little body"). At Joe's party readers learn that "all the children had their Sunday dresses on" including "two big girls in from next door" (*D* 103). These are the two girls who will play the trick on Maria with the saucer. As they are next door, and not part of the family, what is their motive? I suggest they resent Maria not because she is an old woman but because she is an old woman who flirts like a young girl and who expects the same sort of consideration from men that they are hoping to attract.[12] The way Joe sits her down and provides for her (a suitor at her knee) might well sharpen their resentment. They are outraged that she should presume herself to be one of them, and their trick is intended to distance themselves from her and force her to identify with a saucer, designated as "no play," that is normally not allowed in the game.

Maria's girlish ways are evident well before the party. She is still puzzled, even after all the years since her youth, as to why "none of the young men seemed to notice her" (*D* 102). She does not expect them to be chivalrous to an old lady; rather she is surprised that they neglect the opportunity to impress a young girl. Likewise, in the cake shop, the shopclerk's terse question — Was it wedding cake she wanted to buy that was taking her so long? — is again interpreted as a risqué comment to make to a girl rather too young to be thinking of men (I suggest the shopclerk assumes that she is a mother come to shop for a wedding cake for her daughter): "That made Maria blush and smile at the young lady" (*D* 102). A very similar situation occurs to one of the next-door girls at the party at Joe's house, "When one of the next-door girls got the ring Mrs. Donnelly shook her finger at the blushing girl as much as to say: *O, I know all about it!*" (*D* 105, Joyce's emphasis). The irony inherent in Maria's interpretation of other people's teasing of her is that all their teasing, which readers may know to be generated by their perception of her as an old lady, she could equally well view as appropriate to the teasing of a young girl. Why, for instance, is she the only adult allowed to approach the saucers? From her point of view it is because she is yet to be married, like the next-door girls. Mrs. Donnelly's comment that "Maria would enter a convent before the year was out because she had got the prayer-book" is a comment much more appropriate to a young Maria than an old one who is obviously going to remain at the laundry until she is too old to care for herself. The next-door girls are aware of Maria's special status, and their addition of a saucer to Maria's turn represents their bid to expose the absurd claims of a preposterous rival.

Maria's extremely circumscribed life allows her to remain, quite a bit of the time, half-conscious in the illusory mirror-stage state that Lacan designated as the Imaginary Order. There is no one in the story whom Maria sees as anything but a confirmation of the young girl with the tidy little body whom she views every day in the mirror. A drunken older man, for example, is transformed into "a colonel-looking gentleman." It is interesting that this transformation follows from, and depends upon, the young men who inexplicably (from Maria's point of view) ignore her: "She reflected how much more polite he was than the young men who simply stared straight before them" (*D* 103). These young men are not ignoring her—they simply do not see her as a young girl—and so Maria misinterprets their indifference as puzzling behavior in order to infuse her elderly gentleman with something approaching charm. This is what makes Maria so oddly indomitable; she allows a favorite selection of compliments to play constantly like music in the background of her thoughts. She does not view the "colonel-looking" gentleman as a serious flirtation because he is too old for her. For this reason she imagines the attention she pays to him as especially charming for him: "Maria agreed with him and favoured him with demure nods and hems" (*D* 103). What strikes her as so "gentlemanly" about this man is that he acknowledges her bow, bows back, and does not require more of her. Only an old man would still know how to exhibit the courtship manners that the "young Maria" still recognizes. Later, when she realizes she has left her plum cake behind, her shame and disappointment is magnified by the realization that she was more interested in this elderly gentleman than she should have been; she has betrayed the cardinal rule given to young girls,

"Don't talk to strangers!" Significantly, there is no suggestion that she tells anyone at Joe's house about the encounter. In this way, she is once again similar to the next-door girl who blushes at getting the ring but still keeps her own counsel as to how near fruition the prediction is.

Maria's resistance to understanding her place in the Symbolic Order causes her to constantly repeat herself in language and behavior rather than decode her Imaginary meaning into Symbolic meaning (which would force her to move from the fantasy that she is a girl too young to think about marriage to the realization that she is an old maid too old to hope for it). The principle of repetition is Maria's chief strategy for clinging to mirror-stage identifications. At every point where outer realities challenge an inner ideal, she repeats some previous behavior in a constant attempt to relive her history as a young girl in the present ("I was the hope and the pride," as she sings in her song). Another reason, therefore, that she repeats the first verse of *I Dreamt That I Dwelt* is that the second verse has the Bohemian girl dreaming about her movement from the Imaginary Order of "marble halls" and "vassals and serfs at my side" into the Symbolic Order of marriage.

Maria repeats the verse because she does not want to get married; she repeats it because she wants to remain a young girl — and as a sexual outcast from the Symbolic Order (an aging virgin), the fantasy of being a young girl is the only one left to her. Were she to move beyond this fantasy of the first verse, then she would understand the symbolism of the fourth saucer. As it is, all the teasing makes her happy because it supports her view of herself as a young girl. Repetition in Maria's life staves off the insistence of the untold story of growing older that is pressuring the "self" construct of her fictional identity as a young girl. Joe, as I have pointed out, reacts to Maria as though she were his mother, but Maria interprets even his attentions as slightly flirtatious. Her characterization of his attitude toward her is identical to that of the elderly gentleman: "He was very nice with her." He presses gifts upon her (the bottle of stout, a glass of wine, the nuts and nutcracker), and Maria's submission to this "courtship" is presented in the sexually coded phraseology of the romance novel: "So Maria let him have his way and they sat by the fire talking over old times" (*D* 104). Curiously, it is Maria who breaks this mood by introducing the subject of Joe's chief rival for her function as a mother or a lover, his brother Alphy.

There is a polymorphous dimension to Maria and Joe's relation-ship that lends credence to Lacan's assertion that there is no sexual relation — only attempted seductions of the other in an attempt to au-thenticate the myth of one's "self." Maria's repetitive need to see all men as courting the young girl she imagines herself to be is directly at odds with Joe's request that she be the mother who confirms that he is the Phallus that she lacks and, therefore, desires. Lacan describes the dynamic of the sexual relation in terms of Desire and the Phallus this way:

> If the desire of the mother *is* the phallus, then the child wishes to be the phallus so as to satisfy this desire. Thus the division imma-nent to desire already makes itself felt in the desire of the Other, since it stops the subject from being satisfied with presenting to the Other anything real it might *have* which corresponds to this phallus — what he has being worth no more than what he does not have as far as his demand for love is concerned, which requires that he *be* the phallus. . . . [Sexual relations] will revolve around a being and a having which, because they refer to a signifier, the phallus, have the contradictory effect of on the one hand lending reality to the subject in that signifier, and on the other making unreal the relations to be signified. (1982b, 83–84)

Joe sees Maria as the mother who once authenticated his fictional unity; Maria sees Joe as yet another suitor confirming her myth of herself as a young girl. What Joe has or does is irrelevant (he realizes that Maria does not understand his "smart remark," or even what he does when he works); his desire is to be what Maria desires — to be the phallus. This waltz of misrecognition — Maria desires what Joe longs to be — grants each of them a certain yearning subjectivity; but as Lacan makes clear, this subjectivity is obtained by making their relations completely unreal.

The irony is that because Maria is so profoundly helpless and in-significant, because she is so obviously the victim of castration, she is crucial to Joe's sense of "self." Ragland-Sullivan writes: "The primor-dial (m)Other at the mirror-stage, structural base of the ego, becomes confused with woman; and women are consequently seen as secretly powerful. The mother within both sexes therefore implies an unseen dominance. This makes woman — as her displacement — someone to be feared, denied, ignored, denigrated, fought, and conquered — or conversely worshipped and enshrined" (1986, 297). One sees that Maria evinces almost all these negative reactions at some point in the story. My sense is that Joe is nice with her at least partly because he is afraid of her. The young men on the bus ignore her, the next-door girls deny her — all because her function as (m)Other recalls a precastration jouissance that others have forgotten in favor of the apparent certitude of the Phallus and the compensatory substitutive satisfactions of language.

Typically, the masculine subject identifies away from the (m)Other to effectively repress the pain of primary castration and to avoid the unbearable fear of loss of being in the Symbolic Order (the disintegration of personality). For Lacan, castration is not the fear of the loss of an organ, but a fear that the Phallus will prove to have always been unmoored within the substitutive system of language, and this will set the subject afloat in a sea of conflicting sensations that permit no coherent myth of "self." When Joe sees he has failed to seduce Maria into confirming the myth of himself, he calls out for objects — a nutcracker in one instance, a corkscrew in another — that will open things that are otherwise inaccessible to him. From a Lacanian perspective, he is calling for a signifier with a certain signified — a phallic signifier that would prove his true self was not someone else's fiction — that he was a signified enunciator and not a signifier dependent on the discourse of the 'other'. The frightening reality for Joe is that he is dancing to Maria's tune (Maria is his symptom), yet, as he sees by the end of the story, she is singing a song for herself only.

Much has been made of the search for the father in Joyce's fiction. But in this story, as in his work as a whole, one must realize that the dark secret power of the (m)Other is constantly undermining the certitude of masculine subjects in his fiction. In *Ulysses,* for example, Stephen seems fairly sanguine about whether or not he finds a father; what terrifies him is that he cannot get rid of his mother — and Mary Dedalus is every bit as helpless and pathetic, in terms of the Symbolic Order, as Maria. Joe has created very little "self" outside Maria's domain (his "proper mother") and I suspect the breakup of the home was caused by his rivalry with Alphy for Maria's recognition. True, Maria is easily ignored, denigrated, and denied, but this should not blind readers to the fact that she is also feared and that there does not appear to be any way of getting rid of her. Her death will scarcely mitigate her effect on Joe because she is almost dead now as far as her influence in the "real" world represented in the Symbolic Order.

One figure in this story is covertly afraid of Maria, and that is the narrator! The narrator's descriptions of Maria reveal a fascination that someone so tiny and insignificant could also be so dangerous and indomitable. Although the narrator faithfully records Maria's sense of herself as a flirtatious girl, a peacemaker, and someone beloved of the Donnelly family, the narrator is obsessively describing her as "tiny" (when the word Maria would clearly prefer is "tidy"). Moreover, the narrator is trying to slip a message past Maria's fiction of herself to the reader, and the message is Don't be fooled; this apparently pathetic old woman *is really a witch!* Often in fairy tales, most notably in "Snow White," a secretly dangerous, destructive, and powerful woman poses as a helpless old woman. It is curious how the narrator slavishly records all of Maria's favorite compliments, yet still manages to sneak in details that seem to deliberately, even maliciously, contradict her view of herself. The most famous example is the way the narrator dutifully records Maria's insistent description of the old man as a gentleman and then tears the illusion by skillfully employing one of Maria's own phrases: "she thought how easy it was to know a gentleman *even when he has a drop taken*" (*D* 103, emphasis added). The narrator, in one of his several functions (and I am deliberately casting the narrator as masculine), serves as Maria's unconscious, subtly undermining and subverting her conscious sense of herself by selectively weaving what she has repressed back into the fabric of what she thinks she knows.

In a slightly different sense, the narrator also takes on the qualities of a stock masculine character in fairy tales: the enchanted boy or man forced, against his will, to further the evil machinations of a witch. Such a man (e.g., the father of Rapunzel) gives up his autonomy to the witch in a moment of extreme need and then must later endure several hardships to extricate himself from her spell. In "Clay," it is the narrator, as well as Joe, who struggles for individuation. The extreme point of his rebellion is his repetitive description of Maria's face when she is laughing: "The tip of her nose nearly met the tip of her chin" (*D* 101). This image is anatomically absurd and does not qualify as one of her remembered compliments, so readers can only view it as a flashed message from the narrator as to Maria's "real" identity. In a further echo of the enchanted male, the narrator of "Clay" seems willing to flash this message only when Maria's attention is diverted (when she is laughing to cover her confusion and vague sense of embarrassment). The sudden focus on Joe at the close of the story gives me the eerie impression that the narrator has wanted to tell Joe's story all along, but was compelled — by a fear of somehow being deconstructed by Maria's displeasure — to tell Maria's story instead. In other words, the narrator, like Joe Donnelly, fears Maria as a (m)Other: a figure who *appears* to be a perpetual source of nourishment, comfort and love but then turns out to be someone who promises nutrients only as a lure (think of the witch's gingerbread house in "Hansel and Gretel"). The needy subject is then forced to become a frightened slave who must do the witch's bidding to avoid being consumed entirely (the man is allowed to survive only for as long as he can make himself useful). The narrator of "Clay" is struggling to tell his story, which is the same as Joe's, but instead he is almost completely inscribed by Maria's desire.

The narrator's helplessness is particularly apparent when Maria cannot decide where to buy plum cake: "She decided to buy some plumcake but Downes's plumcake had not enough almond icing on top of it so she went over to a shop in Henry Street" (*D* 102). Norris has described her action as "hopelessly dithering between two cake shops," and this is, indeed, the implicit message of the narrator. But what gives the narration such an odd tone is that the excruciating detail that the narrator goes into concerning Maria's least decision seems to present even Maria's hesitations as heroic. The basic strategy of the narrator, besides overtly slipping in "telling" descriptions of Maria, is to validate Maria's desire so overdiligently that the narration produces an effect that is opposite from the one Maria would like to make. The importance of buying or not buying plum cake is so out of proportion to the detail of the narration, that one receives the message Norris observed: this woman is "hopelessly dithering between two cake shops." But if one accepts this immediately, one fails to notice how the narrator seems enslaved to Maria's sense of herself, even as he tries to individuate his own "self" by subverting her fictional constructs.

The hyperdetail in the narration about Maria buying the plum cake seems even more startling when one notices that the narrator, who seems doomed to draw forth every nuance of this purchasing decision, at other points skips whole chunks of time. Significantly, these are the intervals whenever Maria is alone and unlikely to be observed by anyone: the period from when she gets dressed in front of the mirror to "when she got outside"; the period from when she buys the plum cake to when she boards the Drumcondra tram; and the period from when she leaves the tram to when "everybody said: *O, here's Maria!*" *(D*103). What these chronological elisions have in common is that they occur whenever Maria is not imaginatively misrecognizing how other people are viewing her. Maria is such a disturbing force because she has no culturally approved object to her desire. So the narrator declares she is a witch, and once readers receive the message, they are able to break the spell cast on the narrator by discovering "the meaning" of the story. This robs Maria of power because it is precisely her function as something outside the symbolic order (as something that lacks cultural definition or meaning) that causes Joe and the narrator to subsume their own identities in favor of becoming what she desires. The reader, too, becomes just another suitor whom Maria favors with demure nods and hems.

And so critics for thirty years have domesticated the disturbing force of Maria by emphasizing her need for marriage. This interpretation—Maria needs a man—keeps veiled the nonexistent Phallus and, thus, maintains its individuating power. In this sense, the phallus can be seen as the magic talisman that breaks the domination of the witch-like evil (m)Other. This common interpretation of Maria as a frustrated virgin validates the myth of absolute gender complementarity, and insists that Maria would cease to be a disturbing force capable of subverting masculine subjectivity if she were to align herself with the phallus in marriage. How seductively satisfying this reading is! It has been presented often, with admirable subtlety, by various critics, but, at base, it is an argument that puts a veil before the phallus, thus allowing it to continue to perform its function as a phallic signifier. Stripped down to its essence, this interpretation presents the phallus-saving argument that all Maria needs is a good fuck.[13]

This would return her, so the argument implies, to the feminine order of things where she could function as an unambivalent support for masculine subjectivity by masquerading as someone who has found the Phallus in her man. But because Maria is not married, and never will be, this argument avoids a question that remains unanswered, "Who is Maria *now?*" Indeed, "Clay" asks the question "What does a woman want?" and offers two possible answers. The preferred response, from a patriarchial and phallic point of view, is that she wants a man (to get married). The more disturbing answer, which continues to insist in the text, however much one agrees to "understand" Maria, is "Nothing, she simply wants (as does everyone)." For a masculine subject, she is a symbol of the (fictional) unity of masculinity. The readers of "Clay" make the same mistake Freud made when he leaped to his "understanding" of Dora by insisting that her problems stemmed from spurning (when she was fourteen years old) the "healthy" advances of a married, middle-aged man.

But I do not believe that Joyce thinks Maria is a witch. Rather, he is exploring the masculine subject's fear of women who do not fit the mold of femininity. His odd "masculine" narrator shows that the lives of both men and women are impaired by the fact that between them is no sexual relation as such — only fantasies of completeness acted out in the register of masquerade. *The Dublin by Lamplight Laundry,* after all, is a collecting pool for the stream of women who do not run off into the socially accepted tributaries of nun, wife, or emigrant. The Halloween game makes it clear that these are the only (supposedly) "real" choices for a woman short of death. In fact, the main purpose of the game, played exclusively by virgins, is to push forth the supremacy of the symbolic order by proscribing the only choices available to femininity that are, as yet, unclaimed by the patriarchal order. The young girls, at least, are still connected to their fathers and their families. But Maria has no family, nor has she aligned herself with a divine Father by becoming a nun. And, although she lives with women who once traded themselves (as prostitutes) in the phallic economy, she is not a former participant in that system either.

Harmless as she appears to be, Maria would still be frightening and witchlike to masculine subjects because she has not consigned herself to any of the several feminine roles that traditionally support the veiling of the Phallus. When Maria leaves her artificially constructed confinement, the paranoid "masculine" narrator insists on equating her escape from the laundry with that of a dead person leaving the tomb to wreak havoc by walking among the living. In the same way that dead people remind the living of their mortality, Maria's lack of

culturally constructed femininity (or, because she is not a former prostitute, even of *reconstructed* femininity) reminds the masculine subject
of how his gender construction, too, is erected over a void in being.
Joyce shows, in other words, that the terror of the masculine subject
for the internal (m)Other is displaced onto other women. The primordial gaze of the (m)Other within connects the masculine subject to
the precastration jouissance of the mirror stage. But, in doing so, it
leaves the monolithic myth of masculinity and phallic supremacy vulnerable to exposure and dissolution from the same female gaze that
originally sanctioned his presumed certitude.

And what of the reader? No critic has shown any discomfort with
this story (until the recent essay by Norris), yet I find that the text
subverts the reader's fictional unity by insisting that Maria is easily
interpreted both psychologically (she is sexually frustrated and culturally deprived) and allegorically (she is a witch; she is the Virgin Mary;
she is Ireland). The ease and plentitude of these interpretations should
be enough to cast some doubt on them. I have tried to ask more tren-
chant questions such as What's wrong with Joe? This important question is rarely asked because the answer is not at all apparent. Of course,
the answer to "What is Maria's problem?" is even more obscure because
the wrong answer is much more easily reached. To answer this question, the reader and the narrator work together on the "tidy body"
to bring their "selves" to a satisfying climax of interpretation. But how
valid is the readers' certitude and sense of closure? They regard Maria's "mistake" with the same sort of sympathetic dismissal as do the
other characters in the story, but they never see Maria safely home
to her containment center known as Dublin by Lamplight. After watching in exquisite detail her approach to the Donnelly's house, readers
never see her leave; instead the story closes on the image of a man
weeping and pathetically asking a woman (his wife) to tell him where
the corkscrew is. Despite the story ending on Joe's breakdown, readers
continue to explore and explain only Maria, using a contradictory
catalog that includes such labels as witch, Virgin Mary, or Ireland.
Readers do not mind disagreeing on the particulars because all agree
she means something—and that is the main thing—*that she mean something.* In other words, they believe in her. They believe she is saying
something, even though they do not all agree on what it is they hear.
Lacan writes, "for whoever is encumbered with the phallus, what is

a woman? A woman is a symptom" (1982b, 168). For the reader of the story, Maria functions as a symptom. They believe in her desire; they offer themselves as its object inasmuch as they explain what she needs to complete herself and thereby satisfy their own desire through this interpretation (it is the *act* of interpreting that proves satisfying, not the *substance* of the interpretation).

Believing that the celibate Maria has a coherent meaning—whatever it might be—allows readers to celebrate their own unity. They need Maria to make sense of themselves—even as they insist they are only making sense of the text. In the act of detailing her insignificance, they strengthen their own certainty. In noting Maria's castration, they discover that they have the corkscrew necessary to open this text (and, thus, the phallic signifier necessary to open themselves), and what an uplifting and inebriating bottle of wine it is, once they have uncorked it! Maria, "the lost woman," to quote Joyce's letter, hides from us the fact that after castration (loss of mirror-stage unity) the objects of our Desire can never be found, only substituted for. And so Maria's tiny shoulders have supported various interpretations that substitute what she "means" for what critics lack. This process, which appears to end in certitude, merely reenacts the original division that forced the masculine subject to imagine that a woman (Maria) lacks the phallus in order to create the illusion of searching for it. The identity of the masculine subject requires a consistent relation to the phallic term, and the spectacle of Maria's helpless pose wards off unconscious incertitude by permitting soulful interpretations of what she needs, what she desires, and what she stands for. So Maria becomes a nexus of signifying elements that cover the lack of any signified either in this text, in the narrator, or in the identity of the reader.

In short, Maria is essential because of her insignificance. Critics have often remarked that the narrator is on the side of Maria and that he supports her self-delusions as much as possible. This is correct, I think, as far as it goes, but it is not so simple an observation as all that. The narrator assiduously supports Maria's delusions *because* they are delusions, and it is at this point that the reader accepts the narrator's voice as truthful relative to Maria's elaborate fictional dimension. But I argue that the narrator is a fraud because detailing Maria's fictions is not at all the same thing as being the sole possessor of the truth. The narrator's role as a purveyor of truth moves back and forth between the fantasy of his definition of Maria as nothing and his fantasy that she actually may be a powerfully subversive witch. It is easy to overlook that Maria's status as "insignificant" is still powerful enough to vanquish the next-door girls without her even understanding what it is they have done. Indeed, their inclusion of the fourth saucer, and its hasty removal by the "adults," reveals much more about the people at the party than it does about Maria. What it reveals is that they are alive only in relation to their designation of Maria as someone who is dead (and she must not be shown her mistake). Her absence permits their presence and, of course, threatens it at the same time because the structure of their subjectivity depends on Maria as the (m)Other. Maria is every bit as powerful and necessary as the ghosts that crowd the Morkan's house in "The Dead," and it is a small wonder that "everyone" is "so fond of Maria."

Because the people at the party address their demands outside themselves to another, this other comes to represent a fantasized place of subjective certitude—a place that guarantees the value of their subjectivity the way gold in Fort Knox guarantees the value of what is, after all, only paper. In other words, *the conscious truth* about Maria is that she is someone other—disenfranchised, helpless, castrated, *the unconscious truth* is that she is the Other, the source of the discourse that narrates who they imagine themselves to be. Maria is dangerous because she is helpless, and her castration threatens to expose the fact that certitude is structured in relation to something Other that is potentially subversive. Put another way, whereas the narrator's question of identity is directed to the Other via Maria, the question of the reader's identity is directed to the narrator via Maria. In both cases, Maria operates as a symptom, a signifier that embodies a duplicity of meaning that allows unconscious meaning to exist in conscious life. As a symptom, Maria has many of the qualities of a ghost. Halloween is the day when she leaves the laundry—where she has been entombed in their definition of her—and walks among them as if still alive (hence, the fourth saucer seeks to send her back to the laundry, back to her grave). One believes in Maria in order to shore up one's belief in oneself. Jacqueline Rose explains the interaction of the Woman and the Phallus: "To believe in 'The Woman' is simply a way of closing off the division or uncertainty which also underpins conviction as such. . . . The Other crossed through stands against this knowledge as the place of division where meaning falters, where it slips and shifts. . . . The Other therefore stands against the phallus — its pretence to meaning and false consistence. It is from the Other that the phallus seeks authority and is refused" (Mitchell and Rose 1982, 51). As subjects, all are endlessly malleable in the sense that the truth of their being depends on someone else being fiction.

Maria's absolute Otherness secures the narrator's truth (that is to say his claim to truth). Through the narrator, the reader, in the dominant position of the voyeur, gazes at Maria. But is everyone watching her? Nothing is allowed to occur in a dramatic format in this story; instead readers are told of everything that is happening as it happens. The position of the reader in this story is similar to that of someone who has gone to the wrong theatre and must stare at a darkened stage while listening to someone else recount, in as much detail as possible, what is going on in a performance that is elsewhere: "Then Ginger Mooney lifted up her mug of tea and proposed Maria's health while all the other women clattered with their mugs on the table, and said she was sorry she hadn't a sup of porter to drink it in" (*D* 101). Words such as *then* and *while,* phrases such as "and said she was" would all be necessary descriptions to someone seeking to witness the events of this story but is reduced to hearing only a running commentary. The story is told as though readers were standing next to the witnessing narrator and he is constantly noting the spatial and chronological sequence of events to us as if we had been blindfolded. To give another example, readers learn that "she went over to a shop in Henry Street: "*Here* she was a long time in suiting herself" (*D* 102). Why use the word *here* unless it is a verbal cue to tell readers what they otherwise could not see? Likewise, when Maria arrives at the Donnelly house, the first thing readers are told is who else is in the room. If one thinks of the narration as a verbal account to someone who is present, but blindfolded, then the frequent abrupt summary of events — "soon everything was merry again," for instance — can be explained as the result of a narrator rather overwhelmed at having to relay everything to a viewer who can see nothing. By the time one comes to the parlor game — "They insisted then on blindfolding Maria" — one should (if one is not reading defensively and presuming to know what one has only been told) recognize oneself.

Readers are as helpless as Maria. The various interpretations they reach represent the many saucers that they reach for to predict who they will become. And even if their hands were to descend on the saucer with the clay and if they were to realize that it is their own death in life that is being portrayed, the narrator is there to provide "a great deal of scuffling and whispering," and they will understand "that it was wrong that time" and that they have "to do it over again" (*D* 105). Like Maria, readers are forced to dwell in the Real blindness of the Imaginary Order where, batlike, they send out demands for recognition and then determine who they are by the echo that comes back, not comprehending that the echo that returns does not represent their outline but the outline of the Other. They mistake as all there is to see what they can, in fact, only imagine. They cannot objectively determine the meaning of the story because it has been subjectively related, so they create its meaning by individuating a "self" through their interpretation (and interpretation, simply put, is nothing more than the manifestation of desire).

The role of the phallic symbol, Lacan says, "is precisely to supplement the significance of the Other at the very point where it is found wanting. The price of the subject's access to the world of desire is that the real organ must be marked at the imaginary level with this bar, so that its symbol can take up its place as the signifier of this very point where the signifier is lacking" (1982b, 117). And so the lack that underlies readers as desiring subjects (the castration that forces them to use language as a substitutive mode of being) is made positive as the phallic symbol that, in the symbolic order, comes to be the signifier of desire. The castration complex means nothing less for the masculine subject than the fact that men suffer from what I might call "Phallus envy" as much as the feminine subject does. The only difference is that the fact of his penis persuades him to be what does not exist (the Phallus), and this, in turn, causes him to hallucinate what women are in order to believe in himself as a creature of certitude.

In a sense, the reader of this story is like the minister in "The Purloined Letter." The minister is shrewd enough to see through the queen's attempt to hide the incriminating letter. But as soon as he interprets this action by taking the letter, he is displaced to her position. Having been displaced, he is as helpless in relation to the character who occupies his previous position as the queen was to him. Readers learn what Maria seeks to hide, and in doing so, they are able to mistake their understanding of her as knowledge about themselves. But in gazing at Maria, they repress the fact that they are able to do so only because the narrator is looking at them. If their interpretation of Maria's frustrated desire unravels, they become aware that their "selves," which put forward this interpretation are, in fact, dictated by the desire of the Other. "If one does not stress the dialectic of desire," Lacan writes, "one does not understand why the gaze of others should disorganize the field of perception. It is because the subject in question is not that of the reflexive consciousness, but that of desire" (1981a, 89). The narrator's gaze, once realized, startles them out of their voyeuristic mastery of the limitations of Maria and force them to see her in relation to the phallic signifier (that signifier which "authenticates" interpretation) as one of masquerade. In other words, in the end, they have to ask Maria to tell them where the corkscrew is. The narrator, to use a metaphor of Lacan, is a magician who promises not to hide anything from us — to lay his cards on the table. And he can do so without fear of discovery because readers so badly wish to be tricked. "Clay" is really a frightening story to read because the narrator makes it so easy for readers to "see" Maria. This, in turn, allows them to see themselves as not being seen when their interpretation of Maria betrays the fact that their desire is formulated by the desire of the Other.

This is also what makes a woman mystical to the masculine subject: she is pretending to not have what, in fact, does not exist, which means that somewhere, beyond representation, the question of her own sexuality still insists. This is equally true whether a woman has had dozens of partners or none (although patriarchy would label the former woman a "prostitute," and the latter, a "virgin"). An aging virgin is a particularly potent escapee from femininity because there is no way to tell if her failure to be co-opted into the patriarchal order is the result of her "failure" or the fact that the patriarchal order is based on the veiled, and nonexistent, phallus. The safest plan, of course, is to pretend that no mistake has been made. Joyce is aware, I argue, of the dynamic whereby the wicked and the lost — what I am describing as "escapees from femininity" — are domesticated by a paranoid patriarchial culture that sets them to the "good" ("comprehensible") work of washing dirty shirts. In the story "Clay" he shows the impossibility of the woman's position; whether she is regarded as a desireable

object of sexual commerce or whether she is shunned as a bewildering and terrifying enigma, she is seen, willy-nilly, as causing the difficulty that, for speaking beings, is actually inherent in sexuality itself.
The narrator begins his story with the moment when Maria is granted
permission to "go out," and ends it with Joe's breakdown when he cannot locate the corkscrew. For the narrator, this is the parameter of the
story: Maria breaks out and Joe breaks down. Maria has not been
able to let Joe "have his way" because what he wants is not the satisfaction of desire but the confirmation that he possesses the symbol
of desire, the Phallus. In the end, a man (masquerading as masculine) must turn to a woman (masquerading as feminine) and ask her
to tell him what she is taught to pretend to know—where the corkscrew is.

12

Love in the Third Person in "A Painful Case"

Love reopens the door—as Freud put it, not mincing his words—to perfection. . . . That's what love is. It's one's own ego that one loves in love, one's own ego made real on the imaginary level. (Lacan 1988a, 142)

This union exalted him, wore away the rough edges of his character, emotionalised his mental life. Sometimes he caught himself listening to the sound of his own voice. (*D* 111)

James Duffy is able to stay comfortable with himself as long as he does not actually speak to anyone for any length of time about anything of any importance.[1] His rather clever strategy for keeping people at a distance is to overexpose himself in carefully selected public arenas so that he becomes too familiar a figure, in too predictable a manner, to be at all approachable. In other words, he frequents the three different public places—where he works, lunches, and dines— with such consistency and sense of purpose that any overture by others for conversation is foreclosed. In this way he can misinterpret as the unavoidable side effect of his intellectual superiority what is, in fact, his terror when engaging people in conversation. The depth of his isolation is important to him because he uses this as a measure to sound the depth of his intelligence. Indulging the chatter of others interferes with the nurturing relationship he maintains with his own silence.

Duffy's usual pattern of dwelling in the public sphere only long enough to earn a wage and to eat is subject to two exceptions. The first is "his liking for Mozart's music," which "brought him sometimes to an opera or a concert" (*D* 109), and the second is his attendance, for a brief while, at the local meetings of an Irish Socialist party. If one looks at the nature of his participation at these public gatherings, however, one will see that his presence there serves to confirm his isolation rather than mitigate it: "He had felt himself a unique figure amidst a score of sober workmen" (*D* 110). The implication is that he does not speak at these gatherings and that he finds the subject matter of the workmen's conversations to be predictable and trivial: "The workmen's discussions . . . were too timorous; the interest they took in the question of wages was inordinate. He felt that they were hard-featured realists and that they resented an exactitude which was the product of a leisure not within their reach" (*D* 111). In other words, their concerns have nothing in common with his own, and, therefore, he is powerless to impress them with a depth of learning he feels they lack the leisure time to appreciate.

What Mr. Duffy is at pains to find, in a manner he can accept, is recognition. The problem is that he is so extraordinarily paranoid that someone will form an opinion of him that is at odds with his fantasy of himself. He likes to think of himself as beyond caring what others think of him, but the fact is, he is so sensitive to the gaze of others that he cannot bear to engage them unless he is sure they will only see who he imagines himself to be. All those who do not endorse who he thinks he is are relegated to the legions of people who have misunderstood him and are, therefore, best avoided in the future. It is unlikely the men resent his greater leisure or that they even know about it because he has made no effort to communicate with anyone there. More than likely, he assumes that the men resent his larger salary and middle-class employment precisely because it is this fact that verifies his image of himself as "a unique figure" in their midst. They are arguing for what he already has (higher wages) and, should they ever get them, Duffy would be forced to construct a less facile proof of his presumed superiority. Rather than acknowledge that his uniqueness is the result of something as crass and unintellectual as wealth, Duffy rather mysteriously cites the use he makes of his greater leisure time as the feature that distinguishes him from them. But to what

use has he put this leisure? It may have taken him a little time to arrange all his books according to bulk, but what has he produced at
the desk where "writing materials" are "always on the desk?" A full
two months after he terminates the relationship with Mrs. Sinico, the
extent of his literary production appears to be two sentences.

The point I am trying to make is that Duffy's sense of himself,
his reality, engages in a good deal of fantasy. Casual contact with others
must be strictly monitored because, more than likely, others will defy,
quite inadvertently perhaps, Duffy's ideal image of himself. Only people
who consciously devote themselves to divining what his ideal image
is, in order to better support it, will win any sort of allegiance from
Duffy. This, of course, is precisely what Mrs. Sinico does. Duffy insists on presenting his ideas with "exactitude," and he refuses "to compete with phrasemongers, incapable of thinking consecutively for sixty
seconds." What this passion for precise phrasing suggests about Duffy
is that he must keep his thoughts to himself in the absence of any as-
surance that his listener will echo back to him precisely what he "meant"
to say. Not since the narrator of "The Sisters" have readers seen a character so frightened by the inherent treachery of language. Duffy's detailed imaginary fantasies about his own integrity have papered over,
with moi fixations and "other" messages, the primordial lack-in-being
that cannot be symbolized (and, thus, remains unrepresented in the
Real). In contrast to ego psychology, Lacan does not privilege the ego
as the executive that negotiates between desire and reality. Instead,
he writes: "In the human subject there is something which speaks,
which speaks in the full sense of the word, that is to say something
which knowingly lies, and without the contribution of consciousness
. . . this dimension is no longer confused with the *ego*. The ego is deprived of its absolute position in the subject. The ego acquires the
status of a mirage, as the residue, it is only one element in the objectal
relations of the subject" (1988a, 194). It is a construct that bestows
upon the subject a spurious unity that provides the needed coherency
for the individual to search for verification of this (fictional) construct
from others.

This subject who seeks to engage others — a speaking subject — is
actually that second dimension of subjectivity that Lacan calls the je
or *I*: "What do we call a subject? Quite precisely, what, in the development of objectivation, is outside of the object." (1988a, 194). At the
Irish Socialist party meeting, Duffy avoids speaking because he senses

his speech would be met with silence. To have his speech met by the silence of others could intimate that the structure of his moi is primarily a fiction. One speaks most confidently, one believes in oneself most thoroughly, when one senses that one's audience will verify as the truth those lies to which our consciousness has not contributed. Mr. Duffy speaks precisely and consecutively because, like the narrator of "The Sisters," he has a vague premonition that the "truth" he speaks belies the fiction of himself that misrepresents the Real. The full sense of the word, which consciousness does not contribute to in intersubjective communication with others, reveals the unbearable truth that the unity of the ego is a fiction.

Correspondingly, the narcissistic investment in his "self" that Duffy so assiduously protects corresponds to Lacan's view of the moi, or the "ideal ego." This primary narcissism, according to Lacan, is formed as a result of the mirror stage in which the subject mistakes his coherent image for a representation of his unified identity. Later, with a secondary narcissism, the subject seeks out others to validate this earlier (fictional) unity. These others Lacan terms *ego ideals*. Other people serve as the alter ego of the moi, and this dictates the extent to which one loves or hates them (and also suggests why either one of these emotions can turn so unexpectedly into the other). Duffy, like Gabriel Conroy, is protecting an ideal ego that is particularly vulnerable to the effects of interacting with others. Every choice he has made in the construction of his private sphere demonstrates this. He lives in Chapelizod, about three miles outside of Dublin, "to live as far as possible from the city of which he was a citizen" (*D* 103). His room is uncarpeted; there are no pictures on his walls. Most telling of all, "He had himself bought every article of furniture in the room (*D* 103). He has accepted no furniture from relatives or friends, and this fact is a source of some consolation to him. Why? Because even furniture, if it has a history apart from him, possesses a degree of otherness that might make him feel as though he were being watched by a gaze that is hostile to his ideal image of himself. Little Chandler, as I pointed out in my discussion of "A Little Cloud," feels that the furniture his wife picked out possesses a "meanness" that is somehow like the deconstructive "eyes in the photograph." By buying each piece of furniture himself, Mr. Duffy can be assured that the furniture has no history that will contradict the "his[S]tory" of himself.

As Lacan constantly stresses, the gaze of others—which represents the primordial gaze of the Other that can confirm one's unity or subvert it — need not come from any person in the vicinity who is actually looking at one: "The gaze is not located just at the level of the eyes. The eyes may very well not appear; they may be masked. The gaze is not necessarily the face of our fellow being, it could just as easily be the window behind which we assume he is lying in wait for us. It is an *x*, the object when faced with which the subject becomes object" (1988a, 220). At the meetings of the Irish Socialist party, this dynamic had begun to set in with Duffy. As he explains to Mrs. Sinico "He had felt himself a unique figure" (*D* 110). This self-conscious assertion of his autonomy to her actually communicates the opposite message — that his identity felt challenged in this atmosphere and he would like Mrs. Sinico to support his self-serving contention that his discomfort was caused by the fact of his uniqueness. The uncomprehending gaze of the "sober work-men" makes him uncomfortably aware of himself as an object. Significantly, when the party divides itself into three separate sections, Duffy stops attending meetings. This is scarcely surprising when one considers that he had been hoping for something that would allow him to experience himself as unified. This alien group that fragments before his eyes sends him back to the safety of his own room, which, as I have pointed out, contains only objects that have been antiseptically cleansed, as much as possible, of all possible contamination from the gaze of others.

The city of Dublin itself possesses a gaze that Duffy avoids. Not only does he live "as far as possible" from it, but when he takes evening walks he confines them to "the outskirts of the city" (*D* 109). His relationship to the city, which he hates and fears, even though he enters it daily to work and then circles it at night, approximates his relationship to others: "He lived his spiritual life without any communion with others, visiting his relatives at Christmas and escorting them to the cemetery when they died" (*D* 109). Duffy does not acknowledge as pathological his profound aversion to others because he fancies that he needs his leisure time to write (although he rarely does so) and because he fancies himself a disciple of Nietzsche who (at least in Duffy's understanding of him) denounces any adherence to social duties as proof of pettiness.

Duffy uses knowledge gleaned from his carefully arranged books to protect himself from what he cannot afford to know. His ideal ego —

far from being the adaptive dimension of the psyche described by ego psychology—is structured exactly like a symptom (the Lacanian definition of the ego). Conduct that must be undertaken to protect this privileged system is regarded by Duffy as a matter of principle: "Mr. Duffy abhorred anything which betokened physical or mental disorder" (*D* 108). Of course, it is precisely this abhorrence (a strong reaction, surely, to something as trivial as untidyness) that "betokens" Duffy's "mental disorder." What determines relative degrees of happiness is how well one can align one's ideal ego with the alter ego that is produced by our contact with others (ego ideals): "It's the symbolic relation which defines the position of the subject as seeing. It is speech, the symbolic relation, which determines the greater or lesser degree of perfection, of completeness, of approximation, of the imaginary. . . . on the relation to others depends the more or less satisfying character of the imaginary structuration" (1988a, 141). It is not, according to Lacan, "philosophy" or "principles" that hold the human subject together; it is others in their function as mirrors within which one strives to discern the outlines of an ideal ego—that privileged symptom that protects one from knowledge of one's origin in the discourse of the 'other'.

Because Duffy is alone so much of the time, he has perfected, as much as possible, the art of being his own Other: "He lived at a little distance from his body, regarding his own acts with doubtful sideglances" (*D* 108). Here the split at the heart of Duffy's subjectivity is apparent. His body acts, and then his mind distrusts this action to the point of doubting its reality. Where is Duffy while this is going on? Afloat somewhere between an imagined unity and a perceived fragmentation, "He had an odd autobiographical habit which led him to compose in his mind from time to time a short sentence about himself containing a subject in the third person and a predicate in the past tense" (*D* 108). Only the intervention of a third person can tip this seesaw one way or the other (toward a sense of well-being or toward a manifestation of anxiety). Duffy very much wants to be his own third person so that other people might become entirely extraneous to what would then be the closed circuit of his identity. He attempts, through language, to generate a personal Symbolic Order within which he can experience a validation of his existence. He fantasizes about producing the discourse of the Other rather than being dictated by it.

This odd habit might convince Duffy that he *has* lived, but it does very little to persuade him that he *is living*. After all, who is he, or where is he, while he is reciting this sentence, which, in essence, captures how he would like to be described were someone watching him at a given moment? Lacan is clear that the human ego is paranoid, and Duffy's is more paranoid than most (because he is convinced that who he is remains under his conscious control). In a sense, Duffy seeks to confirm his fusion with his mirror image. But to do this, an actual third person is needed. Even the infant relies on the gaze of the mother to confirm the coherent reflection that, in turn, verifies the subject's presumed psychic unity (but only by introducing permanent self-alienation in the form of insatiable desire). Here Duffy strives to treat as inherent and "natural" something that is a symptom. As Ragland-Sullivan points out, "it is others in Real situations who enable the moi to reconstitute itself continually. These others, therefore, hold the human subject together by their recognition and reflection" (1986, 49). These mental snapshots that Duffy takes of himself fade immediately because he has not projected his identity onto something 'other' which is the only way to be recognized and, thus, authenticated, as "real." In others words, desiring the desire of others is the secondary manifestation of a more basic impulse: the desire to be desired.

Duffy can construct an image of himself in the past tense, but he cannot recognize or desire that self in a manner that would reconstitute it: "The human being only sees his form materialised, whole, the mirage of himself, outside of himself. . . . It is through the exchange of symbols that we locate our different selves [mois] in relation to one another" (Lacan 1988a, 140). In short, Duffy cannot be his own ego ideal, but he can be very circumspect about whom he engages to confirm his ideal ego. This "other" who serves as the screen onto which he projects himself will have to be completely unself-absorbed. Such a person he might love but only so long as he could feel that this person's desire corresponded at every point with the precise way in which he needs to be desired. In other words, the relationship, from the point of view of consciousness, would have nothing whatsoever to do with anything Real, and this fact would ensure its ability to completely reflect this reality as accurately as the carefully organized books and personally selected furniture in his room. Of course, what I am leading up to is that Mrs. Sinico is just such a person, and her relationship with Mr. Duffy operates in the manner I have just outlined. The most potent symbolic relation with an "other" is (as Elvis Presley put it) a crazy little thing called love. Lacan's definition is more clinical and, therefore, more precise (but not fundamentally different): "Love is a phenomenon which takes place on the imaginary level, and which provokes a veritable subduction of the symbolic, a sort of annihilation, of perturbation of the function of the ego-ideal. Love reopens the door—as Freud put it, not mincing his words—to perfection" (1988a, 142). It is precisely Mrs. Sinico's early role as "perfection" for Mr. Duffy that makes her later display of need so repulsive to him. In essence, he believed in her, which is to say he believed she verified his ego (which is, in fact, a symptom of his disbelief in himself).[2] When she made it impossible for him to believe in the figure of the Woman that she represented for him, he is suddenly in danger of discovering the disbelief in himself that he has taken such pains to repress. All too predictably, his defense is to abandon her as unnatural and depraved: "It revolted him to think that he had ever spoken to her of what he held sacred" (*D* 115). What he holds sacred, of course, is his ideal image, which he had once let her gaze upon. Mr. Duffy's initial "love" for Mrs. Sinico is yet another attempt to have a third person verify his ideal image.

The one public format that Duffy consistently attends is any concert that features the music of Mozart. This is a relatively safe indulgence because concerts are events that one attends in order to listen; speaking occurs only on the margins of the main event. Curiously, all of Duffy's minor indulgences are described in terms that suggest it is dangerous to desire anything because it can lead unexpectedly to a loss of autonomy: "His liking for Mozart's music brought him sometimes to an opera or a concert" (*D* 109). This liking for Mozart lures him, like a hidden spirit guiding his steps, out into the open where anything might happen. His concertgoing and the time spent at his landlady's piano are characterized as "the only dissipations of his life" (*D* 109). This is a significant term for Duffy's leisure because a dissipation can refer to an amusement or an idle diversion, but the verb "to dissipate" indicates spreading something thin to the point of vanishing. Duffy seems to be in perpetual fear of being absorbed by his surroundings—of dissipating. "One evening," readers are told, "he found himself sitting beside two ladies in the Rotunda" (*D* 109). The description of how he came to be at the same concert as Mrs. Sinico is presented as such a profoundly passive act that one could almost imagine he lost consciousness in his bare room and suddenly "came to" at the concert site. This oddly unconscious locomotion that brings Duffy to the site of his dissipations is all the more surprising in a man who deliberately has the same thing to eat, in the same carefully chosen places, every day of his life. But there are dangerous waters out beyond the islands of working and eating, and Duffy refuses to attempt any sort of navigation that might make him responsible for where he ends up. Outside of the reality of his room, his life is a dream he tolerates by not trying to interpret it.

Mrs. Sinico's opening remark to him sounds the despair of both their lives: "What a pity there is such a poor house to-night! It's so hard on people to have to sing to empty benches" (*D* 109). Both Duffy and Mrs. Sinico have been attempting to "sing to empty benches" for some time — Duffy alone in his barren room and Mrs. Sinico "singing" to her husband whose indomitable indifference toward her is worse than no audience at all. Her remark characterizes her significantly in another sense as well: She is anxious to present herself as an ideal audience for *any* worthwhile performer who is tired of struggling to "sing to empty benches." Not surprisingly, then, when Duffy begins to confide in her a little later, we are told she "listened to all" (*D* 110). He determines, by judging the age of her daughter who has accompanied her, that she is as old as he is. He notes that her general expression "which must have been handsome, had remained intelligent." But what occupies his attention is the "steady" expression conveyed by her eyes. Her gaze is described with the precision one might expect of someone who is erotically entranced (one thinks of Bob Doran's equally detailed description of Polly on her bath night): "The eyes were very dark blue and steady. Their gaze began with a defiant note but was confused by what seemed a deliberate swoon of the pupil into the iris, revealing for an instant a temperament of great sensibility. The pupil reasserted itself quickly, this half-disclosed nature fell again under the reign of prudence, and her astrakhan jacket, moulding a bosom of a certain fulness, struck the note of defiance definitely" (*D* 109). The tension between the pupil and the iris in Mrs. Sinico's gaze reproduces the drama Duffy always feels in relation to the Other. He wants to be surrounded by something that supports and confirms who he imagines himself to be, but because the structure to be confirmed is imaginary, he fears, on another level, engulfment and loss of autonomy. It is Mrs. Sinico's "temperament of great sensibility" that both attracts and frightens Duffy.[3] What will eventually end their relationship is also forecast in this description of her gaze; it will be in that moment when her desire reasserts itself that Mr. Duffy will flee her presence (and decide that the temperament of great sensibility at the center of her gaze is, in fact, a whirlpool into which he, himself, nearly disappeared).

Duffy's strategy, which works in the short-term, is to make *her* the pupil and, thus, repress the danger of becoming dependent on her gaze for his sense of himself. The swoon invited by Mrs. Sinico's gaze allows Duffy to imagine himself as the object of her desire. When the swoon is past, "the reign of prudence" reasserts itself, and then Duffy notices her "bosom of a certain fulness." The more prudent Mrs. Sinico, then, is a maternal figure. She will function for Duffy as what Lacan calls a (m)Other, that is, as a substitute for the original gaze that verified, as the "third person"—Duffy's fusion with his mirror image. In essence, the mother grants an image to the child, but it is an image that he can believe in only because she sees it too. The moment of unification is also a moment of self-alienation that puts the subject in a position where an-other can reconfirm the authenticating gaze of the (m)Other (someone one loves), or nullify it (someone one hates). This structure of the maternal gaze that I have outlined describes what Duffy intuitively fears—that Mrs. Sinico may confirm the unity of himself, but if he submits himself to her gaze (becomes *her* pupil) he risks the very sort of swooning into nothingness that his entire life is organized to prevent. Mrs. Sinico offers herself as the "third person" he has tried to invent for himself. However, because she continues to ex-ist beyond his invention of her as the Woman, he is vulnerable to intimations from the Real should the part of her gaze that demonstrates a "temperament of great sensibility" reassert itself as the gaze of a woman who demonstrates *her own* desire to be recognized as something other than a reflection of him.

The reader sees the relationship only from Duffy's side; his ego ideal creates the "Mrs. Sinico" he needs to know. This creation reflects back to him, as alter ego, his own idealized moi identity. His verbal relationship with Mrs. Sinico will become more and more restrictive until the very fact that she is still alive and not utterly absorbed by his need will register on him as a betrayal on her part. This is an endpoint that is likely to occur in analysis, and Lacan identifies it as follows: "The function of speech . . . become[s] so firmly inclined in the direction of the other that it is no longer even mediation, but only implicit violence, a reduction of the other to a correlative function of the subject's ego" (1988a, 51). Duffy wants to enlist Mrs. Sinico as his "third person"—someone who can "compose in his mind from time to time a short sentence about himself" (*D* 108). He wants, in other words, an external source of "self" that will be constant and unified. To achieve this would be to satisfy Desire because Desire, simply defined, is the insatiable drive for an object that will return the subject to that mirror-stage illusion of unity (sanctified by the (m)Other's gaze) that is the origin of the myth of the "self." There is an implicit violence in the way Mr. Duffy reveals himself to Mrs. Sinico in the "confessional" of her home. Each interview further reduces her to being nothing "other" than a correlative function of Duffy's ego. Her grasping of his hand and pressing it to her cheek forms a third-person sentence along the lines of "I (unpredictable gaze of the Other) love you," rather than "'I' am nothing more or less than the missing object of desire (the permanently benevolent gaze of the 'Other') that you need to complete—and, therefore, completely love—yourself."

After he reads of her death, Duffy's vague sense of what he has done to her begins his breakdown: "Why had he sentenced her to death? He felt his moral nature falling to pieces" (*D* 117). To experience himself as a grammatically self-contained speech unit (a sentence) he imposed upon her the image of his own most perfect "self" and then condemned her (sentenced her) for failing to actualize it. Combining the two denotations of "sentence" and "to sentence," he has "sentenced her to death" by composing his self-rationalizing aphorisms in his "Bile Beans" diary. Zack Bowen points out that "Mrs. Sinico did not begin to drink for a year and a half after Duffy terminated their relationship" (1981–1982, 107). Therefore, Mr. Duffy's feeling of direct responsibility for her death would seem to be an exaggeration. Yet, as Bowen goes on to suggest, "It may very well be the case that Duffy's ego has erroneously prompted him to think that he had condemned Mrs. Sinico to death" (107). What the ego prompts Duffy to believe is not so much erroneous (this implies a correct identity as the basis of Duffy's conscious psyche that knows the truth) as it is a new misrecognition of his unified "self." Like the narrator of "Araby," he adopts a self-denigrating pose to cover, with a slightly altered moi construction, the terrifying gap that has opened up in the Symbolic Order to reveal a glimpse of the Real. In the presence of an acutely responsive audience (Mrs. Sinico), Duffy appears to be able to close the gap at the base of the fictional construct of his ego by speaking it into sentences that she verifies by hearing his sentence correctly. The only aspect of Mrs. Sinico that Duffy knows, of course, is that dimension of her being that has been put into the service of verifying his own. He knows only to the extent that her attentive attitude supplies a mirror within which he sees reflected a substitute object of desire for what he imagines he has lost.

Essentially, the support of her maternal gaze produces for him a natural habitat for his hitherto alienated being that is similar to the jouissance of the subject in the premirror stage: "Her companionship was like a warm soil about an exotic" (*D* 111). She serves as the affirmative third person that he once tried to construct for himself: "this union exalted him, wore away the rough edges of his character, emotionalised his mental life" (*D* 111). His attraction to her role as a reflector reveals that in her presence he pursues, sanctified by her gaze, the lost object of desire that he imagines will complete him. At various times, her role as authenticator slips, and the self-serving quality of his monologue is briefly exposed: "Sometimes he caught himself listening to the sound of his own voice" (*D* 111). Their conversations, held in a "dark discreet room" are described as though the act of rhetorical intercourse was equivalent to the act of sexual intercourse: "Little by little, as their thoughts entangled, they spoke of subjects less remote" (*D* 111). The paradoxical dimension of Duffy's intercourse with Mrs. Sinico is that the more thoroughly he masters the question of her subjectivity, the more he is able to imagine himself as the equivalent of his ideal image. Yet at the same time, the more she complies to his co-option of her as a subject, the more persistently this ideal image is subverted by deeper and deeper intimations of alienation and fragmentation: "He thought that in her eyes he would ascend to an angelical stature; and as he attached the fervent nature of his companion more and more closely to him, he heard the strange impersonal voice which he recognised as his own, insisting on the soul's incurable loneliness" (*D* 111). Because Duffy is not able to see that the source of this loneliness is his increasing subjugation of Mrs. Sinico ("he attached the fervent nature of his companion more and more closely to him"), he locates the division at the base of human desire as being between people, rather than within them. The more Mrs. Sinico supports who he imagines himself to be, the less she will appear to him as a representative of the Other. When her "fervent nature" is *entirely* attached to him, he will become aware, once again, that in all his conversations with her, he has merely been continuing his "odd autobiographical habit" of "compos[ing] in his mind from time to time a short sentence about himself containing a subject in the third person" (*D* 108). Duffy's progressively co-optive relationship with Mrs. Sinico — leading, as it does, to an abrupt termination — demonstrates that the subject alienates himself all the more, the more he seduces an-other into confirming his ego.

It is Mrs. Sinico's actual touch which causes Duffy's "angelical stature" to crash. He assumes that her gesture represents an interpretation of his words (*D* 11). But Mrs. Sinico does not care what his words mean; she cares that they are addressed to her. His belief in her as a symptom has renewed her belief in herself. What he says is of small significance to her compared to the fact that it is her gaze that permits him to speak. She sees herself being seen by him as someone whom he sees seeing him. Lacan characterizes this dialectic of looking, where two people are functioning as ego ideals for one another, as "this double gaze whereby I see that the other sees me, and that any intervening third party sees me being seen. There is never a simple duplicity of terms. It is not only that I see the other, I see him seeing me, which implicates the third term, namely, that he knows that I see him. The circle is closed. There are always three terms in the structure, even if these three terms are not explicitly present" (1988a, 218). Duffy and Mrs. Sinico allow each other to recognize their desire in the Other, but neither can satisfy either themselves or the other. "It is sorrowful," Lacan has said, "that the loved person onto whom one projects Desire and narcissism serves to give proof of the image and pathos of existence. The other reveals the gap of human Desire, but cannot permanently close it" (quoted in Ragland-Sullivan 1986, 81). Duffy says something rather similar to Mrs. Sinico, in their last rhetorical entanglement, after they have "agreed to break off their intercourse: every bond, he said, is a bond to sorrow" (*D* 112). Duffy's pronouncements seem pompous, and even cruel, because they are presented by him as truth, but he will find, to *his* sorrow, that they are more true than he realizes. In more ways than one he is, in enunciating these sentences, pronouncing his own sentence.

All the books and music that Duffy brought to Mrs. Sinico are returned to him via the post, and this is a literal enactment of a psychological truth because his act of bringing them to her was in fact an attempt to mail them to himself after they had been authenticated by the approving gaze of the Other. As Duffy demonstrates, it is one's own ego that one loves while loving a loved one. The ego, which can be understood in this context as Duffy's capacity for misrecognition, is made Real on the imaginary level by Mrs. Sinico's masquerade as the Woman: "So, the subject becomes aware of his desire in the other, through the intermediary of the image of the other which offers him the semblance of his own mastery" (Lacan 1988a, 155). A four-year hiatus extends between Duffy's leave-taking from Mrs. Sinico and his reading of the account of her death in the evening newspaper. In his diary, at some point during this interval, Duffy nominates the sexual urge — the way in which it is encouraged or discouraged — as the divisive force that prevents "love between man and man" and "friendship between man and woman" (*D* 112). Predictably, he is silent about what might occur between women and women (friendship? love?) because he interprets their otherness as a representation of the Other that must be mastered to constitute his being. Significantly, what initially shocks him as he reads of her death is that in the four-year interval since he broke off his intercourse with her, she continued to exist. It is not so much that she is dead now that unnerves him, it is that for four years she continued to live a separate life in distinct variance with his self-serving memory of her. What revolts him is that she has strayed so far from the image of the Woman as to expose the fictional nature of this construct, thus exposing as well the fiction of his identity. Her undeniable suffering restores her 'otherness' in a way that threatens to alter her gaze from one of adoration to one of disdain. He has kept in his mind an image of her gaze at its most benevolent and maternal and allowed it to serve as a specular notarizer of his own self-worth, constantly stamping his third-person sentences as authentic. Helplessly, he will feel this benevolent gaze grow more accusing as the night wears on and the repressed question of her sexuality increasingly impinges on his consciousness. It is the denied of Mrs. Sinico — the "elsewhere" of her sexuality beyond his representation of her — that will allow her to haunt him from beyond the grave.

Although he scorns "the threadbare phrases" of the newspaper account, the journalistic rhetoric is unnerving to him because it selectively misrepresents aspects of her "case" to preserve the image of her as "a lady." Of course, the more the newspaper account tries to leave this representation intact, the more it calls it into question. The headline reads, in direct contradiction of the implied censure of the newspaper account, "Death of a Lady at Sydney Parade." The newspaper account of her life *also* denies the unrepresented elements of her sexuality, as Duffy did, and he is appalled (even as he strives to reject this parallel) to see this clumsy repetition of his own "sentencing" of Mrs. Sinico. The exceedingly fresh quality of his shock and outrage seems to suggest that only a few hours have passed since their last encounter rather than four years! "Not merely had she degraded herself; she had degraded him. . . . His soul's companion!" (*D* 115).[4] At this point the reader realizes what motivated him to end the relationship when he did: she had reached the status of a "third person" for him, and, as such, she was indispensable as a memory *and, thus, dangerous as an actual companion.*[5] He tries to dismiss her supplementary ex-istence (jouissance) in pseudo-Nietzschean terms: "Evidently she had been unfit to live, without any strength of purpose, an easy prey to habits, one of the wrecks on which civilisation has been reared" (*D* 115). But once again it is himself he is condemning because he has allowed the maternal gaze of this same "wreck" to dedicate the truth of the monumental construct of his ego; she was certainly the "wreck" upon which his "civilisation" was reared. Now that she is dead, she is fully a memory and, therefore, no longer *his* memory (that is, a memory that, like Lacan's *objet a,* appears to be precisely what he needs to "complete" his lack-in-being). Her death establishes her as "other" in a manner beyond his ability to misrecognize her, and it is this "otherness" that briefly exposes the fictional nature of the "self" that "sentenced" her to death.

Mrs. Sinico begins haunting Duffy because the memory he constructed of her is undermined by the return of what this construction repressed (a return of the Real) — the question of her desire, which continued to ex-ist beyond the quest for him"self": "As the light failed and his memory began to wander he thought her hand touched his" (*D* 116). The subject is able to believe in the fictional structure of the moi as a symptom because the moi operates as a principle of negation that misrecognizes the other as one's own ego ideal; all other aspects of this other are denied or repressed. Walking in the park, where he had walked with her four years earlier, Duffy experiences the "ghost" of Mrs. Sinico as something very much like what Lacan describes as "presence": "It isn't a feeling that we have all the time. To be sure, we are influenced by all sorts of presences, and our world only possesses its consistency, its density, its lived stability, because, in some way, we take account of these presences, but we do not realize them as such. You really can sense that it is a feeling which I'd say we are always trying to efface from life. It wouldn't be easy to live if, at every moment, we had the feeling of presence, with all the mystery that that implies. It is a mystery from which we distance ourselves, and to which we are, in a word, inured" (1988a, 42). We have seen that Duffy creates a self-generated (and obsessively benevolent) presence with his odd autobiographical habit of formulating a sentence in which he refers to himself in the third person. This deliberate viewing of the "self" as object, using one's own voice, keeps at bay some of the voices that really inform consciousness, voices that occasionally can be overheard at the juncture of the moi and the je (in slips, hesitations, ellipses, and abrupt silences). For the narrator of "The Sisters," this imagined presence acts as an umbrella that screens out the Real and represses the gaze of the Other. Curiously, the touch from Mrs. Sinico, which led to Duffy breaking off his relationship with her is now transposed from the physical realm to the verbal register: "At moments he seemed to feel her voice *touch* his ear" (*D* 117). In addition, the division within his own subjectivity, which had been bridged by her imagined regard for him, reasserts itself as a dual image of her: "As he sat there, living over his life with her and evoking alternately the two images in which he now conceived her, he realized that she was dead, that she had ceased to exist, that she had become a memory" (*D* 116). There is the Mrs. Sinico who authenticated his essential being, and there is this ghostly force beyond that representation that threatens to expose this being as a fictional construct.

In essence, the version of Duffy's moi that he has preserved for four years is fading out (Gabriel will experience a similar sensation at the close of "The Dead"). The gaze and voice of Mrs. Sinico are rapidly gaining force as the alienating presence that he has so long tried to repress. Something 'other' was watching him all the time he imagined that he was looking at himself: "He felt his moral nature falling to pieces" (*D* 117). This moral nature, which I am comparing to Lacan's concept of the fictional moi construction, is really a type of organized ignorance designed to close out the gaze of the Other. One might say that the fragmented moi moves from being the un-acknowledged base of one's personality to being a character trait that is recognized by the subject (as is the case with the narrator in the closing lines of "Araby"). This self-knowledge allows for the submerged formation of a somewhat altered moi, which the humbled subject experiences as having learned something. In this sense, Duffy's more humane recollection of Mrs. Sinico at the close of the story is not so much a restoration of the past as it is a reconstruction of his present. He does not remember her, he re-members himself: "The restitution of the subject's wholeness appears in the guise of a restoration of the past. But the stress is always placed more on the side of reconstruction than on that of reliving. . . . When all is said and done, it is less a matter of remembering than of rewriting history" (Lacan 1988a, 14). What is devastating about the ending of this story is not just that Duffy will suffer a lonely life and unheralded death like the one to which he sentenced Mrs. Sinico (an interpretation with enough poetic justice to comfort more than a few readers); what is devastating is that he forgets her completely in order to re-member himself. Again, like the narrator of "Araby," Duffy puts forth an apparently "self"-deprecating revelation at the close of the story which is in fact a new myth of constancy: "He gnawed the rectitude of his life; he felt that he had been outcast from life's feast" (*D* 117). Poor Duffy. This is exactly the same self-righteousness that allows him to gnaw arrowroot biscuits for lunch every day of his life. Of all things, life's feast is what Duffy can best live without; it is, in fact, what he needs to live without. Mrs. Sinico's death has supplied him with another anecdote about himself that he relates in a short sentence which contains a subject in the third person and a predicate in the past tense: "*He had been* outcast from life's feast" (*D* 108, emphasis added)! Mr. Duffy, in short, is back to his old tricks.[6]

Duffy's self-pity actually reifies him as an ersatz Nietzschean *uber-menschen:* "He had sentenced her to ignominy, a death of shame" (*D* 117). A surge of pride and power is in this statement even though it is posed as self-castigating to obscure its actual function as "self"-indulgence. This thought of himself as the cause of Mrs. Sinico's doom is brought to Duffy's mind by the sight of "some human figures lying" in the park: "Those venal and furtive loves filled him with despair. . . . He knew that the prostrate creatures down by the wall were watching him and wished him gone" (*D* 117). His despair does not arise from the fact that they "wished him gone" (can we really imagine that he wishes they would ask him to join them?) but from the fact that they are allowing themselves to be touched. More than likely, he would see the men at the base of the wall as lost to the fetid charms of Circean women. Like someone with the sexual equivalent of anorexia nervosa, what one might call "pleasure anorexia," Duffy generates self-empowerment by starving himself; it is this precise activity that makes him feel in control and unique (and immune to the gaze of the Other). In this context, his assertion that "no one wanted him" is self-congratulatory! By staring at anonymous people groping each other in what looks like blind and indiscriminate desire (he refers to the lovers as "prostrate creatures"), Mr. Duffy restores the myth that he is a lone figure, a closed-circuit corpus of self-serving third-person sentences built upon the corpse of Mrs. Sinico: "He felt that he was alone" (*D* 117).

13

"It'll be all right when King Eddie comes"
The Pathetic Phallacy in
"Ivy Day in the Committee Room"

> [The role of] the phallic symbol . . . in the subjec-
> tive economy is precisely to supplement the *signifi-*
> *cance* of the Other at the very point where it is found
> wanting. (Lacan 1982b, 117)

> *They had their way: they laid him low.*
> *But Erin, list, his spirit may*
> *Rise, like the Phoenix from the flames,*
> *When breaks the dawning of the day* (D 134–35)

The direct discourse presented in "Ivy Day in the Committee
Room" is in distinct contrast to the indirect narration of Maria's
night out in "Clay." In "Ivy Day" readers need not wait to be told what
has been said, nor do they struggle to reconstruct what might have
been said from a narrator's summary. This story is written very nearly
like a play, and one could print it as such by parenthetically including
the occasional narrative descriptions as stage directions. Whereas "Clay"
opens at the Dublin by Lamplight Laundry, which is full of lost women
of various sorts — no man is likely to enter there — the Committee Room
is a completely male domain where no female would be likely to ven-
ture. All told, seven men come and go in the course of the story: Old
Jack, Mat O' Connor, Joe Hynes, John Henchy, Father Keon, Ban-
tom Lyons, and Crofton. Another four men — two alive, two dead —

are discussed in absentia (Colgan, the labor candidate; Tierney, the nationalist candidate for whom some of the men are canvasing; King Edward, and Parnell). In addition, Hynes's father, Tierneys's father, and Old Jack's son all come up for discussion. These are men talking about men, and women barely are discussed at all, with three notable exceptions (Old Jack's wife, Queen Victoria, and the "Erin" of Hynes's poem). These exceptions, I argue, completely subvert the desire of the men to present themselves as autonomous beings with values, principles, and clearly defined political beliefs.[1]

In both "Clay" and "Ivy Day" a member of the group is called on to publicly perform in a manner that is unexpectedly moving (Maria's song and Hynes's poem), and in both stories there is some difficulty in finding a corkscrew when one is needed. In "Ivy Day" a corkscrew is borrowed and must be returned before the men are done with it: "—Open two bottles of stout, Jack, said Mr. O'Connor. — How can I said the old man, when there's no corkscrew?" (*D* 130). When more men arrive later in the story, the problem arises again: "—Open another bottle of stout, Jack, said Mr. Henchy. O, I forgot there's no corkscrew!" (*D* 133). This constantly misplaced corkscrew is only fitting because the men are forever waiting for something that is always elsewhere (the money from Tierney, the bottles of stout, the ghost of Parnell) to appear among them. Like Joe Donnelly at the conclusion of "Clay," these men are constantly having to ask someone to tell them where the corkscrew is.

The men in "Ivy Day" are not shown in any sort of domestic context. Yet their references to their domestic lives—brief and infrequent though they may be—are extremely significant. "Ivy Day" depicts men in the public realm. Accordingly, they concentrate on their own individuation and the principles that make them consistent and unique. The desire for fusion with the (m)Other is strictly repressed in favor of the control and acquisition of language, law, and culture, sanctified by what Lacan called "the Name-of-the-Father," which grants the subject access to the Symbolic Order. Muller describes the dialectic between imagined fusion with the (m)Other in the mirror stage (Imaginary Order) and the separation from this phase (castration) that inaugurates the child's immersion into the Symbolic Order of language and culture: "For Lacan, the signifier of the mother's desire is the phallus. Thus, in attempting to be the imaginary phallus or completion of the mother the child rejects the limits implied by castration. These limits are the constraints invoked by the Law of the Father, the symbolic father who intervenes in this dual relation, establishes primal repression by structuring desire according to the laws of language, and makes it possible for the child to have a place in a signifying network of kinship relations, sex roles, sanctions, and discourse" (23).

The men of "Ivy Day" are bound together by the historical disasters of their past and the political futility of their present. Their day has been spent canvasing for votes for their chosen candidate, presumably because they hope he will be elected according to due process of law and, henceforth, represent their interests. Yet the only point that all in the room agree upon (to varying degrees) is that the leader they have chosen to support is a fraud. Although the men in the Committee Room seem to care passionately for the concept of Ireland, and they acknowledge it as the larger context that gives each of their lives meaning (as their reaction to Hynes's poem makes clear), the actuality of Irish politics is a subject that disgusts them. Despite the fraudulence and failure of leaders, the men in the committee room continue to long for the idea of moral and unified leadership. In this sense, Joyce's story chronicles the complex politics of subjectivity even more than the vagaries of a local election.

But while the Name-of-the-Father sanctions linguistic orderings such as naming, individuation, and difference, it does so at the price of separating, alienating, and symbolically castrating the subject from the imaginary unity (jouissance) of the mirror stage. Subjectivity is based on a lack that gives rise to what Lacan terms Desire. Language supplies a substitutive satisfaction to the subject, but what it provides is never precisely what the subject lacks. Ironically, then, the subject uses language to substitute for a sense of lack-in-being, but because objects of Desire can never be refound, only substituted for, the subject perpetually searches for the lost unity of the presocial "self" in the mirror stage (sanctioned and approved by the gaze of the (m)Other) even as the public "self" is formed. Far from valorizing the public world of politics where "men can be men," Joyce details how alienated and uncertain the men in the committee room really are. The men who have been canvasing for Tierney, for example, have no real affection for the man or any trust in him as a leader.

Although they believe profoundly in the abstract idea of leadership (embodied by the memory of the dead Parnell), they do not see the man they are working for as anything more than a crafty employer. In a similar vein, Henchy shows an elaborate deference to Father Keon, as though he were a leader, but when the alleged priest departs, readers learn that he, too, is an enigma rather than a source of guidance: "What is he exactly? O'Connor asks. "Ask me an easier one," said Mr Henchy. . . . I think he's what you call a black sheep" (*D* 129). It is implied throughout the story that power is accrued only by compromising principle and depriving other people of choices. Even though the men believe in leadership in the abstract, they know of no leaders — other than the dead Parnell — whom they would defend as uncorrupted. One must compromise to obtain power and then use that power to benefit those who made it possible: "You must owe the City Fathers money nowadays if you want to be made Lord Mayor," Mr. Henchy says. "Then they'll make you Lord Mayor" (*D* 127). The paradox of power in this story is that the men convincingly demonstrate that all power is based on greed and pettiness, yet they talk longingly, and with equal conviction, of a transcendent power that is innate and uncorruptible. They seem able to hold this contradictory view as long as they do not apply it to any living politicians. As Schneiderman remarked: "The function of the Name-of-the-Father is its subversion" (quoted in Ragland-Sullivan 1986, 58). In "Ivy Day," the Name-of-the-Father is bankrupt and, thus, can perform its function only when veiled. It is essentially the illusion of power, but the men pledge allegiance to it just the same.

The current patriarchal leaders in Joyce's story are morally and fiscally destitute. The idea of a power that is moral and good is considered sacred by the men, but every living manifestation of this power is scorned as the self-serving scheme of a manipulative scoundrel. The Phallus, which Lacan stresses does not exist but only represents the law of the Name-of-the-Father, is likewise notable in its absence from the Symbolic Order depicted in "Ivy Day": "—Open another bottle of stout, Jack, said Mr. Henchy. —O, I forgot there's no corkscrew!" (*D* 133). The alienation and unbridgeable otherness that periodically undermines the uneasy camaraderie of the men in "Ivy Day" is a theme that is struck by Hynes when he first enters the room: "—What are you doing in the dark? asked a voice" (*D* 120). None of the men in this story are anybody until they declare their relationships to the transcendent, patriarchal, and Symbolic Order. Whenever a man leaves the room, the others discuss him in relation to one or more of the following points: What was his father like? How does he make his money? What does he want here? Each man is always evaluating his connection to another man in relation to something higher than himself (which, I suggest, has a corollary in Lacan's concept of the Name-of-the-Father). Naturally, they are scornful of men who overtly align themselves with powerful men because this belies the very self-autonomy that the phallus is meant to bestow. Hynes, for example, refers disparagingly to "those shoneens that are always hat in hand before any fellow with a handle to his name" (*D* 121).

Yet they are all waiting for Tierney to pay them or, at least, send them some beer. Henchy has already been put off once because Tierney claims that he "must speak to Mr Fanning. . . . I've spent a lot of money" (*D* 123). Tierney's smooth expression of his superiority over Henchy infuriates him, but he consistently seeks to align himself with it nonetheless. No matter how much he may depise Tierney (whom he calls "the mean little shoeboy from hell"), he remains in awe of what Tierney manages to represent. In the same manner, Henchy is painstakingly deferential to Father Keon, who we learn is "very thick" with Mr. Fanning. The black sheep, Father Keon, may not be a Father at all, and he leaves immediately after seeing that Mr. Fanning is not in the committee room (immediately persuaded, I think, by what a waste of time it would be to talk to *these* fellows). What one can see in "Ivy Day" is the inevitable failure of the Name-of-the-father to substitute for the Desire-of-the-Mother (to unify the subject and, thereby, grant autonomy). This forces the men into elaborate self-deceptions about the nature of leadership, law, patriarchial control, and other structuring landmarks supposedly supplied by the Symbolic Order. The men cling to the abstraction of the "Name-of-the-Father" because it appears to bestow difference and individuality upon them, yet they mock any literal representations of the phallic signifier as elaborate chicanery: "—There's some deal on in that quarter, said Mr. O'Connor thoughtfully. I saw the three of them hard at it yesterday at Suffolk Street corner. —I think I know the little game they're at, said Mr Henchy" (*D* 127). Since the Phallus represents the illusion of unity and power, those masquerading as the possessors of it must be denigrated as impostors to keep this illusion intact.

This story, which seems primarily concerned with masculine prerogative and patriarchal power, actually begins with a conversation between Old Jack and Mat O'Connor that is concerned with, of all things, how best to raise children! Old Jack resumes this conversation (which began before the story opens): "—Ah, yes, he said, continuing, it's hard to know what way to bring up children. Now who'd think he'd turn out like that! I sent him to the Christian Brothers and I done what I could for him, and there he goes boosing about. I tried to make him some way decent" (*D* 119). This complaint inaugurates a subtheme of the entire story—How should fathers parent their sons? Or, to put it more generally, how do boys become men? In Old Jack's case, parenting style consists of beating his son for being too much like him: "—Only I'm an old man now I'd change his tune for him. I'd take the stick to his back and beat him while I could stand over him. . . . He takes th'upper hand of me whenever he sees I've a sup taken" (*D* 119–120). So Jack has beaten him until he's grown too old to continue, and his son too big to stand still. What went wrong? In a masterpiece of myopic reasoning, Old Jack figures his mother must be to blame: "The mother, you know," he confides to Mat O'Connor, "she cocks him up with this and that" (*D* 120). This is the first hint that always underlying masculine failure (or so men believe) is a woman up to her old tricks. To put this another way, a woman who fails to operate as a symptom for the masculine subject must be viewed as willfully treacherous because all other explanations call attention to the permanent lack-in-being at the base of desire.

The second presentation of this rationale occurs when another woman is brought into the men's conversation. She is Queen Victoria, who, so Henchy maintains, never visited Ireland, and who also kept her son King Edward off the throne her whole life. In fact, she *had* visited Ireland—and fairly recently (1900)—although no one in the story seems to know this. So two women are mentioned in the story. One is the Queen of England, and the other is the wife of a caretaker. Despite the extreme difference in their social classes, they have in common that they are both mothers who prevent their sons from achieving phallic power: one does so by nurturing too much, the other by refusing to nurture at all. One "cocks up" her son, the other keeps him out of power until she is dead. The third and final woman mentioned in the story is not an actual person, but a representation of a mother. Precisely because she is not an actual woman, she is the only female who is a staunch supporter of the Phallic Order and also the chief mourner of the tragedy that befell Parnell: "And Erin's hopes and Erin's dreams / Perish upon her monarch's pyre" (*D* 134). The overtly supported male prerogatives of the story insist that women matter very little: they do not vote, they do not canvass, they do not know anything about current events, and they do not frequent taverns to stay informed. Yet I argue that these three mothers—one who nurtures too much, another who does not nurture at all, and a third who fully supports the "Name-of-the-Father" and grieves for her "Uncrowned King"—all represent the pervasive subtext of this story: What makes a boy a man, and what can be done about the gaze of the (m)Other that seems to, by turns, both support and subvert masculinity? My approach may help explain why the men in this story are so peculiarly helpless, even as they actively engage in the patriarchal power struggle of labor and politics. What I am calling the "pathetic phallacy" is the phenomenon whereby the masculine subject seeks to align himself with the phallic signifier that gives rise to the law of the Name-of-the-Father. But this alignment inaugurates Desire: an insatiable lack for which language and culture offer substitutive satisfactions, but nothing that directly provides the imagined fusion with the (m)Other.

This psychic castration that leads to immersing one's "self" into the Symbolic Order permits a subject to use language as a substitutive means for individuating a "self" through Desire, but only by aligning one's identity with the phallus, an object that can only perform its function when veiled. Although the paternal law symbolically castrates a subject, the maternal gaze prevents the subject from becoming a gendered individual. The price for rejecting the intervention of the Symbolic Order, in other words, is psychosis. For the masculine subject, the fear of the internal (m)Other's gaze (which remains the earliest representation for the subject of the authenticating gaze of the Other) is projected onto other women: "Its effect [the castration complex] is to ensure the *signifiance* of the Other at the point where it is wanting. That the Other should thereby act as guarantee is the founding condition for any possibility of exchange, and what must be given up to this is the jouissance of the subject. The castration complex thus designates the passing jouissance into the function of a value, and its profound adulteration in that process. . . . But by becoming the place to which it is transferred, it is the woman who finds herself representing this phallic value" (1982b, 120–21). As Ragland-Sullivan has noted, "The primordial eye that upholds the Symbolic Order is the mother's and therefore female" (1986, 294). But this gaze must be repressed if the phallus is to retain its (illusional) strength as the original signifier that authenticates the subject's story of himself. Any woman who ex-ists beyond the phallic economy (as did Maria) or co-opts its privileges for herself (as did Queen Victoria) or submits to it (as Old Jack's wife has done in relation to her son) will still be reviled as treacherous should circumstances (alcoholism, unemployment, disillusionment in love, physical or fiscal impotence) tear aside the veil that is required for the Phallus to perform its function as a guarantor of meaning and coherency in the fiction of patriarchal reality. In "Ivy Day," the gaze that authenticates masculinity is frighteningly female, and the denigration of the (m)Other (Old Jack's wife, Henchy's Queen Victoria) by the men, as well as the communal worship of her ideal representation (Hynes's "Erin"), is an attempt to domesticate this gaze.

It is significant that the Mother (as Old Jack refers to his wife) is mentioned only once in this story and at a point where there is no real direction to the conversation (Old Jack is alone in the room with O'Connor). What is particularly interesting about this brief mention of the mother is that it is understood between the two men, without any need for further discussion or clarification, that she is to blame for the son's alcoholic abusiveness of the inebriated father. The pathetic phallacy of this father/son relationship is that both men employ alcohol to mask a lack they prefer to ignore, and the gaze of the (m)Other, which upholds their identity structure (such as it is) takes the blame for making them feel something is missing (the female is to blame for the fact of insatiable Desire in the male). Old Jack's designation of his wife as *the* mother instead of *his* mother gives her a generic quality, which is then further reinforced by O'Connor's even more general condemnation: "That's what ruins children" (*D* 120). Surely, Old Jack's wife has not ruined *all* children, but O'Connor accepts and further emphasizes Jack's implied generalization that mothers, by their very nature, ruin their male children by "cocking them up" with "this and that."

The word *cock,* as a verb, means to set at a jaunty angle. The implication in this metaphor is that the mother sets up the man for the fall that occurs when the phallus, which is set up as the basis for the masculine identity structure, proves to be a fantasy object that must be kept veiled if it is to perform its function. "—He's not a bad sort . . . only Fanning has such a loan of him" says Henchy of Tierney after the beer arrives. This is the same man whom Henchy earlier described as a "mean little shoeboy of hell!" who "hasn't got those little pigs' eyes for nothing" (*D* 123), but once the beer arrives, this eases the sting of being at Tierney's beck and call, and Henchy rehabilitates the figure of Tierney except for the fact that he is at the beck and call of Fanning! In other words, he forgives Tierney for everything but being too much like him (this is also the one thing Old Jack would not forgive his son). Much of the stifled animosity circulating among the men in the committee room is their rage at perceiving other men to be as helpless and unprincipled as they are (the only male figure who *now* seems worthy of representing the transcendent phallus without qualification is, as Henchy bluntly points out, dead).

In Lacanian terms, Jack's crude and self-serving observation about the mother has a certain subjective validity. A man, permanently alienated from the objects of his desire by the divisive effects of the mirror stage and the substitutive effects of language acquisition, seeks to be the desire of the mother because he sees this as being the Other of the Other, which would guarantee his unity and, thereby, grant him certitude. But there is no Other of the Other, the Phallus does not exist. But this in no way weakens the masculine subject's insatiable desire to be something impossible. In fact, it is the necessity to be what cannot exist that makes the masculine subject rather helpless to do anything but victimize others in the pursuit of this illusion. The duplicity of "being" inherent in the masculine subject is displaced onto the woman, and her "duplicitous nature" comes to be seen as the outward cause of something that was always already in the subject. A man seeks to return to the presymbolic bliss of mirror unity that the mother's gaze once designated as "real." Later, the gaze of the mother is seen as something hateful and subversive that challenges the supremacy of the phallic signifier. Of course, the Phallus, in its very essence, is already subverted because it signifies the existence of an impossible unity. This fact must be kept veiled for it to serve its illusory function as the origin of meaning and the basis of value and exchange in the linguistic system. So Jack's wife "cocks up" his son, and this grants the son the degree of certainty necessary to begin beating up his father (at least verbally, perhaps physically): "He takes th'upper hand of me whenever he sees I've a sup taken" (*D* 120). This suggests how deeply rooted male violence is in the impossibility of being truly masculine. One sees this pattern elsewhere in *Dubliners* in the increasingly violent actions of Eveline's father and in the closing moments of "Counterparts" where Farrington concludes his debilitating day by beating his son.

The violence between father and son, then, serves to veil the phallic function, even as it further alienates masculine subjects from one another. This violence reduces the relationship between father and son to a power struggle that seems to validate the crippling illusion that power and prestige are the ultrahigh stakes that men compete for within the phallic order. Old Jack elevates the struggle with his son to the level of universal significance: "What's the world coming to when sons speaks that way of their father? [sic]" (*D* 120). Jack's grammatical slip highlights the conflation of Jack's view of his son and his view of all sons in the patriarchial order; his son challenges him, therefore the order of the world is threatened. Patriarchial power is an illusion, and the violence between fathers and sons is a confrontation that purports to validate that illusion but, in fact, threatens to expose it. All the men who come and go in the Committee Room are, whether they like it or not, the sons of Parnell.

Joe Hynes sees the death of Parnell as an event that will leave Ireland forever bereft of power and identity. Henchy and Crofton, however, see an opportunity to replace the dead father with a symbol of patriarchial order that might prove more profitable to Ireland—King Edward.

> —Listen to me, said Mr Henchy. What we want in this country, as I said to old Ward, is capital. The King's coming here will mean an influx of money into this country. The citizens of Dublin will benefit by it. Look at all the factories down by the quays there, idle! Look at all the money there is in the country if we only worked the old industries, the mills, the shipbuilding yards and factories. It's capital we want.
> —But look here, John, said Mr O'Connor. Why should we welcome the King of England? Didn't Parnell himself . . .
> —Parnell, said Mr Henchy, is dead. (*D* 131)

As Rabate notes, "the name of Parnell has been deprived of all political force and turned into a myth, the myth of the dismembered
Father devoured and mourned by the patricidal sons" (1982, 62). In
Mr. Henchy's fantasy, the death of Parnell allows for the coming of
King Edward who will start up all the idle machines in the land and
flood the country with money. In this way the illusion of a phallocratic
order is maintained: the uncrowned king is dead, long live King Edward! I argue that Henchy is neither pro-Parnell nor pro-British but
pro-Phallus! Henchy is not interested in this or that ideology; indeed,
the only shortcoming that he notes about Parnell is the fact that he
is dead.[2] Were Parnell alive, Henchy would continue to gravitate toward
him as keeper of the Phallus: "He was the only man that could keep
that bag of cats in order" (*D* 132).[3] But are these male figures of power
as autonomous as all that? Henchy implicates a third party: "Now,
here's the way I look at it. Here's this chap [King Edward] come to
the throne after his old mother keeping him out of it till the man was
grey" (*D* 131–32). Lacan states, "If the desire of the mother *is* the phallus,
then the child wishes to be the phallus so as to satisfy this desire" (1982b,
83). If, on the other hand, the mother co-opts the Phallus for herself,
the male child is "kept out of it" until her death. With Queen Victoria
dead, King Edward becomes the phallic signifier and represents for
Henchy a boundless source of rejuvenation from which Ireland can
only benefit (and "Ireland" is always synonymous with "Henchy" in
Henchy's mythos). Hence, the death of Parnell is not as significant
to Henchy as the death of King Edward's mother.

Henchy shows ideology to be nothing more than a drive toward
a fantasy of totality that has nothing to do with objective truth. The
image of Ireland reviving itself by aligning itself with the truth of the
phallic order is much more real to Henchy than the fact that England
has colonized Ireland and increased its wealth at his country's expense
and that the post-Parnell political scene provides no incentive for them
to alter that pattern. Henchy, in other words, wants to be a good son
to King Edward, the father of England, now that Parnell, the inadequate father of Ireland, is dead. It does not matter that King Edward
is guilty of the same sexual transgressions that caused Parnell's down-
fall, what does not kill him cannot hurt him as far as Henchy is concerned. Curiously enough, Henchy operates within the group gathered
in the Committee Room as the inverse of Parnell—a sort of anti-Parnell.

Whereas Parnell unified people for the twin purposes of defiance and revolt, Henchy's constant, contradictory patter throughout this story seeks to unify people for acquiescence and passivity. What Henchy needs is subjective capital, that is, an accumulation of certitude and power that he could then devote to the accumulation of more certitude and power. Henchy's belief in a prosperous future sanctioned by the coming of King Edward has nothing to do with truth; instead, it compensates him for the inherent loss in his own being brought about by the trauma of psychic castration. Although Henchy has no use for a dead Parnell, he still has a nearly violent respect for the phallic function represented by Parnell.

When Crofton offers his profoundly dismissive tribute to Parnell ("our side of the house respects him because he was a gentleman"), Henchy is suddenly driven into a paroxysm of delight in which he describes Parnell's indomitable certitude (which he, against all logic, assumes will be endorsed by Crofton): "— Right you are, Crofton!" he says, as he prepares to supplement Crofton's lack of enthusiasm, "He was the only man that could keep that bag of cats in order. *Down, ye dogs! Lie down, ye curs!* That's the way he treated them" (*D* 132). Although Crofton has merely mumbled his comment on his way back to his seat, Henchy is described as "speaking fiercely." Henchy's energy is a crude parody of Parnell's considerable diplomatic skills. But what Henchy admires about Parnell has nothing to do with this or that legislative triumph; what he fantasizes about in relation to Parnell is a certitude and a unity of being that would allow him to address all division (in himself and among others) in no uncertain terms and stand forth as "the only man" capable of keeping "that bag of cats in order." For Henchy, the "truth" that Parnell was better for Ireland than King Edward is as irrelevant as it is undeniable. Henchy does not want to be Parnell, he wants to be the Phallus, which he imagines Parnell once was, and which he believes King Edward to be now. In this sense, the death of mother Ireland is as easy for him to accept as he imagines the death of Queen Victoria was for King Edward.

Joyce's use of italics makes it clear that for the length of time Henchy is shouting *Down, ye dogs! Lie down, ye curs!* he *is* Parnell. Or rather, he becomes what Parnell represents to him: not a leader of Irish nationalism pitted against a British policy of colonialism but a fantasy of totality directly authenticated by the gaze of the Other, and, therefore, indomitable, regardless of whatever forces are gathered against him. Henchy is a caricature of Parnell and he dominates the men in the room by transforming obstacles such as "truth" and "belief" into fantasies of control and unification.[4] Immediately after his speech, he directs Hynes into the room and commands Jack to serve him a beer: "Come in, Joe! Come in! he called out. . . . Open another bottle of stout, Jack, said Mr. Henchy. O, I forgot there's no corkscrew!" (*D* 133). There it is again, the same (?) corkscrew that Joe Donnelly could not find at the end of his evening of posing for the impotent Maria. Henchy had insulted Hynes behind his back as possibly being a spy, but in his present self-induced role as the signifier of all things, he easily absorbs the contradiction of providing for a man he has previously scorned. Yet *he lacks something.* But this implication of impotence does not slow Henchy down. When O'Connor asks Joe to recite the poem about Parnell, Henchy immediately asserts himself as the master of ceremony, and outmaneuvers O'Connor in giving Joe this final cue: "—Out with it, man! said Mr O'Connor. —'Sh, 'sh, said Mr Henchy. Now, Joe!" There is only one weakness to Mr. Henchy's control of Joe's oration: Both before the poem and immediately after its completion he buttresses his domination of the presentation with references to Mr. Crofton. Before the poem: "Did you ever hear that, Crofton? Listen to this now: splendid thing" (*D* 133). And after: "—What do you think of that, Crofton? cried Mr Henchy. Isn't that fine? What?" (*D* 135). At which point, the story ends with the narrator's report to the reader that the taciturn Mr. Crofton has taken up Henchy's invitation to have the final word: "Mr Crofton said that it was a very fine piece of writing" (*D* 135).

And, suddenly, in witnessing Henchy's final compulsive deference to Crofton, readers can understand that all Henchy's verbiage has been, in a sense, produced by Crofton's silence.[5] One recalls, for example, that Henchy prefaced his nearly hysterical support of the power of Parnell by saying "Right you are, Crofton!" Even as Henchy was controlling the conversation of the group, he was being controlled by Crofton's strategically silent presence.[6] Crofton, of course, is an unabashed supporter of the king to whom Henchy has pledged a rather circuitous allegiance to garner for himself the authority to speak "the truth." But the source of Henchy's authority is, in fact, his unconscious fixation on what he imagines Crofton to be thinking. This relationship allows Crofton to be the ultimate controller of the group because what he does not say dictates the extent to which Henchy is spoken by him. Henchy himself inadvertently acknowledges that this has been the case all day. "Between ourselves, you know," he tells O'Connor, "Crofton (he's a decent chap, of course), but he's not worth a damn as a canvasser. He hasn't a word to throw to a dog. He stands and looks at the people while I do the talking" (*D* 129). Henchy's parenthesis—"he's a decent chap"—shows that even his criticism of Crofton is pronounced by Crofton because it partakes of British slang.

One can witness the same effect when Henchy discusses King Edward: "He's a jolly fine decent fellow, if you ask me, and no damn nonsense about him" (*D* 132). His conscious praise of King Edward is, at the same time, unconscious praise for Crofton, who, furthermore, considers this homage no more than his due: "[Mr. Crofton] was silent for two reasons. The first reason, sufficient in itself, was that he had nothing to say; the second reason was that he considered his companions beneath him. He had been a canvasser for Wilkins, the Conservative, but when the Conservatives had withdrawn their man and, choosing the lesser of two evils, given their support to the Nationalist candidate, he had been engaged to work for Mr Tierney" (*D* 130). No one seems to seriously doubt that Tierney is an opportunist who will profit from the death of Parnell by cutting deals with the Conservative party in the name of Parnell's former party. O'Connor makes a feeble attempt to claim that Tierney will not vote to welcome the king, but Hynes brushes this aside ("Is it Tricky Dicky Tierney?"), and O'Connor abruptly abandons all pretense of honor and resigns himself to waiting for his money: "— By God! perhaps you're right, Joe, said Mr O'Connor. Anyway, I wish he'd turn up with the spondulics" (*D* 122). In other words, Crofton does not have to say anything, either when canvassing or when sitting in the Committee Room, because Henchy and everyone else present (except Hynes, who seems too disenfranchised to be a serious threat to Tierney's political ambitions) are essentially working for him and for the Conservative party that he supports. The horrible irony is that Tierney is so much in the pocket of the Conservatives that for them to have posted their own candidate would have been a risky redundancy. There is no more effective way for Crofton to imbue Henchy with Conservative ideology than to silently listen as Henchy imposes the Conservative argument on himself during his self-deceptive assertion of autonomous control over the group gathered before him.

As a representative of the phallic signifier that grants Henchy the authority to speak, Crofton operates as the Other, that is, as the unconscious that underlies and dictates Henchy's speech. Lacan states: "If the unconscious has taught us anything, it is firstly that somewhere, in the Other, it knows. It knows precisely because it is upheld by the signifiers through which the subject is constituted. . . . Obviously the unconscious presupposes that in the speaking being there is something, somewhere, which knows more than he does" (1982b, 158–159). So Henchy is swelled to larger than normal size (one might say "engorged") because he is inhabited by the phallic signifier, but at the same time he is reduced to being no more than a signifier. He is able to speak with authority because he is—in his ex-istence as a creature spoken by the signifier—already spoken. Thus, his ex-istence as Crofton's unspoken message makes him a subject in Lacan's sense of the term.

Hynes represents himself to others as a continued supporter of Parnell, so, for him, Parnell is still alive because *he* represents him. As Henchy notes: "—There's one of them, anyhow . . . that didn't renege him. By God, I'll say for you, Joe! No, by God, you stuck to him like a man!" (*D* 133). One might say that Hynes "stuck to him" in order to be a man. Henchy, however, must declare Parnell dead if he is to be represented by the signifier, "King Edward." Hynes's poem declares that Parnell is immortal, which is why the poem means so much to him, but in doing this he also reiterates that Parnell is dead (it is entitled "The Death of Parnell"), which is why Henchy (and, of course, before him, Crofton) also likes it so much. The truth of the poem pleases two ideologically opposed subjects because it supports equally (though differently) both of their claims to be represented by the phallic signifier.

What I am arguing is that Joyce's most overtly political story in *Dubliners* is not about social politics as much as it is about the politics of the subject who must construct "meaning" in accordance with an arbitrary position relative to the phallic signifier.[7] Henchy speaks with authority because Crofton does not speak at all. Hynes mourns Parnell perpetually (the poem is memorized, and frequently—perhaps compulsively—recited if asked for) because the way Parnell represents him to other subjects means he is not "really" a signifier spoken by other signifiers ad infinitum. All in all, the subjects in "Ivy Day" assert their political and personal autonomy in unconscious (and, therefore, slavish) reference to something that is elsewhere. The communication of Henchy (his *langue*) is contradictory and even absurd, his *parole*, however, is a consistent defense and presentation of his "self" at the expense of other people in the room. Ironically, this same "self" is completely subjugated to the silent Crofton. As a spokesperson, Henchy is like the obedient bottle on the hob that will announce itself in obedience to an influence that is "other." The men in this story do not so much want to be believed as they want to be loved — not by every man but by those others who represent, for them, the regard of the Other (and the "lost" regard of the (m)Other that had staved off the feeling of want-in-being that is the effect of castration).

It is significant that Crofton feels he has two reasons to remain silent.[8] Why two reasons, when even the narrator acknowledges that the first reason was "sufficient in itself"? The second reason is crucial because if Crofton were silent merely because "he had nothing to say," then this would indicate that he was present in the Committee Room as simply an excluded and ineffectual member of the group. But Crofton's awareness of the second reason turns the situation entirely around. He does not speak because the entire monologue of Henchy is unconsciously addressed to him and, in fact, depends on his silence for its presumed authority to subdue and control the others. Thus, Henchy's pose as a free-floating authoritative force is entirely a fraud. Lacan states that "the idea of an organ in glorious monadic isolation, rejecting any tie or relation (whether complementary or antagonistic) in favour of the sole alternative of being or of not being, must refer to an essentially imaginary organ" (1982b, 124). Henchy likes to preface his expressions with preambles that insist he is a source of autonomous authority: "Now, here's the way I look at it" (*D* 131).[9] But as I have tried to show, the *I* who imagines he is speaking (the enunciator) and what the *I* winds up saying (the enunciation) are two quite different things. One insists on "glorious monadic isolation," and the other betrays this pose as a masquerade. The intent of Henchy's conversation is to align the myth of his "self" with the power of the phallic function. This function, once represented by Parnell, is now represented by King Edward and the deliberately silent Crofton whose "absence" from the

conversation wholly determines Henchy's "presence." Henchy's relation to the phallic signifier not only allows him to speak, it speaks
through him and allows him to misrecognize as subjective utterance
what has, in fact, already been spoken by an-Other. So it should not
be a surprise that the other tricky person in this story, besides "Tricky
Dicky Tierney," is Henchy himself. "Did you ever see this little trick?"
he asks. Then he takes "two bottles from the table and, carrying them
to the fire, put[s] them on the hob" (*D* 130).[10] Unable to keep a corkscrew, he is adept at imitating mastery by using a force outside of
himself. Henchy *poses* as a phallic signifier, and as such, he constructs
fictions that stand in as other people's "truth."

Behind the speaking subject who subscribes to the Law of the Father is the even more formative, although repressed, gaze of the
(m)Other. The Phallus is not an original force in the subject. Rather,
it intervenes in the unity of the mother-infant imaginary fusion, thus
introducing the alienating effect of difference and the compensatory
substitutive system of language and culture in the Symbolic Order.
The mastery and individuation that difference, naming, and substitution provide appears to compensate the subject for the loss of mirror-
stage fusion with the mother. But this postcastration individuation
inaugurates Desire and a permanent yearning for the imagined bliss
of this prior state (designated by Lacan as jouissance). Whether a
mother "cocks up" her son (by maintaining a reverential attitude toward
the Phallus, as did Old Jack's wife), or "keep[s] him out of it" (by seeking to assume it for herself, as did Queen Victoria), the result is that
a man must struggle, in one illusory way or another, to be the Phallus
in relation to the female gaze within.

Whether a woman uses her femininity to inflate or deflate masculinity, she represents the absolute 'otherness' that underlies, and potentially undermines, a man's certitude. That is why one can say that
the purpose of the Phallus is its own subversion, and anyone who lines
up his or her identity according to this token is forced to help veil
its fraudulent dimension. What the phallic signifier creates is not meaning but lack, and, henceforth, "meaning" is upheld as something that
obscures that lack. The substitutive Desire inherent in the use of language permits a man to replace imaginary fusion with his own image,
that is, replace jouissance—an illusion authenticated by the gaze of
the mother—with the sort of knowledge that is provided by interpret-

ing the Symbolic Order (interpretation is a form of desire for Lacan). But the "truth" that is thereby attained is always something other than what the subject has demanded to know. The question that subjects ask the Other, through others, about the authenticity of their existence always returns as an echo of the original question; this perpetual question is then misrecognized by the "selves" of the speaking beings as the correct answer.

The failure of the men in the room to complete themselves and become the Phallus is prefigured in the character of Father Keon. Keon has only popped his head into the Committee Room because he is looking for Mr. Fanning. This in itself is significant because Fanning seems to be running the entire operation: Henchy says of Tierney— the man all the men in the room are subordinate to—"[Tierney's] not a bad sort . . . only Fanning has such a loan of him" (*D* 129). Father Keon is the antithesis of an authority figure. His appearance is so polymorphous that even the narrator cannot decide if he is "a poor clergyman or a poor actor" (he is, of course, like other men aligning themselves with the phallus, both and, therefore, neither). Readers also learn that "it was impossible to say whether he wore a clergyman's collar or a layman's." Henchy, who worships the position of patriarchal power, however shabbily incarnated, leaps to his feet and is all attentiveness. When Keon leaves, the subject of his identity remains behind him in the Committee Room: "What is he exactly?" O'Connor asks. "Ask me an easier one," Mr. Henchy replies. They cannot determine where he comes from, what his attachments might be, or how he makes a living. Henchy sounds the theme of all the men in this story when he designates Keon as "an unfortunate man of some kind" (*D* 126). If O'Connor's query, "*What* is he exactly?" suggests that even Keon's humanity is in doubt because his function is obscure, Henchy's reply strengthens this impression: "God forgive me . . . I thought he was the dozen of stout" (*D* 127). The implication is that Father Keon has been "bought out" by Fanning. O'Connor remarks, "Fanning and himself seem to me very thick." The priest who has failed to represent spiritual power has aligned himself with political power; the result is that he and Fanning are "very thick." Emphasis is constant in this story on things "rising," being "cocked up," "thickening"; but the context of all this swelling makes it clear that this effect is another product of self-delusion. "Everything implied by the analytic engagement with human behaviour," Lacan says, "indicates not that meaning reflects the sexual but that it makes up for it" (quoted in Rose 1982, 47). Father Keon represents a rip in the fabric of the phallic order that Henchy cannot bear to acknowledge. "Is he a priest at all?" O'Connor asks. "'Mmm yes, I believe so" is Henchy's unconvincing reply, followed by his awkward attempt to elevate Father Keon to the level of an exception that proves the validity of the rule: "I think he's what you call a black sheep. We haven't many of them, thank God! but we have a few" (*D* 126).

What I am calling "the pathetic phallacy" undermines another discussion about fathers and sons. Henchy tries to diminish the sting of working for Tierney by denigrating his father: "I suppose he forgets the time his little old father kept the hand-me-down shop in Mary's Lane" (*D* 123). He goes on to relate how Tierney's father kept the shop open on Sunday morning "before the houses were open" for those who headed there for an early drink rather than to mass. But Henchy's denigration is all rhetoric. The fact remains that he now depends on Tierney for a drink and that is why he can be dismissed in a high-handed way by him: "*O, now, Mr. Henchy, when I see the work going on properly I won't forget you, you may be sure*" (*D* 127). One learns later that Henchy's forced deference toward Tierney extends to not interrupting him when he is in conversation: "I couldn't go over while he was talking to Alderman Cowley" (*D* 127). Again, it is O'Connor who remarks, as he did relative to Keon and Fanning, that "there's some deal on in that quarter." Despite Tierney's shady heritage, despite Keon's ambiguous status as a priest, these men are the ones cutting deals. In contrast, the men in the Committee Room sit around hoping for a beer, inconsistently defending their various contradictory ideologies, and wondering aloud who they are really working for and why. Hynes's father, in opposition to Tierney's, is characterized by Henchy as "a decent respectable man" (*D* 124). But this compliment is followed by the disconcerting epithet: "Poor old Larry Hynes! Many a good turn he did in his day!" The implication is that Hynes's father was principled and generous, and the result was that he died poor and bequeathed nothing to his son except a frank suspicion of pompous authority (a legacy that has left his son helplessly self-righteous). Despite overwhelming evidence to the contrary, the men in the Committee Room want to see patriarchal power as a sacrament bestowed only upon the great who, having richly proved themselves worthy of it will, therefore, use it fairly.

But trickery and illegality, done cleverly enough, will put a man in a position to patronize and condescend to decent, respectable men. In a small way Henchy accomplishes this very trick when he successfully imposes his outrageous view that King Edward will be good for Ireland. Here, Joyce shows truth to be no more than a contractual agreement consented to by various restless adults who only believe in it to varying degrees. Old Jack goes along with Hynes because what he most desires from powerful men is a pompous display of importance. His disgust with the current Lord Mayor is not remotely political but is purely a matter of style: *"And how do you like your new master, Pat?* says I to him. *You haven't much entertaining now,* says I. *Entertaining!* says he. *He'd live on the smell of an oil-rag"* (*D* 128). Old Jack, in a scandalized tone, goes on to relate that the current Lord Mayor is content to send out for a pound of chops for his dinner. Old Jack does not care who rules, so long as they act like rulers and, thereby, allow him to feel like a worthwhile subordinate securely located farther down in the chain of command. Like the town's people in "The Emperor's New Clothes," he would rather insist on the truth that the king is well dressed, rather than face the 'Real' truth that the Phallus cannot function when it is unveiled.

When Henchy fantasizes about "becoming a City Father," however, he envisions a perverse family of men, cynically displaying a debased version of patriarchal power: "—Driving out of the Mansion House, said Mr. Henchy, in all my vermin, with Jack here standing up behind me in a powdered wig—eh? —And make me your private secretary, John. —Yes. And I'll make Father Keon my private chaplain. We'll have a family party" (*D* 127).

Here one sees the full range of bitterness that these men have toward their own gender. Henchy is enamored of leaders like Parnell and King Edward, but he chafes at having to sidle up to a trickster like Tierney in the hopes of wheedling a drink. Lacan describes the paradox of the castration complex "as a process of cancellation involving the very organ which thereby receives its proper place in the subjective economy" (1982b, 116). In other words, a man becomes symbolically impotent in order to dream of possessing a symbol of infinite power. Because "the subject is constituted in a dependency on the speech of the Other"

(1982b, 116), a subject cannot substitute for the lack-in-being that results from the mirror phase without designating an initial signifier (the phallic signifier) as the thing that inaugurates difference and the substitutive dimension of language. An atmosphere of frustration and lack permeates the atmosphere of "Ivy Day" and accounts for the emotional reaction to Hynes's poem, which reconfirms the existence of the phallic signifier (sanctioned by the (m)Other in the representation of "Erin") in all its abstract purity. Simply put, this is not a political poem but an elaborate male fantasy that restores the mythical unity of masculine subjectivity. The alienating place of the Other (a disunited Ireland) becomes the (m)Other ("Erin") who acts as a guarantor for the masculine fantasy of power and unity (embodied and embalmed in "the memory of Parnell").

Most critics note the paradox that although the poem Joe reads is of rather poor quality, it is still oddly moving not only to his audience in the room but to the reader as well.[11] In my reading, the poem succeeds because its overt purpose (commemorating Parnell) is subverted by Hynes's greater need to describe a state of alienation and disenfranchisement that he has felt all his life (and the other men have felt, too). The several purposes of the poem are to praise the political career of Parnell, to mourn the lost opportunity for a unified Ireland, to insist that Parnell will be honored as the major cause of any future unity in Ireland, and to state that Ireland will still have a permanent stain on its national soul even if a transcendent unity is achieved on some future judgment day. The other men in the room, despite sharp ideological differences of varying degrees, are also deeply moved, with the exception of Henchy. Hynes's poem also recounts the isolating ex-istence that results from a masculine subject being cut off from a myth of unity only to be set adrift in a world of signifiers presided over by a dead Father and a devouring (m)Other, both of whom can only pose as authenticators of the speaking being.

Just as Maria's poem in "Clay" recounts the impossibility of being feminine, Hynes's poem recounts the impossibility of being masculine and also reminds me of Lacan's definition of a man as "he who finds himself male without knowing what to do about it" (1982b, 141). Lacan describes the dynamic between the subject and the phallic symbol as one in which self-alienated subjects mourn the loss of jouissance even as they declare their faith in the transcendent signifier that destroyed this (m)Other fusion. Lacan presents the hopelessly circular self-deception of substitution and masquerade that constitutes the subject's identity. The inherent falseness of the "self" forces the individual to go on noisy crusades for truth and meaning that compensate for a lack-in-being. Hynes's poem revolves around the conceit that because Parnell has been "laid low" by male pretenders ("fell gang of modern hypocrites"), Ireland, as both a woman and a mother, must continue to suffer until someone arises who can fully become what she desires ("for *he* is gone / Who would have wrought *her* destiny").

In a Lacanian sense, Parnell is the darling of the (m)Other's gaze. Other men have owed their sense of certainty to this "uncrowned king," but he was "slain" by these same "coward hounds" whom "he raised to glory from the mire" (*D* 134). What "Erin" has lost by his demise is the possibility of satisfying her desire: "And Erin's hopes and Erin's dreams / Perish upon her monarch's pyre." In this poem, Parnell is not a representative of the phallus, he *is* the phallus, the only man capable of satisfying (m)Other Ireland's desire. The figure of "Erin" corresponds to Lacan's idea of the Woman because "she" does not exist as a woman but only as a representation of one. As such, she guarantees the unity of the masculine subject as well as the existence of the phallic signifier that bestows structure and meaning on the patriarchal order: "He would have had *his Erin famed*, / The green flag gloriously unfurled, / Her statesmen, bards and warriors raised / Before the nations of the World" (*D* 134). She is presumed to have no desire that does not complement what Parnell is able to provide. Unlike an actual woman—unlike Gretta Conroy, for instance—she thinks of no other men in the past. "Erin" is incapable of this sort of betrayal because the question of her own desire is presumed to be what Parnell is questing for. The question of her desire is formulated retrospectively by posing the presumed coherency of Parnell as the answer to what she has always been asking. In this way every nuance of her desire is satiated and his fiction becomes her truth. But at the point where her desire would have been satiated, the intervention of the Name-of-the-Father occurs. This fractures the mother-infant/country-leader dyad and immerses the subject in the Symbolic Order/political order that follows from psychic castration: "He dreamed (alas, 'twas but a dream!) / Of Liberty: but as he strove / To clutch that idol, treachery / Sundered him from the thing he loved" (*D* 134).

What is particularly moving about Hynes's poem for the men in the room is that no "mistake" is made. The dream of "Liberty" (which I read as freedom from Desire), is discovered to be an idol that Parnell is unable to clutch (the way a baby clutches for the absent maternal body that has been replaced by the fragmentary and substitutive satisfactions of the Symbolic Order). This "idol" is also similar to the lost image of mirror-stage unity and autonomy (sanctioned by the gaze of the (m)Other) that the subject clutches to himself when he embraces the myth of masculinity (which denies the effects of castration). But with his death, Parnell begins his resurrection as something immortal. The machinations of his enemies are then portrayed as something that will fall back on their own heads: "May everlasting shame consume / The memory of those who tried / To befoul and smear th' exalted name" (*D* 134). Parnell has become a *transcendent signifier*, permanently supported and authenticated by the gaze of the (m)other: "And death has now united him / With Erin's heroes of the past" (*D* 135). in this state Parnell achieves "the idol of Liberty" (his self-reflective mirror image) that earlier he "strove to clutch."

As a result, he is released forever from the insatiable and interminable substitutive games of language and culture that determine and undermine the ex-istence of the divided subject in the Symbolic Order: "No sound of strife disturb his sleep! / Calmly he rests: no human pain / Or high ambition spurs him now / The peaks of glory to attain" (*D* 135). This is an anthropomorphic description of death that fantasizes about a coherent identity "sleeping" and "calmly resting," free from the substitutive game of language and Desire (high ambition). Parnell seems to have faded out into the very land of the Imaginary Order Maria sings about in "Clay." The idea that the great hero of Irish politics and an unknown washerwoman achieve the same status of "resting" in a pre-Symbolic world of jouissance should alert readers to the powerful psychological appeal of Maria's song and Hynes's poem. Both of these oratory efforts seem pathetic, yet each emerges as poignant because both feature a tragedy inherent in the formation of the speaking subject (castration) that one can never recover from except in fantasies of the past (Maria's song) or illusions about the future (Hynes's poem). "That there must somewhere be *jouissance* of the Other is the only possible check on the endless circulating of significations — but this can only be ensured by a signifier and this signifier is necessarily lacking" (Lacan 1982b, 117). For a brief moment, Hynes's poem supplies this signifier and everyone ("even Mr Lyons") is equally moved. Predictably, Henchy breaks the spell by calling for Crofton's opinion. It is Henchy, after all, who broke an earlier moment of hope with his reminder that for all that Parnell means, he is still dead, and the jouissance of transcendent signification that they imagine is (as it always was) an illusion. King Edward is coming to Ireland with a new boatload of substitutive satisfactions, and Henchy's advice is that they stop fantasizing about a reunion with their (m)Other and prepare to greet their new father ("he means well by us").

In the fifth stanza, readers are told of the "Liberty" Parnell discovered to be imaginary when "treachery / Sundered him from the thing he loved." But something survives this catastrophe/castration, which may yet prove that Parnell did not die in vain or even that he did not really die at all: Mother Ireland exists somewhere beyond representation and comprehension, and the concluding two stanzas of the poem are addressed to this spirit of jouissance that may bring the Imaginary Order and the Symbolic Order into harmony (and erase the distinction between life and death).

> *They had their way: they laid him low.*
> *But Erin, list, his spirit may*
> *Rise, like the Phoenix from the flames,*
> *When breaks the dawning of the day,*
> *The day that brings us Freedom's reign.*
> *And on that day may Erin well*
> *Pledge in the cup she lifts to Joy*
> *One grief—the memory of Parnell.*

One can see in the conclusion of this poem the imposition of the difficulty inherent in human sexuality onto the masculine representation of the 'woman.' "Erin," who is insistently presented in the poem as female, *does not exist*. She is constructed as an absolute category that guarantees that Parnell's fictional unity (and, by extension, all masculine subjectivity) will transcend even death. One can see by this representation of "Erin" how a woman is implicated, without any reference to anything innate in her body or mind, to the role of upholding the validity of the Other, even though she herself—as a speaking subject—is equally subjected to its influence (the question this raises for her is co-opted as the goal of the masculine subject's quest). As Lacan notes, "The man manages to satisfy his demand for love in his relationship to the woman to the extent that the signifier of the phallus constitutes her precisely as giving in love what she does not have" (1982b, 84). A woman operates as a symptom for the man, protecting him from any conscious knowledge that the Other stands against the phallus — that there is no Other of the Other to guarantee phallic meaning — and that, therefore, when a man seeks authority from the Other to validate his significance in a consistent manner, he is always refused. When the masculine subject represents the Other as the Woman, however, this same refusal can be misrecognized as the bestowal of a gift of unity she does not possess. If the masquerade of this spurious authorization should reveal itself, the masculine subject is still protected because it is the Woman who is depriving him of the one thing he needs to complete himself (Queen Victoria keeping King Edward "out of it"), or it is the Woman who gives him a gift that proves to be false (cocking him up with "this and that" as did Old Jack's wife).

In either case a woman is "elevated" (reduced, actually) to the status of the Woman, and is then worshipped for giving to a man, or despised for withholding from him, the gift she has never possessed. On the other side of the gender mirror, a man only imagines who she is and, therefore, can only fantasize what he is asking for — validation for the myth of himself. A woman who is reduced to the role of the Woman ceases to exist for a masculine subject as anything other than a fantastic being (a symptom) that validates the fantasy of himself. Significantly, "Erin's" primary function is to bring about an authentification of the masculine subject that defies dissolution: "Rise, like the Phoenix from the flames" (*D* 135). This feeling of ultimate protection against fragmentation provided by the Woman's gaze is also expressed in the famous phrase of Araby's narrator, "I imagined that I bore my chalice safely through a throng of foes" (*D* 31). Hynes's poem can be seen as a primitive expression of the desire to be the desire of the mother, to be the Phallus. Hynes's poem ends with an image of the mother delivered to satisfaction — Parnell has become her immortal object of "Desire": "The day that brings us Freedom's reign. / And on that day may Erin well / Pledge in the cup she lifts to Joy / One grief — the memory of Parnell" (*D* 135). "The Death of Parnell" records the movement of Parnell from a frustrated life into a death that is beyond Desire. This death is the equivalent of the blissful re-unification (jouissance) that the masculine subject "re-members" from the pre-Symbolic fusion with his own image that was once sanctified by the (m)Other's gaze.

"Ivy Day" begins with a denigration of the mother as a being who ruins men by forcing them into a futile effort to become the phallus ("The mother, you know, she cocks them up with this and that."). The resulting sense of "lack," according to Old Jack's theory, drives men toward drinking and the ritualistic performance of violent acts (he should know because he is an example of this cycle—"I'd take the stick to his back and beat him while I could stand over him—as I done many a time before"). Later in the story, the image of Queen Victoria is invoked to demonstrate the other obstacle to masculine unity—the woman who keeps the phallus for herself. Of course, this is equally a fantasy because she cannot possess what does not exist any more than the man can. By the end of the story, though, in Joe's poem, the image of the Mother appears as a representation ("Erin") and authenticates the male subject as the object of her desire. At the end of Hynes's recitation, the cork flies out of his bottle, but for the first time in the story the trumped up Phallacy of Henchy (opening the bottles without a corkscrew) is ignored: "[Hynes] did not seem to have heard the invitation" (*D* 135). Everyone in the room is moved to silence after Hynes is finished (Henchy, only briefly). They are adrift in the fantasy of a meaningful past that has been lost, a present that is bankrupt, and a future that is permanently elsewhere.

Except Henchy. His call to Crofton to validate the poem is expressed in British slang ("Isn't that fine? What?"), and one sees that Henchy, the would-be ghost of Parnell, is unmoved by the tragedy of incompletion and lost unity in the poem because, for the entire story, *he has already been posing as "complete."* He is, from a psychoanalytical point of view (as well as from the point of view of others) a prick. His being has been inflated (spoken) by the silently superior Mr. Crofton. Henchy's ability to dominate the group is purchased at the price of being "no man," a gnomon posing as a parallelogram. He does not respond to the poem because the control he has exercised over the group is based on the paradox that he is almost purely the voice of the Other: his script is what he imagines King Edward needs to hear in order to recognize him (and Crofton is King Edward's representative in his mind). Throughout the story, he has aligned himself with current representations of phallic power regardless of ideology. Thus, his obstreperous form of allegiance is now devoted to King Edward (presented through Crofton), not because of a shift in politics but because Parnell, as he so decisively puts it, "is dead." This is really the only thing wrong with Parnell from Henchy's point of view.

Henchy wants to recapture the jouissance of mirror fusion where he would be sure who he was, independent from the gaze of others and the unconscious directive of the Other. As Hynes puts it, responding to Henchy's half-joking half-fearful remark that he "expect[s] to find the bailiffs in the hall when I go home": "It'll be all right when King Eddie comes" (*D* 124). This fantastic male orgasm parallels the equally fantastic orgasm of "Erin" in Hynes's poem ("the cup she lifts to joy"). Thus, the two successful climaxes in "Ivy Day" occur only to the two representations of masculinity and femininity in the story. This symbolic mating is strengthened by Henchy's portrayal of King Edward who will come to "Erin" as a suitor and thereby generate "an influx of money" (*D* 131); this would seem to connote "spending" in the Victorian sense of the term![12] Furthermore, the long history of British colonialism suggests that this "courtship" will degenerate into coercion at the first sign of resistance on the part of "Erin."

Political ideology has no truth content as such. Conscious knowledge exists as a complex dialectic between the Other's Desire that authenticates one, and one's relationship with others in which one tries to reflect back to oneself this (imagined) Desire of the Other. All of the men in "Ivy Day" are living within the confines of their own reality reconstruction and seeking to use the discourse of others to confirm this construct. But as Lacan has noted, "the unconscious is the discourse of the other," and one can see in Joyce's story (particularly in the case of Henchy) that the more one denies that consciousness is a tenuous construct, the more one is spoken by the voice of the Other. What the group is ostensibly discussing (the relative merits of Tierney and Colgan, whether or not to welcome the king, the scandalous defiance of sons toward their fathers) is meaningful only in relation to what its use of language represses.

In this story, as in Lacan's theory, "language itself functions as the best of all defenses against unconscious 'truth'" (Ragland-Sullivan 1986, 232). This is the heart of the "pathetic phallacy" in which "truth" serves to obscure the fictional structuration of the subject. Women, by becoming a symptom for the man, are expected to give up the question of their own desire (that is, to become feminine) to serve as the substitutive object that inaugurates the quest for satisfaction of masculine Desire. The committee room in Joyce's story is full of uncrowned kings who have been banished within their own kingdoms. Their futile and desperate nostalgia for a rejuvenation of their kingdoms is summed up in Hynes's sarcastic prediction that "it'll be all right when King Eddie comes" (*D* 124) In grieving for the death of Parnell, they mourn the unveiled phallic signifier within themselves even as they worship the newly veiled phallic symbol of the martyred Parnell. They are inflated by a 'Desire' for a state of unity that would have each of them rise in majestic, monadic isolation. Frightened of the jouissance of the (m)Other, they concentrate instead on wondering when Parnell will appear among them, sanctified by "Erin's" gaze, bidding them all to come again.

14

Mrs. Kearney and the "Moral Umbrella"
of Mr. O'Madden Burke
A Mother's Quest for the Phallus

> As is true for all women, and for reasons which
> are at the very basis of the most elementary forms
> of social exchange . . . the problem of her condition
> is fundamentally that of accepting herself as an ob-
> ject of desire for the man. (Lacan 1982b, 68)

> —I thought you were a lady, said Mr Holohan,
> walking away from her abruptly. (*D* 149)

The society of men that Joyce depicts in "A Mother" is every bit
as hapless and self-deluded as the group of men in the Committee Room. In this story, however, an actual woman intervenes in
the tricky process of keeping the Phallus veiled. She is eventually re-
buffed as the startled group of men first accept her competent services, then seek to ignore her, and finally band together to pronounce
her "not a lady." What she might be, if she is not a lady, is too unsettling for any of the men to contemplate. The desire of the (m)Other
is precisely what the symbolic father is trying to domesticate. The aid
of ladies in this project is crucial (and consequently highly valued)
because the Law of the Father, which poses as the unified ideal that
permits self-hood in the Imaginary and Symbolic orders, is actually
the source of prohibition against any return to the totalized sense of
"self" (jouissance) that once appeared to be sanctioned by the (m)Other's

256

gaze in the mirror stage of the subject. The Phallus, which is represented as a monument honoring the future deeds of the subject is actually the point of lack (a hole) that is the insatiable base of a subject's desire. "A lady" is one who does whatever she can to support what I called in the preceding chapter the "pathetic phallacy." Even if she cannot do much, under no circumstances can she be tolerated if she manages to call its presumably autonomous power into question.

In this context, it is clear to the reader, just as it is clear to the usually befuddled Mr. Holohan, that Mrs. Kearney's initial efforts to make her daughter well-known are irreproachably ladylike. She does not, for instance, directly approach any men in charge of Dublin cultural affairs to sell them on the contribution that her daughter might make to their various projects. Such an approach, regardless of how innocent the proposed contributions might be, would invariably be regarded by the men of the committee as a shocking case of a mother pandering her own daughter. Were she a man, of course, and had she a son, this same approach would be the only one that could possibly garner her any respect from other men. But the fact is that Mrs. Kearney has a nearly unlimited respect for what she imagines men represent (the unifying ideal of the Phallus), and it is the profound degree of this respect that derails her in her later encounter with "the men nowadays," as Lily puts it in "The Dead." The men nowadays are not appreciably different from men long ago, but it is easier for women to imagine dead men who were once worthy of the potent phallic signifier than it is for them to observe living men who prove themselves unworthy on a daily basis. Mrs. Kearney, like Lily the caretaker's daughter, is simply shocked beyond recovery that men are not at all what they take themselves to be, yet they still expect her to pretend that they are! Whereas Lily tries to recover from her discovery by imagining that this may not always have been the case (the men "nowadays"), Mrs. Kearney protects herself by marrying a man she respects "in the same way as she respected the General Post Office, as something large, secure and fixed; and though she knew the small number of his talents she appreciated his abstract value as a male" (*D* 141).[1] This makes clear that Mrs. Kearney did not take on the reality of her husband for "love" (unless her feelings for the General Post Office go beyond what is imaginable) but as a stopgap against a further disappointment in the presumed autonomy of men that was likely to be far greater than the already anticipated disappointment her husband was likely to provide.

Having protected herself from a loss of faith in the Phallic Order that might have proved crushing, she sets about making her daughter's image as feminine as possible in the hopes that through her she might attract the ideal man that she has taken great pains to still believe in. Mrs. Kearney well understands the various expectations on the part of men concerning what women should represent in the self-important atmosphere of the Celtic Revival, and it is this knowledge that inspires the structure and content of her campaign: "When the Irish Revival began to be appreciable Mrs. Kearney determined to take advantage of her daughter's name and brought an Irish teacher to the house. Kathleen and her sister sent Irish picture postcards to their friends and these friends sent back other Irish picture postcards" (*D* 137). Mrs. Kearney, for her own part, does not seem to be particularly moved by Kathleen's Irish name, but she expects that men will be. She packages her daughter in such a way that she might be seen as a living embodiment of the "Erin" of Hynes's poem. In fact, this particular feminine masquerade has become such an expected cliché that the program (which we know Mrs. Kearney designed) closes the first part of the concert "with a stirring patriotic recitation delivered by a young lady who arranged amateur theatricals. It was deservedly applauded; and, when it was ended, the men went out for the interval, content" (*D* 147). There is no question that Mrs. Kearney, like Mrs. Mooney, transforms her desire into a structure that appears to the men to be the mirrored complement of their own desire. But it is equally clear that, in doing so, she is providing no less than what they expect from "a lady." It is when Mrs. Kearney refuses to trick the men any further (when she challenges the authority, and even the existence, of "the committee"), that she is instantly exposed by them as someone who is "not a lady." Mrs. Kearney is so used to providing men with the flawless support they expect that pleasing them is second nature to her. But, in Joyce's story, this second nature unravels to reveal her first nature — an angry woman who believes in the organizing and generating force of the Phallus, and is, therefore, especially disgusted with the unconscious charade whereby the men of the committee insist upon a transcendent and unimpeachable authority that has no objective relationship with either their merits or their sense of fair play.

The story opens with Joyce's presentation of a man with an official title ("assistant secretary of the *Eire Abu* Society") who is helplessly rearranging facts and times with all the men he meets as he frenetically devotes all his energy to approaching no nearer to his goal of organizing a "series of concerts" (*D* 136). No doubt he feels he has chosen to allow Mrs. Kearney into the planning stages of his project because, in his wisdom, he has discerned the need for Kathleen's services. The fact is, he has been at loose ends for some time, and Mrs. Kearney is the first contact he has had that shows any willingness to hem the ragged fringe of his intentions. Mr. Holohan's special talent, which makes him one with the other members of the committee, is his ability to act like a busy man without ever actually getting something done: "Mr. Holohan . . . had been walking up and down Dublin for nearly a month, with his hands and pockets full of dirty pieces of paper, arranging about the series of concerts. . . . He walked up and down constantly, stood by the hour at street corners arguing the point and made notes; but in the end it was Mrs. Kearney who arranged everything" (*D* 136). When Mr. Holohan wanders by to propose that Kathleen be the accompanist for four grand concerts, his errand is the logical endpoint of a process Mrs. Kearney has already set in motion: "People said that she [Kathleen] was very clever at music and a very nice girl and, moreover, that she was a believer in the language movement" (*D* 138). Now, readers already know that Kathleen is indifferent to the language movement (she only knows what a hired tutor has told her. In addition, her later comment about the sadly faded soprano, Madam Glynn ("I wonder where did they dig her up"), puts how "nice" she is into question. Finally Molly Bloom's account (in *Ulysses*) of her musical abilities casts doubt on her cleverness as well. But this is not what people think, so the fiction of Kathleen Kearney, scripted by her mother, serves as the truth. Unbeknown to Mr. Holohan, when he takes the initiative to knock on her door, he is already a part of her plans (which are so much more concrete than his own). Mrs. Kearney uses her hosting duties as an excuse to sit him down. She then imbues him with a sense of purpose in such an oblique and ladylike way that he remains free to interpret his abrupt command of how to proceed with the concert as having somehow sprung up from within him: "She was invariably friendly and advising—homely, in fact" (*D* 138). Her carefully contrived and unadorned simplicity in dealing with him augments, rather than interferes with, his preposterous faith in his organizational abilities.

My analysis so far might be viewed as suggesting that Mrs. Kearney is bitter regarding masculinity and that she cynically plots to meet male needs in a manner that will simultaneously (and surreptitiously) satisfy her own.[2] But, on the contrary, I argue that Mrs. Kearney has a profound regard for masculinity; it is men that she finds infuriating and ridiculous. "Large, secure and fixed" are the adjectives she applies to her husband and to the General Post Office, which sounds phallic enough, but notice that Mrs. Kearney discovers this sort of admirable turgidity only in a building or in the *abstract* (that is to say, *imagined*) value of masculinity. Her actual husband proves to be as adept at supporting the committee as anyone else by observing a silence as profound as the buildings she thinks of in relation to him. His one action is to scurry outside to find a cab when she orders him to do so, but this is also his first opportunity to aid the beleaguered committee by facilitating her departure. Her husband, in other words, is yet another inferior specimen (although less inferior than many) of what she believes masculinity to be.

In fact, during her marriageable years, Mrs. Kearney (as Miss Devlin) carefully arranged herself as a prize exceedingly difficult to capture: "She sat amid the chilly circle of her accomplishments, waiting for some suitor to brave it and offer her a brilliant life" (*D* 136). When the suitors prove to be consistently ordinary, she takes to eating candy in secret "to console her romantic desires." Even after her marriage—and this is a crucial point—"she never put her own romantic ideas away" (*D* 137). But Mrs. Kearney is no Madame Bovary, and what she means by "romantic" we might translate as "competence." After all, it is her own accomplishments that she uses to keep men at bay, and it is these accomplishments that she expects them to match with accomplishments of their own. Her insistence on fair play is in evidence even at this early stage. She does not want them to pay court to the more traditional feminine charms of voice, figure, and supportive gaze; she wants them to prove to her that they represent the phallus whose privileges they claim as their own. Naturally, all the men fail the test because Miss Devlin (who believes in the phallus and all the autonomous, self-originating, lawful, and monolithic power it represents) does not realize that men possess the Phallus only in so much as a woman convinces them that she believes they possess it. And she, for her part, refuses to put the rabbits in their hats and then feign surprise when they pull them out again as proof of their magical "selves." In short, she finds absurd the notion that she should masquerade as the object of their desire. To do this would be to give up her romantic fantasies about the actual existence of the Phallus.

In effect, Mrs. Kearney has a much greater reverence for the "abstract value" of "masculinity" than she does for any particular man. Even more startling, she has a more profound belief in the transcendent power of the phallic order than any of the men on the committee. When first contacted by Mr. Holohan, Mrs. Kearney instantly treats the four-night concert series as something worthy of all her attention and effort: "She entered heart and soul into the details of the enterprise" (D 138). When she witnesses the opening night of the series, she is disturbed by evidence that the whole enterprise is shoddy and unprofessional. But what truly angers her is that the men in charge are neither humiliated nor even concerned about this failure: "There was something she didn't like in the look of things and Mr Fitzpatrick's vacant smile irritated her very much. . . . Mr Fitzpatrick seemed to enjoy himself; he was quite unconscious that Mrs. Kearney was taking angry note of his conduct" (D 140). The vague good humor of the men persists even in the face of having to cancel one of the performances. Predictably, Mrs. Kearney's reaction is to try and force these pathetic specimens of masculinity into acting a little more like the General Post Office. She buttonholes Mr. Holohan and forces him to admit that the series will only run for three nights: "— But of course, that doesn't alter the contract, she said. The contract was for four concerts" (D 140). I suggest, right at the beginning of Mrs. Kearney's increasingly public attack of the committee, that her apparent concern for the money is really a special regard for the contract that she helped design. Her careful invention of Kathleen, conducted over years, finally culminated in the appearance of Mr. Holohan on her doorstep, and this led to the attainment of a nearly lifelong fantasy to make a deal in the masculine world that would reveal her competence in a more meaningful (phallic rather than feminine) way than the "chilly circle of her accomplishments" to which her parents and her society originally consigned her. What she fails to realize, of course, is that the only reason the committee can afford to be cavalier about the dismal prospects of the concert series is that they are counting on adjusting all the various contracts and agreements so that neither their lack of control over the proceedings nor their incompetence will be highlighted. Indeed, to be confident in the midst of a failure is the truest way to imitate convincingly the indivisible unity of the phallic signifier, it is the essence of the masculine masquerade.

Mr. Holohan's evasiveness on this issue panics her further, and she acts immediately on his advice to take up the matter with Mr. Fitzpatrick. He responds as one would expect of a man who wishes to forestall the awkward inquiries of a "lady": he cites the mysterious workings of an organization (the committee/masculinity, to make the comparison explicit) that must convene to resolve the contract issue. "Mr Fitzpatrick, who did not catch the point at issue very quickly, seemed unable to resolve the difficulty and said that he would bring the matter before the Committee" (*D* 141). The authority of something as august as the committee should be instantly acceded to by any woman worthy of the term *lady*, and Mrs. Kearney manages to maintain a slender hold on this pose: "Mrs. Kearney's anger began to flutter in her cheek and she had all she could do to keep from asking: —And who is the *Cometty*, pray? But she knew that it would not be ladylike to do that: so she was silent" (*D* 141). As Gifford points out, Mrs. Kearney is quite mistaken in her insistence that a contract is always honored to the letter in the murky world of semiprofessional music productions (*D* 98–99). No real legal or cultural precedent supports the depth of Mrs. Kearney's rage, a rage that, counterproductively, drives her to doom her daughter's future in the Dublin musical scene (a future that she built up over years). Nor can the issue be money because Mrs. Kearney sacrifices the future possibility of her daughter earning far more than "two Guineas." One is safe, I think, in seeing the force that drives Mrs. Kearney as more psychological than legal.

If one looks back at the atmosphere wherein Mr. Holohan first approached Mrs. Kearney about using her daughter as an accompanist, one can see that Mrs. Kearney went to considerable trouble to make this contract proposal as much like masculine deal making as possible. "She brought him into the drawing-room, made him sit down and brought out the decanter and the silver biscuit-barrel. . . . She pushed the decanter towards him, saying: — Now, help yourself, Mr. Holohan! And while he was helping himself she said: — Don't be afraid! Don't be afraid of it!" (*D* 138). Mrs. Kearney's refrain while Mr. Holohan pours is not exactly vulgar, but neither is it entirely ladylike. It is her imitation of a man (a man like Gallaher, for instance, from "A Little Cloud") offering a drink to another man with a pretentious show of generosity and largesse. By way of contrast, readers might remember the almost unheralded appearance of sherry when women serve liquor to one another in "The Sisters." This imitation of a man will eventually give way to her parody of a man when she insults Mr. Holohan. Mr. Holohan, whose idea of a professional consult is to scribble something on a dirty piece of notepaper and stick it into his already bulging pockets, clearly does not intuit anything about what Mrs. Kearney boisterousness implies, nor does he understand its profound importance to Mrs. Kearney. From her point of view, though, they are two men sitting down to make up a binding contract. She has an opportunity, while still safe within the parameters of being a ladylike hostess, to watch a man seal their contract with a drink.[3]

Although Mr. Holohan does not recognize Mrs. Kearney's departure from her expected gender role, he *is* well aware that two men having a drink at the conclusion of some sort of agreement is a necessary and expected ritual. "— O'Madden Burke will write the notice, he explained to Mr Holohan, and I'll see it in. —Thank you very much, Mr Hendrick, said Mr Holohan. You'll see it in, I know. Now, won't you have a little something before you go? — I don't mind, said Mr Hendrick" (*D* 145). This is the sort of male camaraderie that Mrs. Kearney imprecisely imagines and is anxious to experience. She has spent all her life imagining a "real" man that she has never chanced to meet, and now is her chance to hold herself to the principles of abstract male value that all the men she has ever known abdicate sooner or later. Her cry Don't be afraid of it! to Mr. Holohan nearly betrays her desire that he not pour only a small amount in her presence as though she were a "lady." In this light one can see her effort to meticulously direct her daughter's future as an attempt to place herself at the center of the function that Lacan terms the Name-of-the-Father.

Because she does not suspect that the Phallus is a fraud and that it can only perform its function when veiled, she concludes that it must be the men who are acting in a fraudulent manner. If she were a man, she would force all of them to respect her superior relation to the Phallus: "They wouldn't have dared to have treated her like that if she had been a man" (*D* 148). The peculiar emphasis that I hear in this sentence is that "they" are not men but only impostors, and, there- fore, they could be forced to defer to her *genuine* masculinity if only she were allowed to live up to the abstract value of being a male. If she were a man, of course, she would be as uncertain about the au- thenticity of her presumed autonomy as Mr. Fitzpatrick and Mr. Holo- han. Like them, she would then feel a compelling need to rise above the abject failure of the concert precisely because failure exposes their permanent desire as subjects who are controlled by the Symbolic Order. A woman suffers the same symbolic castration as a man, except that she has nothing to lose. According to the phallic economy set up as the basis of the Symbolic Order, she has already lost it. Put most sim- ply, what Mrs. Kearney does not realize is that, in Lacan's sense of the terms, *men are castrated too* and that their insistence on referring awkward matters to a nonexistent committee—far from revealing their inadequate masculinity—betrays the essence of finding oneself a man and not knowing what to do about it. Moreover, if she were a man, she would hedge against this constantly encroaching incertitude by finding a woman who is "ladylike" enough to reflect back to her the unified mirror image of phallic totality—an image that would then imbue her past with credibility and her future with signficance.[4]

In a deliberate contrast to Mrs. Kearney, Joyce presents the char- acter of Miss Healy, a woman who is as much of a "lady" as any man could desire because she understands the masquerade that is expected of her and does not omit any detail in her performance of it.

> Miss Healy stood in front of [Mr Hendrick], talking and laughing. He was old enough to suspect one reason for her politeness but young enough in spirit to turn the moment to account. The warmth, fra- grance and colour of her body appealed to his senses. He was pleas- antly conscious that the bosom which he saw rise and fall slowly beneath him rose and fell at that moment for him, that the laughter and fragrance and wilful glances were his tribute. When he could stay no longer he took leave of her regretfully. (*D* 145)

Mr. Hendrick appears to be a senior writer for the *Freeman*—too important to actually be subjected to the concert ("concerts and *artistes* bored him considerably"), but, nonetheless, the person who will make sure that O'Madden Burke's account of it appears in the paper. Joyce's description of Miss Healy, presented from Hendrick's point of view, emphasizes the fact of her performance rather than the content of her conversation. To make the point more explicitly, she is talking, but what she is saying could not matter less to him; she is laughing, but her laughter is simply used to convey her homage to Mr. Hendrick. Her laughter, rather than being the spontaneous result of anything she finds humorous, functions as an excuse for her rising and falling chest. What matters to Mr. Hendrick is that this pleasing performance is being staged solely for his benefit. Even the pleased Mr. Hendrick, however, is aware that her performance has been called forth by his "abstract value" as a male (a value he possesses in greater abundance than the obsequious Mr. Holohan, who, although also present, is carefully excluded by Miss Healy to assure Mr. Hendrick further that he is the only one worthy to serve as an audience).

The real signification of Miss Healy's talking and laughing does not reside in anything she is saying but in the fact that the effort of saying it is causing her bosom to "rise and fall slowly" under Mr. Hendrick's watchful and appreciative eye. The spurious nature of their conversation would be disconcertingly obvious, of course, were Miss Healy simply to stand "in front of him" and breathe slowly and heavily, yet she might as well do this for all her "talking and laughing" matters to Mr. Hendrick (except that he could no longer pretend to be interested in her conversation). Significantly, Mr. Hendrick receives her performance as "his tribute." This is a wonderfully ambivalent word for him to use in summing up his attitude toward Miss Healy's performance. A tribute can be something voluntarily given to someone who richly deserves it, but it also implies acknowledgment of submission on the part of the person who offers the tribute and further designates this contributor as forced to offer something in the hopes of being protected rather than attacked. This sort of tribute is paid to people in recognition of what they might be capable of were they to exercise their presumed power. If the recipient country or ruler were ever to betray a lack of power, the tribute would be promptly rescinded. Mr. Hendrick understands that it is what he might do for her that animates Miss Healy. At the same time, he is aware that he will become less and less able to call forth such a tribute as he ages: "He was old enough to suspect one reason for her politeness but young enough in spirit to turn the moment to account" (*D* 145). Joyce brilliantly introduces a subtle poignancy to this man's consumption of Miss Healy's performance: he is young enough, in spirit, but old enough, in fact, to sense that what she admires in him is nothing that he actually possesses, nor is it anything that will save him from old age and death.

To contrast Mrs. Kearney's behavior more directly with Miss Healy's, I suggest that Mrs. Kearney is intolerable to the men because her conduct not only fails to pay them tribute, it implies there is no reason to ever do so because they seem incapable, in her eyes, of acting like men! What makes this story richly humorous is that Mrs. Kearney frightens these bumbling men nearly to death because her high regard for masculinity gives her no option except to view all of them as pathetic examples of what she imagines it should be. The men are held hostage, in other words, by the very myth they are scrambling to protect. Indeed, the men are so unnerved by Mrs. Kearney's chilly assessment of their multiple inadequacies that they hand over half of Kathleen's fee at a moment's notice (an impromptu arrangement that was not part of the original contract) and promise her the other half at the interval!

The hastily produced four guineas makes it clear that the men can be frightened into breaking ranks and conceding to demands without pretending to follow the fictitious procedures of the committee that they normally hide behind. By the end of the first part of the concert, however, the men realize they have compromised their own (illusory) power base, and they insert a face-saving clause: Kathleen will be paid in full but not until after the committee has met. The men are trying to appease a woman's single-minded attack on their all too vulnerable posturing by giving her whatever she demands in a manner that preserves their pretence of having final and absolute power over whether or not they choose to honor these demands. Of course, by conceding to all her demands and then insisting she still must wait until the committee meets, they merely underline the fact that the decision-making power of the committee is a self-serving myth. Mrs. Kearney's response, therefore, is both accurate and telling, "I haven't seen any Committee" (*D* 148). The point is, as Miss Healy's performance for Mr. Hendrick demonstrates, women are supposed to pretend that they see the phallic signifier so that men can imagine, in turn, that what a women looks at (their ideal image) is really there. Significantly, while Miss Healy's "wilful glances" toward Mr. Hendrick are much appreciated because he presumes himself to be their cause, Mrs. Kearney's conduct, which is *truly* willful, is unanimously condemned by the committee. Put more simply, Miss Healy's willful glances, which are, in fact, sycophantic, are accepted as a tribute to Mr. Hendrick's representation of the Phallus, whereas Mrs. Kearney's willfulness undermines this same representation and is, therefore, villified by the men as something not worthy of a lady.

Yet Mrs. Kearney is quite right when she states that she can see no committee. There is no indication in the story that the committee has ever met in a full body; instead, one needs to see the idea of the committee as the men's abstract belief in their own full bodies. The committee is an abstraction that represents the value of masculinity in the same vague way as the existence of the General Post Office. As we know, this structure strikes Mrs. Kearney as being what a man should be — something large secure and fixed" (*D* 141). What enrages Mrs. Kearney is not that there should be such a thing as the committee — she is fully prepared to respect and honor such an idea — what enrages her is that these men have the audacity to excuse their puny organizational skills by pretending that the next meeting of the committee will make everything "large, secure, and fixed."

In essence, her final insult to Mr. Holohan reveals that the issue is not how dare he try and cheat her daughter out of her fee but *how dare he pretend to be a man.* "She tossed her head and assumed a haughty voice: —You must speak to the secretary. It's not my business. I'm a great fellow fol-the-diddle-I-do." (*D* 149). First Mrs. Kearney's insult illustrates the extent to which Holohan's masculinity is a masquerade by stepping into the role of that masquerade herself and assuming "a haughty voice." The effect of her impersonation is to say, "Anyone can be the sort of man you make yourself out to be — even a woman — it is simply a matter of speaking evasively in a sufficiently arrogant tone." What she says in this haughty tone begins as a statement of power and ends in the sort of nonsense language that can be found in the chorus of a children's song. In effect, she demonstrates that what Mr. Holohan says (the content of his speech, or what Lacan calls parole) is as irrelevant as whatever Miss Healy was saying to Mr. Hendrick. What matters is what Mrs. Kearney refuses—the implicit demand his speech makes of her to confirm his "abstract value" as a male. Mrs. Kearney makes herself heard, in a way Miss Healy did not, because she *deliberately* speaks nonsense ("fol-the-diddle-I-do") *from the assumed position* of a masculine subject.

This impromptu burlesque on her part is a sort of linguistic transvestism where a feminine speech pattern cavorts in the borrowed clothes of a "masculine" cliche.[5] When Miss Healy masquerades as the Woman, Mr. Hendrick is "pleasantly conscious" that her rising and falling bosom is a tribute from a lady to a man. Mrs. Kearney, on the other hand, who has resisted masquerading as the Woman, now takes her rebellion one step further and masquerades as someone pretending to be a man. By exposing Mr. Holohan's actual statements as so much absurd chest beating in her burlesque ("You must speak to the secretary. It's not my business."), Mrs. Kearney makes it clear (so she thinks) that her mockery is directed at him as an individual and not against the institution of masculinity as a whole (which she is protecting against the likes of impostors such as he). What Mrs. Kearney fails to understand is that because masculinity, as she envisions it (large, secure, fixed), does not exist (except as an ideal signifier that can only perform its unifying function when veiled), any attack on an individual male must be construed by men as an attack on the very abstract values of masculinity that Mrs. Kearney holds so dear: "After that Mrs Kearney's conduct was condemned on all hands: everyone approved of what the Committee had done" (*D* 149). As Mrs. Kearney might say, if anyone were still listening to her, *what committee* are they talking about? The committee only ex-ists because people need to believe in it. The decision to denounce Mrs. Kearney, which Mr. Holohan and Mr. Fitzpatrick have reluctantly fumbled toward all evening, is now characterized, in a phrase implying autonomy, wisdom, and totality, as "what the Committee had done."

After my discussion of Miss Healy and Mr. Hendrick above, it should not be surprising that the rip Mrs. Kearney has caused in the careful(!) planning of the committee is quickly stitched by Miss Healy in a ladylike manner: "But Miss Healy had kindly consented to play one or two accompaniments" (*D* 149). Miss Healy's kind consent is motivated by a desire to improve her visibility in Dublin music circles and is, therefore, no less crafty and opportunistic than anything of which Mrs. Kearney might be accused (if Miss Healy had no designs on advancement, she would not have been charming in such a calculated way with Mr. Hendrick). Yet, once again, Miss Healy is one who kindly consents — like a lady — and Mrs. Kearney is one who disappoints the committee for failing to be one. Both women are capable and ambitious — an admirable trait in a man — yet Miss Healy is careful to accept, rather than demand. Mrs. Kearney, who begins her quest for recognition in a manner as circumspect and ladylike as does Miss Healy, ends by refusing to pretend that self-serving decisions made by a fragmented and disorganized group of men are anything else but that. The irony is rich, then, when the move to censor her is understood by everyone as what the committee had done.

"The committee" is much like Lacan's view of the ego in that it is a fragmented reality fantasized as a coherent body. The ego of the subject quests tirelessly for meaning, closure, and final solutions. This imaginary closure is intended to close out or domesticate the questioning gaze and desire of the Other. Like Lacan's ego, the committee operates as a structure of exclusion that, because the myth of its autonomy and unity depends on the belief of others, it is permanently paranoid. It is significant that Mrs. Kearney becomes too large a threat to tolerate in relation to the frequency and rapidity of her questions: "And what way did you treat me? . . . I'm *asking* for my rights. . . . I can't get a civil *answer*" (*D* 148–49). Mr. Holohan refuses to countenance Mrs. Kearneys legalistic discourse; all his responses make it clear that he can only hear her questions as proof of some sort of unfortunate gender aberration rather than the protests of a subject who feels wronged. At no time in his responses to her questions does Mr. Holohan address the issue of whether or not she is right (nor do any of the other men). instead he limits himself to a single topic: Is she, or is she not, a lady?: "I'm surprised at you, Mrs Kearney. . . . I never thought you would treat us this way. . . . You might have some sense of decency. . . . I thought you were a lady" (*D* 148–149). The crowning irony regarding the committee, and the central paradox of the story, is that *the committee has done nothing to organize the concert.* As readers learn in the opening paragraph, it is almost entirely the result of Mrs. Kearney's organization.

Mrs. Kearney, who never fully realizes the extent of the condemnation directed against her, tries to renew what she perceives as her individual attack on Mr. Holohan's insufficient manhood: "— I'm not done with you yet, she said" (*D* 149). Mr. Holohan's decisive response — "But I'm done with you" — reflects his confidence that Mrs. Kearney's type, a woman who refuses to perform the masquerade of the Woman (not a lady) — will be thoroughly discredited. And yet the effectiveness of Mrs. Kearney's criticism of him, which is accurate enough, continues to enrage him. The only comfort he can offer himself is bitterly to denounce her ability (which fooled him so soundly) to masquerade as "a lady" (even though one can see by analyzing Miss Healy's "conversation" with Mr. Hendrick that what men view as the behavior of a "genuine" lady is always a performance): "Mr Holohan began to pace up and down the room, in order to cool himself for he felt his skin on fire. —That's a nice lady! he said. O, she's a nice lady!" (*D* 149). It is left to Mr. O'Madden Burke, "poised upon his umbrella in approval" to assure Mr. Holohan that he "did the proper thing" (*D* 149).

To appreciate this wonderfully understated final irony of Joyce's (that is, having Burke act as support for the conduct of the lurching "Hoppy" Holohan while leaning on his umbrella), one needs to turn back in the story to the narrator's initial description of Mr. O'Madden Burke: "He was a suave elderly man who balanced his imposing body, when at rest, upon a large silk umbrella. His magniloquent western name as the moral umbrella upon which he balanced the fine problem of his finances. He was widely respected" (*D* 149).

Mr. O'Madden Burke, if I can intentionally mix my metaphors in an international manner, is the leaning tower of the Dublin General Post Office. It is the apparent association of his name with the law-giving function of the Name-of-the-Father (located, in a way that is safely obscure, back in the committee of Celtic mythology) that provides him with a "moral umbrella" that protects him from creditors and detractors alike. To address a crowd magniloquently is to speak in a bombastic style or manner, and this inflated appreciation of his name accords well with the general theme in this story of keeping the phallus erect whatever the cost. To put it another way, Mr. O'Madden Burke's "magniloquent" name does not represent his financial solvency, but only his ability to remain financially insolvent with impunity. Like the committee itself, Mr. O'Madden Burke would not bear up well under questioning. Readers might also note that Mr. O'Madden

Burke deliberately exploits his Irish name to garner public respect for his masculine gender in the same way that Mrs. Kearney planned to use her daughter's Irish name to garner public approval for her feminine gender. The strategy is identical, and, as a result of it, Mr. O'Madden Burke enjoys recognition as a male ("He was widely respected") and Kathleen has a solid reputation as a young lady ("People said that she was very clever at music and a very nice girl"). And so Joyce balances final male approval of the actions of the committee on Mr. O'Madden Burke's umbrella, with all its shaky moral representations. Masculine order has been resoundingly reaffirmed by the conclusion of the story, yet Joyce's final image suggests that when a woman such as Mrs. Kearney mounts a successful attack against the existence of the committee, the Law of the Father is left with only one shaky leg and a prosthetic Phallus to balance upon.[6]

15

"With God's grace
I will rectify this and this"
Masculinity Regained in "Grace"

What matters, when one tries to elaborate upon some
experience, isn't so much what one understands, as
what one doesn't understand. . . . It is on the basis
of a kind of refusal of understanding that we push
open the door to analytic understanding. (Lacan
1988a, 73)

—Pain? Not much, answered Mr Kernan. But it's so
sickening. I feel as if I wanted to retch off.
—That's the boose, said Mr Cunningham firmly.
—No, said Mr Kernan. I think I caught a cold on
the car. There's something keeps coming into my
throat, phlegm or— (*D* 158–59)

The opening two sentences of this story present a physical parody
of the spiritual phrase, "to fall from grace": "Two gentlemen who
were in the lavatory at the time tried to lift him up: he was quite helpless. He lay curled at the foot of the stairs down which he had fallen.
They succeeded in turning him over. His hat had rolled a few yards
away and his clothes were smeared with the filth and ooze of the floor
on which he had lain, face downwards" (*D* 150). Having begun with
this image of a helpless and anonymous man, Joyce then devotes the
first section of the story to the restoration of Mr. Kernan's physical

balance and the second section to the restoration, with the help of a group of male friends, of his spiritual balance. As Kershner points out, "In a sense, [Mr. Kernan] does not exist until he is claimed by his friend; were it not for Power's intervention, he might well be imprisoned as a penalty for anonymity" (132). The return of "grace" (as well as identity) into the life of Mr. Kernan, which a group of men endeavor to restore to him, can be interpreted as their attempt, through fictional narrative presented as truth, to renew his faith in the myth of a coherent masculine identity.

Mr. Kernan has not only fallen down the stairs, he has also fallen out of the discourse that sustains the identity of his masculine friends. Their plot to rehabilitate him is also a desire to reconfirm the existing patriarchal order that sustains them. In the most general terms, the Symbolic Order surrounds the subject and imposes meaning on its entire history. A signifying system that exists before the subject must be periodically renarrated as the truth if the subject is to be free to find its identity through a discourse with others who subscribe to this same truth. As Lacan stated more than once, subjectivity is not an essence but a set of relationships. If Mr. Kernan drops out of the signifying system that exists before him and determines his identity, then he challenges the presumed certitude of all the other subjects who have participated in the set of relationships that has defined each of them within what they have taken to be the discourse of the other (but which is, in fact, the imagined desire of the Other). To put this another way, Mr. Kernan's drunkenness, which is rapidly increasing in intensity and frequency, must be interpreted by his friends in a manner that reconfirms rather than challenges the signifying system by which their experience of reality is symbolically mediated into self-knowledge.

The narrative of truth that Mr. Kernan's friends weave as they stand about his bedside never mentions that Mr. Kernan's problem stems from his increasingly frequent use of alcohol as an escape from the anxiety and incertitude caused by his slowly failing business. Indeed, as they talk, they begin drinking beer and graduate to whiskey. What these colleagues are doing is using the Imaginary Order (their identificatory relationship with Mr. Kernan) and the Symbolic Order (speech) to reweave Mr. Kernan's reality in a manner that will paper over the lack-in-being upon which he has recently begun to fixate. Although this is not their conscious intention, Kernan's friends offer themselves as a screen on which Kernan's moi (the subject's source of belief and certainty) can interact with its own ideal image through the cliché and social convention of the je (the speaking subject that solicits others to conform the ideal image contained in the moi). Mr. Kernan is the patient, and his friends are all the sort of self-satisfied psychoanalysts of which Lacan so disapproved. They encourage Mr. Kernan to reembrace his ideal image by performing a self-congratulatory ceremony that restores him to "grace" by celebrating the mutually recognized truth of their own fictional structuration as subjects.

The gender myth of masculinity, which functions as a denial of symbolic castration, has the structure of fiction, and this fiction is presented to others by the masculine subject so that they will recognize it as having the structure of truth. What is actually true (what is Real) is what is repressed to facilitate this masquerade of confirmation. The residue beyond the subject's interpretation of his sexual identity as masculine continues to reside in the Real where it can surge forward into consciousness with the sort of inexplicable terror that has been driving Mr. Kernan to drink. If the men can convince Mr. Kernan to *stop* drinking to excess by returning him to the grace of an overarching Symbolic Order that imbues all their lives with meaning, then they can reassure themselves that there is no reason to *start* drinking. If this were not therapy in which the men are treating themselves even more than they are treating Mr. Kernan, they might actually dare to ask him what is bothering him. But it is centrally significant to their strategy that they present him with the solution to his problem without actually inquiring into the details of his anxiety. In other words, they set themselves up as "the ones who know" (a surrogate Other — or ego psychologist!), and Mr. Kernan, because he has lost the thread of his own story, is highly responsive to the opportunity, which they have gathered to offer him, to have his loose ends woven into their narrative of redemption.

The presence of an unknown and unconscious man is an alarming enough sight to cause the manager to call for the law. In doing so he demonstrates the same impulse that Kernan's friends will display: a desire for law (of the Father) and (Symbolic) Order in the face of fallen subjectivity. Moreover, the questions he asks — "Who is the man? What's his name and address?" (*D* 151) — place the reader in similar blind position relative to the identity of Mr. Kernan. By having the reader learn who Mr. Kernan is at the same time that his friends convene to reconfirm who he was, Joyce forces the reader to read two stories: the one he wrote and the one the friends of Mr. Kernan are writing. This, of course, invites the reader to examine the third version of the story, that Joyce has not written — the assertion of the readers' own transcendent subjectivity as they interpret the story. Few interpretations have been written concerning "Grace," but most of the commentary devoted to it imposes a transcendent template of external knowledge (Dante's *Divine Comedy,* the structure of the Trinity, the parable of the unjust steward, the Book of Job) that is authorized to correct the view of the men and show their oblique relationship to the truth.[1] These studies are valid, but they miss what I see as the central point of the story: the necessity of error and misrecognition in the formation of subjectivity.

Lacan insists that one must resist what is understood in order to glimpse the unconscious knowledge that this understanding is designed to block: "What matters, when one tries to elaborate upon some experience, isn't so much what one understands, as what one doesn't understand. . . . One of the things we must guard most against is to understand too much. . . . It is on the basis of a kind of refusal of understanding that we push open the door to analytic understanding" (1988a, 73). In the intrasubjective sharing of a commonly supported discourse, truth promulgates itself in the form of error and can, thus, be seen from an analytical perspective as "the habitual incarnation of the truth" (1988a, 263). All conscious knowledge is based on a fundamental dimension of error because it depends upon "the forgetting of the creative function of truth in its nascent form" (1988b, 19). What one witnesses in watching the men gather about Mr. Kernan's bedside is the nascent form of a creative discourse designed to rehabilitate Mr. Kernan into a fictional structuration that masks unconscious knowledge about the mythic unity of the subject. This fiction then presents itself — *because* of the errors they are based upon, not *despite* them — as truth. What I am suggesting about the typical analysis of this story is that critics gather around it, with the same trepidation as the men crowded into Mr. Kernan's bedroom, armed with metanarratives designed to rehabilitate its frightening portrayal of the fiction of subjectivity. On almost every ecclesiastical point the men bring up, then, there is an element of untruth in what they say.

The point, though, is not that they are "wrong" in relation to some transcendent sense of actual church history that the literary critic valorizes as true but that their fiction takes on the structure of truth within their experience of subjectivity as a set of relationships.

When the police officer arrives, symbol of the law of the Father, he is as much at a loss as the frightened manager. He is in search of information to write down in "a small book" hanging "from his waist." But when he confronts the spectacle of an unconscious and anonymous man, the pages in his little book must remain blank. It remains for another anonymous person, a young man in a cycling suit, to ignore the symbolic ramifications of this man and see directly to his physical needs: "A young man in a cycling-suit cleared his way through the ring of bystanders. He knelt down promptly beside the injured man and called for water" (*D* 151). The constable, seeing a role for himself repeats the order "in an authoritative voice" (*D* 151). The newly conscious Mr. Kernan is immediately wary of the constable and evasively maintains his anonymity in the face of the officer's stubbornly repeated question "Where do you live?" It is clear to Mr. Kernan that he is a public drunk in the discourse of this officer, and this is not the best pathway for him to reenter the realm of the nameable. Instead, his obvious plan is to exit the bar alone—if that is physically possible—and leave no trace of himself behind to be incorporated into a gossipy discourse that might eventually emerge as more true than anything he could say against it. Finally, however, another man comes along (Mr. Power) who recognizes the injured man and, with the same instinctual wariness that McCoy displayed earlier, only addresses him by his first name in front of the constable. Because the constable recognizes Mr. Power, the matter is promptly resolved when Mr. Power promises to "see him home." The constable never learns Mr. Kernan's identity, and no one (including the reader) ever learns who the young man in the bicycle suit was.

I emphasize, in my summary of the opening events of the story, the fact that all the anxiety and drama centers on the issue of anonymity. In a crowded bar, no one noticed Mr. Kernan particularly, but His "fall from grace" is a fall from the Imaginary Order of identification ("Who is the man?") as well as the Symbolic Order of language and others/Other ("Was he by himself? . . . What's his name and address?") All the men present quickly assess their relation to him for one another's benefit: someone remembers he was with two friends, and a curate recalls serving him a small rum. Joyce maximizes this tension by forcing readers to take their places in the bar with everyone else. The relief is palpable when Mr. Power appears from the far end of the bar with his illuminating greeting, "Hallo, Tom, old man! What's the trouble?" (*D* 152). Instantly, "Tom" has a referent—a cause of his existence—and the ominous unsubtle presence of the law immediately recedes: "—It's all right, constable. I'll see him home. The constable touched his helmet and answered: —All right, Mr. Power!" (*D* 152). The unconscious and anonymous man had brought a sudden halt to the activity and conversation in the bar. The question "Who is he?" carries an unusual weight and urgency in this context because the unconscious corollary of it is "Who am I?"

It is not, I suggest, simply that Mr. Kernan is unconscious that alarms the manager but the fact that he is anonymous as well; this combination makes his face frightening: "The manager, alarmed by the grey pallor of the man's face, sent for a policeman" (*D* 151). Partly, of course, he is trying to protect himself in case the man should die, but there is also an urge to understand Mr. Kernan, an urge that he initially demonstrates and that others then take up after him. To put this in a Lacanian context, Mr. Kernan's fall from grace briefly tears a hole in the fabric that is made by weaving threads of the Imaginary and Symbolic orders together to form the tailored cloth of identity. Lurking behind this veil is the unassimilated and unassimilable order beyond identity and language that Lacan called the Real. Of course, it is the literal situation that is painstakingly researched by the manager and the constable; they quickly assess the facts and restore superficial normalcy: "The manager brought the constable to the stairs to inspect the scene of the accident. They agreed that the gentleman must have missed his footing. The customers returned to the counter and a curate set about removing the traces of blood from the floor" (*D* 152–53). This "explanation," agreed upon by the manager and the constable, reweaves the various threads of signification that were temporarily disrupted by Mr. Kernan's fall.

Mr. Kernan is restored to grace, in this immediate context, by having his hat placed back on his head (now that he is upright and can support it). Indeed, this hat and its progress up the stairs is mentioned as if it were equal in importance, if not superior, to him: "One of the gentlemen who had carried him upstairs held a dinged silk hat in his hand" (*D* 151).[2] As soon as Mr. Kernan is decently on his feet, readers are told of this minor action: "The battered silk hat was placed on the man's head" (*D* 152). The reason for the narrator's insistence on noting the material of the hat is made clear when one learns how Mr. Kernan defines "a man": "Mr. Kernan was a commercial traveller of the old school which believed in the dignity of its calling. He had never been seen in the city without a silk hat of some decency and a pair of gaiters. By grace of these two articles of clothing, he said, a man could always pass muster" (*D* 154). *Muster* is a redolent word in the context in which I am placing this story because it means, among other things, to cause to gather, to convene, to come together, to congregate, to pass inspection. A man, it would seem, needs help to "pass muster."

What he needs is something independent of his person that vouches for the authenticity and coherence of himself even to the most casual observer. In the slow reserection of Mr. Kernan up the stairs of the pub, it is his hat that continues to maintain his human dimension. Until he is erect again, and someone is able to clap this hat back on to his head, the disconcertment caused by his sudden and sodden presence as a heap on the men's room floor is a steady cause of unease to the other men in the bar. In the final scene of the story, one finds, once again, that the hat has undergone the same rehabilitative treatment as its owner: "In one of the benches near the pulpit sat Mr. Cunningham and Mr. Kernan. . . . His hat, which had been rehabilitated by his wife, rested upon his knees. Once or twice he pulled down his cuffs with one hand while he held the brim of his hat lightly, but firmly, with the other hand" (*D* 173). Certainly the operation of adjusting the cuffs could have been done more expeditiously had Mr. Kernan allowed his hat to rest, even for a moment, on his knees. But the fact is, he is nervous, and if he cannot wear the hat, he must hold it "lightly but firmly."

One can further appreciate Mr. Kernan's profound attachment to his hat when one notes that all the other men surrender their hats at the door: "The gentlemen sat in the benches, having hitched their trousers slightly above their knees and laid their hats in security. They sat well back and gazed formally at the distant speck of red light which was suspended before the high altar" (*D* 172). The main difference between Mr. Kernan and all the other men is that they accept "the distant speck of red light" as a genuine representation of their coherent identity (they are recognized in the eyes of God/the Other), so they are content to let this speck of red light serve, temporarily, as the cosmic equivalent of their hats. They will, of course, require them again as soon as they leave this august presence. Mr. Kernan, however, must hang onto his hat because he has no particular faith in the Symbolic Order of these candles, which he referred to earlier as "the magic lantern business." In general, his attitude toward Catholic ritual is that it is effective theater but no more genuine than other types of amusement (thus, his attitude is similar to that of Leopold Bloom).

In fact, while recalling the time he saw Father Thomas Burke (accompanied by the Orangeman, Crofton, whom readers met in "Ivy Day"), a particularly popular orator, he refers to his place in the audience as "in the back of the . . . pit, you know . . . the—" It is left to Cunningham to supply hastily the more respectful term which, significantly enough, is "the body" (*D* 165). Mr. Kernan is wary of the retreat proposed to him by his friends because, although they insist the ritual is spiritually sustaining, he has always judged its merits in terms of whether or not it was entertaining. The purpose of the retreat is to reconfirm the unity of the masculine body (and by extension, their particular bodies as they sit in the body of the church) by persuading them to entrust their masculine identity, once again, to the elaborate symbolic Order literalized through the mystical rites of the Catholic church. The retreat conducted by Father Purdon, with its elaborate use of business and financial metaphors, is particularly popular among the Catholic men of Dublin because, in effect, it reminds them that they maintain a certain economic control over their lives (one that women do not share). Money is all too similar to the sacred mystery of grace in that it supplies a Symbolic Order for the masculine subject that forestalls intimations of anonymity and fragmentation.

The issue for a man is how to become his own referent. If one's own hat falters in the performance of this function, then "the red speck of light" can supplement and augment it as the sublime object that "knows" about the loss at the center of being, and promises to compensate for it (although all it can really offer is unending substitutions). For the Catholics who believe in the rituals of the church, this red speck is one manifestation among many (transubstantiation is another) of some knowledge they suppose to represent that law and authority that is necessary to authenticate them. This form of authentification is as self-referential as identifying one's "self" by the quality of one's hat. But one does not believe, typically, in one's hat. The element of belief in the Catholic faith, however, endows the rituals and symbols of the church with the ability to connect directly to the Real. A *retreat,* as the term implies, is meant to be a secession from reality in order to reconfirm *the eternal benevolence* of the Real (precisely when actual circumstances seem to be implying the opposite), which operates within and beyond the experiences of daily life. Going on a retreat offers them future protection against the pain of being ambushed by doubts about their own existence (and it is Mr. Kernan's fall from grace that constitutes just the sort of existential ambush that the retreat is intended to forestall).

Father Purdon's talk, replete with business metaphors, obsessively emphasizes completeness and totality. He makes it clear that lying behind all the symbols and rituals of the Catholic church is an infallible accountant, and they can safely compare and adjust their own ledgers, with reference to His, and be assured that the result will tally *at every point* (thus papering over the lack-in-being that generates the need to do all this accounting in the first place).

> But one thing only, he [Father Purdon] said, he would ask of his hearers. And that was: to be straight and manly with God. If their accounts tallied in every point to say:
> —Well, I have verified my accounts. I find all well.
> But if, as might happen, there were some discrepancies, to admit the truth, to be frank and say like a man:
> —Well, I have looked into my accounts. I find this wrong and this wrong. But, with God's grace, I will rectify this and this. I will set right my accounts. (*D* 174).

The implication of Father Purdon's metaphor is that such a thing as a man exists, and some sublime lawful authority independently maintains the standard of what this man is. Doubting one's manhood, then, need not be as debilitating as doubting the myth of one's fictional unity. What it indicates, instead, according to Father Purdon's remarks, is that a masculine subject requires adjustment vis-à-vis the transcendent standard of masculinity that maintains its inviolable integrity regardless of how far the subject has drifted from the mark. The retreat assures men that, like their hats, masculinity can be rehabilitated.

It is not that Mr. Kernan has no belief in an inviolable standard of a complete and autonomous masculinity—he does—but his standard is literally commercial and has no relation in his mind (at least until Father Purdon's sermon) to the Catholic church: "He carried on the tradition of his Napoleon, the great Blackwhite, whose memory he evoked at times by legend and mimicry. Modern business methods had spared him only so far as to allow him a little office in Crowe Street on the window blind of which was written the name of his firm with the address—London, E. C. " (*D* 154). He has his God—a former salesman named Blackwhite who was, apparently, a legend in the Dublin tea market—but Blackwhite is the dead God of a bygone business era. Mr. Kernan's continued allegiance to this model of a man, in the more impersonal and competitive climate of "modern day business," has reduced him to conducting his increasingly desultory tea sales from "a little office." His memory of Blackwhite seems to hearken back to an earlier time when "men were men," and deals were struck with hearty handshakes. The inadequacy of Blackwhite as a "modern day" role model emphasizes Mr. Kernan's increasing incertitude. His slow, bewildered decline makes him a particularly apt example of Lacan's definition of a man as "he who finds himself male without knowing what to do about it."

Mr. Kernan needs a lesson in what we might call "modern day masculinity," and Mr. Power is just the man for it: "Mr Power, a much younger man, was employed in the Royal Irish Constabulary Office in Dublin Castle. The arc of his social rise intersected the arc of his friend's decline" (*D* 154). The *X* of this intersection marks the spot that Mr. Kernan formulates himself, and his cautious acceptance of Mr. Power's idea of going on a retreat can be seen as his effort to switch from the downward trajectory he is currently on to the upward one of Mr. Power at the point where their interests, although different, intersect.[3] In other words, he may still believe in the "decency of his profession" (where he goes about town in person booking small orders), but no one else seems to notice him. What people recall about him, if they think of him at all, is what he used to be like: "Mr. Kernan's decline was mitigated by the fact that certain of those friends who had known him at his highest point of success still esteemed him as a character" (*D* 154). So, in a larger sense, it is Mr. Kernan's earlier fall from "grace" (from being recognized by others as a masculine subject) that precipitates his actual plunge down the stairs, which this story details in its opening paragraph. The signifying chain that previously connected Mr. Kernan to the veiled and powerful phallus has somehow shifted and left him to seek his peace in the nether world of constant intoxication ("He's been drinking since Friday," Mrs. Kernan tells Mr. Power). In short, Mr. Kernan, despite his silk hat, is no longer capable of "passing muster"; it remains for those friends who remember him as he used to be to shore him up again. By rehabilitating him, they can reassert the efficacy of their own belief system and explain his generally disturbing fall in a manner that strengthens their own necessary systems of error that they present to one another as knowledge.

Significantly, when Mr. Cunningham, Mr. Power, and (to a lesser extent) Mr. M'Coy discuss the special qualities of the Catholic church, they begin by praising the Jesuits, the head of which "stands next to the Pope" (*D* 163). When Mr. M'Coy tries to illustrate their quality by telling a story that shows "they're the boyos have influence," Mr. Cunningham smoothly cuts him off to remark: "The Jesuits are a fine body of men, said Mr. Power" (*D* 163). M'Coy has bumbled by stressing how effective the Jesuits are at material and political matters, when what is currently insisted is how well connected they are as an unfragmented *body*. Yet Mr. Cunningham's point that the general of the Jesuits stands next to the pope is not so very different from M'Coy's cruder assertion that they are "the boyos [who] have influence." The difference between the two remarks — and it is a crucial one — is that the pope is above and beyond the everyday reality that M'Coy insists the Jesuits can manipulate better than anyone else ("if you want a thing well done and no flies about it you go to a Jesuit"). What Mr. Power and Mr. Cunningham wish to stress is the transcendent power of the Jesuits as "a fine body of men" and not those secular successes that betray their own search for recognition as masculine subjects. Even more to the point, as Mr. Cunningham hastily goes on to note, the Jesuits are an order that "was never once reformed" because "it never fell away" (*D* 164). The Jesuit order, unlike the former business order that once made Mr. Kernan a success, will never betray the masculine subject who manages to align his sense of "self" with their precepts. "That's a fact, said Mr. Cunningham. That's history" (D 164). Their order, so the implication runs, has always been immune to the vagaries of time, place, and fashion. It is an order, in other words, that is permanently erect, a transcendent signifier, signifying them, that can never be corrupted or outmoded.

In addition, this order, which never goes out of style, is directly associated with the ultimate exemplar of self-referential masculinity—the pope: "They're the grandest order in the Church, Tom, said Mr. Cunningham, with enthusiasm. The General of the Jesuits stands next to the Pope" (D 163). The pope is the sort of man that Mr. Kernan can look up to—a new legend—like his former "Napoleon," the all but forgotten salesman, Blackwhite. "Some bad lots" may have been pope, as Mr. Cunningham concedes, but "not one of them ever preached *ex cathedra* a word of false doctrine" (D 168). The office of the pope—with a self-authorized infallibility—is that sublime object that is "presumed to know." Although an individual might fall from "grace" (even an individual pope), rehabilitation is always possible because of this transcendent standard. It is significant that Cunningham uses a business term, "bad lots," to describe merchandise (reprehensible popes) who have failed to exemplify the high standards of the manufacturer. A "bad lot," far from challenging the fallibility of the pope, strengthens the need to see *the office* as an infallible signifier of truth. The office of the pope is the ultimate veiled phallus that assures the authenticity of all suffering masculine subjects who experience themselves as signifiers without any outside referent beyond the imagined gaze of the Other.

Although the drives animating the human subject aim repeatedly at this or that desired object that is expected to yield joy, security, and solutions, the object always disappoints by revealing itself as a substitute for the sublime object that is "presumed to know." In the case of the pope's infallibility, however, an office held by a man is declared to be the original signifer from which all other signifiers (subjects) gain their authority as autonomous beings. Indeed, the manner in which Mr. Cunningham narrates the events that led up to the declaration of papal infallibility graphically illustrates how the designation of any signfier as *an original* signifier causes all other signifiers to take on definitive meaning *in relation to it:* "—There they were at it, all the cardinals and bishops and archbishops from all the ends of the earth and these two fighting dog and devil until at last the Pope himself stood up and declared infallibility a dogma of the Church *ex cathedra.* On the very moment John MacHale, who had been arguing and arguing against it, stood up and shouted out with the voice of a lion: *Credo!* . . . Mr. Cunningham's words had built up the vast image of the Church in the minds of his hearers. His deep raucous voice had thrilled them as it uttered the word of belief and submission" (*D* 169–70). Mr. Cunningham's account of this event cannot possibly be historically accurate because John MacHale was not present on July 18, 1870, when papal infallibility was decreed (Gifford 1982, 108). Joyce's point would seem to be, both here and elsewhere in *Dubliners,* that facts have very little to do with what people choose to elevate to the status of truth. Truth is fiction and vice-versa. The "self" is a structured myth that is aligned with whatever fiction is designated by the subject, in discourse with other subjects, as having the coherent structure of truth.

Mr. Kernan promptly moves to align himself with this myth by noting that he saw John MacHale once. His description of the event endows MacHale with the sort of unerring ability to judge character that one might expect of someone who is able to verify his own "self" and, therefore, finds the "selves" of others to be suspect (in other words, MacHale, like the pope, is an infallible judge of character who judges the fallible): "—It was at the unveiling of Sir John Gray's statue. Edmund Dwyer Gray was speaking, blathering away, and here was this old fellow, crabbed-looking old chap, looking at him from under his bushy eyebrow. Mr Kernan knitted his brows and, lowering his head like an angry bull, glared at his wife. —God! he exclaimed, resuming his natural face, I never saw such an eye in a man's head. It was as much as to say: *I have you properly taped, my lad.* He had an eye like a hawk" (*D* 170). Much like Henchy in "Ivy Day," who momentarily *becomes* Parnell while reminiscing over the dead man's former infallibility (shouting out *"Down ye curs"* in Parnell's voice), Mr. Kernan twists his features into a likeness of what he posits as the infallible gaze of MacHale. What Mr. Kernan admires about John MacHale is not his particular religious or political beliefs, but his unshakable certitude in himself that allows him to expose unerringly the fraudulence of others, regardless of how effectively they may posture and preen as being in possession of the phallic signifier. "Properly taped," it might be added, is another commercial term implying the ability to "size up" a man and determine his "true" worth. Gray, who supposedly is at the center of attention giving a speech, is reduced to someone "blathering away" by the hawklike eyes of MacHale. In Kernan's scenario, MacHale becomes the subject who is "presumed to know," and as such, he appears to represent the Real in relation to the hapless Edmund Dwyer Gray.

Infallibility is a conceptual term for the mens' desire for the Phallus, a symbol that, to use Lacan's words, "can take up its place as the signifier of this very point where the signifier is lacking" (1982b, 117). The real male organ becomes "marked at the imaginary level" in order to appear as this symbol. But this condemns human subjects to search perpetually the field of the Other for the site of what they take to be their own truth. A popular orator like Father Tom Burke can attract people outside the Catholic faith because the thundering certitude of his sermons appears capable of checking what Lacan calls "the endless circulating of significations." Indeed, one of his sermons, the subject of which Mr. Kernan cannot recall, leads to an odd sort of communion between Mr. Kernan and the Protestant Orangeman, Mr. Crofton.

> We went into Butler's in Moore Street — faith, I was genuinely moved, tell you the God's truth — and I remember well his very words. *Kernan,* he said, *we worship at different altars,* he said, *but our belief is the same.* Struck me as very well put.
> —There's a good deal in that, said Mr Power. There used always be crowds of Protestants in the chapel when Father Tom was preaching.
> —There's not much difference between us, said Mr M'Coy. We both believe in —
> He hesitated for a moment.
> — . . . in the Redeemer. Only they don't believe in the Pope and in the mother of God.
> — But, of course, said Mr Cunningham quietly and effectively, our religion is *the* religion, the old, original faith. (*D* 165–66)

All human subjects "believe in the Redeemer" in the sense that they require that the Other should act as a guarantee of the fictional unity of the "self" (because it is the only possible site of truth and the place from which the phallic signifier appears to originate).

Still, Mr. Cunningham hastens to reassert the primacy of the Catholic faith by remarking that it "is the religion, the old, original faith." Although the Protestant church might direct a subject's belief in the general direction of the Other, who they trust will redeem them, it is the Catholic church alone that, imbued as it is with this "original faith," is capable of directing the faithful toward the sublime object of desire that is superior to all substitutes. Protestant worshippers may have the same belief in the Other and the same longing for redemption, but they direct this desire to a "different altar," as Crofton puts it. It is this altar, or substitute object of desire, that Mr. Cunningham demotes as inferior because its meaning depends on the *original* signifier that only *the* religion of the Catholic church possesses. This "original signifier," taken to signify them, is represented during the retreat by the "speck of red light" that indicates the presence of the Blessed Sacrament, which bestows grace upon all of them.

In general, then, the structure and symbolism of the Catholic faith, as it is presented at Father Purdon's retreat, shores up the necessary illusion of masculine identity. It would seem, on the face of it, that these men are verifying their identities strictly with reference to other men and without the intercession of women. But this is to forget that the church itself is referred to as "the mystical bride" of Christ. Indeed, what makes all the men a little nervous (especially Mr. Kernan) is the uncomfortably feminine nature of going on a retreat (one recalls Mangan's sister who had to miss the Araby Bazaar in order to attend a retreat). Mrs. Kernan, who is Mr. Kernan's anything but mystical bride, is careful to remain neutral. Yet she endorses the attitude Mr. Cunningham has adopted that they must all go on this retreat because they are a rowdy bunch of two-fisted sinners: "Mrs. Kernan thought it would be wiser to conceal her satisfaction. So she said: — I pity the poor priest that has to listen to your tale. Mr. Kernan's expression changed. — If he doesn't like it, he said bluntly, he can . . . do the other thing" (*D* 171). The point of Mrs. Kernan's gruff assessment of her husband's upcoming confession is to reassure him that he will still be a rascal who will shock the somewhat more feminine priest with tales of his indomitable (albeit, sinful) manhood.

But even this moderate strategy almost backfires because raising the issue of confession (which one now realizes is an issue the other men have deliberately skirted for as long as possible) reminds Mr. Kernan that he will be placed in an inferior position relative to another man; that is, he will confess his weaknesses to someone who will judge him without offering any corresponding confession of his own. The effect of this on Mr. Kernan produces a masculine bluster (not in the least penitent) to the effect that if the priest tries to take advantage of his admission of uncertainty and incompleteness, his endangered moi will retrench itself immediately and tell the priest to fuck off (although the precise phrase he might use remains vague). Mr. Kernan telegraphs in another way that his decision to attend the retreat is more politically motivated than spiritually: "I'll do the job right enough. I'll do the retreat business and confession, and . . . all that business. But . . . no candles! No, damn it all, I bar the candles! He shook his head with farcical gravity. — Listen to that! said his wife. — I bar the candles, said Mr Kernan, conscious of having created an effect on his audience and continuing to shake his head to and fro. I bar the magic-lantern business" (*D* 171). Mr. Kernan's consistent use of the word *business* as an all-purpose filler makes it clear that he sees the male Catholic community as synonymous with the male business community. Given that, the idea of parading around with a candle seems ridiculous. What would the great Blackwhite say? Mr. Kernan is willing to engage in a little mystical theatrics but, as I pointed out before, he will only endure it while keeping a tight grip on his refurbished silk hat (a much more sensible rehabilitation, from his point of view, than all of the "magic lantern business").

The men are willing to admit to a longing for something to verify them, but only if the church can promise them redemption as a reward for such a confession and, thus, assure them that their self-doubt need not be permanent. Accordingly, Father Purdon does just that, assuring them that their souls are like an accounting ledger, prone to getting out of balance from time to time but always amenable to readjustment if they tally their accounts of themselves in relation to the sublime Other (represented on this earth by the infallible office of the pope). Their faith in this sublime Other consists of a belief that the internal unity they crave (jouissance) and believe they have lost is yet redeemable if they realign themselves with the phallus (perceived as the representative of the original object of Desire even though this original object does not and has never existed). In this way, the phallus ceases to be a mere biological organ and becomes instead a symbol of imaginary potency toward which they pledge allegiance. But this elevation of the phallus from organ to symbol also guarantees a permanent alienation in which division and loss must be persistently denied in favor of a fictional unity of identity. In this equation the concept of "grace" can be characterized as the renewed strength to believe in the myth of identity that shores up reality against the inexorable subversion of the Real.

One is in "a state of grace" when what appears to be the sublime object of Desire has not yet revealed itself as yet another substitute. The Symbolic Order that sustains Mr. Kernan's identity has shifted, and he, caught up in a gender myth of a bygone era (exemplified by the forgotten "Napoleon," Blackwhite), has not shifted with it. In the words of the narrator, he has failed to adjust to "modern business practices." As a result, Mr. Kernan has increased his drinking binges in direct proportion to the reduction of his social standing as Mr. Power realizes when he brings him home and sees signs of squalor in the home. Even though Mr. Powers is indubitably on his way up, he must view Mr. Kernan's increasingly visible decline with alarm because, at one time, Mr. Kernan was every bit the "man about town" that Mr. Powers now feels himself to be. In other words, although the men who gather around Mr. Kernan can fairly claim that they have a benevolent intent, the tension in the sick man's room also demonstrates their fear that should Mr. Kernan's "fall from grace" prove to be permanent, should his masculine account remain unbalanced and in default, this foreclosure of gender identity could not fail to pose a threat to their own tenuous *business* of being themselves.[4]

16

"Perhaps she had not told him the whole story"
The Woman as a Symptom of Masculinity in "The Dead"

> The subject goes a long way beyond what is experienced 'subjectively" by the individual, exactly as far as the Truth he is able to attain. . . . This Truth of his history is not all of it contained in his script, and yet the place is marked there by the painful shocks he feels from knowing only his own lines. (Lacan 1981b, 26–27)

> His whole speech was a mistake from first to last, an utter failure. (*D* 179)

A Lacanian plot summary of "The Dead" would present the story as three attempts by Gabriel Conroy, with three different women, to confirm the fictional unity of his masculine subjectivity.[1] In addition, his constant fiddling with the after-dinner speech can be seen as, to use Lacan's phrase, "an attempted seduction of the Other"; Gabriel hopes to confirm his own existence by seducing the audience into authenticating it for him.[2] In his encounters with Lily and Molly Ivors, Gabriel Conroy's defenses and aversions steer him clear of any serious fragmentation of his identity. But Gretta's final disclosure about Michael Furey, which Gabriel perversely elicits from her, brings him to the edge of "that region where dwell the vast hosts of the head." In this region he finds that all of what he thought was solid, resolved, and certain — his identity and the world around him — now appears as a "wayward and flickering existence" (*D* 223).

The successful seduction of the other, through speech, permits the subject to authenticate his own subjectivity because, for the length of time that he is speaking, his belief that the audience believes in him allows him to believe in himself. In the most fundamental sense, Lacan divides the subject in two. The speaking subject he calls je or *I*. The objectlike stable sense of subjectivity, what one might call an ideal sense of one's own identity, Lacan designates as the moi, or *me*.[3] The je tries to bring about, through other subjects, the messages that the moi requires in order to believe in its existence. Lacan offers this analogy to describe the process: "This is what I have called putting the rabbit into the hat so as to be able to pull it out again later" (1982b, 63–64). The moi selects the rabbit, the message that supports its own ego ideal, but it is the je, the speaking subject, that coaxes the rabbit into the hat, that is, causes the proper message to echo back from the subject being addressed to the moi. This echo is never traceable to the actual utterance of the speaking subject but is contained in the utterance unbeknown to them. Only in this fashion can the conscious subject be fully enchanted by the magic of its own being. But because this belief is based on illusion — the magician must forget the origin of his own trick — subjectivity is an illusion dependent on the Other, which only appears to authenticate and complete subjectivity: "If I call the person to whom I am speaking by whatever name I choose to give him" Lacan explains, "I intimate to him the subjective function that he will take on again in order to reply to me, even if it is to repudiate this function" (1982b, 64). Beginning with Lily, each of the women will respond to Gabriel but only to repudiate the function he seeks to assign to them.[4]

Aunt Kate makes this unconsciously astute observation about Lily's consciousness: "She's not the girl she was at all" (*D* 181). This observation sounds the theme of the story. By the end of the evening, Gabriel will not be the man he was at all.[5] Indeed, throughout the Morkan's party he will strive to uphold what Kenner terms a "fiction of self-containment" and what I am calling (in line with Lacanian theory) "the fictional unity of the self." Gabriel is an uneasy man be-

cause he has successfully marketed himself as one who knows everything he needs to know (about carving the goose, keeping Freddy in
line, giving his wife galoshes), but even casual encounters with people
make him uncomfortably aware that much of what he knows is meaningless and serves only to keep him ignorant about the fragmentary
nature of his subjective consciousness (which is all that he *really* knows):
"The subject goes a long way beyond what is experienced 'subjectively'
by the individual, exactly as far as the Truth he is able to attain. . . .
This Truth of his history is not all of it contained in his script, and
yet the place is marked there by the painful shocks he feels from knowing only his own lines, and not simply there, but also in pages whose
disorder gives him little by way of comfort" (Lacan 1981b, 26–27).
Specious knowledge in the service of willful ignorance is a central
strategy for maintaining the fictional unity of the self.

Both the Morkan's party and Gabriel's after-dinner speech emphasize tradition, continuity, stability, clarity, and a comprehendible
universe. Within this setting, individuals attempt to rule over their
personal worlds of identity confusion, shifting modes of subjectivity,
and unpredictable suspensions of conscious thought. The price of all
this superficial order is that the Morkan sisters and their guests, in
attempting to rule everything that is present, are ruled by everything
that is absent. They are ruled by the dead as well as by absent thoughts
that they cannot afford to remember. Much of what they say to one
another in conversation is compulsively banal precisely because what
it is they wish to say is so alarming. What they have forgotten is what
remembers them. Conversation is dangerous, as Gabriel learns, because it is always an attempted seduction of the Other, and one's sense
of self may be subverted as easily as it may be confirmed.[6]

Perhaps because he senses this danger, Gabriel is always anxious
to read correctly from his own script. In the case of the particular evening where we see him, this means getting his after dinner speech
right. He is haunted by a sense that his script is not complete. He
is dimly aware that the missing lines are not completely lost to him,
however much they may be hidden, and that they are perhaps being
spoken by him unawares in his actions and good intentions.[7] Gabriel's
hesitation about whether or not to include the line from Browning
in his speech (the line is never cited in the story, thus forcing the reader,
also, to operate with an incomplete script) has little to do with the

particular line from Browning.[8] Rather, his indecision represents the perpetual effort of the subject to get language to fill in for some vaguely perceived yet fundamental loss. But even though language fills the gap perceived in the "self," it can never do so with the object that originally caused it, but only with countless substitutions for it. Gabriel's obsession with the inadequacy of the after-dinner speech is an illustration of the constant sense of loss and incompleteness that the conscious subject struggles to overcome by using language in a manner intended to seduce the voice of the Other into confirming, rather than undermining, one's belief in the fictional unity of the "self."[9]

What Gabriel really longs to restore to his conscious story are the missing pages still legible in his unconscious and also indirectly operative in his subjective consciousness. "The unconscious," Lacan says, "is that chapter of my history which is marked by a blank or occupied by a falsehood: it is the censored chapter. But the Truth can be found again; it is most often already written down elsewhere" (1981b, 21). It is written, for instance, in his confused panicky reaction to Lily's bitter retort about "the men nowadays"; it can be read again in his own bitter retort to Gretta about a possible trip to the west of Ireland, "You can go if you want to." At a different point in the evening, he will recall his mother's comment that Gretta is "country cute," but he will not connect this recollection to his rudeness to Gretta. Even though he is consciously annoyed by the unfairness of his mother's comment, he unconsciously supports it (in fact, he merely restates it in a different form) when he makes his retort to Gretta about going west by herself. He fails (refuses?) to understand that when he answers her in this manner, it is his dead mother who is speaking.[10] Indeed, Gabriel's mother is quite a presence for Gabriel at the Morkan's party—almost the guest of honor. She speaks a good deal of Gabriel's life for him. She was considered by Gabriel's aunts to be "the brains carrier of the Morkan family." Her picture hangs above the piano, and in it she is "pointing out something" to Gabriel's brother, Constantine.

Gabriel is not in the picture—not actually, anyway—but later one learns *he loves to review books:* "The books he received for review were almost more welcome than the paltry cheque. He loved to feel the covers and turn over the pages of newly printed books. Nearly every day when his teaching in the college was ended he used to wander down the quays to the second-hand booksellers" (*D* 188). Gabriel's mother, in this photograph from which Gabriel is absent, is "pointing out something" in a book; it is a lost page that Gabriel has been searching for ever since. Knowing that she has viewed this missing page in a photograph from which he is absent, he would like to review it; then he would know what it is that she desires; then he could become whatever it is. Gabriel is not in the photograph, and his mother is not at the party; these two absences create Gabriel's present consciousness and its insatiable need to be recognized by what is elsewhere (this phenomenon he will describe as "Distant Music" at the close of the story). Those pages of history not accessible to consciousness still are read aloud by the conscious subject in ways that disguise their unconscious source, and they assure that the subject's conscious script will always seem incomplete.[11] The subject's identity is doubly precarious because it conceals a division within the subject and because it is also the product of a division between the subject and the Other.

"After Lacan," Ragland-Sullivan maintains, "reality, rationality, and objectivity appear as comforting illusion — *points de capiton* — amid the truths of plurality, ambiguity, and uncertainty" (1986, xvii). Points de capiton, as I have mentioned, is intended by Lacan as an allusion to the buttons that hold down and give form to upholstered furniture. The upholstery has no inherent form; shape is provided by the buttons of reality, rationality, and objectivity. One has only to think of dreams to imagine the original shapelessness of our subjectivity before these buttons are put in place. From this critical perspective, one can see why the first sentence of "The Dead" presents such a remarkably compressed characterization of Lily. Each clause in the sentence presents the point of attachment of a different points de capiton whereby she gives the particular form to her subjective consciousness that she can misrecognize as her identity.

When "The Dead" opens, Lily is busy. She is occupied not only with answering the door and taking coats but also with the business of using this occupation to help fictionalize for herself the seamless quality of her consciousness: "Lily, the caretaker's daughter, was literally run off her feet" (*D* 175).[12] Her name, Lily, designates her as a unified entity — something that can be labeled or called upon. It is a unified word, not fragmented, that represents what she takes to be the totality of her subjectivity. The coherent reflection she identifies in the mirror (misrecognizes) and the sense of self that returns to her via the Other is named Lily. She answers to the name, which is to say she believes it. She is Lily when she answers and Lily when she thinks although not Lily when she dreams or when she muses. Speak the names of daydreamers aloud, and they will resume their presumed identity with a guilty start. "Man has only to dream," Lacan says "to see re-emerging before him that vast jumble, that lumber room he has to get by with" (1982b, 159). "The caretaker's daughter": Here is a phrase that is less subjective, more categorical. This phrase is more important to other people than it is to Lily. She does not call her father "the caretaker"—other people do—but as the certitude of her identity depends on the regard of others, she becomes for herself what she imagines others see when they look at her.

While occupied, she anchors her identity with reference to her father's occupation. She is literally run off her feet. Literally? No, not literally. She is very much on her feet. "Literally run off her feet" is the cliché that provides her with an image of how she imagines other people would perceive her at the moment. What might they say if asked to comment about her rushed movement through the hall? A figure of speech figures her existence for her. She imagines herself in terms of a spoken phrase ("literally run off her feet" is a cliché precisely because it has been *said* so many times) and assumes the author of the phrase authenticates her as well. She is a conscious subject unconsciously basing her myth of a unified identity on what is, in fact, a reflected image that emanates from the voice of an imagined Other. Through the reflection of itself in the Other, the subject fantasizes a specular self that is seamless and total. But this cohesion of self never actually occurs. Identity, begun as a fantasy, never becomes anything else. In the conscious mind of the subject, however, the fantasy is mythologized, idealized, and represented in culture and worshipped as the truth. The Other, Rose states, "appears to hold the 'truth' of the subject and the power to make good its loss. But this is the ultimate fantasy" (Mitchell and Rose 1982, 32).[13]

One can guess that, on a strictly physical level, Lily is tired. But to give this feeling meaning and identify it as her own she must imbue it with a subjective dimension by transforming it into language she imagines could be spoken about her. But who is this invisible other to whom she has become a subject in order to exist? Conceivably, it might be any number of people, but even before Gabriel arrives, he is on Lily's mind because Aunt Kate and Aunt Julia are fretting about his tardiness. Readers are introduced to her significations in the opening of the story so Gabriel can enter the story (take shape) in relation to them. Gabriel, as readers soon see, regards Lily as a little girl and himself, in relation to her, as an avuncular, solicitous adult. What would he think if he saw that Lily "had to scamper along the bare hallway to let in another guest"? (*D* 175). He would think this was tiring work for a little girl. Because he has a fondness for clichés, he might remark that Lily "was literally run off her feet." This sets the stage for Lily and Gabriel to shatter as mirrors for each other in the exchange that follows.

When Gabriel hears himself inquired after by Aunt Kate, he sings out, "Here I am as right as the mail, Aunt Kate!" (*D* 177). It is his signature piece, just as the opening sentence of the story is Lily's. Gabriel delivers himself to the party as though he were a package. He will spend the rest of the evening trying not to be unwrapped although the possibility of this is immediately put in doubt because Lily comes forward to take his hat and help him remove his coat. If he is a package, readers will see later that the wife he has created in his mind is the bow that holds the wrapping in place. Immediately upon Gretta's departure from his side to join the ladies upstairs, Gabriel's subjective sense of himself is newly influenced by the presence of Lily as an informing object: "—Is it snowing again, Mr. Conroy? asked Lily. . . . Gabriel smiled at the three syllables she had given his surname and glanced at her. . . . Gabriel had known her when she was a child and used to sit on the lowest step nursing a rag doll" (*D* 177). Gabriel absorbs two messages from her question: the actual content of her question and her pronunciation of his name. It is the latter message that most affects him although he will not allude to it directly in his response to Lily. Hearing the three syllables given his name, Gabriel smiles because it asserts their difference and his superiority. Only then does he glance at her. When he does, he does not see the objective spectacle of Lily at all. He sees, in his mind, "a child . . . on the lowest step nursing a rag doll" (*D* 177).

Lily, as I have already suggested, often imagines her identity in relation to Gabriel's regard, both when he is there and when he is not. Now she prompts him with a question that is, in fact, an invitation for him to address her as though she were a small girl. The "light fringe of snow" on Gabriel's overcoat, an overcoat that she is helping him take off, actually gives her the answer to the very question it prompts her to ask. Put another way, knowing it is still snowing allows her to properly frame a question that will activate his role as the avuncular male adult, which is necessary if she is to maintain a sense of "self" in his presence. Gabriel does not disappoint: "Yes, Lily . . . I think we're in for a night of it" (*D* 177). He does not simply answer "yes" or "it is snowing again." Rather, he begins his response with "yes, Lily" the manner in which Gabriel, the adult teacher, would address a student or a child. His further response is still not an answer to her question but a forecast. In the secure position she has helped create for him, he can tell her more than whether or not it is snowing; he can tell her for how long. In the certainty of "self" with which she invests him, he can predict the future — of himself or the weather. Knowing everything about what has been assures him continuity in the process of becoming what he imagines he will be.

Next, feeling so much the teacher, Gabriel asks if she is still in school. Her response begins to derail their mutually affirming dialogue: "O no, sir . . . I'm done schooling this year and more" (*D* 178). Strange that Gabriel did not know that; but then the Lily he is speaking to exists for him as a child nursing a rag doll. Although the schooling question is delivered in "a friendly tone," his prediction of her upcoming marriage is delivered "gaily." This move from "friendly" to "gaily" bespeaks uncertainty, a slight recklessness born of mild confusion. Gabriel ignores the growing fragmentation of his subjective consciousness by increasing the apparent certainty of his social demeanor. But he has strayed from his point of certitude, and his question about her "young man" tears it altogether. Lily's unexpected reply ("The men that is now is only palaver and what they can get out of you") makes it clear that he should have confined his self-confirming predictions to the weather (*D* 178). Lily has shattered as a mirror for Gabriel, but, unwittingly, he shattered one for her first by asking a real woman a question better asked of a little girl in a fairy tale (of course, she is that unreal to him). Lily has delivered her retort by glancing at him over her shoulder. He breaks away from this gaze immediately: "Gabriel colored as if he felt he had made a mistake, and, without looking at her . . . flicked actively with his muffler at his patent-leather shoes" (*D* 178). Gabriel avoids Lily's gaze and instead stares into his polished shoes as he searches for a return to certainty. His abrupt decision to give her a coin is a desperate attempt to return to his initial treatment of her as a child.[14]

This interaction leads to the rapid disintegration of Gabriel as a speaking subject: "'Just . . . here's a little'" is Gabriel's inarticulate explanation for the sudden gift. There is, suddenly, no literal message to his utterances. If Gabriel were able to fill in the gaps of this statement (the je), he might hear the silent discourse of the moi speaking directly: "Just (let me get away). Here's a little (exchange to reconvert you into what I need you to be)." What I have added to Gabriel's je utterance is my own approximation of what Lacan calls the *parole* of the spoken word. *Parole* is not the actual word chosen or the literal message conveyed but the implicit message woven into speech that asks for love and recognition. *Palaver* means to talk profusely or to cajole, which is also what the moi does. Lily is quite right when she says, "the men that is now is only all palaver"; she now hears what men say to her as merely a vehicle for what it is they would have her understand about them. As any masculine subject would, he glimpses himself in the new mirror of Lily's description. She becomes, for an instant, an accurate reflector of his state rather than a fanciful mirror for his ideal self.

Gabriel terminates the exchange with Lily by "thrusting [a gold coin] into her hands" (*D* 178). This gesture is followed by his abrupt withdrawal. Their social intercourse is terminated in a manner that mimics sexual intercourse.[15] More than that, his imposition of the gold coin mimics the exchange whereby a man buys a woman's sexual compliance for the purpose of gender confirmation. A prostitute, after all, agrees to *act* as the perfect sexual complement for a man in exchange for a fee. The man, through an act of will similar to forgetting the mythical component of his conscious subjectivity (that is, forgetting that he has put the magical rabbit in the hat), "forgets" that the performance has been paid for and seeks to witness it as a natural fact. Cast in the role of being the phallus (and Lacan's point is that the divided subject in man causes him to permanently *cast* women in this *role*), the woman does not exist. It is this mythical entity that Lacan means to designate when he writes "the Woman" and crosses a line through the word *the.* His point, as Rose suggests, is "not that women do not exist but that her status as an absolute category and guarantor of fantasy (exactly *The* Woman) is false (The)" (Mitchell and Rose 1982, 48). Woman is "the place onto which lack is projected and through which it is simultaneously disavowed—the woman is a 'symptom' for the man" (1982, 48). The Woman is a symptom that the man believes in order to keep at bay the fragmentary, nonidentificatory, premirror phase that permanently undermines his subjective consciousness: "A woman is a symptom. . . . What constitutes the symptom—that something which dallies with the unconscious—is that one believes in it. . . . In the life of a man, a woman is something he believes in. He believes there is one, or at times two or three, but the interesting thing is that, unable to believe only in one, he believes in a species, rather like sylphs or water-sprites" (Lacan 1982b, 168). The Woman exists, as does Tinkerbell, because a man believes in her; *a* woman ex-ists, relative to a man's perception, because he believes her to be what she is not in order to disbelieve that he is not who he imagines himself to be.

When Lily's comment interrupts Gabriel's fantasy of completion, he attempts the exchange anyway, compelled to misrecognize her in accordance with his fantasy. His encounter with her has been a dalliance with his own unconscious; he has glanced into "the lumber room that he has to get by with." Outside the drawing room door, he feels "discomposed by the girl's bitter and sudden retort. It had cast a gloom over him that he tried to dispel by arranging his cuffs and the bows of his tie" (*D* 179). Having been discomposed from within, Gabriel devotes elaborate care to his outward composition (that supposedly self-contained image that is intended to indicate to himself and others his unified identity). In this attempt at recovery, Gabriel is seeking to forestall a dissolution of identity that will, nonetheless, happen to him at the close of his day. After each of Gabriel's three encounters with women who fail to adequately pose as a symptom (as the Woman), he scurries into a corner to obsessively polish the fiction of his identity as though it were a talisman he must brighten whenever circumstances tarnish it.[16] This supports Lacan's contention that subjective consciousness is largely formed on absence; on what has not been thought, said, or remembered; on a lack that is ever present because it must be forgotten again and again. At that later point, he will be forced to acknowledge that the apparent outward unity of his mirror reflection (a neat appearance with cuffs properly arranged, etc.) bears no real resemblance to the permanent division within him that his misrecognition of women incompletely masks. Immersion into the Symbolic Order of language makes one a master of substitutions, but also a permanent outcast from the kingdom of the real.

This strictly symbolic control of the unity of one's subjective consciousness permanently alienates the subject from any direct contact with the actual world of his unconscious: "To be human is to be subjected to a law which decenters and divides. . . . The subject is split; but an ideological world conceals this from the conscious subject who is whole and certain of a sexual identity" (Mitchell and Rose 1982, 26). Instead of acknowledging the "forced labor of this discourse without escape," as Lacan describes it, Gabriel instead glances at his notes for his after-dinner speech. The notes, too, are in disarray, and he can generate no confidence in them. The wording of the speech has no meaning, any more than his audience, except inasmuch as he imagines it will formulate an audience reaction that he can believe in as a confirmation of the unity of his subjective consciousness.[17] But he is becoming conscious of the implicit strategy in his speech. The normally unconscious dimension of his spoken message (what Lacan calls the parole) now becomes apparent to him and is, thus, rendered ineffective. On the level of parole, the Browning quote is there to invite from his audience authorization for his viewing of himself as someone with refined tastes and a superior education. But if *he* understands his manipulation of the text and his contempt for them as intellectual peers, they will too, and his covert invitation to them will be exposed: "They would think he was airing his superior education. He would fail with them just as he had failed with the girl in the pantry. He had taken up a wrong turn. His whole speech was a mistake from first to last, an *utter* failure" (*D* 179, emphasis added).[18] Once again, he fears a failure of utterance. Of course, utterance always fails to confirm the ideal ego that Lacan calls the moi. What the conscious subject finds intolerable is knowledge of this. One cannot become aware of the perpetual failure of language to join the moi and the je into a unified whole without also becoming aware of the fact that masculine subjectivity is a cultural construct that only appears to exist in the gap between the two. Desire is the result of the hopeless attempt to join the two through language (which is the very thing that maintains the split). To become truly self-aware is to become aware of the myth of the self.

The encounter with Molly Ivors begins much less auspiciously than the one with Lily because Molly Ivors is much more a peer, and, thus, the various strategies by which Gabriel might seduce her into reflecting his ideal image back to him are more limited. A dance of Lancers has been arranged and Gabriel discovers that Miss Ivors is his partner. Lancers is an elaborate group dance, a bit like square dancing, in which various geometric patterns are formed by masculine/feminine couples during the dance. In the myth of masculinity and femininity, the problem of the fragmented and incomplete subject is made to "disappear" by insisting that the two genders complement each other in a way that is innate and absolute. The hypersymmetrical action and reaction of the dance acts as an ironic counterpoint to the frightening misrecognition that occurs between Gabriel and Molly Ivors even as they are participating in this dance which insists, in its elaborate repetitions and predictable returns, on the myth that the masculine and feminine entities complete each other.[19]

Significantly, the description readers get of Molly Ivors offers an immediate challenge to this cultural myth of masculinity and femininity: "She did not wear a low-cut bodice" (*D* 187). Gabriel sees Molly Ivors only as what she is not. He automatically superimposes an image of the Woman on Molly Ivors. Her *failure* to accurately correspond to the visual image of the Woman is precisely what makes her visible. This may explain Gabriel's curiously floundering assessment of her after they have parted as "the girl, or woman, or whatever she was" (*D* 190). Gabriel cannot identify Miss Ivors because there is nothing about *her* (either in appearance or manner) that might help identify *him*. Her brooch features "an Irish device"—that is, it has a signification for her that is not meant to signify anything to him. What is lacking about her is what dominates. The absence of the low-cut bodice announces that Miss Ivors does not dress in accordance with what she imagines the male viewer wishes to see. Her refusal to masquerade is what makes her performance compelling.[20]

"'Who is G. C.?'" Molly Ivors asks Gabriel, thereby again sounding the central question of this story or of anyone's story (*D* 187). Gabriel is once more reduced to a confused state. He feigns ignorance, but Molly Ivors persists. She is his peer—a fact as awkward and threatening as the absence of a low-cut bodice—and he cannot "risk a grandiose phrase with her" (as he certainly would with Lily or his aunts or even Gretta.) Her style of questioning is aggressive and persistent.

One might say, then, that it is completely unfeminine. But not *completely;* Molly Ivors keeps Gabriel off balance by acting the part of the Woman just long enough to skirt his defenses so she can stun him with her masculine interrogation: "He avoided her eyes for he had seen a sour expression on her face. But when they met in the long chain he was surprised to feel his hand firmly pressed. She looked at him from under her brows for a moment quizzically until he smiled. Then, *just as the chain was about to start again,* she stood on tiptoe and whispered into his ear: —West Briton?" (*D* 190, emphasis added). She understands that playing the Woman is a performance that men cannot afford to see as a masquerade because they must believe in it in order to imagine themselves. She is the most disconcerting person at the party because she maintains, publicly, an ironic distance from her own social performance. "Just as the chain was about to start again" refers, of course, to the resumption of the dance of Lancers (where masculine and feminine genders compulsively complement one another). But it also suggests that the initial feminine behaviour of Molly Ivors has relaxed Gabriel to the point where the chain of associations he associated with a representation of the Woman is about to resume. Molly Ivors uses the key junctures of a dance of compulsive gender complementarity to break disconcertingly with the masquerade of the Woman. Molly Ivors, by not acting the part of the Woman, or rather by acting it perversely, has failed to operate as a symptom protecting Gabriel from disconcerting knowledge of the inchoate promptings of his unconscious that constantly undermines his subjective consciousness. The symptom, according to Lacan, acts as a signifier of a signified repressed from the consciousness of the subject. Women properly masquerading as the Woman can serve as a symptom for the man because they effectively stand in for the loss and division that the masculine subject refuses to acknowledge. Rather than functioning as a symptom for him, Molly Ivors becomes an unanswerable question ("What does woman want?"). She concludes her vivisection of his subjectivity with the comment "of course you have no answer."[21] By playing at being the Woman, she has lured him much further into the morass of his own unconscious than Lily's bitter retort.[22] Because her appearance and behavior unsettle his specious phallic function and because she offers evidence of a life outside the role he would compulsively assign to her, Gabriel cannot imagine

she has any existence at all: "Had she really any life of her own behind all her propagandism?" (*D* 192). Precisely because she so clearly
has a life of her own (even leaving the party by herself for another
engagement), he cannot imagine it. "Throughout the story," Munich
observes, "Gabriel awkwardly confronts various women — and feels as
if he has failed, as if the women speak [a] language different from
his own, or at least as if they speak a code with words he knows but
with different meanings" (1988, 129). Or, as I argue in the case of
Molly Ivors, as if she knew she *was* his code and refusing this role
gives her access to a language that is the unconscious of what he
thinks he knows. He must retreat from her and fiddle with the conscious language of his after-dinner speech, not only to neutralize Miss
Ivors but to neutralize the language of his unconscious as well. The
speech Gabriel delivers is being written by the speech he cannot afford to give.

When Miss Ivors leaves abruptly, Gabriel stares "blankly down
the staircase" (*D* 196). Having been in pitched battle against the
blasphemous Miss Ivors, her sudden departure leaves his subjectivity
suspended. He is rescued by Aunt Kate who "at that moment" calls
out, "Where is Gabriel? . . . Where on earth is Gabriel?" (thus echoing Molly's question "Who is G. C.?" (*D* 196). At "the moment" this
is asked, Gabriel is staring "blankly" down the staircase; he is nowhere
"on earth": "There's . . . nobody to carve the goose!" Aunt Kate adds,
to which Gabriel responds "with sudden animation," "Here I am, Aunt
Kate! . . . ready to carve a flock of geese if necessary" (*D* 196). Gabriel
takes his place at the head of the table, thrusts his fork "firmly into
the goose," and, for the first time since addressing Lily, feels "at ease"
(perhaps because he has finally found something he can unequivo-
cally master). At the conclusion of the carving, Gabriel seats himself,
telling the company "kindly forget my existence," which makes the point
that he believed they were remembering his existence for him all the
while he stood confidently at the head of the table. His after-dinner
speech emphasizes, with hypnotic frequency, tradition, continuity, and
repetition. He mentions, just to select a handful of phrases, "as in years
past," "not the first time," "every recurring year," "a tradition that is
unique," "for many and many a long year to come." This litany earns
him "a healthy murmur of assent" (*D* 203). Ragland-Sullivan observes
that Lacanian theory shows that "individuals make the world of their

thought equal to their own conscious understanding of it" (1986, x). This, in a general sense, is the function that Gabriel's speech performs for himself and his audience. In his speech he shrinks the world to the size of their understanding of it, although, of course, it will expand again beyond him when he imagines the snow falling everywhere on all the living and the dead.

The party quickly breaks up after this punctuation that Gabriel has provided. He is confident once again of his integrity and his place in the universe, which moves readers into the final phase of the story. He stands in the dark, gazing up a staircase, and he sees "a woman . . . standing near the top of the first flight, in the shadow also" (*D* 209). He sees, in other words, a figure that represents the species he believes in, one that stands as the symptom that protects him from certain knowledge of the incertitude of his subjective consciousness. Only after a moment does he realize that this "woman" is also *his wife.* As his wife, she represents to him his private, unlimited access to "woman"—that enchanted species that Lacan says masculine subjectivity equates with sylphs and water sprites. Gabriel is moved by her stillness. The shadow she stands in has made the panels of her skirt "appear black and white." She is as though captured in a photograph; her attention is focused on something that has caused her desire. Gabriel wishes to be this distant music, to be the cause of her desire. [23] What is it that women want? Lacan's answer to Freud's most famous question is that they simply want; and the man's desire, what he wants, is to be what he imagines they want, hence, the first question.

Gabriel gazes at his wife and yearns to hear the song that appears to be the cause of her desire. What he in fact yearns for is to become the cause of desire for the image of woman he sees before him: "There was grace and mystery in her attitude as if she were a symbol of something. He asked himself what is a woman standing on the stairs in the shadow, listening to distant music, a symbol of" (*D* 210). Of him, of course. Gabriel desires to be the desire of the Woman—of Lily, Molly Ivors, or Gretta—because she/they, as symptom, can then provide what he lacks, or rather protect him from realizing that he lacks anything. As Lacan describes it, "To *believe in?* What does it mean? If not to believe in beings in so far as they are able to say something . . . he believes that the symptom is capable of saying something, and that it only needs deciphering. The same goes for a woman, except that one believes her effectively to be saying something. That's when things get stopped up—to believe *in,* one believes *her.* It's what's called love" (1982b, 169).

The actual woman, or even her actual body, is not what man approaches in the sexual act. Lacan says, "Images and symbols *for* the woman cannot be isolated from images and symbols *of* the woman. It is representation . . . of feminine sexuality . . . which conditions how it comes into play" (1982b, 90). If he could paint his wife in this attitude, Gabriel thinks, he would call it *Distant Music.* In this regard, Gretta is Gabriel's symptom, something that, he is sure, if he could only hear it, would complete him. The symptom emits something of infinite value yet is indecipherable—like distant music. As long as man believes in the Woman, he imagines he is on the verge of understanding the secret of his own certitude. In fact, the woman as symptom protects him, by her enigmatic masquerade as the Woman, from understanding the fantasy of himself. The complex and contradictory demands that the instability of masculine subjectivity places on a woman ensures that whatever relationship there is between the masculine and the feminine, it must be based on fantasy and misrecognition.

> [Relations between the sexes] will revolve around a being and a having which, because they refer to a signifier, the phallus, have the contradictory effect of on the one hand lending reality to the subject in the signifier, and on the other making unreal the relation to be signified.
>
> This follows from the intervention of an "appearing" which gets substituted for the "having" so as to protect it on one side and to mask its lack on the other, with the effect that the ideal or typical manifestations of behaviour in both sexes, up to and including the act of sexual copulation, are entirely propelled into comedy. (Lacan 1982b, 83–84)

Gretta's "attitude" on the stairs is precious to Gabriel. He is excited because he feels he owns what he sees. When she rejoins the group downstairs, he notes that "she [is] in the same attitude" and "a sudden tide of joy went leaping out of his heart" (*D* 212). This is called love, but what has caused her to assume this attitude has nothing to do with him.

Even more devastating, his lack of existence as the cause of her desire has allowed a dead man to return from the grave and replace him. If he has not been in his wife's thoughts all the time, then where on earth is Gabriel? His thoughts are described as "rioting through his brain, proud, joyful, tender, valorous." He recalls "moments of their secret life together;" these moments "burst like stars upon his memory" (*D* 213). Although these moments are highly specific and of short duration, "he longed . . . to make her forget the years of their dull existence together and remember only their moments of ecstasy" (*D* 213–14). He wishes to freeze those moments during which he feels most secure in relation to her assumed role as the Woman. Of course, all these moments of assocation that he is so dependent upon are based on fantasy; the fiction of his subjectivity depends on Gretta being what she is not and on her giving him what she has never possessed.

Acting continues to be the operative word in the relation of the sexes depicted in "The Dead" because Gabriel's sense of what will happen later, when he and Gretta are alone at the Gresham hotel, is as carefully and imaginatively planned as the writing and directing of a play: "They would be alone together. He would call her softly: —Gretta! Perhaps she would not hear at once: She would be undressing. Then something in his voice would strike her. She would turn and look at him (*D* 214). Gabriel's interior monologue trails off into silence because there is no literal message that can give voice to his *parole*. He can only talk up to the moment in which he imagines she looks at him, the point where he sees in her eyes that he is the object of her desire. All this will be triggered, fantastically enough, by "something" in his voice that she will hear and correctly interpret, even though he, the author of this script, cannot say what this "something" is.[24] As Lacan says, the "truth of [the masculine subject's] history is not all of it contained in his script, and yet the place is marked there by the painful shocks he feels from knowing only his own lines, and not simply there, but also in pages whose disorder gives him little by way of comfort" (1981b, 27).

When Gretta kisses him and calls him "a generous person," he pathetically misinterprets this as a prelude to his sexual scenario: "Perhaps her thoughts had been running with his. Perhaps she had felt the impetuous desire that was in him" (*D* 217–18). This is vital to him because if she has not felt it, then he has no way of being sure that he has felt it either (any more than Lily can imagine herself as being harassed and tired without reference to some cliché that might be spoken about her, which she can imagine contains the secret discourse of the Other). The idea is not to understand the content of the message from the Other (there is no message) but to be convinced it is there if only she could hear it. According to Lacan, the obsession with absolute complementarity crosses the Woman through and relegates her to the realm of fantasy. The Gretta that Gabriel believes in, the one from whom he hears the distant music that he longs to decipher, is nowhere present in the room. "Tell me what it is Gretta," he wheedles, referring to the cause of her pensive mood, "I think I know what is the matter. Do I know?" (*D* 218). He is still convinced, against rising odds, that she is in his scenario and that he knows what the matter is, even though, like the "something" in his voice, he depends upon her to tell him what it is he knows (that is to say to tell him *who* he is). Her bursting into tears, which to Gabriel is shocking proof that her thoughts were not parallel to his at all, causes him to look up and suddenly notice his reflection in the mirror: "He caught sight of himself in full length, his broad, well-filled shirt-front, the face whose expression always puzzled him when he saw it in a mirror" (*D* 218). His glance into the mirror is both reassuring to him and puzzling. His image is coherent; how could he appear so unified and feel so discomposed?

Gabriel's questioning of Gretta about Michael Furey is centered on one theme: "someone you were in love with?" he asks first, followed by "O, then, you were in love with him?", and finally "I suppose you were in love with this Michael Furey" (*D* 219–20). The difference in the statements is the progression of pronouns from "someone" to "him" to the name "Michael Furey"; the language solidifies as Michael moves from being a ghost to taking on a distinctive human shape. The other variation concerns tone. The first question is asked "ironically," the next in a straightforward manner, and the last, no longer a question, is delivered in a manner that is "humble and indifferent." As Michael Furey finds form, Gabriel fades. Lacan talks about something he characterizes as "the fading of the subject." Lacan's term, adapted from Ernest Jones, is *aphanisis:* "The subject appears on one side as meaning and on the other as *fading,* disappearance" (1982b, 15–16 n. 2).[25] When Gretta says of Michael Furey, "I think he died for me," Gabriel feels his subjectivity fading out altogether: "A vague terror seized Gabriel at this answer as if, at that hour when he hoped to triumph, some impalpable and vindictive being was coming against him, gathering forces against him in its vague world. But he shook himself free of it with an effort of reason" (*D* 220). Gabriel learns suddenly, and beyond any ability of his to equivocate, that Gretta will not authenticate that "something" in his voice that connects him to his belief in the Woman and his own phallic function.

Worse than that, he learns that "while he had been full of memories of their secret life together . . . she had been comparing him in her mind to another" (*D* 219-20). This exposes to him as fantasy the entire history of their relationship: "He watched her while she slept as though he and she had never lived together as man and wife" (*D* 222). He is seeing her for the first time as a woman and not the Woman. The price of this privileged glimpse into the Real is that the falsity of his subjective consciousness, and all its myriad deceptions, attacks him at once and divorces him from his own reflection: "A shameful consciousness of his own person assailed him. He saw himself as a ludicrous figure, acting as a pennyboy for his aunts, a nervous well-meaning sentimentalist, orating to vulgarians and idealising his own clownish lusts, the pitiable fatuous fellow he had caught a glimpse of in the mirror" (*D* 219-20). Now he has no role to play, no audience to seduce into verifying the secret messages about himself that he has smuggled past even his own consciousness (so he might greet it as authorization for the myth of himself when it returns to him in inverted form from Lily or Molly Ivors or Gretta, but always from the Other, the third position that is being invited to speak in any conversation of two people).

Following this moment of authentic analytic consciousness, which Gabriel experiences as an "attack," he looks around the room and his eyes are drawn to two items of clothing: "A petticoat string dangled to the floor. One boot stood upright, its limp upper fallen down: the fellow of it lay upon its side" (*D* 222). The simple petticoat string, normally a detail one would expect to inflame Gabriel's plan of mastering Gretta further, is now seen only for what it is, with no associational value. The petticoat string is useless as a catalyst for, or focus of, male fantasy. And next to it is the boot, a "limp" phallus. In this little allegory of the boot and the petticoat string is an opposite scenario from Gabriel's fantasized chain of events and emotions. Gabriel is half-conscious and adrift in the gap of his own Desire: "His own identity was fading out into a grey impalpable world: the solid world . . . was dissolving and dwindling" (*D* 223). "The solid world"— that which is created and maintained as a result of the belief in the Woman—only appears solid. "The grey impalpable world," Lacan's "lumber-room," has always been there, but has been kept at bay by an act of faith in a symptom called the Woman.

But Gabriel's reality, the purely associative world that he calls "solid" now fades as does his soul—that bridge across the gap of desire that exists only until one attempts to walk across it. The fading of the subject leads to a terrifying awareness of a permanent division in a unity of "self" that was, itself, once believed to be permanent. So Gabriel believes the time has come for him to set out on his journey westward away from the Dublin/fictional self that he thought he knew, toward the Galway/want-in-being that he has refused to acknowledge. He must read the censored chapters of his history, the ones that refute the unity of his subjective consciousness and are, therefore, not consciously known. Joyce ends "The Dead" with Gabriel adrift between the "lumber-room" of the unconscious and the carefully crafted scenery of subjective consciousness; his fictional unity, what a woman is a symbol of, cannot, for the moment, be found.[26]

17
Boxing My Own Corner

> The ego experiences reality not only in so far as it
> lives it, but in so far as it neutralises it as much as
> possible. (Lacan 1988b, 100)

> My intention was to write a chapter of the moral his-
> tory of my country and I chose Dublin for the scene
> because that city seemed to me the centre of paraly-
> sis. I have tried to present it to the indifferent public
> under four of its aspects: childhood, adolescence, ma-
> turity and public life. The stories are arranged in this
> order. (Joyce 1975, 83)

While looking over what I have written in the preceding pages,
I am reminded most strongly of the goal I announced in my
introduction, namely, that this book would suggest new ways to read
and teach Joyce's stories and that it would do so by suggesting new
ways to read oneself as a reader. The problem, as I see it, is not that
one needs to learn more about Joyce, but that one thinks one knows
more than one does. As Felman puts it in her Lacanian discussion
of the dynamics of teaching and learning, "Ignorance . . . is not a
passive state of absence, a simple lack of information: it is an active
dynamic of negation, an active refusal of information" (1987, 79). Readers and teachers of Joyce's fiction sometimes minimize the disturbing
challenge to their "reality" that his texts make. My reading of *Dubliners* abandons the traditional clarity of linear progression as well as
the steady accumulation of "meaning" in order to explore the gaps,

silences, elisions, deferred actions, self-delusions and false consisten-
cies that I see as the dominant discourse of this collection.

The greatest teaching does not so much present facts as it generates a linguistic atmosphere in which the student and, ineluctably, the
teacher, too, experience more fully the possibility of a stable truth,
the congenital uncertainty of any ideological premise stated as a given,
and the necessarily predetermined structure of whatever is presented
as new. Instead of looking to the Other for truth, one needs to recognize that the Real of Desire and lack are what make the teacher's position as presumed master possible. "[The verbal slip] is the radical
facet of the non-meaning which all meaning possesses" (Lacan 1988b,
280). Yet lecturers who "slip" are often deemed to be "not in control"
of their subjects. Such an accusation is frightening because to not be
in control of one's subject is to not be in control of one's "self" *as* subject. And yet explicating the tension between certitude and the void
is the essence of great teaching. What teaching Joyce's fiction should
teach everyone is that the "truth" about his fiction is not what one
comes to understand, but what defies explication. Teachers are often
most pleased when their students accept the "knowledge" they offer.
Yet both Freud and Lacan make it clear that benign acceptance of
another's point of view is the sincerest form of complete dismissal.
Education, both for analysts and their analysands and for teachers
and their students, should generate resistance. The point is not to
strengthen or develop the reader's ego or the writer's theme, but to
point out the manner in which it is already subverted. One symbolizes existence because something is missing; reading merely to "understand" reduces the stories to just another series of disappointing
substitutive replacements for a lack-in-being one wishes to deny. Interpretation is desire, but a Lacanian approach offers the possibility
of examining why one needs to know instead of misrecognizing what
one needs to see as what one has learned.

What one demands to know is what one desires to be true, so what
one learns is how to have more conviction about the truth of one's
individual fictions. It goes without saying — *everything* goes without saying, which is why one needs to talk about it — that I am skeptical about
the degree of my success in avoiding all the interpretive traps about
which I philosophize. In writing this book, I have certainly experienced,
from time to time, the sensation of satisfaction, completion, certainty,

closure, and resolution that almost certainly mark the points where my discussion of the stories is strategically ignorant. Both the instruction and the construction of the ego — the primary purpose of any "normative" educatory experience — can only be accomplished by neutralizing what the Real has to teach everyone. There has been much debate recently on what value, if any, the college learning experience holds. The remarkably solid and secure atmosphere of the college setting, insulated, as it often seems to be, from the real world, seems to invite students to nurse their preexisting prejudices to fruition in the four allotted years.

But this same controlled atmosphere is also well-suited for the unsettling process of reading the book of oneself. Such an interpretive act is a frightening, invigorating experience, impossible to sustain (and, therefore, akin to a Joycean epiphany). It is an experience during which learning provides a glimpse of what one needs to unlearn and, thereby, forces one to dwell in the truly instructive realm of not knowing. "Meaning must not be revealed to [the subject], it must be assumed by [the subject]" (Lacan 1988a, 29). The best analysts, Lacan says, "are always trying to find out what posture the subject could possibly take up, what find he could have made, in order to get himself into a position such that everything we might say to him will be ineffective" (1988a, 30). Because their work is intentionally obscure, willfully elliptical, and arrogantly contradictory, neither Lacan nor Joyce are often designated good teachers. But their frustrating style, which is apparently indifferent to an audience's reception of it, actually shows enormous respect for the impossible structure of what people so breezily refer to as "the human condition." What teachers feel the students need to know rarely coincides with what they actually communicate to them. Joyce is an effective teacher, that is, an effectively disconcerting teacher, because he mounts the royal throne of the Other dressed in the disorganized motley of the court jester. As a writer, he plays the fool to our studied interpretations with all their would-be King Lear majesty and disingenuous grandeur. "What's a joke? — if not the calculated irruption of non-sense into a discourse which seems to make sense" (Lacan 1988b, 280). A student entering a classroom, or a reader encountering Joyce, should be like the person who enters a room just as the crowd gathered within erupts into laughter. The student's potentially pleasurable urge to discover the source of the laughter would then be profitably tempered by the illuminating fear that he or she may be the source of the joke.

The idea of the modern curriculum that organizes literature according to decades, centuries, or epochs, is similar to the idea of modern ego psychology that presents consciousness as a historical contingency that neutralizes the future by explaining the past. The goal of such aggressive reality formations is not ignorance but misrecognition. Such expedient misrecognition is the invariable structure that underlies any lesson too easily learned. What is unique about "live" classroom teaching is that the process of misrecognition may, at times, be set in motion in a way that makes the "attachments" of a subject/pupil visible (the "blind spots" of point de captions that shape one's opinions. Certainly learning may take place when individuals read texts for themselves, but lecturing and classroom discussions generate an instructive distortion of the Real that is not merely a new illusion in the questionable shape of a fact, but the exposure of old illusions too long misrecognized as the truth. Indeed, what must be learned in the classroom is not what the book means but how the subject produces meaning when confronted with whatever resists immediate comprehension.

Increasingly, I find that my role as a teacher is not to facilitate comprehension in the students but to make problematical their own eagerness for answers. Teachers tend to view bored students as those who are not listening or trying to learn; conversely, teachers appreciate hardworking students as those actively engaged in their education. But is boredom always and only the manifestation of inattention? Is it not at least as likely that a bored student is one who is surfeited by useless answers and rather desperately in need of self-evident questions (questions that provide evidence of the construction of the "self")? Lacan poses a question to his fellow analysts that might usefully be addressed to my fellow teachers: "Can you really, you analysts, in all honesty, bring me testimonies of these splendid typical developments of the *ego* of subjects? These are tall stories. We are told how this great tree, man, has such a sumptuous development, how throughout his existence he overcomes successive trials, thanks to which he achieves a miraculous equilibrium. A human life is something entirely different!" (1988b, 155). There is no question, as this quote makes especially clear, that Lacanian theory is antihumanist; but it is most decidedly prohuman. Lacan's protest against humanism, stated most simply, is that it is a school of thought that denies the complexity of the human condition it purports to examine ("A human life is something entirely different!").

Overly structured closure and artificially induced conclusions present a body of knowledge that is the philosophical equivalent of the mythically coherent body imagined by the subject relative to his or her mirror image. The ego of the subject is already proficient enough at neutralizing reality without engaging the "tall stories" of the humanist tradition. Significantly, the anxiety of the teaching profession has focused more on the problem of what to teach than on the more complex issue of how difficult it is to teach anything at all. Postmodern anxieties about the fragmented nature of subjectivity have been projected onto the need to find the Holy Grail of a perfect syllabus. Such contentious discussions begin with the false assumption that what teachers intend to teach becomes precisely what the student learns. By what sleight of hand are teachers able to talk about "keeping alive the great tradition" when the only thing their students know for sure is that there is no such thing? What teachers misrecognize as a tradition that must somehow continue to be is something quite different, even if equally powerful — their nostalgia for a unity and coherency that never was. The choice seems to be either to represent every known form of literature in the classroom or to jettison the idea of multiple perspectives and gratefully return to the seductively singular idea of the one true mother — the "body" of the "great tradition." The only thing innately "great" about this tradition, of course, is one's tremendous need for it. The urge to return to it is akin to the subject's urge to return to the Imaginary Order wherein one may be in love with the apparent unity embodied in one's reflection.

Generating constant alternative syllabi, however, has generated a different sort of insatiable desire. Just as moving from the Imaginary Order to the Symbolic Order facilitates exchange at the price of unity, literature departments generate as many subdepartments as necessary to accommodate, and then isolate, any number of alternative perspectives. The fractious result is a superficially coherent department deeply divided about what constitutes a worthwhile education. Eventually, teachers come to view as worthwhile only what they imagine occurring in their own classrooms. Perhaps one reason the discussion of *what to teach* has become so shrill is that one very rarely asks Why do I like to teach? There is a fairly widespread conviction among the general, nonacademic, populace that teachers teach because they are self-indulgent. A typical response is to say, "No, I do it for the sake of the students." But this does not ring very true any more because, increasingly, teachers are imposing a predetermined agenda on them (presumably one that embodies what they need to know), which students find frankly puzzling when they do not find it too uninteresting to reward further scrutiny. In this context, boredom seems to be a form of unenthusiastic hostility on the part of the students. Paradoxically, if teachers view their own presence in the classroom as a given, then their efforts to present a classroom experience that is meaningful may only produce one that is, from the student's point of view, irrelevant and, therefore, easily dismissed. Teachers may like to think of their role as bringing light where before there was only darkness but, as Lacan suggests, to be human is something entirely different.

Perhaps teachers are not so much self-indulgent as "self"-indulgent, that is, they construct a sense of certitude in them"selves" by deconstructing everything else.

> Whereas Freud took it upon himself to show us that there are illnesses which speak . . . and to convey the truth of what they are saying, it seems that as the relationship of this truth to a moment in history and a crisis of institutions becomes clearer, so the greater the fear which it inspires in the practitioners who perpetuate its technique. . . .
>
> For precisely on account of the strength of the forces opened up by analysis, nothing less than a new type of alienation of man is coming into being, as much through the efforts of collective belief as through the selective process of techniques with all the formative weight belonging to rituals: in short, a *homo psychologicus*. (Lacan 1982b, 63–64)

Just as the psychiatrist's office can be viewed as a confessional with more comfortable seating, the classroom easily becomes a church with an unacknowledged doctrine. As such, the holy ritual enacted through the sacraments of term papers and final exams instructs the faithful on what to believe, while the individual at the lectern/pulpit is viewed as the unapproachable voice of God/the Other. The very strength of the forces opened up by poststructural theory has made the classroom itself the one structure exempt from deconstruction, and the teacher him- or herself as the one ahistorical given. Yet, as Grosz has pointed out recently, "The certainty the subject brings with it in its claims to knowledge is not, as Descartes argued, a guaranteed or secure foundation for knowledge. It is a function of the investment the ego has in maintaining certain images that please it. Rather than a direct relation of recognition to reality, the ego only retains a premedi(t)ated, i.e., imaginary or preconstructed, Real" (Grosz 1990, 48). Few contemporary thinkers accept the equation "I think therefore I am," yet its hastily enshrined replacement, "I teach therefore I am," is very much with us. Lacan's point that the aim of the drive is recognition, not this or that object, is instructive; it is not what one teaches, but what one imagines other people see when they perceive one teaching that attracts one to teaching (or any other) profession. The stated goals written into and supposedly embodied by a syllabus or curriculum distort something else that is not written down elsewhere. Of course one must distort in order to be comprehensible, but one should not misrecognize the result as comprehensive.

Like the symptom that is "written" in the sand of the flesh, one can benefit from, yet cannot decipher, one's own meaning both after one designs the course and while one is in the process of teaching it. Indeed, one benefits from one's construction of meaning in direct proportion to how indecipherable it is. The symptom, according to Lacan, is discernable in "traditions and legends which, in a heroicized form, transport my history. It represents, in a form antithetical to meaning, "distortions necessitated by the linking of the adulterated chapter with the chapters surrounding it, and whose meaning will be reestablished by my exegesis" (1981b, 21). The text in the classroom — any text — is the *objet a* that permits the illusion of direct communication. Neither the student nor the teacher has a direct relationship to the text; rather, "The subject doesn't have a dual relation with an object with which he is confronted, it is in relation to another subject that his relations with this object acquire their meaning, and by the same token their value. Inversely, if he has relations with this object, it is because a subject other than himself has relations with this object, and they can both name it, in an order different from that of the real" (1988b, 255).

Teachers need students in order to productively misrecognize both what they love to teach and what they presume students need to know. "Without the *petit a,* something is missing. . . . And why? Because the subject is only ever supposed. It is its condition to be only supposable. If it knows anything," Lacan says of the subject, "it is only by being itself a subject caused by an object — which is not what it knows, that is, what it imagines it knows. The object which causes it is not the other of knowledge. The object crosses this other through. The other is thus the Other" (1981b, 164). Why is it teachers appear before the students exuding the absurd confidence of Gabriel at the head of a well-laden table, announcing to all concerned that they are ready to carve up a flock of texts if necessary? Would it really be counterproductive to acknowledge that the "fading out" of their own identities underlies their stance as a given, their pose as those who know?

Grosz reports "Many saw [Lacan's] seminars as a kind of intellectual/sexual tease; his indirect, elliptical, evasive, but always suggestive lecture technique remains striking for the promise of a 'knowledge' (the gratification of a desire to know) which recedes the closer it comes" (Grosz 1990, 15). The point of an effective striptease is to appear to the audience as one perpetually about to reveal "everything" by simultaneously prolonging the inevitable disappointment of appearing before them as what they always knew they were about to see. But, if one removes a veil to reveal another veil, and then removes this to reveal another, eventually the unavoidable topic for discussion becomes the purpose of veils (to hide what is not there), and the false act of posing as the one for whom the truth behind the veil is well known. Joyce, of course, was a fiction writer and not a teacher per se, but even his earliest comments relative to his own fiction show a subtle sense of himself as a profane jester dancing in the sacred courtyard: "I am writing a series of epicleti — ten — for a paper. . . . Look out for an edition de luxe of all my limericks instantly" (Scholes 1969, 259). The reference to the stories as epicleti is often quoted, but the context of the comment is rarely noted (it is a letter to Constantine Curran, one of several friends for whom Joyce consciously posed), and the second comment about limericks is never given equal weight. Yet the two comments mirror one another.

Epiclesis refers to a prayer that invokes the Holy Spirit; as such, it is a call, voiced from within a coherent discourse, for something beyond the discourse to interrupt and reveal the structure of its erroneous certitude. The basic movement of a limerick is to move from a measured statement of fact to a sudden and antic revelation. The stories in *Dubliners* derive their elliptical nature from the structure of the prayer and the joke. Both are rhetorical forms that build to dissolution rather than resolution; both are forms that assume truth may best be glimpsed just at the point where certitude collapses into laughter or awe. "I cannot alter what I have written," Joyce wrote to Grant Richards: "All these objections of which the printer is now the mouthpiece arose in my mind when I was writing the book. . . . Had I listened to them I would not have written the book. I have come to the conclusion that I cannot write without offending people" (Scholes 1969, 269). To come to the conclusion that what one writes will offend is to develop a style of writing designed to forbid oneself the sort of conclusions that would make one's work inoffensive. Again, this is not a commonly cited passage when scholars look for evidence of Joyce's intention in writing the stories.

And yet Joyce's admission to Richards that he heard voices while working on *Dubliners* is, to me, his most profound comment concerning the collection. Throughout most of his correspondence with Richards, he characterizes the publisher's calls for omissions and revisions as too absurd for discussion. But here he says something quite different; he says that he *has* heard the voices for which the printer now serves as a "mouthpiece." More than that, the special quality of his prose is the result of having listened to, and then refuted, whatever those free-floating voices said to him. "It is not my fault," he protested to Richards, "that the odour of ashpits and old weeds and offal hangs round my stories" (Scholes 1969, 286). Whose fault then? Perhaps the fault of the voices he had to refute, the voices that, when relayed without resistance as in the case of Richards and his printer, make the speaker a "mouthpiece" or, in Lacanian parlance, make the supposed signified just one more signifier in an uninterruptable chain. Writing a novel that endorses the "voices" and makes them sound "real" (the "ingredients" of a "bestseller"), is, as Joyce confided to his brother, not much of a trick: "If I had a phonograph or a clever stenographist I could certainly write any of the novels I have read lately in seven or eight hours" (Joyce 1975, 56). Such novels do not attempt to craft a prose style that first encapsulates these voices and then interrupts them by using the self-destructive formula of prayers and jokes.

But Joyce proves unduly optimistic about his ability to become a mouthpiece for the extant voices of the Symbolic Order, which would then dictate a novel through him in a few hours. As he also stated to Stanislaus, "Were I to rewrite the book as G. R. suggests 'in another sense' (where the hell does he get the meaningless phrases he uses) I am sure I should find again what you call the Holy Ghost sitting in the ink-bottle and the perverse devil of my literary conscience sitting on the hump of my pen" (Joyce 1975, 110). Invoking something beyond the readily understood voices by using the discourse of these same voices is a matter of conscience with Joyce. It is his particular perversion that he hears an innocuous phrase like "in another sense" or "did he . . . peacefully" (from "The Sisters") and then must wonder, like Eveline with her dust, where it comes from. It is the throwaway phrases that Joyce dismisses as truth and yet cherishes as enigma; like Lacan, he never accepts language as a given. This is the sort of Holy Ghost that the stories (epicleti) are designed to invoke, yet in doing so they attract the more domesticated Holy Ghost sitting on the hump of the printer's blue pencil: "O, one-eyed printer! Why has he descended with his blue pencil, full of the Holy Ghost, upon these passages and allowed his companions to set up in type reports of divorce cases, and ragging cases and cases of criminal assault — reports, moreover, which are to be read by an 'inconveniently large section of the general public'" (Scholes 1969, 268). Of course, Joyce knows the answer; journalists use the same sort of "meaningless phrase" that Joyce here puts in quotes; but when they use such phrases *they mean it!* That is, they know how to write without offending people (the very sort of writing Joyce finds most offensive). The newspaper account of Mrs. Sinico's death is a case in point, and the meaningless phrase in its headline, "A Painful Case" becomes the richly enigmatic title of Joyce's story.

By contrast with journalistic prose, Joyce, using the phrase "a man with two establishments to keep up," signifies that a man has a mistress by employing the actual words used by people who wish to convey this very fact while apparently remaining ignorant of its sexual implications; the phrase merely calls attention to the ownership of two different houses but by doing so highlights more effectively what takes place inside of them. All sensuality has been removed from the phrase;

it is exceedingly modest. But the phrase calls attention to what it needs to leave out, and it is really Joyce's "offensive" use of a repressed discourse that frightens Richards into believing he may be arrested should he print it. Additionally, the printer's circling of this phrase with a blue pencil became the first indication of the sort of inarticulate misgivings that would delay the publication of *Dubliners* for many years, yet Joyce's impromptu analysis of the printer's character betrays a coy satisfaction on Joyce's part that the "scrupulous meanness" of his prose style has proved to be offensive in a manner even more insidiously subtle than he could have dared to hope: "His marking of the . . . passage makes me think that there is priestly blood in him: the scent for immoral allusions is certainly very keen here" (Scholes 1969, 268). Olfactory stimulants—odor, or scent—seem to be among Joyce's favorite metaphors for describing stories he hopes will be offensive but only in a supersubtle way that will be difficult to identify right away and, therefore, impossible to dismiss: "There was a heavy odour in the room," the narrator of "The Sisters" tells us "—the flowers" (*D* 14). This narrator, like Joyce, delays revealing the source so that readers can participate in his initial dread that it might be the corpse.

In fact, the strategic presence of the flowers with their "heavy odour" unintentionally signals the possible presence of the odour they effectively mask. Throughout *Dubliners* Joyce shows a special fondness for using meaningless phrases to reveal precisely what the phrase was intended to obscure; it is "such a gentle way to put it," Joyce wrote to Stanislaus, rather smugly referring to his use of the phrase "Dublin by Lamplight." His brother did not understand Joyce's peculiar use of the phrase because Joyce intended the phrase to look like one thing and "smell" like another; it is an irony of Joycean proportions that Joyce's own brother displayed a less keen scent for "immoral allusions" than the one-eyed printer with his "blue pencil, full of the Holy Ghost." The Holy Ghost of censorship, it seems, is often a match for the Holy Ghost of jouissance.

Sheldon Brivic, in his book on Lacan and Joyce, opens with the statement that "the uncertainties involved in Lacan's system . . . stimulated my awareness of uncertainties in Joyce" (1991, ix). He goes on to warn that "to put [Joyce's] ideas into definite form is to violate them" (1990, 1). I agree, and very few critics nowadays try to put *Ulysses* or *Finnegans Wake* into "definite form." To interpret *Dubliners* discerning its form has far and away been the most popular approach. Scholars who do so, however, may be easily excused once one understands that the first writer to put *Dubliners* into definite form was Joyce: "My intention was to write a chapter of the moral history of my country and I chose Dublin for the scene because that city seemed to me the centre of paralysis. I have tried to present it to the indifferent public under four of its aspects: childhood, adolescence, maturity and public life. The stories are arranged in this order" (Scholes 1969, 269). Joyce gave this organized schema to Richards early in their correspondence when there was still ample reason for Joyce to believe that the censorship difficulties might be easily sidestepped. "My intention . . . to present . . . arranged . . . order," all these no-nonsense words appear to be those of a responsible writer soberly discussing his craft; they are intended to be music to soothe the nervous ears of Grant Richards.

If Dublin is "the centre of paralysis" what is the periphery—Ireland, England, the world? What were the other choices that he presumably discarded? Is one to believe that Joyce thought seriously of picking another city? Dublin was the center of Joyce's universe; he could no more "choose" not to write about it than a fish could "choose" not to swim. More accurately, *he* felt paralyzed when attempting to write differently than everything that surrounded him. The four aspects that Joyce reveals here are remarkably unhelpful—childhood, adolescence, maturity, public life—so what? The description of a Van Gogh painting in an auction catalogue would, no doubt, be equally illuminating. Several gifted scholars have written brilliant essays on *Dubliners,* but I have never read anything interesting about this (constantly cited) schema. I suggest that it is impossible to do so. Joyce intended his schema to be reassuring. It is his attempt to write without offending anyone (and one can be glad, if this is a sample of such writing, that he did not do it very often). The point of the schema, specifically, is to appease Richards's increasingly diffuse anxiety that something bad will happen if he publishes the stories. More generally, the schema is a dense parody of the paralysis that occurs when meaningless phrases are imposed in order to give "definite form" to a subtly odiferous work. No, Joyce is posing here. He is posing as the responsible, omniscient writer who establishes his intentions and then chooses his material accordingly—just the sort of thing one might do when setting out to write something quickly with the help of a clever stenographer. Indeed, for Richards's benefit, Joyce seems to be doing a passable imitation of George Moore, the sort of stable and safe writer that any publisher in financial difficulties would be thrilled to represent. Where Richards has said, in an apprehensive tone, "There is a heavy odour in the room," Joyce has reassuringly replied, "the flowers." In this book, I have tried to Re-Joyce *Dubliners* by reopening this reassuring statement of the facts: —The flowers . . . yes . . . but something else . . .

Notes
Works Cited
Index

Notes

1. Spilling Whiskey on the Corpus:
Jacques Lacan and *Dubliners*

1. "There is no such thing as knowledge in the pure state, for the strict community of ego and other in desiring the object initiates something completely different, namely recognition" (Lacan 1988b, 51). Ragland-Sullivan characterizes the "human tendency" that both Lacan and Joyce regard as a type of myth making: "The human tendency is to try to explain what is by things from the outside or by impersonal innate tendencies, rather than by deficiencies and dissymmetries in being and knowing" (1990, 69). In another context she states, "Lacan's teaching faults traditional philosophy for never having fully understood that meaning only exists at all because it can refer to perceptions already structured (ordered) in a realm of repressed (unconscious) representations (references)" (1990, xvi).

2. "The symptom is first of all the silence in the supposed speaking subject. If he speaks, he is cured of his silence, obviously. But this does not tell us anything about why he began to speak" (Lacan 1981a, 11) Ragland-Sullivan states: "The symptom is the more-than-us in us which destroys us. But we cling to our symptoms because they are familiar and give us a sense of being unified and consistent. . . . Lacan gave Joyce a new name: "Joyce the symptom." by rewriting the spelling of symptom (a late-learned Greek borrowing) with the letters of its archaic Old French spelling — sinthome — Lacan said he was giving Joyce a new (old) name. The sinthome is that which is singular in each person, as ordered by every subject's experiences of taking on a gender identity" (1990, 70).

3. "The displacement of the signifier determines the subjects in their acts, in their destiny, in their refusals, in their blindness, in their end and in their fate, their innate gifts and social acquisitions notwithstanding, without regard for character or sex, and that, willingly or not, everything that might be considered the stuff of psychology, kit and caboodle, will follow the path of the signifier" (Lacan 1988c, 43–44).

4. "What the unconscious does is to show us the gap through which neurosis recreates a harmony with a real — a real that may well not be determined" (Lacan

1981a, 22). "Just as what is rejected from the symbolic register reappears in the real, in the same way the hole in the real that results from loss, sets the signifier in motion. This hole provides the place for the projection of the missing signifier, which is essential to the structure of the Other" (Lacan 1982a, 38). The Real, like all of Lacan's theoretical concepts, is complex depends on other terms for its significance. Ragland-Sullivan's description of the Real in reference to Lacan's seminars on Joyce emphasizes that the Real is beyond representation, even though representation constantly tries to symbolize it: "Language produces a Real which does not have any corresponding reality. Thus, it is difficult even to know when one is in the presence of the Real. . . . Even though the Real is the expulsion of, even the aversion to, meaning, Millot points out that the only way it can be treated is by being symbolized. . . . Lacan emphasized that without an internalized representation of a border or an identity limit, a subject is open to the chaos of the Real, which wreaks havoc on subjects who have little or no sense of a self that has a name and some characteristic properties. Without our 'legal fictions,' Lacan argued, psychosis waits in the wings, attesting to the human incapacity to think oneself human unless one already has a firm conceptualization of a position in a given Symbolic order" (1990, 79).

5. "The entire dialectic which I have given you as an example under the name of the *mirror stage* is based on the relation between, on the one hand, a certain level of tendencies which are experienced . . . as disconnected, discordant, in pieces . . . and on the other hand, a unity with which it is merged and paired. It is in this unity that the subject for the first time knows himself as a unity, but as an alienated, virtual unity" (Lacan 1988b, 50). Shoshana Felman summarizes the late difficulties that the subject will face as a result of the fictional structuration of the totalized and totalizing ego: "The mirror thus epitomizes perception as a visual centering anchored in the misperception in the denial — of one's own castration: the apparent fullness of the image in the mirror is an objectification of the gaze which, in substantifying the image as an object, elides from it the very insufficiency experienced by the subject. Facing his mirror image, the child perceives himself as king (all powerful, all seeing), in much the same way as the subjects, in 'The Emperor's New Clothes,' attribute sovereignty to the king so as to deny their own unfitness" (Felman 1988, 103).

6. "The core of our being does not coincide with the ego. . . . the ego isn't the *I*, isn't a mistake, in the sense in which classical doctrine makes of it a partial truth. It is something else — a particular object within the experience of the subject. Literally, the ego is an object — an object which fills a certain function which we here call the imaginary function. . . . The eccentricity of the subject in relation to the ego" (Lacan 1988b, 44). "As distinct from other psychoanalytic theories of the ego, for Lacan the ego is not an autonomous synthetic function of the subject, but only the delusion of such a function. The outcome of a series of narcissistic identification, the ego is the mirror structure of an imaginary, self-idealizing self-alienation of the subject. It is a structure of denial: denial of castration (through a unified self-aggrandizement) and denial of subjectivity (through objectification of others and self-objectification)" (Felman 1987, 11).

7. Lacan's metaphor, "point de capiton," refers to the buttons used in upholstered furniture to secure the formless cushioning to the preexisting wooden frame;

by designating strategic points of attachment, they cause the final product to look like a chair.

8. Kaja Silverman offers a succinct summary of ways in which the subject "attaches" him- or herself to the Symoblic Order: "Not only does language provide the agency of self-loss, but cultural representations supply the standard by which that loss is perceived. We look within the mirror or those representations — representations which structure every moment of our existence — not only to discover what we are, but what we can never hope to be and (as a consequence) hopelessly desire. . . . The subject not only learns to desire within the symbolic order; it learns what to desire. It is there taught to value only those objects which are culturally designated as full and complete. . . . Lacan indicates that the subject's desires are manufactured for it. The factory — the site of production — is the symbolic" (1983, 177).

9. Stories such as "Araby" and "Clay" show up routinely in high school and undergraduate anthologies; they are often accompanied by a one or two-page explanation of the "difficulties" that Joyce has "intentionally" introduced into the stories to make them more interesting. In a sense, the format of students' first exposure to Joyce's fiction implies that this is the "essential" Joyce and the later experimentation is a fantastic embroidery anchored to this "realistic" work. Thus, *Dubliners* is the essential "self," and the later fictions are variations of this "self." In fact, the fictional structure of the "self" is Joyce's topic from the beginning.

10. MacCanell's description of "the great irony of the word" gives an interesting echo of the hallucinatory quality of the subject who uses language: "The great irony of the word is that, by negating [the Real] it introduces what is not, but does so in the guise of what is. It creates the 'truth' of Being by the 'fiction' of the word" (1986, 45).

11. My proposal here is similar to one made by Patrick McGee in the introduction to his study of *Ulysses:* "The model proposed here (based on the critical practice of Lacan and Derrida) presupposes gaps in the reader that are symptoms of gaps and silences in the symbolic order itself" (1988, 9). Robert Con Davis also attempts to apply Lacanian theory to the study of narrative: "Going in precisely the opposite direction from Holland (and from other versions of ego psychology), Lacan shows that the reader's mind is not an independent agent, a separate and discrete entity that so simply may respond to, accept, reject, or assess a pre-existent text" (1983, 1,002). Although I agree with his contention that Lacanian theory decenters the reader, I disagree with Davis's further assertion that the text operates like the unconscious. To me, this invites the formation of a sort of mystical "New Critics" where the text contains an essential truth that must be teased out of it. The text operates more as a symptom of the writer and the reader — as something that blocks unconscious knowledge of subjectivity even as it presents a narrative weave that is full of holes.

12. McGee's elaboration of Joyce as a symptom is worth quoting in full: "Implicitly, Lacan says that if Joyce's work illustrates psychoanalysis as a symbolic process, it also refuses it as an ideology, just as it refuses the ideologies of the church, the nation-state, art, and so on, from which it nevertheless draws all of its symbolic material. As Lacan stresses, Joyce is a symptom, and a symptom is the articulation of a contradiction between the structure of art and the desire of the artist, between

the constituted subject and the subject-in-progress, between the law binding the subject and the law's other, the process of symbolic exchange" (1988, 9).

13. Elsewhere, Lacan describes the symptom of consciousness as "a symbol written in the sand of the flesh" (1981b, 44).

14. Elizabeth A. Hirsh links the layered structuration of the ego with the dynamic of the mirror stage that I have outlined: "Lacan theorized the genesis of the ego as a series of alienating identifications inaugurated by the subject's assumption of and captation by his own specular image during the Mirror Stage. . . . In his theory the image functions as a prosthesis, a pseudo-totality that permits the subject, by a phantasmatic detour, to evade the lived lack congenital to (his) human being. At the same time, in subject-ing him to the gaze that returns his look in the mirror, the Mirror Stage prefigures and vehiculates the moment when castration will propel the subject into the order of the Symbol (and vice-versa)" (1986, 1). By her description "castration" is pyschic and symbolic rather than a simple fear of the loss of the male organ. In this sense, both men and women are castrated. The masculine gender myth denies this by seeing the feminine as physically castrated.

15. Lacan's disparages any psychoanalytical theory that privileges the ego as the core of "normality" in the subject (ego psychology) throughout his work. The following objection, formulated by him in 1953, might be seen as basic to his thought on this topic: "Such is the fright that seizes man when he unveils the face of his power that he turns away from it even in the very act of laying its features bare. So it has been with psychoanalysis. Freud's truly Promethean discovery was such an act, as his works bear witness. . . . In fact the emphasis on the resistance of the object in current psychoanalytic theory and technique must itself be subjected to the dialectic of analysis, which cannot fail to recognize in this emphasis an alibi of the subject" (1977, 34–35).

16. "For the phallus is a signifier, a signifier whose function in the intrasubjective economy of analysis might lift the veil from that which it served in the mysteries. For it is to this signified that it is given to designate as a whole the effect of there being a signified, inasmuch as it conditions any such effect by its presence as signifier" (Lacan 1982b, 79–80). Alice Jardine summarizes the relationship of the feminine subject to the phallic signifier: "If woman is not All, she nevertheless has access to what he [Lacan] calls a 'supplementary *jouissance*'—beyond Man, beyond the Phallus. This 'extra' *jouissance* is a substance. . . . Most importantly, this substance *jouissance* is of the order of the infinite; it cannot be understood consciously, dialectically, or in terms of Man's Truth—for it is what we have always called 'God'. . . . Feminine *jouissance* will, therefore, be posited as the ultimate limit to any discourse articulated by Man. It is, however, only the first of a series of such limits, which, through metonymy, will all be gendered as feminine" (1982, 61). My own feeling, in line with what Jardine outlines here, is that Lacan details the unconscious structure of the obsessively conscious patriarichal order so that its basis in fantasy and illusion can be explored in detail.

17. "The original union of I and the (m)Other, that is, the illusory perception of an integral self which is signified by having or being the phallus, is lost. The lack of the phallus then signifies a lack-in-being, assumed by the symbolic order that

transforms . . . the relationship between the Ego and the self. . . . It is the desire for the phallus which represents difference as absence and as such derives the signifying process as language to recover it—'it' being the ultimate meaning and true identity" (Rauch 1987, 29–30).

18. "When any speaking being whatever lines up under the banner of women it is by being constituted as not all that they are placed within the phallic function. It is this that defines the . . . the what?—the woman precisely, except that *The* woman can only be written with *The* crossed through. There is no such thing as *The* woman, where the definite article stands for the universal. There is no such thing as *The* woman since of her essence—having already risked the term why think twice about it?—of her essence, she is not all" (Lacan 1982b, 144).

19. This situation is rapidly changing. The *James Joyce Quarterly*, criticized in the past as a journal that ignores European theory, recently produced a special issue entitled "European Perspectives of Joyce." A second special issue on "Joyce between Genders: Joyce and Lacan," edited by Sheldon Brivic and Ellie Ragland-Sullivan, is scheduled in 1991.

20. "The unconscious is that part of the concrete discourse in so far as it is trans-individual, which is not at the disposition of the subject to re-establish the continuity of his conscious discourse. . . . The unconscious is that chapter of my history which is marked by a blank or occupied by a falsehood: it is the censored chapter. But the Truth can be found again; it is most often already written down elsewhere" (Lacan 1981b, 20–21). Lacan's view of the unconscious as everywhere present in the conscious supports my central thesis that his theory is particularly apt for studying what Joyce has called "the mystery of consciousness."

21. Jean-Michel Rabate offers a definition of Lacan's Other in relation to the narrator of "The Sisters": "The child encounters language issuing from the beings that surround it, and whereas it can identify these beings as others similar to itself, there is also within them another agency at work enabling them to speak language and marking them as having submitted to the Law. It is this mysterious element of the beings surrounding the child that Lacan has called the Other (the capital letter marking the irreducible difference between this real of being and the realm of the imaginary where the other simply appears as the mirror image of the self)" (1982, 56).

22. "The price of the subject's access to the world of desire is that the real organ must be marked at the imaginary level . . . so that its symbol can take up its place as the signifier of this very point where the signifier is lacking. . . . It is as his pay-ment to this place that the subject is called upon to make the dedication of his cas-tration—the negative mark bearing on the organ at the imaginary level (the lack of phallic image in the image desired) is positivised as the phallic symbol, the signi-fier of desire" (Lacan 1982b, 117). Mykyta offers a valuable insight into how the cas-tration complex plays itself out in the relationship between the masculine and femi-nine: "In order to be able to reproduce man as a speaking subject, as a human being, he must position himself in reference to castration which he does by seeing woman as castrated. On the other hand, if woman accepts the truth of her 'castrated' posi-tion, she must also accept that this truth entails speaking in the silences and mar-

gins of discourse, ultimately entails a renunciation of practical power—Oedipus blinded, Oedipus in the position of a woman. Furthermore it means giving up even a negative specificity since woman's condition as the 'not-all' is only the figuration of an aspect of the male condition that the male does not wish to confront—his feeling of not being whole projected onto a woman's lack of an organ" (1983, 56). For a further discussion of how to include an awareness of the construction of subjectivity while teaching Joyce's fiction, see my essay, "Authorizing the reader: Student 'Freewriting' as a Method for Teaching Joyce" (1991b).

2. The Free Man's Journal:
The Making of His[S]tory in "The Sisters"

1. What I offer here is a selective and hurried survey of different extratextual approaches to "The Sisters," from Levin and Shattuck's ingenious 1948 discussion of *Dubliners* in relation to Homer to Kershner's recent and fascinating account (1989) of the popular culture sources that make up the different "voices" one hears in the stories. Walzl offers a detailed comparison of the *Irish Homestead* version and the later version. The comparison is still provocative, particularly in the way Walzl argues that Joyce's rewrite made "The Sisters" a more fitting introduction to the collection as a whole (1973). Ghiselin's 1956 article is still one of the best treatments of the inter-relationships among all the stories. Fritz Senn's much more specific examination (1965) of Joyce's play on language in the opening paragraph of "The Sisters" makes it clear that *Dubliners* was not an apprenticeship work by an author not yet sure of his craft. My Lacanian approach in this volume, which assumes a very sophisticated technique on the part of Joyce, is indebted to these two early articles that show how *Dubliners* is characteristic of Joyce's later works.

2. Don Gifford goes on to the state, "Traditionally the men of Irishtown were employed in intermittent, pick-up jobs on the docks at the mouth of the Liffey and at the terminuses of the two canals that encircle Dublin" (1982, 34).

3. I am paraphrasing for my analysis a description that Lacan offers of the Real: "The question which arises at this point in my exposition is the following, answering to the notion of consistency insofar as consistency presupposes demonstration—what could be supposed to be a demonstration in the real? Nothing supposes it other than the consistency for which the cord is acting here as the support. . . . When the thread shows through, it means that the weave is no longer disguised in what is called the fabric. *Fabric* is everywhere and always metaphorical in use—it could easily serve as an image of substance. The formula *wearing down to the thread* clearly alerts us sufficiently to the fact that there is no fabric without weave" (1982b, 163).

4. Ragland-Sullivan's description of the Other is worth quoting here because her definition of the conscious subject's relationship to the Other echoes the boy's frightened, yet fascinated, relationship to what he terms "a maleficent being": "The Other(A) is the place of the unconscious and thus is either a dark-faced and absent

part of oneself which one must flee or a mysterious force which one renders divine and proceeds to worship" (1986, 297).

5. Brandy Kershner's discussion of this story intersects with mine at several points, although he uses the theory of Bakhtin. The following passage may suggest where we agree and where we differ: "As Bakhtin insists, the languages that surround him, with their concomitant ideological structures, are the only means of thought and speech available to the boy. He cannot escape them, however alien he feels them to be. They are the world, and they articulate his consciousness. This fact, more than any vacancy at the center of languages, is responsible for the tone of inescapable menace that pervades the story and hovers around the theme of language" (1989, 30–31). I argue that a vacancy is at the center of the subject, which makes words substitute objects for this lack-in-being. I agree that there is no "vacancy at the center of languages." Yet, although the boy is, to a certain extent, articulated by their speech, his silence also disarticulates them (they can scarcely talk at all in his presence). Using language to control others is a two-way street. Eliza, in particular, fears the journal of this little free man precisely because it is not yet written.

3. The Detective and the Cowboy:
Desire, Gender, and Perversion in "An Encounter"

1. Senn's observation about the human quality of the old man is worth quoting in full because it mirrors a basic assumption of my reading of the story: "Above all he is meant to portray something generally human — fallible, corrupt, disappointed humanity, not simply someone to despise (as most critics seem to do), but also someone in whom we may recognize ourselves." (1969, 32–33).

2. For an excellent discussion of popular culture in this story, complete with references to primary sources, see Brandy Kershner's *Chronicles of Disorder:* "All three Harmsworth magazines participated in the new upsurge of romanticism modified by realistic detail that characterized popular literature of the 1880s and 1890s. . . . All three also were unusual in featuring a heroine, whose part in the stories was negligible — usually consisting in blundering into the clutches of the nearest villain — but who was often, at least in *The Marvel*, given a head-and-shoulders illustration of her own. Thus the girl hovered like a mysterious icon above the male adventures, intimately connected with them in wholly unspecified ways. . . . In both these boys' magazines and the monologue of the old man, the young girl with beautiful hair serves as putative goal and justification for a narrative that in fact demonstrates her irrelevance" (1989, 34). Of course, in a Lacanian framework, the disembodied woman is not "irrelevant" but marginalized. She ex-ists beyond the limit of the discourse as the absence that permits the hero's presence. As for her becoming a pull-toy between the villain and the hero, this role makes her the object of exchange that authenticates the moral order of the adventure and establishes "what's at stake" if the hero loses. In the movie *Batman*, the entire plot circles around the question of who has a better right to rape Kim Basinger — the Joker or Batman. The Basinger character never does

a thing to help herself or to alter the plot, yet everything that happens is related to her negligible role as the object of exchange (who wears the negligee).

3. Kershner argues for this construct as well. He talks about the effect of "popular fictions" on the young boy. What I am suggesting is that the myth of "femininity" and "masculinity" are the two most popular fictions by which the subject denies the effect of symbolic castration. "In the perspective of popular fictions, it seems clear that the social distinction the boy-narrator makes a gesture toward abandoning at the end is not his intuitive sense of superiority as artist, but a pernicious fiction enunciated first by the priest and then inadvertently deconstructed by the old josser. . . . 'An Encounter' does not recount the defeat of imagination by reality, because the 'imagination' that inspires the outing is mass-produced and the 'reality' the boys encounter is merely another genre of popular fiction" (1989, 46). I agree with this assessment, but I think Lacanian theory suggests why one form of popular fiction becomes more popular than another, thus making it possible and profitable to mass-produce it. Mahony's "reality" is not the same reality that the narrator "encounters" because his masculinity has been scripted by a different genre of popular fiction. Why did Wister's *The Virginian* create a format that still endures, whereas countless other Western adventures did not? The myths of "masculinity" and "femininity" shift in the way they are embodied in popular fiction (whether an advertisement, a movie hero, or a novel), and here Bakhtin seems particularly useful. Lacan, however, explores the cause that makes subjectivity itself a fictional text. I agree with Kershner (and Bakhtin) that one constructs oneself by borrowing overheard "voices," but Lacan wants to know why self-sufficiency is impossible. Kershner's use of Bakhtin is compelling in the way that it details how the particular popular fictions of the late Victorian era inform and manipulate the characters in Joyce's fiction; Lacan's theory examines why the subject needs this "voice" at all.

4. In this sense, the old man approximates a perverse role that Jean-Michel Rabate assigns to Joyce himself: "Nowhere is perversion more virulent than in a discourse which attempts to articulate the truth of the subject in his own division, and this is where psychoanalysis and religion exhibit their common logic, a logic Joyce merely displaces, or rather warps" (1982, 56).

5. MacCabe defines two types of perverse structures: one a playful perversity that temporarily deviates from normalcy, and the other a radical perversion. I certainly characterize the old man's perversion as radical in MacCabe's sense of the word: "We must distinguish between a perverse structure which, while suspending the either/or of sexual difference and investigating the non-disjunctive nature of discourse, undertakes this suspension and investigation only with the guarantee that the process will be ended and denied, and, on the other hand, a perversion so radical that there is never any question of arresting the process" (1979, 124). Actually, MacCabe's second variation of perversion is the only viable one; "temporary" perversion is neurosis (the dream that one is perverse).

6. Indians were often regarded as "Satanic" by western colonizers, which made it a duty, rather than a moral burden, to eradicate them. The British were equally anxious to see the Irish as treacherous, savage, and unredeemable in order to justify the various politically expedient purges that occurred over the centuries.

4. The Question and the Quest:
The Story of Mangan's Sister

1. Harry Stone, to cite one example, is comfortable declaring that "all women, for Joyce, are Eves: they tempt and they betray" (1965, 392). Stone, like many male critics of the sixties and seventies, shows the same self-indulgent perspective on women as the narrator of "Araby," but I do not think this does justice to the complexity of Joyce's perspective.

2. Bernard Benstock writes: "Of all the fierce winds of controversy surrounding Joyce the most volatile remains that of the impact of the theories of Jacques Lacan" (1988b, 16). My approach here is informed by Lacanian theory, but my primary purpose is to problematize Joyce's representation of Mangan's sister and show it to be far more subtle than the perspective of the narrator.

3. As Ellie Ragland-Sullivan explains, "Lacan maintained that mind is not a unity; personal reality is built up by structures, effects, and the fragments of perceived fragmentations. Reality, therefore, is to be assessed in details, allusions and wisps of meaning" (1986, 187). The Real is what lies beyond representation; although it cannot be directly apprehended, it is always a threat to the subject's reality.

4. As Lacan explains, "When any speaking being whatever lines up under the banner of women it is by being constituted as not all that they are placed within the phallic function . . . except that The woman can only be written with The crossed through. . . . There is no such thing as The woman since of her essence . . . she is not all" (1982, 144).

5. Later in this same chapter, Devlin makes the general point, which I am also making in a more specific way, that "the critical complaint that Joyce's women are male-defined seems to me one-sided" (1988, 143).

6. Devlin says of Bloom's attitude toward Gerty McDowell, "He does not envision the female eye as being possibly prurient, sexually intrusive, as being the organ of kinetic stimulation, as a compromising eye that secretly enjoys naughty sights" (1988, 137).

7. This is also how a woman comes to be seen as standing in the place of the Other and believed by the man to guarantee the reality of all his fantasies about himself and assure him of the authenticity of his masculine sexuality.

8. In a similar dynamic, one never sees the contents of the letter that changes hands in Poe's story. Because there is no certain signified, the signifier speaks through the subject.

5. Wondering Where All the Dust Comes From:
Jouissance in "Eveline"

1. "Instead of having a penis and being a subject, for man, woman as the object of desire, woman as a whole, as a veiled hole, becomes the phallus" (Mykyta 1983, 54). Lacan also discusses the imaginary dimension of the phallus and its crucial distinction from any biological organ: "It is of course obvious that the idea of

an organ in glorious, monadic isolation, rejecting any tie or relation (whether complementary or antagonistic) in favour of the sole alternative of being or of not being, must refer to an essentially imaginary organ, even if this image is that of a real organ, namely the penis, or, more precisely, the penis in its privileged state of tumescence and erection" (1982b, 124).

2. One of the few critics who comments upon Eveline's subtle yet intense relationship with her dead mother is Brandabur: "Gradually, the protagonist in Eveline convinces herself she is her dead mother. . . . She identifies with her dead mother as with a tribal god" (1971, 26–27). Brandabur's first observation is too simplistic, but his second one is in line with one of the points I am making: that which is beyond representation (jouissance) bears an uncanny resemblance to that realm beyond knowledge, which one sees "as through a glass darkly," that is traditionally associated with God the almighty Father (and the supposed source of the authority of the "Name-of-the-Father"). Lacan designates the force beyond representation as the Real: "Just as what is rejected from the symbolic register reappears in the real, in the same way the hole in the real that results from loss, sets the signifier in motion. This hole provides the place for the projection of the missing signifier, which is essential to the structure of the Other" (1982a, 38).

3. In his discussion of the conclusion of "Eveline," MacCabe's assertion that Eveline's paralysis at the close of the story is a "linguistic disorder" might be better described as beyond the order of linguistics, thereby exposing the social construction of language. But this fails to take into account that Eveline's silence is in direct communication with the "final craziness" of her mother: "Eveline is unable to escape from a life of servitude to her father because finally she cannot allow herself to be defined in terms of the demands addressed to her by her father. But insofar as she is defined by these demands, in so far as they provide the only articulation of her experience, she cannot find any space in which her own desire could speak. It is no wonder that she is speechless at the end because the paralysis which freezes her in her tracks is a linguistic disorder" (1979, 32).

4. In making this a central theme of the story, Joyce may have been specifically reacting to the popular pornographic novel *Eveline*. In this novel, Eveline introduces her exploits by citing the fact that her family does not allow a woman to circulate beyond the family without first "using" her sexually: "There are at least two families of high and ancient aristocratic pretensions, whose loud-tongued, drinking, gambling male descendents openly boast that they have never allowed a maiden of their noble line to pass, as such, out of the family and into the arms of her spouse. Ours is a third, only we are not so simple as to publish the fact" (quoted in Kershner 1989, 69). Kershner quotes this passage to support his claim that "Joyce suggests that there are several levels of reality here." These levels, in a Lacanian context, might be best described as a knot whose strands include the Real, the unconscious, the gaze, and reality. Once entwined, the "knot generates a presumably distinct entity (the "knot" of subjectivity) that is no more than the imaginary space among all the various strands.

5. Although not working within a Lacanian framework, Senn has noted the quality of "elsewhereness" in Joyce's stories and finds it pervasive enough in "The

Boarding House" to describe it: "The story's technique is one of 'elsewhereness'" (1986, 406).

6. Brivic discusses the metaphor of the veil both in Lacan's theory and Joyce's fiction. "To pass beyond the veil is to go into the realm of dream, a realm in which, according to Lacan, the gaze shows itself. Lacan emphasizes here that coherence and self-consciousness are impossible in dream. The dream state of vision cannot be apprehended by the organized mind of waking except in distorted, fragmented, indirect form. After all, the waking mind is constituted by the looping of the veil that conceals the gaze" (1991, 109). This is significant for my reading of the final moment of "Eveline" where the veil slips and neither Eveline nor Frank, for different reasons, can see one another even though, from the reader's conscious perspective, they gaze fully into one another's face.

7. Benstock observes that Eveline's earning potential is the most highly specified of any character in *Dubliners:* "Her role as a wage earner is an essential characteristic, and her salary the only specifically quantified one in *Dubliners.* . . . Eveline's wages are an open secret (her father certainly knows the precise amount), since she is not the sole determiner of her financial situation" (1988a, 200–201). This observation seems in line with my point about how frightening this supplementary income is within the phallic economy of the Hill household. For a more detailed discussion of women as objects of exchange in the phallic economy, see my "Women on the Market: Commodity Culture, 'Femininity,' and 'Those Lovely Seaside Girls'" (1991).

8. Bowen has also observed that readers who accept Frank's final observation of Eveline as an epiphany can only do so by "ignoring or discounting" Eveline's: "Eveline's epiphany of the whirlpool and Jack as the person who would drown her is counterbalanced by the last epiphany of the story, the caged animal, a revelation from Jack's perspective and presumably his insight. Readers who accept this last epiphany must do so at the risk of ignoring or discounting Eveline's. But there is little evidence other than the reader's predisposition to suggest the truth or falsity of either" (1981–1982). Bowen's observation is right on target, although I suggest that the "predisposition of the reader" may be considerably influenced by the gender of the reader. This story has a masculine ending followed by the disconcerting blankness of a feminine ending (which serves to undermine, as Bowen's comments suggest, the truth of the masculine ending).

9. "By placing the roots of the pleasure principle in the Imaginary union between infant and (m)Other, Lacan redefined the pleasure principle as *jouissance* or a sense of Oneness, and reshaped the reality principle to refer to the separation evoked by language and law (castration), which ends the mirror stage. Pleasure is therefore destined to be bitter-sweet and deceptive ever after. It proceeds paradoxically along the Desiring path of investing passion in simultaneous efforts to recreate the bonds of an impossible unity through substitutes and displacements and, thereby, to deny the reality principle of Castration" (Ragland-Sullivan 1986, 139).

10. Riquelme also reads *Dubliners* as providing different layers of story telling to the reader. His interpretation of this closing line in "Eveline" may highlight our similarities and differences: "The language of narration manages to work in at least two ways at once. While it expresses what the character's actions and feeling mean,

it also announces through figuration its difference from any mode of thinking or speaking available to the character either in the narrative action or as a result of that action. . . . As an admission that Eveline's state of mind is beyond the reach of referential language, the act of shifting styles itself represents that state of mind which cannot be rendered adequately through psychonarration quoted monologue, and narrated monologue. . . . The act of representing in the final paragraph counters Eveline's refusal to give any 'sign of love or farewell or recognition' [D 41]. The teller's stylistic farewell recognizes her state" (Riquelme 1983, 111). I support the distinction Riquelme makes between "teller and tale" in *Dubliners*. But I still think he privileges the teller of these stories more than Joyce did ("the teller's stylistic farewell recognizes her state"). There is, as Riquelme convincingly argues, a "teller" who knows more than the character's stories can reveal—but the most subversive thing this teller knows, I argue, *is that all reality is fiction*. Thus, it is not Eveline who "refuses to give any sign" (the semiotics of her body language speak volumes) but the "teller" himself who is rendered speechless and must allow a self-revealing metaphor (Eveline's expression as inhuman—an animal) to stand in as "the whole story."

11. This conclusion was suggested, in part, by an observation of Lacan: "Naturally we ended up in Christianity by inventing a God such that it is he who comes!" (1982b, 146).

6. Living for the Other in "After the Race"

1. Marilyn French also suggests a connection between Jimmy "living" the desire of his father and his subsequent feeling of being unreal: "The elder Doyle wants the young man to fulfill his own desires for status, for class. . . . Jimmy can find pleasure only in the idea of being part of this world, not in the reality" (1978, 454).

2. Kershner analyzes Doyle as a would-be musketeer: "The major fragment of ideology operative in the story is one lifted directly from popular literature. Jimmy's vision of youthful fellowship, the good life available to young sophisticates who are above the common herd, is rooted in Dumas's *Three Musketeers*" (1989, 74).

7. Men in Love:
The Woman as Object of Exchange in "Two Gallants"

1. Although Irigaray (1985) does not always make the relationship of her ideas to Lacan clear, my sense is that when she talks about women existing as nothing but an exchange object within the phallic economy, she is talking about the construct Lacan called "the Woman." A further point that Lacan makes, which Irigaray does not seem to endorse, is that the phallic economy is extremely fragile because it is based on an object of exchange *that does not exist* (however much women may be persuaded to *masquerade* as this object of exchange). What women are in the Real, outside this masquerade (what they are beyond representation), ex-ists as a further threat to the Symbolic Order in the form of jouissance (as a form that threatens to

permeate the protective envelope of reality that protects the Symbolic Order from the Real).

2. Irigaray sees the woman as "losing herself" in the masquerade of femininity, but this implies a prior, "whole," self that Lacan would disallow. In Lacan's view, a woman's subjectivity is divided as much as a man's; differences occur because a patriarchal culture offers her no myth to offset this symbolic castration other than the gender myth of femininity that insists she must pose as not all to authenticate the phallic totality of the masculine subject. For a discussion supporting Irigaray's critique of Lacan, see *Jacques Lacan: A Feminist Introduction* (Grosz 1990).

3. With the character of Molly Ivors, as I will discuss later, Joyce presents a woman who deliberately deconstructs femininity by alternating between womanly mannerisms and blunt assertions (thoroughly confusing and vanquishing Gabriel in the process).

4. Kershner, from a different critical perspective (that of Bakhtin), brilliantly makes the case that Joyce's use of the word *gallant* in his title is not ironic: "The story of Corley and Lenehan simply lays bare the heart of gallantry without romantic mystifications" (1989, 83). Joyce does so by presenting the woman who has attracted their attention as also stripped of all romantic mystification. She has value, as Irigaray puts it, "only in that she can be exchanged. In the passage from one to the other, something else finally exists beside the possible utility of the 'coarseness' of her body. But this value is not found, is not recaptured, in her. It is only her measurement against a third term that remains external to her, and that makes it possible to compare her with another woman, that permits her to have a relation to another commodity in terms of an equivalence that remains foreign to both" (1985, 176).

8. Ejaculations and Silence:
Sex and the Symbolic Order in "The Boarding House"

1. In *Joyce's Anatomy of Culture* Cheryl Herr offers a fascinating and detailed presentation of the importance of the Dublin music hall on Joyce's later work (1986).

2. Kershner notes that Doran's "most striking feature . . . is that he is virtually without point of view; he is at the mercy of any social pressures that can be brought to bear on him. . . . as soon as he has established a possible point of view upon the affair, he is overwhelmed by the opinions he ascribes to Mrs. Mooney, the priest, and people in general. Their views periodically blind him to his own" (1989, 90). I agree with Kershner's contention that the voices of others form Doran's "point of view." There is no such thing, however, as "point of view" in any essential sense. What one presents as a "point of view" is an amalgamation of what one imagines as the points of view of others; a subject is a signifier for another signifier (another subject), and a point of view is the result of masquerading as one who is a signified (as one who has the phallus). "Point of view," as the phrase suggests, also involves the imagining of the gaze of the Other as well as an-other.

3. "Language belongs to the Symbolic Order, and in Lacan's view, it is through language that the subject can represent desires and feelings, and so it is through the

Symbolic Order that the subject can be represented, or constituted" (Ragland-Sullivan 1986, 82).

4. Margot Norris discusses Lacan's concept of the "demand for love" in relation to "The Dead" and suggests that Gretta Conroy and Ibsen's Nora are treated like children when what they desire is recognition as subjects: "For women, especially, what Lacan calls 'the demand for love' and which more closely resembles being nurtured, having the emotional security of knowing that one's physical needs will be supplied, being treasured as a valued and cherished object — that is, relations more proper to the parent-child relation — is easier to achieve than recognition and significance as a subject. Nora is a perfect example of a woman whose relationship to her husband is patterned on such a model of 'demand for love'. . . . Gretta enjoys a similar oppressive and infantile nurturance without recognition in her marriage" (1989, 489). The demand for love, which purports to be about nurturing is, finally, like *any* demand, a desire for recognition. From a social and cultural perspective, a woman is taught to be more appreciative of whatever security she is offered, and it is deemed unfeminine for her to expect something more.

5. Norris cites the same passage, and goes on to make a point about Ibsen's Torvald and Gabriel that is similar to the point I am making about Bob Doran: "In respectable bourgeois men like Torvald or Gabriel, where adultery is prohibited, this divergence toward the other woman takes the form of transforming the wife herself into another woman, into the stranger or the bride" (1989, 490). As I point out later in this chapter, Bob Doran "has affairs" with different women by frequenting the music hall. Inside the Empire theater, the original of Polly continues to perform even if Polly herself has become self-consciously respectable (as the narrator of "Cyclops" would have readers believe). Kershner also discusses the multiple layers of Polly's sexual role playing in a manner that describes, I think, what Lacan designates as "the masquerade of femininity": "She is impersonating a 'good girl' impersonating a harlot (or whatever the tantalizing ellipses signify) impersonating a "naughty girl," and she assures her auditors that they need not pretend to take her for anything better. Yet because this is a putatively ironic, 'teasing' performance, she is of course asking her listeners to take her for nothing of the kind. The roles are all 'sham,' but what lies beneath?" (1989, 91). It is not "what lies beneath" but what lies beyond, unrepresented female desire that operates as something supplemental to masculine desire (thus, undermining it).

6. This seems to support Irigaray's point about women having an identity imposed upon them according to what a masculine subject needs to see: "Women's social inferiority is reinforced and complicated by the fact that woman does not have access to language, except through recourse to 'masculine' systems of representation" (85).

7. As Irigaray also notes: Women are thus in a situation of specific exploitation with respect to exchange operations: sexual exchanges, but also economic, social, and cultural exchanges in general. A woman 'enters into' these exchanges only as the object of a transaction unless she agrees to renounce the specificity of her sex, whose 'identity' is imposed on her according to models that remain foreign to her" (1985, 85).

8. Kershner notes, "To speak of Polly as hypocritical, as many critics do, is

to miss the point of her perfectly poised unconsciousness" (1989, 91). My lengthier analysis of this scene agrees with Kershner's premise and goes on to try to account for the place of the unconscious female in the phallic economy. She operates like the placeholder zero that permits the illusion of linearity and teleology that becomes the his[S]tory of the masculine subject.

9. *"Reynold's Weekly Newspaper,* a radical London Sunday newspaper, started in 1850 as a fourpenny record of social and political scandals. From a conservative point of view, its politics were 'rude,' and Reynolds was characterized as 'a formidable spokesman for the most irreconcilable portions of the community'" (Gifford 1982, 65). Doran, of course, is all too reconcilable to "the community," partly because he allows this newspaper to be the "spokesperson" for that ten percent of himself that either sits alone in the Empire or, when inebriated, publicly exhibits "delirium."

9. "Why had he married the eyes in the photograph?" The Gaze in "A Little Cloud"

1. Stephen Dedalus goes down a street much like this one before his first encounter with a prostitute at the close of book 2 of *Portrait.* Stray female voices calling out to men is also a dominant feature of the atmosphere of the "Circe" chapter of *Ulysses.*

2. Gifford says of these student balls: "Baedecker's notes that 'many of these entertainments [are] 'got up' for the benefit of strangers, numbers of the supposed visitors being hired as decoys by the lessee of the saloon'" (1982, 70).

3. This collapsing of a hostile gaze with the orange tie—signifier of a hostile political force (British imperialism)—is worth noting, although I am not attempting a political analysis of *Dubliners* or this story per se.

4. Kershner's reading of this story, from the perspective of Bakhtin, bears some resemblance to my Lacanian reading—particularly in the way he characterizes the conversation of Little Chandler and Gallaher as a violent game of co-optation and one-upsmanship: "For all the vulgarity and banality of his friend's existence, which Chandler dimly recognizes, he still aspires to 'live bravely, like Gallaher'. . . . And from his own socio-linguistic situation, Gallaher obviously aspires after the aesthetic and scholarly elevation with which he vaguely associates Chandler. . . . Indeed, the crowning irony of their violent dialogic encounter is that both combatants, with their diametrically opposed phenomenologies of inclusion and exclusion, aspire after identical linguistic identities. Yet neither can recognize this, because the identity of each is founded on the tactic of self-definition through opposition to the other (1989, 99–100). Lacan would stress that oppositional self-definition is mutually illusory (and, thus, mutually hostile). The Lacanian approach has also allowed me to discuss the various gazes that inform identity (as will become even more clear in my discussion of "the eyes" that Little Chandler married).

5. These women, of whom he can say nothing, operate as a symptom that frames the silence of his lack-in-being: "The symptom is first of all the silence in the supposed speaking subject. If he speaks, he is cured of the silence, obviously.

But this does not tell us anything about why he began to speak" (Lacan 1981a, 11).

6. Nadel looks at this same passage when discussing the "feminine qualities" of the Jewish woman, which often embody "sensuality, warmth, allure, and air of temptation. . . . These features stood in stark contrast with the stern, hard, cold women of Europe whose temperament was haughty and whose sexuality was repressed. . . . In 'A Little Cloud,' Little Chandler becomes painfully aware of the difference between Occidental and Oriental, Irish and Jewish women" (1989, 159). I emphasize, however, that Little Chandler is comparing his wife's picture to an image that, like the voice of the anonymous reviewer of his nonexistent collection of poems, guarantees his ideal image as one that is coherent and unified. The difference between European and Jewish women, like the difference between a madonna and a whore, reflects a division in masculine subjectivity (rather than anything inherent in female sexuality) because they constitute *representations* of femininity that are perceived as enriching or thwarting the truth about the phallus. The allure of imagined eyes of voluptuous Jewish women titillates Little Chandler's masculinity much like the "stray voices" that cause him to "tremble like a leaf" when he takes walks down narrow and unknown streets.

7. This reduction of Annie Chandler to a pair of eyes, in order to better compare her to the eyes Gallaher has talked about, seems to support Irigaray's contention that the pleasure of masculine sexuality is essentially an economic pleasure: "Does pleasure for masculine sexuality, consist in anything other than the appropriation of nature, in the desire to make it (re)produce, and in exchanges of its/these products with other members of society?" (1985, 184). For a further discussion of the relationship of the Lacanian gaze to Little Chandler's furniture, as well as the relationship between shopping and sexuality, see my chapter, "The 'Lifestyle' of Molly Bloom: The Performative as Normative" (1991e).

10. *In No Case Shall the Said Bernard Bernard Bodley Be . . . :* Repetition and Being in "Counterparts"

1. Kershner also takes particular note of Alleyne's conversational strategy and quotes Bakhtin to good effect. "Parodic repetition is clearly a fundamental category of dialogic interchange. Bakhtin discusses it under the general heading of parody: ' . . . In the ordinary speech of our everyday life such a use of another's words is extremely widespread, especially in dialogue, where one speaker very often literally repeats the statement of the other speaker, investing it with new value and accenting it his own way — with expressions of doubt, indignation, irony, mockery, ridicule, and the like.' . . . Certainly in the interchanges of 'Counterparts,' where the mocking appropriation of the antagonist's words is generally carried out by men in the real or imagined presence of female onlookers, the element of aggression is highlighted. Conversation becomes less the exchange of information than a ritual of domination and submissions" (1989, 102). One should note particularly that Alleyne interrupts Farrington *first* and then mocks him by repeating his fragment back to him *as if Farrington had intended it to be a complete sentence.* From a Lacanian perspective, Alleyne's strategy

emphasizes Farrington's absence of subjectivity and makes him a more abject reflector of Alleyne's ideal image (at least from Alleyne's point of view). As I will clarify later in my discussion of this story, the presence of female onlookers is a central catalyst of Farrington's temporary victory over Alleyne and his mounting inclination for violence after the female artiste in the pub rejects his gaze.

2. In a personal conversation, Kimberly J. Devlin also identified the presence of Miss Delacour as an essential influence on the behavior of the two men.

3. Irigaray's comment about "the exchange of women" as the basis of patriarchal culture seems appropriate here: "The society we know, our own culture, is based upon the exchange of women. Without the exchange of women, we are told, we would fall back into the anarchy(?) of the natural world, the randomness(?) of the animal kingdom. The passage into the social order, into the symbolic order, into order as such, is assured by the fact that men, or groups of men, circulate women among themselves" (1985, 170). In the triangle Joyce presents, however, Miss Delacour has a powerful role as the one who authenticates masculine subjectivity.

4. This is in line with an observation Robert Scholes makes concerning the title of the story: "The title of this story suggests both the harmonious balance of counterpointed musical parts and the anonymous interchangeability of cogs in a great machine" (*D* 93). Of course "the harmonious balance," seen in the light of Lacanian theory, is a rather horrific one where what must be kept in harmony by dominating others (the moi and the je) is, in fact, permanently cacophonous.

5. In Joyce's fiction the Virgin Mary is frequently presented as the one woman who will continue to gaze at men with pity and forgiveness no matter what they have done and no matter how persistently they fail to mend their ways. There is the temperance retreat that Gerty MacDowell overhears in the "Nausicaa" episode of *Ulysses,* and Stephen Dedalus makes a point of hurrying to the chapel to pray to the Virgin Mary after he has been in Nighttown.

11. Where the Corkscrew Was:
The Purpose of Insignificance in Joyce's "Clay"

1. Edward Brandabur offers a fairly standard version of this reading: "The omitted last verse would refer to her earlier rejection of a suitor who had made vows which her heart had been able to withstand: for Maria a memory fraught with pain and, perhaps, in view of her superficial smugness, an element of spinsterish relief. She still has, after all, her nice, tidy little body intact, even if her wishes are not quite so tidy" (1971, 73). Brandabur's fear and distaste for Maria's avoidance of sex with a man is barely in check here. He seems particularly scornful of her "tidy" body which he associates with the fact that it is still "intact." He further comforts himself with the thought that the virginal Maria has "untidy" thoughts that are strictly concerned with all the sexual encounters with men she has inexplicably declined to experience. In all these regards he shares the tone of the narrator who, I suggest later in my discussion, views Maria, rather hysterically, as a dangerous witch set loose on the unsuspecting Donnelly family.

2. Deneau offers the basic argument that Maria is pathetic and should not be regarded as a transcendent symbol (1972, 26–45). I, too, see a danger in recuperating Maria through allegorical interpretations. My point, however, is that Maria's insignificance makes her essential for the production of other people's certitude.

3. Homer Obed Brown offers an example of this approach: "The reader is made aware, through the narrator, of the hopelessness of her condition, but the separation between this knowledge and her ignorance of it is complete. Her blindfolding, near the end of the story, which cuts her off from an awareness of what she has touched and its relevance to her, is parallel to her figurative blindness to the truth of her life as the narrator reveals it" (1972, 32–33). One can see here, rather clearly, that a privileging of the narrator as the possessor of absolute and incontrovertible truth permits the transcendence of the critic. For a discussion of how Maria uses the objects of her everyday world to anchor her reality, see my chapter "Classical Kitsch: Art and Mass-Production in Joyce's Fiction" (1991c).

4. Norris's statement is a bit too all-inclusive. Brandabur, for example, refers to Maria's "neurotic cunning" (1971, 70), and he takes issue with Noon's contention that Maria is "a modern work-a-day saint" (1955, 93–95). Brandabur counters. "My analysis is obviously not in accord with Father Noon's opinion: sanctity is irreconcilable with the kind of self-deception operating in Maria. I cannot imagine Joyce seriously presenting in Maria a portrait of sanctity" (1971, 73). Male critics seem to want to view Maria as either an allegory of saintliness or as Other in such a profound way that there is something creepy (witchlike) about her.

5. French states, "Maria . . . is more problematic than the other characters, for her blindness does seem to enable her to live without suffering" (1978, 461). I explore that paradox a little later.

6. Kershner argues that "what she asks is that Joe's feelings toward her remain those of child to mother" (1989, 109). My own sense is that Maria sees Joe as yet another suitor now that he has grown up (and she has not) and that it is Joe who reveals—with his oft-repeated phrase about her being his "proper mother"—that he experiences her gaze as that of what Lacan calls the (m)Other. The fact that Maria obsessively remembers compliments does not mean that other people have no unconscious motives *of their own* when pronouncing them.

7. Kershner notes that "the song articulates Freud's 'family romance,' the infantile fantasy that the child's mundane parents are impostors, while the real parents are aristocrats" (1989, 109). I agree, but add that Lacan's reinterprets this fantasy as another manifestation of the subject's longing for the mythic unity of the Imaginary Order.

8. "[The] jubilant assumption of his specular image by the child at the *infans* stage, still sunk in his motor incapacity and nursling dependence, would seem to exhibit in an exemplary situation the symbolic matrix in which the I is precipitated in a primordial form, before it is objectified in the dialectic of identification with the other, and before language restores to it, in the universal, its function as subject. . . . This forms situates the agency of the ego, before its social determination, in a fictional direction, which will always remain irreducible for the individual

alone . . . whatever the success of the dialectical syntheses by which he must resolve as *I* his discordance with his own reality" (Lacan 1977, 2).

9. Kershner argues that Maria "eventually succeeds in affirming whatever is the case" (1989, 105). That is her intention, of course, but she fails frequently, particularly here where she does not understand Joe's story (and does not understand how important it is to him that she understand it). In this story, everyone has a personal version of "what is the case" based on individual needs.

10. My analysis challenges a generalization by French about male attitudes toward women in *Dubliners:* "Although women may function busily in the background, men tend to ignore them or take them for granted; when men think about women, they think about unknown or imagined women, who seem to offer sexual pleasure" (French 1988, 269). One needs to see that the men in *Dubliners* are, in fact, paralyzed with fear over the unpredictable reality of the women in their day-to-day lives (and, thus, they daydream about the unambivalent woman whom French describes).

11. I am presenting in more detail a phenomenon that French notes: "They treat her as if she were a very young girl—and that is how she sees herself. . . . her image of herself as a late adolescent is deluded" (1982, 243).

12. Norris states: "The point of the children's joke is to make prim, 'genteel' Maria recoil in shock and disgust at the sensation of touching 'excrement'—only to reveal to her, on removal of the blindfold, the harmless garden dirt. The embarrassment would be self-inflicted: the victim would be betrayed by her own 'dirty' mind" (1987, 212). This explanation seems plausible to me; I am attempting to go further than this by suggesting *why* they might wish to embarrass her so profoundly.

13. Lacan cites the spuriousness of this argument with equal bluntness: "What was tried at the end of the last century, at the time of Freud, by all kinds of worthy people in the circle of Charcot and the rest, was an attempt to reduce the mystical to questions of fucking" (1982b, 147).

12. Love in the Third Person in "A Painful Case"

1. Suzanne Katz Hyman makes much the same observation: "Duffy must be able to see himself as a fixed and knowable subject within the conventional, ordered frame of things; but it is exactly this frame of things that women can disrupt. In other words, Duffy is depicted as a traditional male, supporter or guarantor of rational structures, while Mrs. Sinico is proposed as exactly that which can threaten such structures" (116). My analysis sees "The woman" as a more ambivalent representation than this because it is a representation that undermines masculinity precisely because it is the only thing that can authenticate it. What makes Mrs. Sinico so terrifying to Mr. Duffy is that he mistakes her as representing the benevolent gaze of the Other and then is shocked to catch a glimpse of her own desires as a subject.

2. Lacan offers a further definition of "love": "Were one dealing with beings who could not say anything, who could not pronounce what can be distinguished as truth and falsehood, then to believe in them would have no meaning. . . . the same

goes for a woman, except that it can happen that one believes her effectively to be saying something. That's when things get stopped up—to believe in, one believes her. It's what's called love" (1982b, 169).

3. This "deliberate swoon of the pupil into the iris" mimics the later swoon of Gabriel Conroy as well as the swoon of the young Stephen Dedalus into the arms of a prostitute. The female gaze in Joyce's fiction is often a whirlpool into which the masculine subject is invited to plunge.

4. Bowen's entire article is useful for the doubt it casts on the epiphanies as moments of privileged truth or insight. He cites the train moving through the final scene "like a worm with a fiery head" as "another of the comically inspirational and neo-Platonic images that Joyce often uses to illuminate these moments of presumed truth" (1981–1982, 108).

5. Heumann observes, "By refusing communion with Mrs. Sinico, Duffy maintains the separate state that is his essential being. . . . He cannot have both Mrs. Sinico and the self he has chosen: that much was clear to him at their parting" (1981, 92). Heumann's identification of the "self" Duffy "has chosen" as "his essential being" contains a contradiction because one does not "choose" one's essence. I agree with Heumann's second point that Duffy's "chosen self" is incompatible with a Mrs. Sinico who evinces Desire of her own, but, of course, I do not see this "self" as "his essential being." Far from compromising his "essential being," she authenticates it, and when her actions threaten the truth of this authentification, he flees from her presence.

6. Hendricks and West are equally unimpressed with Duffy's final misery: "With the quiet irony of the final word Joyce challenges us to realize that Duffy, alone but no longer lonely, has returned gladly to the anesthetic self-sufficiency that he enjoyed to begin with" (1977, 714). Kershner cites this same passage and finds support for this perspective in the newspaper account that so upsets Duffy: "Duffy, of course, is horrified at having a part of his own experience reflected so banally in the public media. So absolute is his contempt for the public that he is probably incapable of realizing fully the links between this example of reportorial narration and his own inner narrative. . . . For Duffy is at base a creature of cliché, much like Little Chandler but with a somewhat more sophisticated disguise of originality. . . . the dialogical confrontation with the newspaper article shakes his very sense of self" (1989, 115–16). Of course, my contention is that Duffy's his[S]tory (what Kershner calls "his very sense of self") is also a piece of yellow journalism in the way that it falsifies the Real to produce a (fictional) coherency that successfully poses as objective reality.

13. "It'll be all right when King Eddie comes": The Pathetic Phallacy in "Ivy Day in the Committee Room"

1. This story has been analyzed in considerable detail for its symbolical, historical, and allegorical properties but only rarely for its psychological one. For the historical dimension, see Stern 1973 (228–39) and Fairhall 1988 (289–304). Blotner traces the story's allusions to the Last Supper and sees Parnell in allegorical relationship to Christ (1957, 210–17) as does Horowitz (1984, 145–54). O'Grady has a

somewhat psychological approach to the story; he uses Nietzschean theory to explore how the characters use history to efface personal guilt (1986, 31–42).

2. Kershner notes "the arbitrary nature of [Henchy's] commitment" (1989, 120).

3. Kershner also notes, as a general observation, that "Henchy is merely trying to associate himself with any apparent source of money and power" (1989, 123).

4. Kershner characterizes Henchy as someone who dominates the dialogue of the story: "Henchy . . . shows himself a master of ostensibly nonpolitical rhetoric that is nonetheless ideologically charged" (1989, 120).

5. Here I divert from Kershner's fine analysis of Henchy because Crofton is not factored into his discussion of the peculiarly successful dominance over the group by Henchy.

6. Rabate does take Crofton into account in discussing Henchy: "Crofton's arrival releases the longer and most sustained speech by Mr. Henchy" (1982, 61).

7. Delany does not take a psychoanalytic approach to this story, but his observation in passing also suggests that "local politics" is not the primary subject of this story: "For the real contest in this election is not between Socialist and Nationalist but rather, as so often in Irish politics, between a decadent present and a retrospectively glorified past" (1972, 262–63).

8. Rabate is the first to note this peculiar attitude of Crofton: "The void of the enunciated word is not really sufficient, for we have to understand what matters most is the *a priori* position of superiority he assigns to himself. Enunciation can reveal this position, without any material being spoken" (1982, 61).

9. Kershner offers an excellent analysis of these prefaces: "Henchy's qualifiers function proleptically as if to assure the listener that he is not simply deriding at random but is exercising reasoned judgement" (1989, 121). Of course, I am trying to demonstrate that Henchy's derision is not random at all but spoken in an unconscious attempt to seduce Croton into approving of him.

10. Kershner draws attention to this parallel between Henchy and Tierney (1989, 122).

11. Boyle was the first to make this point (1963, 3–9).

12. French makes a point relative to my emphasis on seeing the story as more concerned with gender identity than politics: "Politics is seen as governed by the desire for instant gratification rather than by principle" (1978, 463). For a further discussion of history in Joyce's fiction from a Lacanian perspective, see my chapter, "Joyce and Lacan: The Twin Narratives of History and His[S]tory in the 'Nestor' Chapter of *Ulysses*" (1991d).

14. Mrs. Kearney and the "Moral Umbrella" of Mr. O'Madden Burke: A Mother's Quest for the Phallus

1. Margot Norris, discussing Nora in *A Doll's House* and Gretta in "The Dead," states: "Both Nora and Gretta fail to find in their husbands a freedom of anxiety in the face of the other that would give the men a mastery worthy of the women's recognition. . . . Ontological slavishness [of men] in the social realm prevents the

woman from granting the man mastery as 'another man,' either literally another man, as in the case of Gretta, or to an idealized version of the man, as in the case of Nora" (1989, 490). This is an astute observation and something that needs to be more generally noted. But, of course, women who expect perfect men and reserve their "respect" for only them are doing as great a disservice to themselves and to men as those men who do the same thing to women.

2. David Hayman, for instance, seems to take this view: "'A Mother', as Joyce later thought of it and as he doubtless intended, is the clearest exposition of the theme of the dominant female, a type he despised, feared and might have married. . . . She has turned a superficial culture into a whip with which to flog the males who cross her path or into a means of cozening them" (1969, 123–24). But Hayman seems to fear *his* image of Mrs. Kearney at least as much as he maintains Joyce did. His image of her bestriding the bottoms of well-whipped males would seem more appropriate to Bella Cohen (who is, by and large, an invention of Bloom's — a representation of one dimension of *his* desire, rather than an "exposition" of a woman's desire). Hayman's reading takes no notice of *how easily* the "dominant" Mrs. Kearney is routed at the close of the story by the very group of men who have amply demonstrated their hilarious incompetence throughout the story. Jane E. Miller has also noted Hayman's remarkably vituperative attack upon Mrs. Kearney: "Hayman also loses his critical bearings in his strong disapproval of Mrs. Kearney, whom he describes as 'a sour presence, a succubus among the drinking and the good cheer'" (1990, 409).

3. Sherrill E. Grace, in an interesting (and badly needed) reassessment of Mrs. Kearney states the following: "Mrs. Kearney takes art seriously insofar as she puts time and effort into careful preparation and wants the performances to go smoothly and well, but it is the men who carry the day after all, and art is reduced almost to the level of farce by their laziness, timidity, and parsimony" (1988, 277). I support Grace's insight here but not her initial assumption. It is not "art" that Mrs. Kearney cares for *but organization and contracts.* As Grace's own observation emphasizes, Mrs. Kearney's "time and effort" is devoted to "careful preparation," and what she wants is not to witness great "art" but for "the performances to go smoothly and well." Miller also cites Mrs. Kearney's primary concern as "persistence and perfectionism" (1988, 417).

4. Grace points out the importance of this word *lady:* "which occurs three times as frequently here as in any of the other stories. Lady is the key, the ephipanic word in 'A Mother.' . . . She is acceptable as a lady because of what it means to be one; a lady must be decorous and decorative, passive, silent, long-suffering, and dependent on male chivalry. By being a lady, she provides a flattering mirror to the male society strutting before her" (1988, 278–79). In the Lacanian framework that I am using, a "lady" supports *the illusion* of the phallic term. Hugh Kenner remarks in *Dublin's Joyce* that the "genitals of Dublin are gelded," and Grace responds to this in her analysis: "If Mrs. Kearney is made a female scapegoat in the story, as I think she is, then it is because she is forced to carry the guilt of the gelded man and his paralyzed city" (1988, 279). I quite agree, except that I maintain that men, *in order to repress the fact that they never had the Phallus in the first place,* develop elaborate fears that

women will geld them (as in the myth of Samson and Delilah). Castration anxiety, in other words, once transformed into the gender myth of masculinity, helps the man to imagine that, in the Symbolic Order, he and the (nonexistent) Phallus are still somehow attached.

5. Kershner stresses that Mrs. Kearney's verbal slip "betrays her lower-middle-class origins." To illustrate his point, he adds, "*'I'm a great fellow fol-the-diddle-I-do'* is more reminiscent of Simon Dedalus on a binge than of the woman who had aspired to demand "What is the *Cometty*, pray?'" (1989, 128). Kershner's choice of example also supports my point that this insult is a shocking transformation where one who has played "the lady" suddenly burlesques the stereotypical blowhard, n'er do well, nincompoop male Dubliner (thus, she performs a devastating parody of the crafty tongued masculine Dubliner, of which Simon Dedalus is the most colorful example).

6. "With his phallic umbrella, finely balanced, and his previously mentioned 'moral umbrella,' a 'magniloquent western name' . . . veiling his economic impotency, Burke ironically represents the paternal lawgiver as the figure of justice" (Valente 1991, 435). Valente's interesting discussion of this story emphasizes the inherent contradictions in any system of justice. Of particular value is his discussion of justice in the public and private spheres as it relates to gender construction and Lyotard's notion of *differend.* In line with Lyotard's notion, the committee may represent and may have been intended to represent, an inept imperialist force—unfair and disorganized—which continutes to operate successfully because it controls the idioms that constitute "right" and "wrong," what is "fair" and "unfair," and what is "reasonable" and "unreasonable."

15. "With God's grace I will rectify this and this": Masculinity Regained in "Grace"

1. Joseph E. Baker associates Power, Cunningham, and McCoy with the trinity (1965, 299–303); Robert S. Jackson interprets the story in the light of the "unjust steward" parable (1961, 719–24); Francis X. Newman sees the actual source for the story's structure as The Book of Job rather than Dante's *Divine Comedy* (1966, 70–79).

2. Helene Cixous mentions the progress of Mr. Kernan's hat: "Tom's hat has been rehabilitated, his soul can be refurbished by the Jesuits" (1972, 40).

3. Cixous, reasonably enough, is puzzled by the energy Mr. Power devotes to Mr. Kernan's rehabilitation: "Mr. Power, a converted Protestant without real convictions, wants to make him 'turn over a new leaf,' though we never find out exactly why" (1972, 39). My feeling is that he knows anyone wishing to continue prospering in the Dublin (masculine) business community can never be Catholic enough, and his organization of Mr. Kernan's rehabilitation will offset what might be perceived as some of his faults (keeping a barmaid as a mistress, for instance). It is clear that the Dublin business community is fickle and ruthless in its willingness to punish those who seem to take the Catholic faith lightly. This might also explain why the decidedly non-Catholic Tom Kernan would treat his visitors with the same cautious hospitality one might expect him to extend to Rotarian's or any masculine members of

an influential network of commerce. "Grace" and financial credit seem synonymous in the day-to-day business practices of Dublin.

4. Kershner also sees Mr. Kernan as a clear and present danger to what he calls "the community." The difference in our approach, if not in our conclusions, is that I see Kernan's "fall from grace" as a specific threat to the social contract of masculinity (which is also a social construct), and Kershner sees it, in a less gender-inflected way, as a threat to the identity of anyone in the community. "Kernan the good husband and adequate businessman is also a hopeless drunkard, but his society cannot afford to admit that there may be a connection between these identities. What Kernan 'says' cannot be allowed to be 'spoken.' Thus his friends will attempt to cover his silences and distortions with acceptable speech of their own, or better, with a publicly approved rhetoric like that of the church. If Kernan can be 'drawn in' to a conversation, can be taught to speak properly—that is, as everyone else does—then the threat he poses can be nullified" (1989, 132).

16. "Perhaps she had not told him the whole story": The Woman as a Symptom of Masculinity in "The Dead"

1. Brown also sees these encounters as the fundamental structure of the story and anticipates the tenor of a reading like mine: "The story of Gabriel Conroy seems tailor-made for feminist interpretation. Gabriel's evening consists of a succession of significant encounters with women" (92).

2. Like any seducer, Gabriel is not interested in the audience, per se, only on what he can persuade them to do for him: "What did he care that his aunts were only two ignorant old women?" (*D* 192). As I clarify later, Lily's comment that "the men that is now is only all palaver and what they can get out of you" (*D* 178) is an apt description of masculine subjectivity from a Lacanian point of view.

3. Ragland-Sullivan offers this description of how the je and moi struggle to constitute a sense of self: "The *moi* is an ideal ego whose elemental form is irretrievable in conscious life, but it is reflected in its chosen identificatory objects (alter egos or ego ideals). The subject of speech . . . is distinct from the subject of identifications, . . . but they interact all the same" (1986, 3–4).

4. Kershner specifically cites Lacanian theory as an apt perspective for analysis of "The Dead": "But perhaps the most suggestive recent formulation of woman's position is that of Lacan, who argues that "The Woman" does not exist, in that 'phallic sexuality assigns her a position of fantasy.' Woman is sought by men to fill the lack or absence that they experience as a corollary of consciousness. Further, Lacan teasingly argues that the 'jouissance that goes beyond,' the '*jouissance* of the body' that is associated with the place of women, is the domain sensed by mystics—the realm of the supplementary, which has often been interpreted theologically. Lacan takes courtly love to be symptomatic of this set of relationships, a way in which a man as speaking being attempts to take responsibility for the impossibility of erotic love. Given the theological resonance of 'The Dead' to which so many commentators have attested, Lacan's formulation seems particularly relevant" (145).

5. Kenner makes the general point, about several characters in *Dubliners,* that they resist the giving of themselves because "this recognizes the fact of otherness, of a portion of being neither susceptible to his control nor violable to his gaze" (1956, 60).

6. French cites examples throughout the collection in which what is missing silently undermines the consciousness of the characters (1978, 443–72).

7. I am offering a detailed psychological explanation for what Walzl has long identified as Gabriel's "deep, basic, self-distrust and timidity" (Bowen 1985, 211).

8. Munich sees more significance in what the quote *might have been* than I do. Much of her article is persuasive, but I do not think her thesis about why Gabriel needs women depends on what the Browning quote is.

9. "Language introduces us to an existence which can never be satisfied, for, as a condition of our speech, something is always missing" MacCabe goes on to make the further point that "in Joyce's text the division between signifier and signified becomes an area in which the reader is in (and at) play—producing meaning through his or her own activity" (1979, 2). The reader reacts to the gaps in the text of *Dubliners* just as Gabriel reacts to the figure of Gretta on the stairs: "If I just had that information, if I could just hear the 'Distant Music', I could achieve some sort of permanent resolution." In attempting to seduce the voice of the Other, the subject is actually engaged with his own unconscious which Lacan defines as "the discourse of the Other."

10. Herring notes that one of Joyce's notes for *Ulysses* is "Dead govern living" (1987, 30). I am arguing that this principle of uncertainty—where the living unwittingly give the dead life by unconsciously observing their former strictures—is also a governing principle of "The Dead."

11. Herring makes a similar point that, in the story "Clay," Maria "habitually blocks out what is troublesome, the result here being that her secret and persistent dream is unveiled dramatically" (1987, 65).

12. Kenner was the first to analyze Joyce's use of a "neutral" narrator who actually echoes phrases and sentence constructions of the character being described. Kenner calls it the "Uncle Charles' effect," after a character in *Portrait* (1978, 52).

13. Mitchell, in her introduction to Lacan's essays on feminine sexuality, summarizes the plurality (and the attempts to impose certainty on this plurality) that characterizes the fundamental split in the human subject: "Lacan's human subject is the obverse of the humanists'. His subject is not an entity with an identity, but a being created in the fissure of a radical split. The identity that seems to be that of the subject is in fact a mirage arising when the subject forms an image of itself by identifying with another's perception of it. . . . Lacan's human subject is . . . a being that can only conceptualise itself from the position of another's desire" (Mitchell and Rose, 1982, 5).

14. Brandabur argues that "Gabriel anticipates the paralysis which will befall him. . . . Throughout the story, personal encounters disturb his poise until he finally gives in to the annihilation he has not only anticipated but invited" (1971, 116). I am arguing quite the reverse, that Gabriel's strategies of aversion are formidable, but he need not "invite" the annihilation for it to occur because subjective consciousness is a house divided against itself and any number of trivial events can severely threaten it.

15. "The point is Gabriel's need to prevail over Lily by reducing a human relationship to commerce" (Bauerle 1988, 115). She later identifies, correctly I think, his addition of the phrase "hyper-educated" as a thrust at Molly Ivors. But my argument is that he wants to master these women because their break from the role of "The Woman" is so threatening to him. Rape is, among other things, an act of desperate force in the face of what is perceived as a chronic threat to the integrity of one's masculine subjectivity. Although I agree that this is not too strong a description of some of Gabriel's *initial impulses,* I do not think he can be judged as a rapist solely on the evidence of impulses.

16. "The malevolent realities surrounding the innocent protagonist of the first part of the book are now part of the texture of life." Kenner goes on to note that in the latter part of *Dubliners* is a "multiplication of spectres, of choices negated, passions unexplored, opportunities missed, aspects of the self denied" (1956, 48).

17. That is fairly easily done with regard to his doting aunts, of course, but after his encounter with Miss Ivors, he fears her "quizzical" eyes as something that will mar his audience with himself at the after-dinner speech. He inserts (thrusts?) a sentence into the speech that will neutralize her presence and maintain the audience as a polished mirror for his composed self.

18. "Isolated by education, temperament, and egotism, Conroy is defeated by forces that conspire against him, and by his ultimate awareness of inadequacy as a man" (Herring 1987, 71). Herring's sentence is an admirably concise statement of the standard way of viewing Gabriel's "failure" by the end of the story, so I note here where I differ from this view. The forces that conspire to defeat Gabriel come from within. He is inadequate, but no more so than anyone else who benefits and suffers from using the Symbolic Order of language to define himself. In his dissolution and failure one sees him in a gap, a moment between the heartbeats of subjective certainty (what Stephen Dedalus terms 'an enchantment of the heart'). Gabriel never fails to recover although he always fails to do so permanently.

19. The party itself, as well as Lancers, represents this ideological world: "Never once had it fallen flat," readers are told of the party in the opening paragraph, "for years and years it had gone off in splendid style" (*D* 175). Yet many things fall flat at the party (or, in the case of Freddy Malins, threaten to); what "goes off in splendid style" is the *performance* required by the assembled group to systematically ignore the ellipses, hesitations, and miscues that constitute the actual discourse of the party. The suggestion of theatrical success in the phrase "gone off in splendid style" is appropriate. As Kenner has noted (1956, 65), the guests do not talk about art, they talk about performers in relationship to a particular performance on a given night, transcending mere identity to become a popular myth (that is, they talk about versions of their own ideal selves).

20. Similarly, when Gabriel sees Gretta on the stairs, he will first identify her as "the woman" then as "his wife" (twice), but never as Gretta. After she discloses her belief that Michael Furey "died for me," Gabriel sees her for what seems to be the first time: "He watched her while she slept as though he and she had never lived together as man and wife. His curious eyes rested long upon her face and on her hair" (*D* 222).

21. As my analysis of this scene makes clear, I cannot agree with Bauerle's description of Gabriel as "the interrupter, the would-be chieftain, the man with the last word" (1988, 117). Quite the contrary, he is pathetically vulnerable to Miss Ivors's brilliant attack.

22. The most vicious epithets about the feminine gender seem to be reserved for a woman who deliberately plays at being "The Woman," perhaps because this is particularly devastating to the maintenance of masculine subjectivity.

23. Brivic also states that Gabriel is excited by her excitement, not simply by her figure: "Gabriel is sexually stimulated, for the first time in the story, by the excitement this music has generated in her" (1980, 89).

24. "A consummate pretender, Gabriel has in the course of a few minutes played every role, from tender lover to indignant husband. . . . He must both express and feel affection in devious ways, by identification" (Brandabur 1971, 122). I agree, but again, so must all men. Brandabur goes on to posit a "true self" behind Gabriel's posing that has a "wistful and sympathetic desire for affection." But posing, as long as one remains ignorant of one's performance, *is* the self. And when one acknowledges a pose, the result is humiliation, not enlightenment. Kershner also characterizes Gabriel as a "stage-manager." His description of Gabriel's taste in drama as "theatricality of a low order" suggests to me that, like Bob Doran, some of what he finds erotic is determined by the way femininity is depicted on the popular stage: "Once they have arrived at the hotel he goes to considerable trouble to arrange the proper lighting for his seduction of Gretta. Like a stage-manager he has the porter remove the candle and then stands in a position of dramatic dominance with his back to the light from the street, watching her for a beat as she undresses, and then calling her name. Gabriel's imagination is highly theatrical, and despite his claims to literary sophistication, it is theatricality of a low order. His desire revolves about the tableau, that staple of nineteenth-century popular entertainment" (1989, 144).

25. Eggers suggests a similar dynamic between Gabriel and Gretta, where Gretta gains individuality as Gabriel's identity slips. But Eggers sees this as somehow mutually affirming, which I do not: "As Gabriel feels his identity slipping from him, he becomes more complex and human, and as Gretta asserts her individuality, she also becomes more ambiguous and real" (1981, 393).

26. "We make our destiny, because we talk. We believe that we say what we want, but it is what others wanted, most particularly our family, which speaks us. . . . We are spoken, and because of that, we make of the accidents that push us, something 'plotted.' And, actually, there is a plot—we call that our destiny" (quoted in Ragland-Sullivan 1988, 118). Ragland-Sullivan goes on to suggest how to apply Lacanian insights to a text that could almost serve as a motto for what I attempt in this chapter "Lacan says our only tool in knowing anything about the enigma of a symptom is the equivoque that attends to the vacillations in language, resonances, the questionable, uncertainties, double senses. . . . Interpretation must work with this tool" (Ragland-Sullivan 1988, 121).

Works Cited

Attridge, D., and D. Ferrer, eds. 1984. *Post-Structuralist Joyce: Essays from the French.* London: Cambridge Univ. Press.

Baker, J. E. 1965. "The Trinity in Joyce's 'Grace.'" *James Joyce Quarterly* 2: 299–303.

Barr, M. S., and R. Feldstein. 1989. *Discontented Discourses: Feminism, Textual Intervention, Psychoanalysis.* Chicago: Univ. of Illinois Press.

Bauerle, R. 1988. "Date Rape, Mate Rape: A Liturgical Interpretation of 'The Dead.'" Scott, *New Alliances,* 113–25.

Beja, M. 1983. "One Good Look at Themselves: Epiphanies in *Dubliners.*" Cohn, Peterson, and Epstein, 3–14.

———, ed. 1986. *James Joyce: The Centennial Symposium.* Chicago: Univ. of Illinois Press.

Benstock, B. 1978. "Joyce's Rheumatics: The Holy Ghost in *Dubliners.*" *Southern Review* 14:1–15.

———, ed. 1982. *The Seventh of Joyce.* Bloomington: Indiana Univ. Press.

———. (1988a) "The L.S.d. of Dubliners." *Twentieth Century Literature* 34, no. 2:191–210.

———, ed. 1988b. *The Augmented Ninth.* Syracuse, N.Y.: Syracuse Univ. Press.

Blotner, J. L. 1957. "'Ivy Day in the Committee Room': Death without Resurrection.'" *Perspective* 9:210–17.

Boheemen, C. van. 1987. *The Novel as Family Romance: Language, Gender, and Authority from Fielding to Joyce.* Ithaca, N.Y.: Cornell Univ. Press.

———. 1988. "Deconstruction after Joyce." Scott, 29–36.

Bowen, Z. 1981–1982. "Joyce and the Epiphany Concept: A New Approach." *Journal of Modern Literature* 9, no. 1:103–14.

———. 1982. "Joyce's Prophylactic Paralysis: Exposure in *Dubliners.*" *James Joyce Quarterly* 19, no. 3:257–73.

————, and James F. Carens. 1985. *A Companion to Joyce Studies.* Westport, Conn.: Greenwood.

Boyle, R., S. J. 1963. "'Two Gallants' and 'Ivy Day in the Committee Room.'" *James Joyce Quarterly* 1, no. 1:3–9.

————. 1969. "Swiftian Allegory and Dantean Parody in Joyce's 'Grace.'" *James Joyce Quarterly* 7:11–21.

Brandabur, E. 1971. *A Scrupulous Meanness: A Study of Joyce's Early Work.* Chicago: Univ. of Illinois Press.

Brivic, S. 1980. *Joyce between Freud and Jung.* New York: Kennikat.

————. 1987. "The Other of *Ulysses.*" Newman, Robert, 187–212.

————. 1991. *The Veil of Signs: Joyce, Lacan, and Perception.* Chicago: Univ. of Illinois Press.

Brown, H. O. 1972. *James Joyce's Early Fiction: The Biography of a Form.* Cleveland, Ohio: Press of Case Western Reserve Univ.

Brown, R. 1985. *James Joyce and Sexuality.* London: Cambridge Univ. Press.

Burgin, V., J. Donald, and C. Kaplan, eds. 1986. *Formations of Fantasy.* London: Methuen.

Chadwick, J. 1984. "Silence in 'The Sisters.'" *James Joyce Quarterly* 21, no. 3:245–55.

Chayes, I. H. 1946. "Joyce's Epiphanies." *Sewanee Review* 54:449–67.

Church, M. 1968. "Dubliners and Vico." *James Joyce Quarterly* 5:150–56.

Cixous, H. 1972. *The Exile of James Joyce.* New York: David Lewis.

————. 1984. "Joyce: The (R)use of Writing." Attridge and Ferrer, 15–30.

Cohn A. M., R. F. Peterson, and E. L. Epstein, eds. 1983. *Work in Progress: Joyce Centenary Essays.* Carbondale: Southern Illinois Univ. Press.

Cronin, J., and Ormsby, F. (1972) "A Very Fine Piece of Writing: 'Ivy Day in the Committee Room.'" *Eire* 7, no. 2:84–94.

Davis, R. C., ed. 1983. *Lacan and Narration: The Psychoanalytic Difference in Narrative Theory.* Baltimore, Md.: Johns Hopkins Univ. Press.

Delany, P. 1972. "Joyce's Political Development and the Aesthetic of *Dubliners.*" *College English* 34, no. 2:256–68.

Deming, R. H., ed. 1970. *James Joyce: The Critical Heritage, 1902–1927.* New York: Barnes and Noble.

Deneau, D. P. 1972. "Joyce's 'Minute Maria.'" *Journal of Narrative Technique* 2:26–45.

Devlin, K. J. 1988. "The Female Eye: Joyce's Voyeuristic Narcissists." Scott, *New Alliances,* 135–43.

Dilsworth, T. 1986. "Sex and Politics in 'The Dead.'" *James Joyce Quarterly* 23, no. 2:157–71.

Duffy, E. 1986. "'The Sisters' as the Introduction to *Dubliners.*" *Papers on Language and Literature* 22, no. 4:417–28.

Eggers, T. 1981. "'What is a Woman . . . a Symbol of ?'" *James Joyce Quarterly* 18, no. 4:379–95.

Engel, M. 1971. "*Dubliners* and Erotic Expectation." *Twentieth Century Literature in Retrospect.* Edited by Reuben A. Brower, 3–26. Cambridge, Mass.: Harvard Univ. Press.

Fairhall, J. 1988. "Colgan-Connolly: Another Look at the Politics of 'Ivy Day in the Committee Room.'" *James Joyce Quarterly* 25, no. 3:289–304.

Feeley, J. 1982. "Joyce's 'The Dead' and the Browning Quotation." *James Joyce Quarterly* 20, no. 1:86–96.

Feldstein, R., and Sussman, H., eds. 1990. *Psychoanalysis and . . .* New York: Routledge.

Felman, S. ed. 1982. *Literature and Psychoanalysis, The Question of Reading: Otherwise.* Baltimore, Md.: Johns Hopkins Univ. Press.

———. 1987. *Jacques Lacan and the Adventure of Insight: Psychoanalysis in Contemporary Culture.* Cambridge, Mass.: Harvard Univ. Press.

Felman, S. 1988. "The Real of the Tragedy of Desire: Lacan's Psychoanalysis, or The Figure in the Screen." *October* 45:97–108.

Fischer, T. 1971. "From Reliable to Unreliable Narrator: Rhetorical Changes in Joyce's 'The Sisters.'" *James Joyce Quarterly* 9:85–92.

Flieger, J. A. 1990. "The Female Subject: (What) Does Woman Want?" Feldstein and Sussman, 54–63.

French, M. 1978. "Missing Pieces in Joyce's *Dubliners.*" *Twentieth Century Literature* 24:443–72.

———. 1982. "Joyce and Language." *James Joyce Quarterly* 19, no. 3:239–55.

———. 1988. "Women in Joyce's Dublin." Benstock, *Augmented Ninth,* 267–72.

Friedrich, G. 1965. "The Perspective of Joyce's *Dubliners.*" *College English* 24:421–26.

Gallop, J. 1982. *The Daughter's Seduction: Feminism and Psychoanalysis.* Ithaca, N.Y.: Cornell Univ. Press.

———. 1985. *Reading Lacan.* Ithaca, N.Y.: Cornell Univ. Press.

———. 1990. "Why Does Freud Giggle When the Women Leave the Room?" Feldstein and Sussmann, 49–53.

Garrison, J. M. 1975. "*Dubliners:* Portraits of the Artist as a Narrator." *Novel* 8:226–40.

Gates, R. A. 1982. "Tom Kernan and Job." *James Joyce Quarterly* 19, no. 3:275–87.

Gelfant, B. 1988. "A Frame of Her Own: Joyce's Women in *Dubliners* Reviewed." Benstock, *Augmented Ninth,* 263–66.

Ghiselin, B. 1956. "The Unity of Joyce's *Dubliners.*" *Accent* 16:75–88, 196–231.

Gibbons, T. H. 1967. "Dubliners and the Critics." *Critical Quarterly* 9:179–87.

Gifford, D. 1982. *Joyce Annotated: Notes for Dubliners and A Portrait of the Artist as a Young Man.* Berkeley: Univ. of California Press.

Gillespie, M. P. 1986. "Aesthetic Evolution: The Shaping Forces behind *Dubliners.*" *Language and Style* 19, no. 2:149–63.

Givens, S., ed. 1948. *James Joyce: Two Decades of Criticism.* New York: Vanguard.

Godin, J. G. 1988. "Sur le Sinthome." Benstock, *Augmented Ninth,* 210–14.

Grace, S. E. 1988. "Rediscovering Mrs. Kearney." Benstock, *Augmented Ninth,* 273–81.

Grosz, E. 1990. *Jacques Lacan: A Feminist Introduction.* New York: Routledge.

Hart, C. 1969a. "'Eveline.'" Hart, 48–52.

———. 1969b. *James Joyce's Dubliners: Critical Essays.* London: Faber.

Hayman, D. 1969. "'A Mother.'" Hart, 122–33.

Heath, S. 1986. "Joan Riviere and the Masquerade." Burgin, Donald, and Kaplan, 45–61.

Hendricks, W., and M. West. 1977. "The Genesis and Significance of Joyce's Irony in 'A Painful Case.'" *ELH* 44:701–27.

Henke S. 1983. "James Joyce and Women: The Matriarchal Muse." Cohn, Peterson, and Epstein, 117–31.

———, and E. Unkeless, eds. 1982. *Women in Joyce.* Chicago: Univ. of Illinois Press.

Herr, C. 1986. *Joyce's Anatomy of Culture.* Chicago: Univ. of Illinois Press.

———. 1989. "Fathers, Daughters, Anxiety, and Fiction." Barr and Feldstein, 173–207.

Herring, P. F. 1987. *Joyce's Uncertainty Principle.* Princeton: Princeton Univ. Press.

Heumann, M. J. 1981. "Writing—and Not Writing—in Joyce's 'A Painful Case.'" *Eire* 16, no. 3:81–97.

Hirsh, E. A. 1986. "'New Eyes': H. D., Modernism, and the Psychoanalysis of Seeing." *Literature and Psychology* 32, no. 2:1–10.

Horowitz, S. H. 1984. "More Christian Allegory in 'Ivy Day in the Committee Room.'" *James Joyce Quarterly* 21, no. 2:145–54.

Hyman, S. K. 1981. "'A Painful Case': The Movement of a Story Through a Shift Voice." *James Joyce Quarterly* 19, no. 2:111–18.

Irigaray, L. 1985. *This Sex Which Is Not One.* Ithaca, N.Y.: Cornell Univ. Press.

Jackson, R. S. 1961. "A Parabolic Reading of James Joyce's 'Grace.'" *Modern Language Notes* 76:719–24.

Jardine, A. 1982. "Gynesis." *Diacritics* 12:54–65.

Jones, E. C. 1989. "Preface." *Modern Fiction Studies: Feminist Readings of Joyce.* 35, no. 3:407–17.

Joyce, J. 1966. *The Letters of James Joyce.* Vols. 2 and 3. Edited by Richard Ellmann. New York: Viking.

————. 1969. *Dubliners: Text, Criticism and Notes.* Edited by R. Scholes and A. W. Litz. New York: Viking.

————. 1975. *Selected Joyce Letters.* Edited by Richard Ellmann. New York: Viking.

Kershner, R. B. 1989. *Joyce, Bakhtin, and Popular Literature: Chronicles of Disorder.* Chapel Hill: Univ. of North Carolina Press.

Kenner, H. 1956. *Dublin's Joyce.* Bloomington: Indiana Univ. Press.

————. 1978. *Joyce's Voices.* Los Angeles: Univ. of California Press.

Kloss, R. J. 1974. "The Function of Forgetting in Joyce's 'Clay.'" *Hartford Studies in Literature* 6:167–79.

Lacan, J. 1977. *Ecrits.* New York: Norton.

————. 1981a. *The Four Fundamental Concepts of Psychoanalysis.* New York: Norton.

————. 1981b. Wilden.

————. 1982a. "Desire and the Interpretation of Desire in *Hamlet.*" Felman, *Literature and Psychoanalysis,* 11–52.

————. 1982b. Mitchell and Rose.

————. 1988a. *The Seminar of Jacques Lacan: Freud's Papers on Technique 1953–1954.* New York: Norton.

————. 1988b *The Seminar of Jacques Lacan: Freud's Papers on Technique 1954–1955.* New York: Norton.

————. (1988c) "Seminar on 'The Purloined Letter.'" Muller and Richardson, 28–54.

Lawrence, K. 1987. "Paternity, the Legal Fiction." Newman, R. D., 89–97.

Leonard G. M. 1990. "A Fall from Grace: Masculine Subjectivity and the Construction of Femininity in Hitchcock's *Vertigo.*" *American Imago* (Fall–Winter): 271–92.

————. 1991. "Women on the Market: Commodity Culture, 'Femininity,' and 'Those Lovely Seaside Girls' in *Ulysses.*" *James Joyce Studies: An Annual* (June): 27–68.

————1991. "Joyce and Lacan: The Twin Narratives of History and His[S]tory in the 'Nestor' Episode of *Ulysses.*" In *Joyce in Context,* edited by Timothy Martin and Vincent Cheng, 57–66. Cambridge Univ. Press.

————. Forthcoming. "Authorizing the Reader: Student 'Freewriting' as a Method for Teaching Joyce." In *Images in Joyce,* edited by Fritz Senn and Bonnie Scott, Monte Carlo: Princess Grace Irish Library.

Leonard, G. Forthcoming. "Classical Kitsch: Art and Mass Production in Joyce's Fiction." In *Images in Joyce,* edited by Fritz Senn and Bonnie Scott. Monte Carlo: Princess Grace Irish Library.

————. Forthcoming. "the 'Lifestyle' of Molly Bloom: The Performative as Normative" In *The Real Molly Bloom,* edited by Richard Pearce. Madison: Univ. of Wisconsin Press.

Levin, R., and C. Shattuck 1948. "First Flight to Ithaca." Givens, 47–94.

MacCabe, C. 1979. *James Joyce and the Revolution of the Word.* London: Macmillan.

———. 1982. *James Joyce: New Perspectives.* Bloomington: Indiana Univ. Press.

MacCannell, J. F. 1986. *Figuring Lacan: Criticism and the Cultural Unconscious.* Lincoln: Univ. of Nebraska Press.

Mahaffey, V. 1988 *Reauthorizing Joyce.* Cambridge: Cambridge Univ. Press.

Mandel, J. 1985. "The Structure of 'Araby.'" *Modern Language Studies* 15, no. 4:48–54.

McGee, P. 1988. *Paperspace: Style as Ideology in Joyce's Ulysses.* Lincoln: Univ. of Nebraska Press.

McGuiness, A. E. 1974. "The Ambience of Space in Joyce's *Dubliners.*" *Studies in Short Fiction* 11:343–51.

Miller, J. E. 1990. "'O She's a Nice Lady!': A Rereading of 'A Mother.'" *James Joyce Quarterly* 28, no. 2:407–26.

Mitchell, J., and J. Rose, eds. 1982. *Feminine Sexuality.* New York: Norton.

Muller, J. P., and W. J. Richardson 1988. *The Purloined Poe: Lacan, Derrida, and Psychoanalytic Reading.* Baltimore: Johns Hopkins Univ. Press.

Munich, A. A. 1988. "'Dear Dead Women,' or Why Gabriel Conroy Reviews Robert Browning." Scott, 126–34.

Mykyta, L. 1983. "Lacan, Literature and the Look: Woman in the Eye of Psychoanalysis." *Sub-Stance* 39, no. 12:49–57.

Nadel, I. B. 1989. *Joyce and the Jews: Culture and Texts.* Iowa City: Univ. of Iowa Press.

Nebeker, H. E. 1976, "James Joyce's 'Clay': The Well-Wrought Urn." *Renanscence* 28:123–38.

Newman, F. X. 1966. "The Land of Ooze: Joyce's "Grace' and the Book of Job." *Studies in Short Fiction* 4:70–79.

Newman, R. D. and W. Thornton, eds. (1987) *Joyce's Ulysses: The Larger Perspective.* Newark: Univ. of Delaware Press.

Noon, W. T., S. J. 1955. "Joyce's 'Clay': An Interpretation." *College English* 17:93–95.

Norris, M. 1987. "Narration under a Blindfold: Reading Joyce's 'Clay.'" *PMLA* 102:206–15.

———. 1989. "Stifled Back Answers: The Gender Politics of Art in Joyce's 'The Dead.'" *Modern Fiction Studies: Feminist Readings of Joyce* 35, no. 3:479–503.

O'Grady, T. B. 1986. "'Ivy Day in the Committee Room': The Use and Abuse of Parnell." *Eire* 21, no. 2:31–42.

Pearce, R. 1988. "Voices, Stories, (W)holes: The Politics of Narration." Scott, *New Alliances,* 79–85.

Rabate, J.-M. 1982. "Silence in *Dubliners*. MacCabe, 1982, 45–72.

―――. 1983. "A Clown's Inquest into Paternity: Fathers, Dead or Alive, in *Ulysses* and *Finnegans Wake*." Davis, 73–114.

Ragland-Sullivan, E. 1986. *Jacques Lacan and the Philosophy of Psychoanalysis*. Chicago: Univ. of Illinois Press.

―――. 1988. "More French Connections." *James Joyce Quarterly* 26, no. 1:115–27.

―――. 1990. "Lacan's Seminars on James Joyce: Writing as Symptom and 'Singular Solution.'" Feldstein and Sussmann, 67–86.

Rauch, A. 1987. "I and the (M)other. Why the Ego's Narcissism Can Be Exploited by the Media." *Literature and Psychology* 33, nos. 3, 4:27–37.

Riquelme, J. P. 1983. *Teller and Tale in Joyce's Fiction: Oscillating Perspectives*. Baltimore, Md: Johns Hopkins Univ. Press.

Riviere, J. 1986. "Womanliness as a Masquerade." Burgin, Donald, and Kaplan, 35–44.

Rose, J. 1986. *Sexuality in the Field of Vision*. London: Verso.

Schneiderman, S. 1971. "Afloat with Jacques Lacan." *Diacritics* 1, no. 2:27–34.

Scholes, R. 1969. "'Counterparts.'" Hart, 93–99.

―――, and A. W. Litz, eds. 1969. *Dubliners: Text, Criticism and Notes*. New York: Viking.

Scott, B. K. 1984. *Joyce and Feminism*. Bloomington: Indiana Univ. Press.

―――. 1987. *James Joyce*. Brighton, Sussex: Harvester.

―――. 1988. *New Alliances in Joyce Studies*. Newark: Univ. of Delaware Press.

Senn, F. 1965. "'He Was Too Scrupulous Always': Joyce's 'The Sisters.'" *James Joyce Quarterly* 2:66–72.

―――. (1969) "'An Encounter.'" Hart, 26–38.

―――. (1986) "'The Boarding House' Seen as a Tale of Misdirection." *James Joyce Quarterly* 23, no. 4:405–13.

Silverman, K. 1983. *The Subject of Semiotics*. New York: Oxford Univ. Press.

Smith, P. 1983. "Crossing the Lines in 'A Painful Case.'" *Southern Humanities Review* 17, no. 3:203–9.

Snead, J. A. 1988, "Some Prefatory Remarks on Character in Joyce." Benstock, *Augmented Ninth*, 139–47.

Somerville, J. 1975. "Money in *Dubliners*." *Studies in Short Fiction* 12:109–16.

Stern, F. C. 1973. "'Parnell is Dead': 'Ivy Day in the Committee Room.'" *James Joyce Quarterly* 10, no. 2:228–39.

Stone, H. 1965. "'Araby' and the Writings of James Joyce." *Antioch Review* 25, no. 3:375–410.

Valente, Joseph. 1991. "Joyce's Sexual Differend: An Example From *Dubliners*." *James Joyce Quarterly* 28, no. 2:427–43.

Voelker, J. C. 1982. "'Chronicles of Disorder': Reading the Margins of Joyce's *Dubliners*." *Colby Library Quarterly* 18, no. 2:126–44.

Walzl, F. L. 1973. Joyce's 'The Sisters': A Development." *James Joyce Quarterly* 10:375–421.

————. 1982. "Dubliners: Women in Irish Society." Henke, *Women in Joyce*, 31–56.

Wilden, A., ed. 1981. *Speech and Language in Psychoanalysis: Essays by Jacques Lacan*. Baltimore, Md.: Johns Hopkins Univ. Press.

Williams, T. L. 1989. "Resistance to Paralysis in *Dubliners*." *Modern Fiction Studies: Feminist Readings of Joyce* 35, no. 3:437–57.

Index

Reading *Dubliners* Again
was composed in 11 on 13 Baskerville on Digital Compugraphic equipment
by Metricomp;
with display numerals in Baker Argentina #1
by Dix Type;
printed by sheet-fed offset on 50-pound, acid-free Natural Smooth,
bound over binder's boards in Holliston Roxite B,
and with dust jackets printed in 2 colors by
Braun-Brumfield, Inc.;
and published by
Syracuse University Press
Syracuse, New York 13244-5160

Irish Studies

Richard Fallis, *Series Editor*

Irish Studies presents a wide range of books interpreting important aspects of Irish life and culture to scholarly and general audiences. The richness and complexity of the Irish experience, past and present, deserves broad understanding and careful analysis. For this reason, an important purpose of the series is to offer a forum to scholars interested in Ireland, its history, and culture. Irish literature is a special concern in the series, but works from the perspectives of the fine arts, history, and the social sciences are also welcome, as are studies that take multi-disciplinary approaches.

Selected titles in the series include: